N

Aristotle and the
Metaphysics

'This is an excellent book, written with great lucidity and engaging the reader directly with the problems of Aristotle's *Metaphysics* . . . The book reads with ease, even at the most difficult of stages. I found it positively enjoyable to read.'

Mary Margaret McCabe, *Kings College, London*

'[This book] is well written and philosophically acute. It will prove a most worthwhile addition to the series, and will be helpful for under-graduates and graduates taking options in Aristotle's *Metaphysics*.'

David Charles, *Oxford University*

Aristotle is perhaps the most important figure in Western philosophy and his *Metaphysics* is a benchmark in the history of philosophy.

Aristotle and the Metaphysics introduces and assesses:

- Aristotle's life and the background to the *Metaphysics*
- The ideas and text of the *Metaphysics*
- The continuing importance of Aristotle's work to philosophy.

Vasilis Politis is lecturer of philosophy at Trinity College Dublin.

Routledge Philosophy Guidebooks

Edited by Tim Crane and Jonathan Wolff

University College London

Aristotle and the Metaphysics Vasilis Politis
Rousseau and the Social Contract Christopher Bertram
Plato and the Republic, Second edition Nickolas Pappas
Husserl and the Cartesian Meditations A. D. Smith
Kierkegaard and Fear and Trembling John Lippitt
Descartes and the Meditations Gary Hatfield
Hegel and the Philosophy of Right Dudley Knowles
Nietzsche on Morality Brian Leiter
Hegel and the Phenomenology of Spirit Robert Stern
Berkeley and the Principles of Human Knowledge Robert Fogelin
Aristotle on Ethics Gerard Hughes
Hume on Religion David O'Connor
Leibniz and the Monadology Anthony Savile
The Later Heidegger George Pattison
Hegel on History Joseph McCarney
Hume on Morality James Baillie
Hume on Knowledge Harold Noonan
Kant and the Critique of Pure Reason Sebastian Gardner
Mill on Liberty Jonathan Riley
Mill on Utilitarianism Roger Crisp
Wittgenstein and the Philosophical Investigations Marie McGinn
Spinoza and the Ethics Genevieve Lloyd
Heidegger on Being and Time Stephen Mulhall
Locke on Government D. A. Lloyd Thomas
Locke on Human Understanding E. J. Lowe

Routledge Philosophy GuideBook to

Aristotle and the
Metaphysics

Vasilis
Politis

Routledge
Taylor & Francis Group

LONDON AND NEW YORK

First published 2004
by Routledge
11 New Fetter Lane, London EC4P 4EE

Simultaneously published in the USA and Canada
by Routledge
29 West 35th Street, New York, NY 10001

Routledge is an imprint of the Taylor & Francis Group

© 2004 Vasilis Politis

Typeset in Aldus and Scala by
Florence Production Ltd, Stoodleigh, Devon
Printed and bound in Great Britain by
MPG Books Ltd, Bodmin

British Library Cataloguing in Publication Data
A catalogue record for this book is available from
the British Library

Library of Congress Cataloging in Publication Data
Politis, Vasilis.
   Routledge philosophy guidebook to Aristotle and the
   Metaphysics/Vasilis Politis
      p. cm.
   Includes bibliographical references and index.
   1. Aristotle – Metaphysics.   2. Metaphysics.
   I. Title: Aristotle and the Metaphysics.   II. Series:
   Routledge Philosophy Guidebooks.
   B424. P65 2004
   110 22   2003058658

ISBN 0–415–25147–8 (hbk)
ISBN 0–415–25148–6 (pbk)

CONTENTS

ACKNOWLEDGEMENTS

Special thanks are due to: the third- and fourth-year students at Trinity College Dublin, and especially Peter Dudley, Francis Fallon, Richard Hamilton, Colin Higgins, Scott O'Connor, Damien Storey, Stefan Storrie and Gry Wester. I would also like to thank my friends and colleagues who have in various ways been of help with this project, and especially Lilian Alweiss, Bert van den Berg, John Connolly, Klaus Corcilius, John Dillon, Brian Garvey, Vassilis Karasmanis, James Levine, Bill Lyons and Brendan O' Byrne; the referees, David Charles and Mary Margaret McCabe, for their invaluable comments; and, last but not least, Cordula.

1

ARISTOTLE'S
METAPHYSICS

1 What is the *Metaphysics* about? The question, 'What is being?'

The work that we have here under the title 'the *Metaphysics*' (*ta meta ta phusika*) is a series of fourteen books, all or most of which were written by Aristotle (384–322 BC). They belong to his latest period of work. Therefore the *Metaphysics* belongs to what Aristotle wrote after founding (in 335 BC) his own school of philosophy in Athens: the Lyceum or Peripatos. This means that, even if we take into account that the *Metaphysics* must have been written over an extended period of time, Aristotle must have produced the work some years after leaving the Academy, Plato's school in Athens; for he became a pupil of Plato (427–347 BC) at the age of seventeen, and he remained in Plato's school, first as a pupil and later as a relatively independent researcher, for some twenty years. But he left the Academy after Plato died.

However, Aristotle did not write the *Metaphysics* as a single work, and even the individual books (or sets of books) in it may not be finished works. Only after his death, and probably between 200 and 100 BC, were these fourteen books arranged and published in the order in which we now have them. The title itself, 'the *Metaphysics*', is not Aristotle's, but was probably devised by Andronicus of Rhodes when he put together the edition of the collected works of Aristotle (first century BC).

He probably devised this title (*ta meta ta phusika*, 'the [books] that come after the *Physics*') to indicate that, in his view, the *Metaphysics* belongs naturally after another work by Aristotle, the *Physics*. We may suppose that Andronicus thought that this is the natural place of the *Metaphysics*, because he thought that the study of all things and of things simply in so far as they are beings, i.e. metaphysics as characterized by Aristotle, comes naturally after the study of changing and material things, the things with which we are directly familiar from sense perception and experience, i.e. physics as characterized by Aristotle. For we will see that if there is anything that the fourteen books have in common, and that justifies collecting them together as a single work, the *Metaphysics*, it is the centrality of a single overall investigation. This is the investigation into all things and into things simply in so far as they are beings: things that are. So the title, 'the *Metaphysics*', may perhaps indicate what Aristotle's *Metaphysics* is about, but it does so only in an indirect and not immediately perspicuous way. We have of course become accustomed to thinking that the *Metaphysics* is evidently about metaphysics, and there is nothing wrong with thinking this. But Aristotle does not himself use this term, 'metaphysics', and when he wants to indicate what his present study is about, he uses terms such as 'wisdom' (*sophia*), 'first philosophy' (*prōtē philosophia*), and 'first science' (*prōtē epistēmē*).

Still, the *Metaphysics* is about some one thing and there is a single theme. This is the question, 'What is being?' (*tí to on*; *to on* means 'being', 'that which is'). The *Metaphysics* is about the question 'What is being?' in two ways. On the one hand, Aristotle raises this question; he undertakes a long search for an answer to it; and eventually he offers an answer. On the other hand, he also reflects on the question itself, what it is to raise it and to search for an answer to it, and even whether it is possible to search for an answer at all. As we would say, he also considers how metaphysics is possible. So let us begin by concentrating on the central question in the *Metaphysics*, 'What is being?'

First of all, the question 'What is being?' is about being, not about the noun 'being' or the verb 'to be'. It is about what it is for something to be, not about what it is for us to think or say of something that it is. Of course, how we think and speak, when we think or say of something that it is, may in various ways be important when we ask the question 'What is being?' and 'What is it for something to be?' But still, this question is not about how we think and speak when we think or say of something that it is; it is about being and what it is for something to be.

So what is this question about? Of what are we asking, 'What is being?' and 'What is it for something to be?' Aristotle evidently thinks that we are asking this question of beings (*onta*), things that are; i.e. we are asking of a being, something that is, what it is for that thing to be. But he also supposes that we are already familiar with beings, prior to our raising this question; and it is of such familiar things that he thinks that we may want to ask this question. So he thinks that we are familiar, pre-philosophically and from our ordinary experience, with beings; for beings are directly apparent to us and present to us, they are all around us and make up the world which we inhabit. It is of such familiar things that he thinks that we may want to ask 'What is it for something to be?': humans, plants, animals, which we encounter around us; the sun, the moon and other planets, which we see in the sky and which are central to our conception of motion, time and space; even the whole universe which appears to us to be made up of all these things. Of course, once we ask 'What is it for something to be?' of such familiar things, we may go on to ask this question also of things that are not directly apparent or present to us, but in whose existence we believe on other grounds. But this is a second step, and we must begin with the beings with which we are already familiar.

But it is important to recognize that when Aristotle asks, 'What is being?', he intends this question to be understood in a particular way. For, as he understands it, this is not primarily the question, 'What is there?'; it is above all the question, 'What is it for something to be?' The question 'What is there?' asks for a complete general description of what there is; we may say that it asks for the *extension* of being. But the question, 'What is it for something to be?', asks of anything that is, what it is for that thing to be. It asks for an explanation of why something that is is, or in virtue of what something that is is. We may say that this question asks for the *essence* of being, and for an explanatory account of the essence of being. Aristotle says (e.g. at the opening of book IV) that he wants to investigate 'being *qua* being', by which he means that he wants to investigate beings, and to investigate them simply *in so far as* they are beings, things that are. But this is precisely to investigate what it is for something to be – the essence of being. So metaphysics, as Aristotle understands it, is not so much the search for a complete and general description of what there is; it is above all the search for an explanation of why something that is is, or in virtue of what something that is is.

From the very beginning of the *Metaphysics* (in book I, chapter 2) Aristotle characterizes metaphysics, or what at this stage he calls 'wisdom' (*sophia*), as a search for explanations (*aitiai*, which can also be translated as 'causes') and explanatory knowledge (*epistēmē*), i.e. knowledge *why* something is as it is. This kind of knowledge we may call 'scientific knowledge' and 'science'; and Aristotle repeatedly speaks of metaphysics as a search for such knowledge (*epistēmē*). In particular, he says that metaphysics is the most fundamental science (*prōtē epistēmē*, see VI. 1, 1026ª29), for it is the search for the most fundamental explanations. These explanations he calls 'first explanations' and 'first principles' (*prōtai aitiai, prōtai archai*); and he says that they are explanations of *all* beings (*panta*) and of *everything* there is. But he thinks that such fundamental and universal explanations are, precisely, explanations of what it is for something – *anything* – to be.

We will gradually become more familiar with the basic question of metaphysics, 'What is it for something, anything, to be?' But it is worth emphasizing that Aristotle from the outset associates the search for an answer to this question with a search for explanatory knowledge (*epistēmē*), i.e. knowledge *why* things are as they are. So the basic question of metaphysics can also be formulated as, 'Why are the beings (*ta onta*) beings, things that are?' This must not, of course, be confused with the question, 'Why are there beings, things that are?' In general, we must not confuse questions of the type, (1) 'Why are there things that are F?', with questions of the type, (2) 'Why are the things that are F F?' The basic question in the *Metaphysics*, 'What is it for something, anything, to be?', is associated with questions of type 2, not type 1.

Finally, it is worth noting that Aristotle does not think that this basic question of metaphysics, 'What is being?', is his own invention. On the contrary, in a memorable passage at the centre of the *Metaphysics*, he emphasizes that this question is as old as the trees, never ceasing to be 'that which is sought after' (*to zētoumenon*) and 'a source of puzzlement' (*to aporoumenon*):

> Indeed, that which is always, both now and long ago, sought after and which is always a source of puzzlement, i.e. the question, *What is being?*, . . .
>
> (VII. 1, 1028ᵇ2–4)

From the beginning of the *Metaphysics* (I. 3–10) it is clear that he thinks that earlier thinkers have just as much been engaged in the investigation of being in general and as a whole (see, e.g. I. 3, 983ᵇ1–3). Here (in I. 3–10) he enlists a wide variety of earlier thinkers in this shared search: Thales, Anaximenes, Empedocles, Anaxagoras, Pythagoreans and, above all, Plato, who is only recently dead.

2 Sources of the question, 'What is being?'

But why does Aristotle think that we may want to ask this question, 'What is being?'? At the opening of the *Metaphysics* (I. 1), he argues that it is because we are human that we want to ask this question. He argues that all animals desire some kind of knowledge (*to eidenai*), and in particular sense perception (*aisthēsis*). But one thing that distinguishes us humans from other animals is that we desire not only any kind of knowledge of which we are capable, including knowledge that other animals desire, but also explanatory or scientific knowledge (*epistēmē*), which is knowledge of explanations (*aitiai*). But further, he argues that explanatory knowledge requires knowledge of what things are, their essence; for it is by knowing what a thing really is, its essence, that we can explain why the thing is as it is. For example (this is based on Aristotle's example in I. 1), it is by trying to know what a certain illness really is, its essence, that a scientifically minded physician may try to explain why this illness is as it is and behaves as it does: why it has the symptoms, causes, and consequences it has; why it responds to one treatment but not another, etc.

So, in general, Aristotle argues that it is simply because we are human that we search for science and explanatory knowledge (*epistēmē*); and explanatory knowledge requires knowing the essence of things. But he also argues (in *Metaphysics* I. 2) that metaphysics is the most fundamental kind of explanatory knowledge; it is the knowledge of the most fundamental explanations and the explanations of all things. But this, precisely, is the knowledge of what it is for something to be, i.e. it is the knowledge of the essence of being and the answer to the question 'What is being?' So he argues that it is because we are human that we want to ask the question, 'What is being?' and 'What is it for something to be?', and that we want to search for an answer to this question.

However, in the course of books I and III of the *Metaphysics* there emerges what appears to be a different account of why we may want to ask this question, 'What is being?' For Aristotle argues (in III. 1) that what in general motivates us to ask questions about being, and to search for answers, are particular *aporiai* that present themselves to us about being – *aporiai* in the sense of particular problems and puzzles that we are puzzled about. He goes on (in III. 2–6) to set out some fifteen *aporiai* about being. But before doing so, he argues (in III. 1) that it is precisely such *aporiai* about being that motivate us to search for what being is, and that if we are not puzzled about such problems and puzzles, then we cannot even begin to search for what being is. This suggests that Aristotle thinks that the question, 'What is being?', is not some arbitrary question that we may or may not want to raise; it is rather a question that presents itself to us as a problem and puzzle (*aporia*), or as an immediate consequence of similar problems and puzzles which present themselves to us. In general, it will emerge that *aporiai* about being are absolutely central in the *Metaphysics* and indeed to the whole project of the *Metaphysics*, the project of searching for what it is for something, anything, to be. Aristotle's method in the *Metaphysics* is fundamentally based in *aporiai* (see Chapter 3).

So Aristotle thinks that the question, 'What is being?', is not just any kind of question, but an *aporia*; i.e. a problem and puzzle that presents itself to us and makes us puzzled about it. This fascinating view arguably goes back to Plato, especially in the dialogue *Sophist* (242bff.), where Plato argues that we are thoroughly perplexed and puzzled about being. Plato identifies a particular source of this puzzlement, which he too calls *aporia*. For he argues that our puzzlement about being springs above all from our encounter with different views about what there really and fundamentally is. He points out that some people (the pluralists) argue that, really and fundamentally, there are different kinds of things, but others (the monists) argue that, really and fundamentally, there is only one kind of thing (*Sophist* 242b–245e). Or again, some people (the materialists) argue that only changing and material things really are, but others (the immaterialists) argue that only changeless and immaterial things really are (*Sophist* 245e–249d). But Plato objects that there is a problem with all these views. The problem is not so much that we do not know which view is true, but rather that we do not even really understand what each view means (*Sophist* 243b). For he argues that unless we basically ask what being is and what is the essence of being, i.e. unless we ask the question 'What is being?', we cannot properly ask what things there really are, i.e. we cannot properly ask, 'What is there?' So, unless we ask what being is, we cannot properly ask such questions as whether the things that really are are one or many, material or immaterial, etc. Plato concludes that if we want to ask such questions as, 'Are things fundamentally material or immaterial?', we must also ask the basic question, 'What is being?' and 'What is it for something to be?' But he thinks that so far no one has adequately asked this question. In general, Plato's point appears to be this. If we want to make any completely universal claims, i.e. claims of the form 'All things are, basically and fundamentally, such and such (e.g. material)', then we must at the same time raise the basic question, 'What is it for something, anything, to be?' We must do so in order to justify, and indeed in order properly to understand, any completely universal claim that we may want to make.

It appears that this is also Aristotle's overall view – and in this he may have been influenced by Plato. This overall view says that the question, 'What is being?', is not just any kind of question, which we may or may not want to ask; it is rather an *aporia*, a problem and puzzle which, for particular reasons, presents itself to us and makes us puzzled about it. Thus early in the *Metaphysics* (I. 2) Aristotle argues that it is *aporiai* that originally motivate us to ask universal questions about what there is. He goes on (in I. 3–10) to set out a number of different universal claims that previous thinkers have held about what there is. He then (in III. 1) argues that without particular *aporiai* about being, we cannot at all search for what being is. He goes on (in III. 2–6) to set out some fifteen *aporiai* about being, which it is his aim to answer in the remainder of the *Metaphysics*. Finally (at the opening of book IV), he expressly raises the question, 'What is being *qua* being?', i.e. 'What is it for something, anything, to be?' (Here we should note that books I, III and IV belong together. Book II, on the other hand, is only later inserted between books I and III.)

So it appears that the question, 'What is being?', as Aristotle understands it, springs from certain problems and puzzles that may present themselves to us when we think about, and encounter others thinking about, what there fundamentally is and what things are fundamentally like. In general, it appears that the question, 'What is being?', springs from certain problems and puzzles – *aporiai* – that present themselves to us when we are inclined to make completely universal claims, claims of the form, 'All things are, basically and fundamentally, such and such (e.g. material).' It is the reflection on such completely universal claims, and puzzles generated by such claims, that may prompt us to ask the basic question, 'What is being?' and 'What is it for something to be?' – and to begin to search for an answer.

This also suggests that when Aristotle argues (in the opening two chapters of the *Metaphysics*) that it is because we are human that we want to ask questions about the essence of things, and in particular to ask about the essence of being itself ('What is it for something to be a being, something that is?'), he has in mind a particular characteristic of being human: to be human is to be subject to puzzlement (*aporia*) about particular puzzles and problems (*aporiai*). This is not, of course, the only thing that is characteristic of being human. But it is such puzzlement that ultimately prompts us to ask about being itself and to search for what being is.

This also shows, it is worth noting, that Aristotle does not think that the question, 'What is being?', springs simply from what we ordinarily and pre-philosophically think and say, when we say that something is or is not; for example, when we say that there are trees in the garden or that there are no trees in the garden. For it is evidently not in an ordinary and pre-philosophical frame of mind that we ask such questions as, 'Are things fundamentally material or immaterial?', and in general that we are inclined to make completely universal claims. Rather, completely universal questions and claims are, precisely, philosophical and, broadly speaking, metaphysical.

In general, metaphysics, as Aristotle understands it, has its source in certain problems and puzzles that may present themselves to us in a natural and forceful way. But this is not a source outside metaphysics. On the contrary, the problems and puzzles – *aporiai* – that are the source of metaphysics are themselves metaphysical problems and puzzles, i.e. problems and puzzles that emerge when we reflect on completely universal questions and claims. In this regard, Aristotle's conception of metaphysics differs in a very important way from certain typically modern conceptions, which argue that if metaphysics is possible at all, it is possible because it is based in something outside it: epistemology; or logic; or ordinary language; or something else, perhaps our way of life. We will later return to this important difference between Aristotle's conception of metaphysics and certain typically modern conceptions (see Chapter 3§§2–3). The difference is that whereas modern conceptions of metaphysics will typically search for the source of metaphysics, indeed for the source of the very possibility of metaphysics, outside of metaphysics, e.g. in logic or epistemology, Aristotle argues that the source of metaphysics, and indeed of its possibility, lies within metaphysics itself.

This also suggests that we, just as much as Aristotle or Plato, may want to ask the question, 'What is being?' For philosophers today, or some philosophers at any rate, are just as much asking questions such as, 'Are things material or immaterial – and, especially, mental – or perhaps both?' Or, 'Are all things physical or are there non-physical things?' Or, 'Are all things particulars or are there universals?' Or even, 'Are things what they are independently of us or are they what they are only relative to us and to how we conceive of them?' In general, the tendency to ask completely universal questions and to make completely universal claims has not gone away or diminished. But we too may find that somehow such questions are associated with the basic question, 'What is being?' and 'What is it for something, anything, to be?' So we too may think that it is natural and perhaps reasonable to ask this question. Of course, this does not mean that we *must* ask this question. For we may want to resist its source, i.e. resist seriously asking, and taking seriously those who ask, such questions as whether things are fundamentally material, or whether there are universals, or whether things are what they are independently of us, etc. In general, we may want to resist the tendency to make any universal claims and to raise any universal questions. But this would be to resist metaphysics altogether, even if metaphysics is understood broadly to mean the search for what there is and what things in general are like. But although today this is perhaps a widespread attitude, it is by no means a shared one, and metaphysics broadly speaking is as much alive now as it was then. It is also questionable whether it really is possible successfully to resist making any universal claims or raising any universal questions, without resisting philosophy, and indeed an important tendency within science, altogether.

We have seen that Aristotle thinks that the basic question of metaphysics, 'What is it for something, anything, to be?', is rooted in certain metaphysical *aporiai*, i.e. in certain puzzles and problems that arise when we reflect on certain questions about things in general and all things. Here it may be useful to distinguish three general kinds of metaphysical *aporiai* that will become prominent in the *Metaphysics*, and which we will take up at length later.

First, one kind of metaphysical *aporiai* is associated with the question of how things can have properties, and in general how something can be true of something. This question goes back especially to Aristotle's earlier work, the *Categories* (see Chapter 4§4). We will return to this fundamental relation, i.e. the relation *x is true of y*, in a moment (see §4) and again at length later (Chapters 4§4 and especially 7§3 and §§5vi, v, viii). There we will also consider certain fundamental *aporiai* to which this question gives rise, and how Aristotle answers them.

Second, a further kind of metaphysical *aporiai* is associated with the question of how things can be intelligible and subject to explanation. This question goes back especially to Aristotle's earlier work, the *Posterior Analytics*. Later we will consider Aristotle's theory of explanation (Chapter 2§3), and later again certain fundamental *aporiai* to which this question gives rise, and how Aristotle answers them (Chapter 7§5viii–x, also Chapter 8).

Third, a final kind of metaphysical *aporiai* is associated with the question of how things can change, and in particular how things can change in such a way that they can be subject to explanation. This question goes back to Aristotle's earlier work, the *Physics*. Later we will consider Aristotle's theory of change and changing things (Chapter 2§4), and later again certain fundamental *aporiai* to which this question gives rise, and how Aristotle answers them (Chapter 7§5vi, vii, ix).

3 A central distinction in the *Metaphysics*: Being in general *versus* primary being (*prōtē ousia*)

Of central importance in the *Metaphysics* is Aristotle's distinction between *being* in general (*to on*) and *primary being* (*prōtē ousia*, often simply *ousia*; see below for our choice to translate *prōtē ousia* as 'primary being' and not as 'primary substance', which is the usual English translation). He first introduces this distinction in IV. 2, but it becomes prominent in books VII–IX, the central books of the *Metaphysics*. We will consider this distinction at length later (in Chapters 4§§1–3 and 7§§1 and 4), but it is important to draw attention to it straight away. Aristotle introduces this distinction in order to address the basic question of metaphysics, 'What is being?' and 'What is it for something to be?' For he argues that in order to address the question, 'What is being?' and 'What is it for something to be?', we need to address the question, 'What is primary being?' and 'What is it for something to be in the primary way?' In particular, he argues that if we want to search for what being is and what it is for something to be, we must do so by searching for what primary being is and what it is for something to be in the primary way.

This argument, which concludes that we can search for what being is only by searching for what primary being is, serves to introduce the notion, *primary being* (*prōtē ousia*, often simply *ousia*), and to introduce the distinction between being in general (*to on*) and primary being. This notion, *primary being*, and the distinction between being in general and primary being, will become absolutely central in the *Metaphysics*. For in the central books of the *Metaphysics*, books VII–IX, Aristotle will search for an answer to the basic question of metaphysics, 'What is being?', and he will eventually offer an answer, precisely by searching for, and eventually offering an answer to, the question, 'What is primary being?' Let us briefly anticipate the argument for the conclusion that we can search for what being is only by searching for what primary being is (for the full argument, and the full account of the notion, *primary being*, see below, Chapter 4§§1–3).

It will emerge that the basic question of metaphysics, 'What is being?' and 'What is it for something, anything, to be?', gives rise to a fundamental *aporia* about the very possibility of metaphysics: how is it possible even to conceive of being, in general and as a whole, and meaningfully to ask, 'What is it for something, anything, to be?'? Aristotle will raise this *aporia* in book III, the book of *aporiai* (see the third *aporia*, 997^{a}15–25, and part of the seventh *aporia*, 998^{b}22–27). Summarily, the *aporia* is this: we cannot conceive of being by distinguishing it from not-being, but neither can we conceive of being as the sum of all the kinds of beings that there are. So, apparently, we cannot conceive of being at all, either by distinguishing it from something outside it, i.e. from not-being, or by distinguishing it from what is inside it, i.e. by conceiving of it as the sum of all the kinds of beings that there are and in general as the sum of everything that there is.

It is in order to answer this *aporia* about the possibility of metaphysics that Aristotle will (in IV. 2) introduce the notion, *primary being*, and the distinction between being in general and primary being. Summarily, the answer to the *aporia* is this. Suppose that we cannot conceive of being, in general and as a whole, either by distinguishing it from something outside it or by distinguishing it from what is inside it. Perhaps we can still conceive of being, if we suppose that there is a distinction between things that are beings simply in virtue of themselves (i.e. primary beings) and things that are beings in virtue of their relation to those things (i.e. non-primary beings). For then we can conceive of being, in the following way: by supposing that anything that is, i.e. any being, is a being *either* simply in virtue of itself and not in virtue of its relation to other things (in which case it is a primary being) *or* in virtue of its relation to a primary being (in which case it is a non-primary being).

This way of introducing the notion, *primary being*, also shows what Aristotle means by primary being and how he distinguishes between primary beings and non-primary beings. For something to be a primary being is for it to be a being, something that is, simply in virtue of itself (*kath' hauto*) and not in virtue of its relation to other things; whereas for something to be a non-primary being is for it to be a being only in virtue of its relation to other things, namely, a primary being. (See Chapters 4§3 and 7§4 for a fuller account of the general notion, *primary being*.)

But it is important to recognize that this general notion, *primary being*, is not yet Aristotle's answer to the question, 'What is primary being?' On the contrary, it will emerge that he thinks that this question, 'What is primary being?', is one that he shares with other thinkers that have raised the basic question of metaphysics, 'What is being?' But he thinks that different thinkers have defended very different answers to just this question, 'What is primary being?' For example, materialists argue that it is above all the basic material elements of physical bodies, such as the elements fire, water and earth, that are primary beings (see VII. 2, 1028^{b}8f.). But Plato and the Platonists argue that what is primary being above all is certain eternal beings that are distinct from (*para*) the sense-perceptible and physical things; i.e. they argue that the forms (*eidē*) are the primary beings (see VII. 2, 1028^{b}18f.). So Aristotle thinks that just as he shares the basic question, 'What is being?', with other thinkers, so the question, 'What is primary being?', is a shared one (see Chapter 7§1).

Aristotle thinks that the question, 'What is primary being?', is common to very different thinkers, and that very different answers can be defended in response to it. This has one immediate and very important consequence: it is wrong to translate *ousia* as 'substance', or *prōtē ousia* as 'primary substance'. The terms *ousia* and *prōtē ousia* in Aristotle are usually translated as 'substance' and 'primary substance' (at least by English-speaking critics, for this translation is much less common by, for example, German critics). But this is a mistake. For the claim that *prōtē ousia* is substance is a particular answer to the question, 'What is *prōtē ousia*?' It is not what the term *prōtē ousia* means in the question, 'What is *prōtē ousia*?' The Latin term *substantia*, which literally means 'that which lies under', translates Aristotle's term *to hupokeimenon*, i.e. 'that which lies under' (from *hupokeisthai*, 'to lie under'). It is true, as we will see, that in his earlier work, the *Categories*, Aristotle argued that *prōtē ousia* is simply *to hupokeimenon* (see Chapter 4§4). But this is a particular view about what *prōtē ousia* is, i.e. a particular answer to the question, 'What is *prōtē ousia*?' It is not what the term *prōtē ousia* means or what the question 'What is *prōtē ousia*?' is asking. We have chosen to use the term 'primary being' for *prōtē ousia* and in general for *ousia*.

4 Three candidates for primary being: The particular; the universal; and the essence

Aristotle thinks that very different answers can be defended in response to the question, 'What is primary being?' But it will emerge that he thinks that three candidates for primary being, i.e. three competing answers to the question, 'What is primary being?', are especially important. These are:

(1) the particular;
(2) the universal; and
(3) the essence

(see VII. 3, 1028^{b}33–36, discussed in Chapter 7§3). Indeed, it will emerge that Aristotle will defend the third candidate: primary being with regard to each thing is the essence of that thing (see Chapter 7§5iv). We will consider these candidates at length later (in Chapter 7, especially §§2–3 and §5 especially ii, iii–iv, and viii). But can we perhaps, at the beginning, stand back and in some way see why Aristotle thinks that just these are particularly important candidates for primary being? This will also help to explain what Aristotle means by 'a particular' (*to kath' hekaston*), 'a universal' (*to katholou*), and 'an essence' (*to ti estin, to ti ēn einai*). Here is an attempt to do so.

Consider first the two candidates, the particulars and the universals. They appear to be rooted in a certain most general conception of the structure of things: things are distinguished into things and their properties, i.e. into things and things that are true of them. So the following structure is fundamental to things in general:

something is true of something.

Aristotle uses the phrase *ti kata tinos* for this structure. Or, in a formulation with which today we are more readily familiar:

F is true of something,

or simply,

something is *F*.

Here it is natural to think that *F* is a universal (*to katholou*), i.e. it is a single thing that can be true of other things and of many things. For example, suppose that it is true of Socrates that he is five foot tall; then it is natural to think of the property, *five foot tall*, as a universal, i.e. as a single thing that can be true of other things (e.g. of Socrates) and of many things (e.g. Socrates, Plato, etc.). In general, *F* is a single thing in the sense that it is just the one property it is, *F*, as opposed to any other property, *G*, *H*, etc. And evidently it can be true of other things and of many things; i.e. *a* is *F*, *b* is *F*, etc., where *a*, *b*, etc., are not identical with *F*.

It is also natural to think that the thing of which the property, *F*, is true is a particular (*to kath' hekaston*), e.g. Socrates. Aristotle will argue that the things of which other things are true are, precisely, particulars. They are particulars in just this sense: while other things are true of them, they are not themselves true of other things. For example, being five foot tall is true of Socrates; but Socrates is not true of another thing. Particulars are, in this sense, ultimate subjects of predications (*hupokeinena*), i.e. they are what other things are ultimately true of, but they are not themselves true of other things. But it is important to emphasize that to speak of a particular in the sense of an ultimate subject of predication (*to hupokeimenon*) is not to speak of a particular as we encounter it in experience, and in general it is not to speak of a particular in a wide and loose sense of 'a particular'. In a wide and loose sense of 'a particular', a particular may naturally be thought to include its properties. For example, Socrates, as we encounter him in experience, is the particular that is human, five foot tall, snub-nosed, etc. But the particular (e.g. Socrates), in the sense of the ultimate subject of predication, is what these properties are true of (for the notions of the particular and the ultimate subject of predication, see Chapter 4§4).

So the following structure is fundamental to things in general: *something is true of something*. Here it is crucial to emphasize that the relation, *x is true of y*, is a relation between things. It is not a relation between words or parts of sentences. This is easily overlooked, especially since the adjective 'true of' is easily confused with the adjective 'true'. It is natural to think that the adjective 'true' is not applicable to things; it is rather applicable to sentences, or statements, or propositions, i.e. to things that we say or think, or to what we mean when we say or think something. So it easy to suppose that the same holds good of the adjective 'true of', i.e. that it likewise is not applicable to things, but is rather applicable to parts of sentences, etc. But this is a confusion, and in general it is crucial not to confuse the adjective 'true' with the adjective 'true of'. For the adjective 'true of', unlike the adjective 'true', is applicable to things. For example, if Socrates is five foot tall, then this property, not the phrase 'five foot tall', is true of Socrates, not the word 'Socrates'. It is also important to note that if, following Aristotle, we call this relation, *x is true of y*, the relation of 'predication', we mean a relation between things, not between words or parts of a sentence. For the phrase 'something is predicated of something' (*ti katēgoreitai tinos*), and in general the term 'predication' (*katēgoria*), may, on the contrary, suggest a relation between words or parts of a sentence. But it is clear that in general Aristotle conceives of this relation as holding between things (see e.g. the opening of the *Categories*).

But now suppose that we reflect on this basic structure of things, *something is true of something*. Then we may naturally find ourselves in the following vexing and apparently inescapable dilemma – or *aporia*. On the one hand, it appears that the things of which the universals are true, i.e. the ultimate subjects and the particulars, are more basic than the universals. For it is natural to think that universals are beings, things that are, only in virtue of their being true of other things. This side of the dilemma especially attracts Aristotle, in the earlier work, the *Categories*. On the other hand, it appears that the universals are more basic than the things of which they are true. For it is the universals that determine what in general the things of which they are ultimately true, i.e. the ultimate subjects and the particulars, are like. In other words, an ultimate subject and a particular depends, for its determination, on its relation to the universals, i.e. the relation *being something that universals are true of*. This side of the dilemma especially attracts Plato.

But if we reflect long enough on this dilemma, it may appear to be inescapable and irresolvable. Now we are pulled one way, i.e. towards thinking that the ultimate subjects and the particulars are the primary beings. Now in the opposite way, i.e. towards thinking that the universals are the primary beings; and then back again. Can we step off this see-saw? One way of doing so, and apparently this is Aristotle's way in the *Metaphysics*, is to argue that an ultimate subject of predication and a particular does not after all depend, for its determination, on its relation to the universals. On the contrary, an ultimate subject of predication and a particular is determinate *simply in virtue of itself (auto kath' hauto)*. This means that there is something, some *F*, that the subject and the particular is, simply in virtue of itself and not in virtue of its relation to something else, the universal *F*. We may then use an already current phrase for precisely this, i.e. for what an ultimate subject and a particular is simply in virtue of itself; i.e. we may say that this is *the essence (to ti estin, to ti ēn einai)* of an ultimate subject and a particular. So we start from two original candidates for primary being, i.e. the particulars and the universals; and we introduce a third candidate, i.e. the essence of the particulars, in order to answer an *aporia* that originates when we reflect on the two original candidates.

Perhaps this was just Aristotle's path. He started from the one side of the see-saw, i.e. from the view of Plato that the universals are the primary beings. He went over to the other side of the see-saw, i.e. to his view in the *Categories* that it is simply the ultimate subjects and the particulars that are the primary beings. He eventually, in the *Metaphysics*, resolved to step off the see-saw by arguing that the essence of the ultimate subjects and the particulars is, above all, primary being.

We will see that Aristotle will argue (in the central books of the *Metaphysics* and especially in book VII) that primary being is neither simply the universals nor simply the ultimate subjects and the particulars; it is rather the essence of the ultimate subjects and of the particulars (see Chapter 7§5ii, iv, viii). But the important thing is how he conceives of *essence* here. For he will argue that the essence of an ultimate subject and a particular is not something different from and true of the ultimate subject and the particular whose essence it is. On the contrary, the essence of an ultimate subject and a particular is what the subject and the particular is *simply in virtue of itself* (see below, Chapter 7§5v). Evidently this also means that the essence is not simply a universal, and perhaps that it is not a universal at all (see below, Chapter 7§5viii). In general, Aristotle will argue that the relation between a particular (e.g. Socrates) and its essence (e.g. being human) is fundamentally different from the relation between a particular and those things that are different from it and true of it (e.g. five foot tall, healthy, etc.). For while the latter relation is a relation between two things, one being true of the other, the former relation, i.e. the relation between a particular (e.g. Socrates) and its essence (e.g. being human) is a relation between a thing and itself.

This also helps to clarify what Aristotle means by the essence (*to ti estin, to ti ēn einai*). For it shows that he argues that particulars, indeed the changing particulars with which we are directly familiar from sense perception and experience (e.g. Socrates), have an essence, i.e. there is something that they are simply in virtue of themselves (*auta kath' hauta*). This stands in contrast especially with Plato, who argues that only universals have an essence, and that particulars depend for their determination on their relation to universals. But this fundamental disagreement about what things have an essence takes place against the background of a shared general conception of essence: the essence, E, of a thing, x, is what x is simply in virtue of itself and in virtue of its being the very thing it is, x. Or, less formally: the essence of a thing is what we know when we know the answer to the question, 'What is this very thing?'

5 Does Aristotle assume essentialism in the *Metaphysics*?

Let us call 'essentialism' the view which says that:

(1) there are things that have an essence; and
(2) what the essence of a thing is does not depend on how we refer to that thing or in general how we think or speak about it.

There is no doubt that Aristotle holds this view. But does he simply assume essentialism in the *Metaphysics*, or does he defend it? If he simply assumes essentialism, then this may be a cause of concern. Indeed, we may think that there is a particular cause of concern especially if we are impressed by Quine's argument against essentialism (see e.g. Quine 1953). So we may think that there is a basic cause of concern about Aristotle's *Metaphysics* before we have even started looking at it.

Two responses are appropriate to this cause of concern. On the one hand, even if Aristotle simply assumes essentialism in the *Metaphysics*, Quine's argument against essentialism ought not to be a cause of concern. For the conception of essentialism that Quine's argument is directed against is crucially different from Aristotle's conception of essentialism. On the other hand, we will see that Aristotle does not simply assume essentialism in the *Metaphysics* – rather he defends this view.

Quine's argument against essentialism is directed against a particular conception of essentialism. According to this conception, if E is *essentially* true of a thing, x, then the proposition 'x is E' is not only a necessary truth – so much is agreed on by any conception of essentialism. Rather, the proposition 'x is E' is an a priori truth, i.e. its truth can be established independently of sense experience; indeed, it is an analytical truth, i.e. it is true simply in virtue of the meaning of the terms in it. Let us call this, 'the purely semantic conception of essentialism'. In general, purely semantic essentialism holds that an essential truth is not only a necessary truth – so much is agreed on by any conception of essentialism – rather it is an a priori and indeed an analytical truth.

Quine's argument is directed against the purely semantic conception of essentialism. The argument, basically, is that whether E is *essentially* true of a thing, x, will depend on how we refer to the thing, x. For whether the proposition 'x is E' is an a priori and an analytical truth depends on how we refer to the thing, x. For example, whether being H_2O is *essentially* true of water will depend on how we refer to this thing, water. If we refer to it as 'any stuff that is H_2O', then evidently it will be *essentially* true of water that it is H_2O. For evidently the proposition 'Any stuff that is H_2O is H_2O' is a priori and analytical. But if we refer to water as, e.g. 'Any stuff that is identical in kind with this stuff (pointing to a sample of water)', evidently it will not be *essentially* true of water that it is H_2O. For evidently the proposition 'Any stuff that is identical in kind with this stuff (pointing to a sample of water) is H_2O' is neither a priori nor analytical.

Suppose that Quine's argument against essentialism succeeds. What it succeeds in showing is that what the essence of a thing is depends on how we refer to that thing. This undermines essentialism because essentialism holds, on the contrary, that what the essence of a thing is does not depend on how we refer to that thing. But Quine's argument against essentialism succeeds only if essentialism is understood in a purely semantic way, i.e. if it is thought that an essential truth is not only a necessary truth – so much is agreed on by every conception of essentialism – rather it is an a priori and indeed an analytical truth.

Aristotle's conception of essentialism is not a purely semantic conception. So Quine's argument does not really touch it. What is important
is that Aristotle does not assume that if E is essentially true of a thing,
x, then the proposition 'x is E' is an a priori or an analytical truth. Indeed
the notions of a priori truth and of analytical truth are conspicuous by
their absence in Aristotle. He thinks that essential truths are necessary
truths, but he does not associate such necessary truths with a priori or
analytical truths. We may say that Aristotle's conception of necessity,
i.e. the kind of necessity that is based on essence, is a metaphysical
and not a semantic conception. In general, we will see that, in Aristotle,
the metaphysical conception of essence and necessity is associated with
the search for explanations and explanatory knowledge – with science
(see Chapter 2§3). So, even if Aristotle simply assumes essentialism
in the *Metaphysics*, Quine's argument against essentialism ought not
to be a cause of concern.

Here it is also worth emphasizing that since the time when Quine
offered the argument against the purely semantic conception of essentialism, a variety of philosophers have defended a conception of essentialism
that is not purely semantic, and indeed is rather associated with explanations and science. This is true, in different ways, of, for example, Saul
Kripke, Kit Fine and David Armstrong. It is also notable that these
philosophers can be said, in one way or another, to defend an Aristotelian
conception of essentialism.

So far, we have seen that, even if Aristotle simply assumes essentialism in the *Metaphysics*, Quine's argument against essentialism
ought not to be a cause of concern. But does Aristotle simply assume
essentialism in the *Metaphysics*? Even setting aside Quine's argument,
this would be a cause of concern. For metaphysics, as Aristotle characterizes it, is a 'first philosophy' and a 'first science'. But then how could
it depend on central but unexamined presuppositions? If it did, there
would be a philosophy and a science – perhaps epistemology, or logic –
that is even more primary, namely, one that examines and assesses these
central presuppositions. Indeed, it will emerge that Aristotle is careful
not to 'beg the question' against a radical opponent, i.e. not to presuppose something that a radical opponent would, precisely, question (see
IV. 4, 1006ª15–18).

We will see (in Chapters 5–6) that Aristotle does not simply assume
essentialism in the *Metaphysics*. On the contrary, he does what he can
to defend this view. First (in IV. 4), he addresses a radical opponent that
argues that things do not have an essence at all, whether this essence
depends or does not depend on how we conceive of things. Against this
opponent Aristotle argues that if things did not have an essence, then

we could not distinguish things from one another, and in general we could not think or speak about things (see Chapter 5, especially §8). Second (in IV. 5–6), he addresses a radical opponent that argues that even if things have an essence, i.e. enough of an essence for us to be able to distinguish them from one another and in general to think and speak about them, still it is not the things themselves that have an essence, but only things as we conceive them. Against this opponent Aristotle argues that the best explanation of why things as we conceive them have an essence is that the things themselves have an essence, and he challenges the opponent to offer a better explanation (see Chapter 6, especially §5).

Finally, it is important that any concern that we may have about essentialism should be a specific and well-articulated one. After all, essentialism can be formulated in a way that ought not to be a cause of general concern. For at its root, essentialism is the view that, with regard to any thing that we are thinking of, it is always appropriate to ask, 'What is this very thing?' One reason why this question ought not to be a cause of general concern is that this question, precisely, does not beg any questions, i.e. it does not presuppose anything that can be questioned. For example, we might think that this question, 'What is this very thing, x?', presupposes that there really is such a thing, x, and that it is what it is independently of us. But this would be a mistake. For example, if we ask, 'What is this very thing, a goatstag?', we may answer that a goatstag is, precisely, an imaginary being; and we may use this answer, for example, to argue that we are at considerable liberty to suppose that a goatstag is as we imagine it to be, because it is, precisely, an imaginary being. Or again, if we ask 'What is this very thing, art?', we may answer (rightly or wrongly) that art is, precisely, what we call art. But to assess such an answer, or even to arrive at it, we will have to ask the question, 'What is this very thing, art?' So this Socratic type question, 'What is this very thing, x?', is perhaps a truly radical question, i.e. one that it is always appropriate to ask and that does not presuppose anything.

6 The structure and unity of the *Metaphysics*

Aristotle did not write the *Metaphysics* as a single work, and even the individual books (or sets of books) in it may not be finished works. Partly because of this, the question, what is the structure of the *Metaphysics* and to what extent does the *Metaphysics* amount to a single unified project?, is especially difficult to answer. On primarily textual grounds, i.e. grounds that are largely independent of issues of interpretation, the following is relatively uncontroversial. First, books I, III and IV are written together and intended to form a relatively continuous work (book II is a later insertion). Second, books VII, VIII and IX, the so-called central books of the *Metaphysics*, are likewise written together and intended to form a relatively continuous work. Third, book XII is written as a largely self-contained work which can, at least to a large extent, stand on its own. Fourth, books XIII and XIV are written together and intended to form a relatively continuous work. Similar points can be established, on primarily textual grounds, with regard to some of the other books. But we may set this aside here. For we will largely concentrate on the above four sets of books: I, III, IV; VII–IX; XII; and XIII–XIV. However, we will consider books XIII–XIV only to the extent that they bear on Aristotle's criticism of Plato's theory of forms.

But let us turn now to the question of thematic unity, i.e. the unity of a single unified project. If we concentrate on these four sets of books in the *Metaphysics* (I, III, IV; VII–IX; XII; and XIII–XIV), we may naturally ask to what extent there is a single theme that runs through them all. Certainly there is a single theme that connects the first set (I, III and IV) and the second set (VII–IX). This is, precisely, the question, 'What is being (*to on*)?' and in particular 'What is being *qua* being?', i.e. 'What is it for a being to be a being?' This question is expressly raised at the opening of book IV. But it is immediately (in IV. 2) associated with the question, 'What is primary being (*prōtē ousia*, often simply *ousia*)?' And book VII immediately takes up and, together with books VIII and IX, answers this central question, 'What is primary being?'

So there is a single continuous theme that connects the first set (I, III and IV) and the second set (VII–IX), and this theme is provided by the basic question of metaphysics, 'What is being?', and by the view that this question must be addressed by addressing the question, 'What is primary being?' Whether this theme also extends to book XII is less clear. For it may appear that book XII is not so much concerned with the question, (1) 'What is it for a being to be a being?' It is rather concerned with the question, (2) 'Why are there the kinds of beings that there are?', and in particular, 'Why are there beings that are changing and material, but whose change is intelligible and subject to explanation?' However, it is arguable that book XII addresses not only question 2 but also question 1. In that case, book XII is after all also concerned with the basic question of metaphysics (see Chapter 8§11).

But it appears that this thematic unity, which is provided by the questions, 'What is being?' and 'What is primary being?', also extends to Aristotle's criticism of Plato's theory of forms, especially but not only in books XIII–XIV. For it will emerge that Aristotle sees Plato and himself as engaged in a shared project, the project of searching for primary being (*ousia*). And he thinks that he shares with Plato the general notion of primary being (see Chapters 7§4 and Chapter 9). Indeed, when Aristotle criticises Plato's theory of forms, he does so against the background of thinking that he and Plato are engaged in this shared project – the search for primary being. In general, the criticism is that while Plato asked the right question, 'What is primary being?', and indeed while he gave an answer that is in general correct, namely, that primary being is the essence of things, he defended a mistaken conception of essence. For Aristotle argues that Plato was mistaken when he argued that changing things do not have an essence and that only the forms, which Plato conceived as separate and distinct from changing things, have an essence.

The *Metaphysics*, therefore, to the extent that it constitutes a single unified project, is unified by the question, 'What is being?', and by the view that this question must be addressed by addressing the question, 'What is primary being?' But is it Aristotle's aim, especially in books VII–IX, to defend a single overall answer to the question, 'What is primary being?', i.e. a systematic theory of primary being? And does he offer such an answer in books VII–IX? Again, these questions require taking up controversial issues of interpretation. But we will argue that this is Aristotle's aim and that he does offer such an answer, i.e. a systematic theory of primary being and, thereby, of being in general and as a whole (for a summary of his answer, see Chapter 7§5i).

7 About this companion to the *Metaphysics*

Aristotle's *Metaphysics* is a difficult work. It is also one of the most dense pieces of philosophical writing. So what one says about it will not be easy either, even if one tries not to presuppose anything in particular. Things are not made easier by the fact that we have chosen regularly to quote from the *Metaphysics*. But without Aristotle's words, or a translation of them, there is nothing to focus on, and things are unlikely to come to life. (All translations are the author's, except where indicated.)

There is no way of making the *Metaphysics* easy or straightforward. But we have in two ways tried not to make it unnecessarily difficult. First, we have tried to concentrate above all on Aristotle's questions, especially the central questions, 'What is being?' and 'What is primary being?' Second, we have tried to concentrate on one theme or issue at a time, and to use a few quotations with regard to it. The sections in each chapter constitute such thematic units, and the intention is that the reader should concentrate on just a few sections at a time, ideally with the text of the *Metaphysics* at the side. The titles of the sections indicate the theme or issue contained in them. At the end of the companion there are suggestions for further reading.

We have not tried to cover the *Metaphysics* exhaustively. Rather, we have concentrated on the following sets of books: I, III, IV; VII–IX; XII; also XIII–XIV, to the extent that they bear on the criticism of Plato's theory of forms. For it is especially in these books that the overall theme of the *Metaphysics*, which is provided by the questions, 'What is being?' and 'What is primary being?', is manifest (see §6 in this chapter).

With regard to what we have concentrated on, we have tried to do so in a thorough and, on the whole, exhaustive way. However, with regard to the central books, books VII–IX, we have had to limit ourselves to book VII – which is after all the heart of the *Metaphysics*.

Finally, the interpretation of the *Metaphysics*, both as a whole and in detail, is a source of considerable controversy. We have decided on the whole not to get involved too much in detailed issues of interpretation. However, certain issues of interpretation, especially in books IV and VII, make a decisive difference to how we understand the central questions of the *Metaphysics*, 'What is being?' and especially 'What is primary being?', and to how we understand Aristotle's answer. So we have chosen to concentrate on these issues of interpretation in the relevant places (see especially Chapter 4§2 and Chapter 7§5v and viii). In general, where we have explicitly considered different interpretations, we have first set out our interpretation, then considered a different interpretation under the heading, 'Alternative interpretation'.

2

METAPHYSICS AS THE SCIENCE OF THE ULTIMATE EXPLANATIONS OF ALL THINGS

(Book I)

1 Metaphysics as the science of the ultimate explanations and principles of all things

In the first two chapters of the *Metaphysics*, Aristotle asks what metaphysics is. His aim here is to give an initial general characterization of metaphysics. He will argue that metaphysics is a kind of knowledge, namely, explanatory knowledge (*epistēmē*) – or what we may call science. By 'science' we will mean simply and generally: some kind of explanatory knowledge. This must be distinguished from a more narrow use of the term 'science', which is perhaps more common today, to mean the empirical or the exact sciences. But Aristotle thinks that there are different kinds of explanatory knowledge, different sciences, and he argues that metaphysics is one of them; it is the science of the first explanations and the first principles of all things. Later (in book IV, chapter 1) he will characterize metaphysics as the science of being *qua* being; it is the science that investigates things that are, and investigates them simply in so far as they are. Later again (in IV. 2, but especially in book VII) he will characterize metaphysics as the science of primary being (*prōtē ousia*, often simply *ousia*). But first let us consider Aristotle's characterization of metaphysics as the science of the first explanations and the first principles of all things, before we ask how this is related to the other two characterizations.

The *Metaphysics* opens with the statement that we humans desire knowledge (*to eidenai*; also, in general, *gnōsis*); and we desire knowledge not only for its consequences and its practical benefits, but also for its own sake. Aristotle goes on to describe how, in general, knowledge develops from its most basic form, which he thinks consists of sense perception, for example, sight, to its highest form, wisdom (*sophia*, this is the term that he uses here for what we call metaphysics). But he emphasizes that it is particularly difficult for us humans to attain this kind of knowledge, and that wisdom is the most difficult cognitive achievement for human beings (982ª23–25). This, he says, is because the kind of knowledge distinctive to metaphysics is 'furthest removed from the senses' (982ª25). This suggests that metaphysics is more the desire and the search for wisdom and less the actual achievement of wisdom; it is *philosophia* rather than simply *sophia* (see 982ᵇ12f.). Later (in VI. 1) he will in fact refer to metaphysics as 'philosophy' (*philosophia*, 'the desire and search for wisdom') and 'first philosophy' (*prōtē philosophia*); but also as 'first science' (*prōtē epistēmē*).

Therefore Aristotle thinks of metaphysics as the search for the highest form of knowledge, which we desire for its own sake and not for its consequences. In general, he distinguishes two levels of knowledge, lower and higher knowledge; and he argues that metaphysics is a higher kind of knowledge, indeed the highest kind. Lower knowledge is knowledge of facts; i.e. it is knowledge *that* something is the case, but without knowing the explanation of why it is the case. Higher knowledge, on the other hand, is knowledge of explanations (*aitiai*, which can also be translated as 'causes'; see below for the translation of *aitia*); i.e. it is knowledge *why* something is the case (981ª24f.). For example (our example, not Aristotle's), it is one thing to know that grass is green, another to know why it is green. The former kind of knowledge we may call purely factual, the latter is explanatory knowledge: science. Or again (this time Aristotle's example), it is one thing to know that fire is hot, another to know why it is hot (see 981ᵇ11–13). We will consider this central distinction between purely factual knowledge, on the one hand, and explanatory knowledge, on the other hand, in a moment. But it is crucial to observe that Aristotle argues that these two kinds of knowledge make up two levels of knowledge; for he argues that explanatory knowledge is knowledge 'more strictly' or 'more properly' (*mallon*) than non-explanatory knowledge (see 981ª24–25).

So Aristotle distinguishes between non-explanatory knowledge, on the one hand, and explanatory or scientific knowledge (*epistēmē*), on the other hand; and he argues that explanatory knowledge is higher than non-explanatory knowledge, i.e. it is more strictly or more properly knowledge. But he thinks that metaphysics is a kind of explanatory knowledge, a science. This leads him to ask (at the opening of I. 2) what kind of explanatory knowledge metaphysics is:

> So it is evident that wisdom [*sophia*, i.e. metaphysics] is a science [*epistēmē*] of certain principles and explanations [*archai* and *aitiai*]. But since this is the science that we are seeking, this is what we must consider: what sort of explanations and what sort of principles is wisdom [i.e. metaphysics] the science of?
>
> (I. 1–2, 982ᵃ1–6)

He answers that metaphysics is the science, i.e. the explanatory knowledge, of 'the first explanations' and 'the first principles':

> this [i.e. wisdom, metaphysics] must be the science [*epistēmē*] that considers the first principles [*prōtai archai*] and [the first] explanations [*aitiai*].
>
> (982ᵇ9–10)

He clarifies what he means by 'the first explanations' and 'the first principles' as follows:

> It is through them and from them [i.e. the first principles and the first explanations] that the other things are known; but they [the first principles and the first explanations] are not known through the things under them.
>
> (982ᵇ2–4)

In other words, the first principles and explanations are what provide explanatory knowledge of other things – the things 'under them' – but other things do not provide explanatory knowledge of the first principles and explanations. In general, Aristotle argues that if something has an explanation, it has a final and complete explanation, i.e. an explanation that does not itself have a further explanation. So he rejects the view that, if something has an explanation, then that explanation may itself have a further explanation, which may itself have a further explanation, and so on without end. (We will return to the question of why he holds this view and what he means by a complete explanation.)

This final and complete explanation of a thing he calls 'the first explanation' of the thing. He also calls it 'the first principle'; for in general he means by a principle (*archē*): 'the starting-point from which a thing either is, or becomes, or is known' (V. 1, 1013ª18–19).

So Aristotle thinks that one characteristic of metaphysics is its being the knowledge of the first or ultimate explanations of things. But there is a second characteristic of metaphysics, which is equally important, for he argues that metaphysics is the explanatory knowledge of 'all things' (*panta*, 982ª8–10, ª21–25). So metaphysics searches for the explanations of all things, i.e. explanations that explain something not only about some things, but about all things. It is, as he says, 'the universal science' (*hē katholou epistēmē*, 982ª22), the science of all things:

> Having explanatory knowledge *of all things* [*to panta epistasthai*] will necessarily be distinctive of the person that most properly possesses the universal science [i.e. metaphysics].
>
> (982ª21–22)

Two things, therefore, are characteristic of metaphysics as Aristotle conceives it. First, it is the knowledge of first or ultimate explanations, explanations that are not themselves subject to further explanation. Second, it is the explanatory knowledge of all things, i.e. knowledge that explains something not only about some things, but about all things.

Let us begin by clarifying some central points about this conception of metaphysics, and some of the background to it.

First, we have in general chosen the term 'explanation' as a translation of *aitia*, rather than 'cause' – although often it will be useful also to use the term 'cause' as translation. The reason for this choice is simply that, as Aristotle in general uses the term *aitia*, an *aitia* is whatever it is, in reality, that answers the question, 'Why?' (*dia tí*). In other words, an *aitia* is *that because of which* such and such is the case (the *di' hoti*); or simply, as Aristotle often says, *the because* (*to dioti*). But it appears that the English term 'explanation' best captures this concept, and that the term 'cause' is too narrow. In other words, all causes provide answers to 'Why?' questions, but not all answers to 'Why?' questions are provided by what in English is naturally called 'a cause'. For example, a law of nature provides an answer to a 'Why?' question, e.g. why water boils at a certain temperature; but it would be unnatural to say that the law of nature causes water to boil at a certain temperature. Of course, the choice of 'explanation' rather than 'cause' as translation of *aitia* must not be associated with modern views, themselves controversial, about the distinction between explanation and causation. In particular, it must not be associated with the modern view that says that *explananda* (i.e. things that are explained) and *explanantia* (i.e. things that explain) are facts, whereas effects and causes are things or events. Most important, it must not be associated with the modern view that says that explanations are dependent on, whereas causes are independent of, how we conceive and describe the world.

Second, Aristotle thinks that every science, and not only metaphysics, searches for first and ultimate explanations of things; for he thinks that each science searches for the first and ultimate explanations of all the things that belong to a particular kind. For example, biology searches for the ultimate explanations of living things; geometry searches for the ultimate explanations of extended things; etc. Metaphysics, on the other hand, searches for the first and ultimate explanations not of one kind of thing as opposed to another, but of all things.

Third, the phrase 'to know all things' is crucially ambiguous; it can mean 'to know *everything* about all things' or it can mean 'to know *something* about all things'. When Aristotle asserts that metaphysics is the search for the first explanations of all things, he does not mean that such explanations will explain *everything* about all things; he means that they will explain *something* about all things. In fact it will emerge that he thinks that the first explanations of all things explain something very definite about all things: why each and every thing is a being, something that is, in the first place. So metaphysics is 'the universal science' (*hē katholou epistēmē*, 982ª22), the science of all things; but it is the universal science because, above all, it investigates something very definite about all things: why each and every thing is a being – something that is.

Fourth, he says that the metaphysician will, ideally, have knowledge of all things 'to the extent that this is possible, and not by having knowledge of each one of them' (982ª9–10). There are two important points in this clarification. First, the metaphysician will not know each and every particular thing that there is, for example each tree in each wood; rather, they will know all things in a general way. This is true of every science; for every science knows things not as particulars, but in a general way. Forestry, for example, does not know each tree in each wood, but trees in general, i.e. the general kind, *trees*. Second, the metaphysician will not know things in a general way in the way in which the other sciences do; for such knowledge would simply amount to the sum of the special sciences, each of which searches for knowledge of one kind of thing as opposed to another. Rather, the metaphysician will know all things in a completely and radically general way, i.e. simply in so far as each thing is a being, something that is, and not in so far as it is one as opposed to another kind of thing.

Fifth, metaphysics, the knowledge of the first explanations and first principles of all things, is the knowledge that we acquire last, if we search for it and acquire it at all; and it is a kind of knowledge with which we are least familiar. We may naturally call such knowledge, knowledge of *ultimate* explanations. The knowledge that we acquire first is sense perception (*aisthēsis*) and experience (*empeiria*), and this is the knowledge with which we are most familiar; it is only later that we, or some of us at any rate, search for explanatory knowledge (*epistēmē*). But the kind of explanatory knowledge that is metaphysics we acquire only last, if we search for it and find it at all. Aristotle emphasizes that metaphysics is a kind of knowledge with which we are least familiar, when he says that this kind of knowledge 'is furthest removed from the senses' (982ᵃ25). Since he thinks that we are least familiar with this kind of knowledge, metaphysics, it is only natural that he should be at pains to provide an initial general characterization of metaphysics and to clarify what kind of knowledge this is.

Therefore, at the opening of the *Metaphysics*, Aristotle characterizes metaphysics as the science of the ultimate explanations of all things. But later (at the opening of book IV), he characterizes metaphysics in a different way: as the science of being *qua* being. This means that metaphysics is the science that investigates beings, and investigates them simply in so far as they are beings, things that are. It is the science that investigates the essence of being, or what it is to be a being. How are these two characterizations of metaphysics related? Aristotle appears to think that the first characterization (metaphysics as the science of the ultimate explanations of all things) leads to the second characterization (metaphysics as the science of being *qua* being and of the essence of being). For he thinks that the explanations for which metaphysics searches – the ultimate explanations of all things – explain above all this about all things: why each and every thing is a being – something that is.

In particular, the relation between the characterization of metaphysics as the science of the ultimate explanations of all things and the characterization of metaphysics as the science of being *qua* being appears to be this. Broadly speaking, an ultimate explanation of a thing, x, is the explanation of the essence of that thing, x. So the ultimate explanation of *all things* (*panta*) is the explanation of the essence of all things and of being as a whole (*katholou*, see IV. 1, 1003ᵃ23–25, where he argues that the science of being *qua* being is the science of being as a whole). But apparently what all things essentially share, if they share anything essentially, is above all their being beings – things that are. So the ultimate explanation of *all things* is the explanation above all of all things simply in so far as they are beings, things that are – so it is the explanatory knowledge and the science of being *qua* being.

In general, Aristotle characterizes metaphysics in three ways in the *Metaphysics*:

> M1. Metaphysics is the science, i.e. the explanatory knowledge, of the first or ultimate explanations of all things.

> M2. Metaphysics is the science of being *qua* being; i.e. it is the science that investigates things that are, and investigates them simply in so far as they are.

> M3. Metaphysics is the science of primary being (*prōtē ousia*, often simply *ousia*).

We have seen that, apparently, he thinks that the first characterization, which he states at the opening of the *Metaphysics*, leads to the second, which he first states at the opening of book IV. The relation between the second and the third characterization we will consider later (see Chapter 4§§1–3).

So metaphysics, as it is characterized at the opening of the *Metaphysics*, is a kind of explanatory knowledge – a science; and it differs from other kinds of explanatory knowledge (other sciences) in that it is the science of the ultimate explanations not of some things as opposed to others, but of all things. But there is a further interesting feature in Aristotle's initial characterization of metaphysics. For (in I. 1) he distinguishes between two general kinds of explanatory knowledge: science (*epistēmē*) and art (*technē*); and he characterizes metaphysics as a science as opposed to an art. Both science and art are kinds of explanatory knowledge. But art (*technē*) is the explanatory knowledge of how to act and especially how to produce and in general bring about things. For example, Aristotle distinguishes between, on the one hand, a skilled craftsman (*cheirotechnēs*), who knows, for example, how to build a house, but does not know the principles of house-building or why houses must be built according to certain principles, and, on the other hand, a master-craftsman (*architektōn*), who also knows the principles of house-building and why houses must be built according to certain principles (I. 1, 981ᵃ30–ᵇ2; 981ᵇ31–982ᵃ1). But he contrasts art (*technē*) with science (*epistēmē*), and he argues that science is the kind of explanatory knowledge that is not concerned with bringing about anything, but is concerned simply with knowing why things are as they are. As we would say, science is explanatory knowledge that is purely theoretical, whereas art is explanatory knowledge that is practical and, especially, productive.

Aristotle does not further clarify the distinction between these two general kinds of explanatory knowledge: science (*epistēmē*) and art (*technē*). He points out that the difference between them was discussed in the *Ethics* (981^{b}25–26; see *Nicomachean Ethics*, book VI, especially chapters 3–4). But he emphasizes that metaphysics is a science as opposed to an art. In a remarkable piece of history and sociology of science, he argues that in general science is not concerned with the necessities of life, or with what is useful, or with pleasure; it is rather the fruit of leisure (*scholē*):

> Hence when all such things [i.e. the kinds of knowledge that are concerned with what is necessary, useful, or pleasant] had already been established, the sciences were discovered that are not concerned with pleasure or with what is necessary; and they were first discovered in those places in which people enjoyed leisure. This is why the mathematical sciences were first developed in Egypt, because there the priestly class was granted leisure.
>
> (981^{b}20–25)

Evidently Aristotle thinks that the practice of science emerges only when leisure is available, because he thinks that only when leisure is available can we develop or realize the desire for the kind of knowledge that is desired for its own sake and not for its consequences and practical benefits, and he thinks that the desire for this kind of knowledge is natural to us humans. But he also appears to think that the practice of science constitutes a leisurely activity, perhaps the highest sort of leisure, precisely because this activity is desired not for its consequences or practical benefits, but for its own sake.

We saw that in general Aristotle ranks explanatory knowledge higher than non-explanatory knowledge, i.e. he thinks that explanatory knowledge is more strictly knowledge than non-explanatory knowledge (981^{a}24–25). But it is striking that he also ranks science higher than art:

> the theoretical [kinds of explanatory knowledge] are considered more wise than the productive ones.
>
> (982^{a}1)

He thinks that this is an accepted opinion, but he also agrees with it. So it seems that Aristotle thinks that purely theoretical explanatory knowledge (i.e. science) is more strictly knowledge than the kind of explanatory knowledge that is concerned with bringing about things (i.e. art). However, we must not misunderstand this view. For when he speaks of explanatory knowledge that is 'theoretical' (*theōrētikē*), i.e. of science as opposed to art, he does not mean what we may mean by 'purely theoretical knowledge' or 'science', especially when we use these terms loosely and popularly. To us these terms may suggest a search for knowledge that is altogether divorced from life; but for Aristotle, if anything, the opposite is true. He thinks that such knowledge is desired not for its consequences, but for its own sake, but he also thinks that the search for such knowledge, and the enjoyment and contemplation of it once found, is a central constituent in the happy life, the life worth living for a human being (see especially *Nicomachean Ethics*, book X).

2 How explanatory knowledge differs from sense perception and experience

At the opening of the *Metaphysics* (I. 1) Aristotle argues that there is a fundamental difference between sense perception (*aisthēsis*) and experience (*empeiria*), on the one hand, and science (*epistēmē*) and art (*technē*), on the other hand. Each of these is a capacity for knowledge, and we humans possess all of these capacities, whereas other animals possess only sense perception and, to a limited extent, experience. But the fundamental difference between the first two and the last two capacities for knowledge is this: sense perception and experience are capacities for knowing that something is the case, but not for knowing why it is the case; science and art, on the other hand, are capacities for knowing why something is the case. So, unlike sense perception and experience, science and art are capacities for explanatory knowledge, i.e. knowledge of why something is the case or why it is as it is.

The distinction between non-explanatory knowledge and explanatory knowledge is absolutely central in Aristotle. But it is particularly important to recognize what capacities for knowledge he thinks are capacities for explanatory knowledge, and especially what capacities he thinks are not capacities for explanatory knowledge. For he argues that neither sense perception (*aisthēsis*) nor experience (*empeiria*) are capacities for explanatory knowledge.

By 'sense perception' (*aisthēsis*), he means the capacity for knowledge associated with the senses – sight, hearing, touch, smell and taste – both each sense in isolation and the senses taken together. By 'experience' (*empeiria*) he means a particular capacity for knowledge, which is generated from sense perception and memory:

> But from memory is generated experience in human beings [but he
> has just said that other animals also possess experience, though to
> a limited extent]. For many memories of the same thing produce the
> capacity for a single experience [of that thing].
>
> (I. 1, 980^{b}28–981^{a}1)

The memories that he has in mind are evidently memories associated
with previous sense perceptions. So when he says that experience
is generated from sense perception and memory, he means that if an
animal has perceived many particular things that are all alike, for
example, many particular trees, and if it also remembers these particular things, then this animal may – especially, but not exclusively, if it
is a human being – develop the capacity for a single experience of such
things, for example, of trees. By 'a single experience' he means, apparently, a single thought (noēma, see 981^{a}6), i.e. a thought with a single
general content; e.g. the thought of trees. Such a general thought will
not be of any particular tree, but of trees in general; for example, it will
be the thought that trees have leaves, or that trees provide useful shelter
from the sun, etc. If this is what Aristotle means here, to develop experience (empeiria) is to develop a capacity for general thought.

So Aristotle appears to think that what distinguishes sense perception from experience is this: sense perception is a capacity for particular knowledge, for example, the knowledge of this particular tree or
that particular tree; experience, on the other hand, is a capacity for a
kind of general knowledge, for example, general knowledge of trees,
such as the knowledge that trees have leaves, or that trees provide
useful shelter from the sun, or (to mention his own example) that
fire is hot (see 981^{b}12–13). That this is his view is confirmed when
he says:

> For it belongs to experience to form the supposition that when Kallias
> was suffering from this disease, this drug did him good, and simi-
> larly in the case of Socrates and many individual cases.
>
> (981^{a}7–9)

In these lines, Aristotle is describing the practice of a physician who
relies exclusively on sense perception (aisthēsis) and experience
(empeiria), but does not possess explanatory knowledge (technē and
epistēmē). In other words, he does not at all know how to explain why
his patients behave as they do, and perhaps he is not interested in such
knowledge; but he is familiar with common ailments of people and how
to treat them effectively. To begin with, this physician has perceived a

number of particular cases which are all similar: Kallias behaves in a certain way, is administered a certain drug, and responds in a certain way; Socrates behaves in a similar way, is administered this drug, and responds in a similar way, etc. But the physician may naturally go on to form the general thought: patients that exhibit such and such behaviour generally respond in such and such a way to such and such a drug. We should note, however, that this physician does not put forward any explanatory hypothesis to explain why a certain kind of drug has a certain kind of effect on a certain kind of illness. Aristotle argues that the capacity to form such general thoughts, based on the particular cases familiar from perception, belongs to experience. So he characterizes experience as a capacity for general knowledge; and he distinguishes this from the capacity for particular knowledge, which he associates with sense perception.

Aristotle's distinction between sense perception and experience is itself interesting, but what is especially important for our purpose is his assertion that neither sense perception nor experience constitutes or is sufficient for explanatory knowledge – knowledge of why things are as they are:

> However, we believe that knowledge [*to eidenai*] and understanding [*to epaïein*] belongs more [*mallon*, 'more strictly', 'more properly'] to art [*technē*, but also science, *epistēmē*] than to experience, and we suppose that people who possess art are wiser than those who possess experience . . .; and the reason for this is that the former know the explanation [*aitia*], but the latter do not.
>
> (981ᵃ24–28)

So the physicians who rely on sense perception and experience may, in virtue of their capacity for experience, form general thoughts, and they may know that such thoughts are true. But Aristotle argues that this neither constitutes nor is sufficient for explanatory knowledge – knowledge of why things are as they are. In general, he argues that the capacity to form general thoughts, e.g. the thought that fire is hot (i.e. not this or that particular fire, but fire in general; see 981ᵇ12–13), is not yet the capacity to explain things, and it is not sufficient for this latter capacity. So he thinks that, to explain things, more is required than general thoughts or the knowledge that such thoughts are true.

It is worth emphasizing Aristotle's view that experience is not sufficient for explanatory knowledge. For he thinks that experience does indeed provide us with a kind of general knowledge: it provides us with non-explanatory general knowledge (e.g. the general knowledge that fire is hot, or that trees have leaves, or that swans are white). But he appears to think (e.g. from what he says about the procedure of the non-scientific physician) that the general knowledge that is based on experience is based on what we may call induction by enumeration: 'this particular fire is hot, and that particular fire is hot, and that . . . ; therefore, all fire is hot'. Each of the steps in such an induction involves a piece of particular knowledge (e.g. the knowledge that this fire is hot), and particular knowledge is acquired directly from sense perception. But the induction also goes beyond sense perception; for it generates general knowledge on the basis of many pieces of particular knowledge, each of which is acquired through sense perception. We should note, however, that the term in Aristotle, *epagōgē*, which is commonly translated as 'induction', is crucially broader than induction by enumeration; for although apparently it includes induction by enumeration, it includes also the putting forward of explanatory hypotheses.

Perhaps the kind of reasoning that Aristotle associates with experience (*empeiria*) may involve more than simply induction by enumeration; it may also involve an ability to recognize relevantly similar cases. We may think of an effective but non-scientific physician. But what is particularly important for our purpose is Aristotle's view that the kind of reasoning that is associated with the capacity for experience (*empeiria*), whatever exactly it may involve, is not sufficient for explanatory knowledge; for he thinks that experience provides non-explanatory general knowledge, but not explanatory general knowledge. Evidently he thinks that there is a fundamental distinction between non-explanatory general knowledge (e.g. the knowledge that fire is hot) and explanatory general knowledge (e.g. the knowledge why fire is hot); and the former is not sufficient for the latter.

This view may perhaps seem puzzling, especially if we arrive at it from a Humean philosophy of science which argues that general knowledge cannot go beyond induction by enumeration. But there is also something very plausible about a view which says that while no more than induction by enumeration may be required for non-explanatory general knowledge, what is required for explanatory general knowledge is explanatory theories. Aristotle argues that the putting forward of such theories, or 'universal suppositions', as he calls them here (*katholou hupolēpseis*, see 981ª6–7), will involve reflecting on the general knowledge already arrived at through experience:

> Art [*technē*, i.e. the kind of explanatory knowledge relevant to, for example, medicine] comes about when a single universal supposition

about the similar cases is generated from a variety of thoughts belonging to experience.

(981ª5–7)

For example (from his example in 981ª7–12), the non-scientific physician may possess the general knowledge that patients who exhibit such and such behaviour generally respond in such and such a way to such and such a drug. But the scientific physicians will ask, what is it about such patients and such drugs that make them interact with such results? In asking this question they will be reflecting on the general thoughts already present in the general knowledge of the non-scientific physicians, i.e. the thoughts of *such patients*, *such drugs* and *such behaviour*. But they will want to put forward a universal hypothesis to explain why these things are related in the way in which the non-scientific physicians already know that they are related.

However, it is worth emphasizing (as Aristotle does in lines 981ª7–12) that when the scientific physicians put forward a universal hypothesis to explain why these things are related in these ways, they may need to revise the initial, non-scientific conception of the things involved. We may, incidentally, note that in general Aristotle speaks of *the phainomena* (*ta phainomena*) to refer to things as we initially and pre-scientifically perceive them and think of them. For while the non-scientific physician will talk of patients exhibiting certain familiar symptoms of illness (e.g. high fever), of certain drugs (e.g. the herb sage), and of certain familiar symptoms of recovery (e.g. reduction of the fever), the scientific physician will want to identify what the illness is and what it is about it and the drug that explains why they interact in a certain way, a way whose visible manifestation is the patient's recovery. Such revision of the initial, non-scientific conception of the things involved – of the *phainomena* – will, he says, involve distinguishing the patients into a single scientifically known kind (*eidos*), i.e. the kind associated with the scientific knowledge of the illness in question, the illness which was initially known simply by certain familiar symptoms such as high fever (see 981ª10–12; here he refers to the illness by using the terms 'bile' and 'phlegm', these apparently being the latest and most advanced terms of medicine at that time). In general, the search for explanation as Aristotle conceives it is the search for the correct way to distinguish things into natural kinds. But this search may involve considerable revision of our initial conception of things.

So Aristotle thinks that there is a fundamental distinction between two kinds of general knowledge: non-explanatory general knowledge and explanatory general knowledge. And he thinks that two different capacities for knowledge are associated with general knowledge: experience is the capacity for non-explanatory general knowledge; science and art are the capacities for explanatory general knowledge. But how are sense perception and experience, on the one hand, related to science and art, on the other hand? And are they related at all? How Aristotle understands this relation is perhaps not so clear at the opening of the *Metaphysics*. But if we draw on what he says elsewhere (especially at the end of the *Posterior Analytics*, II. 19), the following view emerges:

> Sense perception (*aisthēsis*) is necessary and sufficient for particular knowledge (e.g. the knowledge that this particular tree has leaves).

> Experience (*empeiria*) is necessary for non-explanatory general knowledge (e.g. the knowledge that trees have leaves); and perception and experience are jointly necessary and sufficient for such knowledge.

> Science or art (*epistēmē*, *technē*) is necessary for explanatory general knowledge (e.g. the knowledge why trees have leaves); and perception, experience and science or art are jointly necessary and sufficient for such knowledge.

This shows that Aristotle thinks that there is a progression and ascent of knowledge, with three main steps. The first step is particular knowledge, which is acquired through sense perception. The second step is non-explanatory general knowledge, which is acquired through experience. The third step is explanatory general knowledge, which is acquired through science or art. These steps are related as follows: each step is necessary for taking the next, but not sufficient. In other words, each step relies on the previous step, but it also goes decisively beyond it.

Aristotle makes a further claim at the opening of the *Metaphysics*, which is central to understanding his distinction between non-explanatory and explanatory knowledge: experience is knowledge of particulars, but science and art are knowledge of universals. He says:

> Experience is knowledge of particulars [*ta kath' hekasta*], but art [*technē*; but he intends the point to be true also of science, *epistēmē*] is knowledge of universals [*ta katholou*].
>
> (981ª15–16)

So non-explanatory knowledge, including experience, is knowledge of particulars, for example, particular trees; but explanatory knowledge is knowledge of universals. We will see that by 'universals' here he means above all: natural kinds, kinds associated with distinctions in reality.

Aristotle's claim that non-explanatory knowledge, including experience, is knowledge of particulars and not also of universals may appear puzzling, since he also thinks that experience is a kind of general knowledge: it is non-explanatory general knowledge. For how can he think that experience is knowledge of particulars and not also of universals, but also think that experience is a kind of general knowledge? Apparently he must think that there are two different kinds of general knowledge:

(1) general knowledge that is only of particulars and not also of universals; and
(2) general knowledge that is of universals as well as particulars.

So experience belongs to the former kind of general knowledge, but not to the latter.

The important thing here is that Aristotle does not think that all general knowledge is knowledge of universals. Rather, he thinks that only explanatory general knowledge is knowledge of universals; non-explanatory general knowledge is only of particulars, although it is general knowledge of them. We may ask, how puzzling is his view that experience, though it is a kind of general knowledge, is knowledge only of particulars and not also of universals? This depends on what he means by 'a universal' (*to katholou*). If he means 'a general thought' or 'a general concept', or the content of general thoughts and concepts, then the view will be very puzzling and arguably incoherent. For he thinks that experience involves general thoughts (e.g. the thought that fire is hot: not this or that fire, but fire in general; see 981[b]11–13). On the other hand, if by 'a universal' he means 'a natural kind' and 'a distinction in reality', then his view will not be so puzzling. For he may think that not every general thought or knowledge is the knowledge of a natural kind and a distinction in reality. He may think rather that only a certain kind of general thought and knowledge is the knowledge of natural kinds and distinctions in reality: explanatory general thought and knowledge. In general, Aristotle thinks that only through the search for explanations and explanatory knowledge can we acquire knowledge of universals, i.e. real universals: universals that correspond with natural kinds and distinctions in reality. Indeed he thinks that explanations are themselves elements in reality, they are not simply elements in our thought. And such real explanations are, precisely, universals.

Alternative interpretation

On a different interpretation of Aristotle's conception of experience (*empeiria*), experience does not involve general thought at all; it involves only a plurality of particular thoughts, and particular memories of particular thoughts. So, on this interpretation, experience does not, for example, involve the thought: such and such patients generally respond to such and such a drug in such and such a way. It involves only the thought: in the cases of Socrates, Kallias, etc. (i.e. the number of particular cases that one has actually experienced), such and such a drug has produced such and such a response. (This interpretation is defended by, for example, Bolton 1991: 6–7.) This interpretation is motivated by the view that experience does not involve knowledge of universals, or even strictly universal knowledge, i.e. knowledge of the form: *all* Fs *without exception* are Gs. But the interpretation is not convincing. It is true that experience does not involve knowledge of universals; for we have seen that the knowledge of universals requires knowledge of explanations, and experience does not involve such knowledge. It may also be true that experience does not involve strictly and unexceptionally universal knowledge; for it is explanations that are strictly and unexceptionally universal. (We will return to this point later.) But it does not follow that experience does not involve general knowledge. We have seen that Aristotle's distinction between experience (*empeiria*) and scientific knowledge (*epistēmē, technē*) is *not* the distinction between particular and general knowledge. The distinction between particular and general knowledge is rather that between sense perception (*aisthēsis*), on the one hand, and *empeiria* and *epistēmē*, on the other. Rather, Aristotle's distinction between experience (*empeiria*) and scientific knowledge (*epistēmē, technē*) is the distinction between general knowledge that is not explanatory and general knowledge that is explanatory.

In the remainder of this chapter we will provide some important background about Aristotle's conception of explanation (this chapter, §3) and his conception of the explanations and causes of changing things (this chapter, §4). In the next chapter we return more directly to the text of the *Metaphysics*.

3 Aristotle's general conception of explanations and explanatory knowledge

i The search for explanations and what it is based on

At the opening of the *Metaphysics* (I. 1–2) Aristotle argues that metaphysics is the science of the ultimate explanations of all things. He goes on (at the opening of I. 3) to remind the reader that in the *Physics* he had developed a theory in which he had distinguished four different basic kinds of explanations and causes of things, and in particular of changing things: the formal cause; the material cause; the efficient cause; and the final cause. But it is important to note why he mentions the theory of the four causes here:

> for we say that we know each thing precisely when we suppose that we know its first explanation [or 'its first cause', *prōtē aitia*].
>
> (I. 3, 983ª25–26)

So he thinks that knowledge, at its best, requires knowledge of explanations; and ultimately it requires knowledge of first, i.e. ultimate, explanations. This is also a reminder of the theory of explanatory knowledge that he developed in the *Posterior Analytics*. So let us stand back from the text of the *Metaphysics* and consider Aristotle's general conception of explanatory knowledge, or science (*epistēmē*). We will begin with his account of what it is to search for explanations, and what this search is based on.

At the opening of the *Physics*, Aristotle characterizes the search for explanations as a 'path' or 'road' (*hodos*) that we take up:

> from what is better known and more clear *to us*, towards what is better known and more clear *on account of [its] nature* [*tēi phusei*].
>
> (*Physics* I. 1, 184ª16–18)

Here he also refers to 'what is better known and more clear *on account of [its] nature*' as 'what is better known and more clear *without qualification* (*haplōs*)'. In the *Posterior Analytics* (71ᵇ29–72ª5) he makes the same point, but he also clarifies that:

> By what is more basic [*proteron*, 'prior', 'more primary'] and better known *to us* I mean what is closer to sense perception; and by what is more basic and better known *without qualification* [i.e. on account of its nature] I mean what is further removed from sense perception.

> But it is the things that are most universal that are furthest removed
> from sense perception; and it is particulars that are closest to sense
> perception.
>
> (*Posterior Analytics* I. 2, 72ª1–5)

So, when we search for explanations, we must start from something
that is already clear or evident (*safes*) to our senses, for example that
plants grow. And it is of such evident things that we may go on to ask:
why are these things as they are (or as they appear to our senses)?
For example: why do plants grow? To search for an explanation is to
search for the answer to a 'Why?' question (*dia tí*; 'Why?'). But we
can only ask 'Why?' questions if there is something that we already
know or something that at least is already evident to us. This means,
Aristotle argues, that we can search for explanations only if, to begin
with, there is something that we know, or that is evident to us, directly
and without this knowledge involving a search for explanations. And
he argues that such direct and non-explanatory knowledge is, precisely,
sense perception. It is also worth emphasizing that he does indeed
conceive of sense perception as a kind of knowledge, even though it is
non-explanatory knowledge. So he does not think that it is only
through explanations that we can acquire any knowledge at all. This
more extreme view is apparently Plato's. At the same time, we should
also recall his central claim, which says that explanatory knowledge
(*epistēmē*) is 'more strictly' (*mallon*) knowledge than non-explanatory
knowledge. So knowledge does, in the end and at its best, require
explanatory knowledge.

What we are searching for when we search for explanations is,
evidently, answers to 'Why?' questions. But Aristotle thinks that such
answers will refer directly to the things themselves and their features.
So he thinks that when we ask a 'Why?' question, we are asking something of the things themselves; for example, why plants grow. But
he also thinks that the answer that we are searching for will appeal
directly to the things themselves and their features; for example,
plants grow because they take up and process nutrients in certain ways.
In other words, he conceives of both *explananda* (i.e. what we ask
'Why?' questions of) and *explanantia* (i.e. what provides the answer
to 'Why?' questions) as things and their features, and he conceives of
explanation as a relation simply between two sets of things and their
features – a metaphysical relation. The one set is the *explananda*; the
other set is the *explanantia*; and the relation is: *X explains Y*. It is not
so clear, however, to what extent there is a real worry or concern in
Aristotle that explanations may in general be relative to us and to our

conception of things. He is clearly a realist about explanation, but it is not so clear whether this realism is a considered position or it is merely a result of the issue between realism and anti-realism about explanation not being a live one for him. But we must not simply assume that this issue is not a live one for him; for we will see later (in Chapter 6) that it is very much a live issue for him, whether in general our thought and knowledge is about the things themselves or it is only about things as they appear to us and as we conceive them.

Let us look closer at this 'path' or 'road' (*hodos*), i.e. the path from what is more clear (or evident) and better known *to us*, towards what is more clear and better known *on account of its nature* and *without qualification*. What is more clear (or evident) and better known *to us* is, he says, what is closer to sense perception. This view seems on the whole plausible and unproblematic; for it means that, in order to search for explanatory knowledge, we must ultimately start with non-explanatory knowledge (or apparent knowledge that is non-explanatory), and such knowledge is acquired through sense perception. But what does he mean by 'what is more clear and better known *on account of its nature* and *without qualification*'? Clearly, he means what is explained, or better explained: hence what is understood, or better understood. (On a different reading, he means what is explicable and intelligible, i.e. capable of being explained and understood, but the two readings are similar enough.) But we should note that Aristotle's general view about the relation between knowledge and explanation is not simply that what is explained is better *understood* than what is not explained; so much is stating the obvious, since it is evidently through explain-ing things that we understand them. Rather, his view is that what is explained is better *known* than what is not explained. For he argues that explanatory knowledge is knowledge more strictly than non-explanatory knowledge.

But why does he think that what is known in such a way that its explanation is also known is 'more clear' (*safesteron*), than what is known in such a way that its explanation is not known? And why, indeed, does he think that what is known in the former, explanatory way is 'better known' (*gnōrimōteron*) than what is known in the latter, non-explanatory way? In other words, why does Aristotle think that explanatory knowledge is knowledge more strictly than non-explanatory knowledge? At the root of this centrally important view is a view that is itself absolutely central to Aristotle. For he argues that to search for the explanations of things, things with which we are already familiar from sense perception and experience, is to search for divisions in reality and natural kinds. But he argues that things are distinguished into kinds simply because of what they are – their nature or essence – and not because of how they appear to us or how in general we conceive them. So we can see why he thinks that explanatory knowledge is 'more clear' than non-explanatory knowledge, and why things are 'better known' when their explanations are known than when their explanations are not known. This is because he argues that it is when we know real distinctions and natural kinds that we have the clearest and best knowledge of things. For he argues that it is this knowledge that enables us to distinguish things adequately – to distinguish them as they are distinguished 'by nature' and 'on account of their essence and nature' (*tēi phusei*). So this, in the end, is why Aristotle thinks that explanatory knowledge is knowledge more strictly (*mallon*) than non-explanatory knowledge; this is because it is explanatory knowledge that enables us to distinguish things as they really are distinguished in themselves.

ii The nature and requirements of explanations

Aristotle's theory of the nature of explanation is rooted in Plato's. In the dialogue *Phaedo* (95ef., a passage with which Aristotle was familiar) Plato considers the nature of explanation. He points out that he is first of all concerned with explanations of phenomena in nature – phenomena that involve change and changing things. Plato argues that an explanation must satisfy a number of requirements: (R1) it must be completely general, or universal; (R2) it must be uniform; and (R3) it must be complete or capable of being completed. He argues further that (R4) purely materialist explanations, explanations that are based simply in the material constituents of things (e.g. that a thing is made of flesh and bones), do not satisfy these requirements; hence they are not, by themselves, adequate explanations. Finally, in his famous theory of forms, he argues that (R5) explanations are based in the essence of things. But he argues that the essence of things are separate and distinct from changing things, the things with which we are directly familiar from sense perception. In the course of the *Metaphysics*, Aristotle will argue that Plato's view of essences, i.e. the view which argues that essences are separate and distinct from changing things, is fundamentally mistaken (see below, Chapter 9). But this disagreement takes place against the background of a shared conception of explanation and a shared view that explanations are based in the essence of things.

Let us briefly review these requirements for explanation.

R1. GENERALITY

If we want to explain a particular thing, e.g. why this particular plant grows in a certain way, the explanation must appeal to something about plants in general, not just this plant.

R2. UNIFORMITY

If we explain a particular thing in a certain way, then we must explain in the same way any other thing that is of the same kind. Conversely, if we explain two particular things in the same way, then we must suppose that the two things are of the same kind. In short, this means: same *explanandum* (i.e. what is explained) if, and only if, same *explanans* (i.e. what explains). Or, in other words: same cause if, and only if, same effect. For example, if we explain in a certain way why a particular plant grows as it does, then we must explain in the same way the growth of any other thing of the same kind; i.e. either any other plant or any other plant of that specific kind. Conversely, if we explain in a certain way the growth of one particular plant, and explain in the same way the growth of another particular plant, then we must suppose that the two things belong to the same kind.

R3. COMPLETENESS

Each particular explanation must be complete. In other words, it must not give rise to the need for a further explanation. So there are first and ultimate explanations, i.e. explanations that do not themselves have further explanations.

It is important not to misunderstand this requirement, i.e. the requirement of completeness. For it does not mean that there cannot be an infinite series of causes and effects. On the contrary, Aristotle thinks that there are infinite series of causes and effects. For example, he argues that the cause of the generation of each living thing is an already generated thing of the same kind, and he argues that this series of causes and effects extends infinitely backwards in time. But then how can there be a complete explanation of the generation of a particular thing (e.g. of this rosebush)? There can be a complete explanation, because the way in which a generated thing explains the generation of a new thing is exactly the same way whichever set of two things, a parent and an offspring, we consider (for this point in general, see Chapter 7§5ix). For the mode of explanation is, quite generally, this: the explanation and cause of the generation of each living thing is an already generated thing of the same kind.

What, then, does the requirement of completeness mean? Apparently, it means, above all, that, if a particular 'Why?' question has an answer, then it has a single, determinate and well-defined answer. For suppose that the answer to a 'Why?' question could not, in principle, be completed. In that case, only part of the answer would be determinate and well-defined, and it would, necessarily, be indeterminate what the remaining part is. In other words, there would, necessarily, be a remaining part that could be any number of things. So there would not be a single, determinate, and well-defined answer to the 'Why?' question.

With regard to particular things, and kinds of things, such as this rosebush and rosebushes in general, the requirement of completeness means that if there is an answer to the question, 'Why is this thing as it is and why does it behave as it does?', then there is a single, determinate and well-defined answer to this question. It will emerge that Aristotle (and Plato) thinks that this answer will be provided by the essence of the thing in question. For he argues that if a thing has an essence, then it has a single, determinate and well-defined essence (see Chapter 7§5iii). And in general he argues that the explanation of why a thing is as it is and behaves as it does is ultimately provided by the essence of that thing. In this sense, the explanation of each particular thing, and kind of thing, must be complete.

But again it is important not to misunderstand this point. For when Aristotle claims that the explanation of each particular thing, and kind of thing, must be complete, he does not mean that it must explain all the facts about the thing. What he means is that it must explain, in a complete way, all the facts about the things that are part of its essence, i.e. part of what it is to be that very thing (and perhaps also all the facts that follow directly from those facts). Indeed, he thinks that it is impossible to give a complete explanation of *everything* about a thing; for he thinks that each thing has indefinitely many accidental properties, hence there are indefinitely many facts about each thing (see e.g. 1007ª14–15).

To see what he means by the claim that the explanation of each particular thing, and kind of thing, must be complete, we may compare our own likely response to such a question as, 'What is water?', posed in a scientific context. For if we answer that water is H_2O, it is natural to suppose that this is a complete explanatory answer (within the context of the theory of chemistry) to this question. At any rate, the fact that indefinitely many things are otherwise true of water will hardly constitute an objection to our supposition that this answer, 'Water is H_2O', gives (within the context of chemistry) a complete explanatory account of what water is.

R4. REJECTION OF SCIENTIFIC MATERIALISM

Plato and Aristotle argue that purely materialist explanations fail to satisfy the requirements of explanation, and especially the requirement of uniformity. Their argument is along the following lines. Suppose that we ask why this particular thing behaves in a certain way, and we answer that this is because it is made of certain materials, e.g. flesh and bones. Still, we may ask why the fact that the thing is made of these materials is associated with the thing's behaving in this way and not in another way. After all, we can imagine a world in which a thing that is made of the same materials behaved in a different way. In Plato's memorable example (*Phaedo* 98–99), the same bones and sinews that make up Socrates and that are in fact associated with his behaving in one way (e.g. his staying where he is, in prison) could have been associated with his behaving in a different way (e.g. his running away from Athens to the provinces). But if all that we have recourse to is purely materialist explanations, this question ('Why are these materials in this thing associated with the thing's behaving in this way and not in another way?') is in principle unanswerable. So purely materialist explanations fail to satisfy the requirement of uniformity, and in particular the requirement: if same *explanans* or cause (e.g. same bones and sinews), then same *explanandum* or effect (e.g. staying here, not running away). But we should note that Plato and Aristotle allow that an explanation may appeal to the material constituents of things, provided that this is not all that it appeals to. So the material constituents of a thing are not sufficient for explaining why the thing behaves as it does, but they may be necessary for explaining this.

R5. ESSENTIALISM

Explanations are based in the essence of things. For example (from Aristotle's example in *Metaphysics* I. 1), it is by trying to know what a certain illness really is, its essence, that a scientifically minded physician will try to explain why this illness is as it is and behaves as it does: why it has the symptoms, causes, and consequences it has; why it responds to one treatment but not another, etc. Another example: to explain why trees have leaves, we must know the nature of trees, or plants in general, i.e. what it is to be a tree or plant. So in general Aristotle and Plato think that it is by knowing what a thing really is, its essence, that we can adequately explain why the thing is as it is.

This means that explanatory knowledge requires knowledge of what things are, their essence. But it is worth emphasizing that this view does not mean that we can know the essence of things independently of searching for explanatory knowledge; neither does it mean that the essence of things is something that we know first, before we go on to explain anything. On the contrary, knowledge of the essence of a thing, if we acquire it at all, is something that we find only at the end of the search for explanatory knowledge about that thing. So the view is not that we can search for explanatory knowledge about a thing only if we already know the essence of that thing; the view is that knowing the essence of a thing is what constitutes finding explanations about that thing that are complete and fully adequate.

We should also note that if something is true of something *essentially*, then it is true of it *necessarily*, but the converse is not the case. For example, if it is true of Socrates essentially that he is human, then Socrates is necessarily human; or if it is true of the property *red* essentially that it is a colour, then the property *red* is necessarily a colour. So, according to essentialism, explanations ultimately are based in certain necessary truths about things, namely, those necessary truths that are essential truths about those things.

There are at least two general reasons why, although all essential truths are necessary truths, not all necessary truths are essential truths. First, on Aristotle's characterization of essence, an essential truth about a thing, x, is a truth in virtue of what this thing, x, is, simply in virtue of itself and not in virtue of its relation to other things. So in this sense an essential truth is non-relational. But a necessary truth may be relational; in particular, it may be the consequence of the relation between two things and their essences. For example, it may be a necessary truth that Socrates is distinct from the Eiffel Tower. But, on Aristotle's non-relational conception of essence, this is not an essential truth. It is rather a consequence of essential truths about Socrates, the Eiffel Tower, space, time, and perhaps other things too.

Second, and perhaps more important, there may be a mutual and two-way necessary relation between two things, but there may only be a one-way essential relation between them. In Plato's famous argument from the dialogue *Euthyphro* (9–11), it may be a necessary truth both that things that are good are desired by the gods and that things that are desired by the gods are good. But, Plato argues, it is because of the essence of things in so far as they are good that they are desired by such perfect beings as the gods; it is not because of the essence of things in so far as they are desired by the gods that they are good. We may or may not agree with Plato's particular conclusion, but his general point appears plausible: a two-way necessary relation between two things is compatible with a one-way essential relation between them.

We should also note that the essence of a thing determines what kind of thing it is and to what general kind it belongs. For example, if Socrates is human essentially, i.e. in virtue of his being the very thing that he is, and if Plato is human essentially, i.e. in virtue of being the very thing that he is, then Socrates and Plato belong to the same general kind, *being human*. So to search for the essence of things is also to search for the general kinds to which things belong. Aristotle thinks that what distinguishes different sciences is that they investigate things that belong to different general kinds. For example, biology investigates living things, and investigates them in so far as they are living things; geometry investigates extended things, and investigates them in so far as they are extended, etc. Metaphysics, on the other hand, investigates simply beings, and it investigates them simply in so far as they are.

Aristotle shares with Plato these fundamental requirements for explanation (R1–5) – though they disagree fundamentally about what things have essences. But in the *Posterior Analytics* Aristotle developed a theory of the structure of explanation and explanatory reasoning, based on his theory of the structure of deductive reasoning, which he developed in the *Prior Analytics*. According to this theory, explanatory reasoning, which he calls 'demonstration' (*apodeixis*), is a kind of deductive reasoning (*sullogismos*). For a piece of deductive reasoning to constitute a demonstration, it must be an explanatory deductive reasoning (*sullogismos epistēmonikos*, see *Posterior Analytics* I. 2, $71^{b}17$–19). This means that the truth of the premises in the deductive reasoning must not only entail that the conclusion is true, it must also explain why the conclusion is true. To do so, the premises must in general be more explanatory than the conclusion. So Aristotle thinks that explanatory knowledge (*epistēmē*) aims at demonstration, i.e. at using deductive reasoning to derive explanatory conclusions from more explanatory premises; and he thinks that there are premises that are most explanatory and cannot themselves be explained further. These are the premises that state the first and ultimate explanations.

Finally, there is a basic supposition in Aristotle's (and Plato's) conception of science, which is so evident to him that he nowhere expressly states or considers it (the same is true of Plato). But this supposition is one that we may disagree with, so it is important to make it explicit.

R6. SCIENTIFIC REALISM

It is things that have explanations, and explanations are themselves things and features of things. So explanations are things and features of things, not what we think or say about things. Of course, if we know things that explain other things, and, if we know that, and how they explain other things, then we have explanatory knowledge of things. And Aristotle thinks that such knowledge can be stated in statements.

Still, explanations are things, not our thoughts or statements about things. As we would say, he thinks that explanations are independent of us, our thought and our language. So he thinks that essences, too, which is what explanations are based in, are independent of us, our thought and language. The same is true of the general kinds to which things belong, since it is the essence of a thing that determines to what general kind it belongs. So in general Aristotle thinks that explanations, essences and kinds are independent of us, our thought and our language.

iii The relation of metaphysics to the other sciences

Aristotle conceives of metaphysics as a science: a search for explanatory knowledge. To this extent metaphysics is like the special sciences, e.g. biology; for all the sciences search for explanatory knowledge about their peculiar area of interest. In general, the difference between metaphysics and the other sciences is that each of the other sciences searches for explanations of some things, but not all, and their area of interest is some one kind of thing as opposed to other kinds. Metaphysics, on the other hand, searches for explanations of all things and of being as a whole.

But how is metaphysics related to the other sciences? Is it simply that whereas the other sciences are specialized and search for explanations of only some things and some one kind of thing, metaphysics is the universal science (*hē katholou epistēmē*, 982ᵃ27), which searches for explanations of all things and of being as a whole? If this is Aristotle's view, then metaphysics will apparently run parallel to the other sciences, with no interaction. In other words, metaphysics will ask more general questions than those asked by the special sciences, but otherwise its method will be the method of the special sciences. We may recall that in general the method of a special science is to start from what we already know through sense perception and experience, and to search for explanations of what is known through this prior knowledge. So (on the present interpretation) metaphysics will likewise start from sense perception and experience, and will search for explanations of what is known in this way. The difference between metaphysics and the specialized sciences will be simply that the questions that metaphysics asks of what is known through sense perception and experience will be more general than those asked by the special sciences. (For a defence of this line of interpretation, see Bolton 1996: 231–280.)

But this interpretation does not seem plausible. For we will see (in Chapter 3) that, as Aristotle conceives it, metaphysics does not start from sense perception and experience, at least not directly. It starts rather with certain general and abstract *aporiai* ('puzzles', 'problems'). Thus, at the opening of book III, the book of *aporiai*, he emphasizes that this is the method that he wants to adopt in metaphysics: a method based in *aporiai*. But it is unnatural to think that the *aporiai* that he has in mind here have their source directly in sense perception and experience. For none of the fifteen *aporiai* that he lists in book III, and which it is his aim to engage with and eventually to answer, appear to have this source. They are too general and abstract to originate directly in sense perception and experience. More important, these *aporiai* contain concepts that appear to be not at all familiar to us directly on the basis of sense perception and experience. This is above all true of the central concept of *primary being* (*prōtē ousia*, often simply *ousia*), which occupies an important position in these *aporiai*. But it is also true of the very concept of *all beings* and *being as a whole*, which is absolutely central to his characterization of metaphysics. Indeed it seems wrong to think that even such central concepts in Aristotle's metaphysics as those of *particulars, universals* and *essence*, which likewise occupy an important position in the *aporiai*, originate directly in sense perception and experience.

In general, our sense perception and experience do not directly provide us with a recipe for how the things that we know by their means must be conceptualized in order to be intelligible and subject to explanation. So concepts such as those of *particulars, universals* and *essence* appear rather to be concepts that the special sciences presuppose when they search for explanations of what is initially known through sense perception and experience. So the special sciences, when they seek to explain things, presuppose that there are particulars, universals and essences – they do not themselves ask questions about these presuppositions. With regard to the central concept of *primary being*, it is even arguable that this concept comes from within metaphysics itself, once metaphysics raises certain general *aporiai* about all beings and being as a whole. The same can be said of the concept of *all beings* and *being as a whole*, i.e. this absolutely central concept of metaphysics originates within metaphysics itself.

This suggests a very different view of how metaphysics is related to the special sciences. In searching for explanations of things that are initially known through sense perception and experience, the special sciences make use of certain fundamental concepts and certain fundamental assumptions – assumptions to the effect that these concepts really apply to reality. But metaphysics examines these concepts and assumptions themselves, and it does so by engaging with and trying to answer certain fundamental *aporiai* ('questions', 'puzzles', 'problems') which have their source in these concepts and assumptions. In this sense we may even say that metaphysics is the foundation of the sciences. Of course this does not mean that it is a master science from which the other sciences can be derived. Neither does this mean that metaphysics is purely a priori and can ignore the specialized and more empirical sciences. Rather, metaphysics is, as he says, 'furthest removed from the senses' (982ª25), but it is still related to the senses, even if only indirectly. So metaphysics does not run parallel to the other sciences, rather it interacts and intervenes with them. For it asks questions about presuppositions which originate in other sciences and in general in the search for knowledge and especially explanatory knowledge. (For this line of interpretation, see Wieland 1975.)

This interpretation is suggested by what Aristotle says in *Metaphysics* VI. 1 (although the reading of this chapter is controversial). But it is especially suggested by the method that he adopts in metaphysics, the *aporia*-based method, and by the particular *aporiai* that he sets out and concentrates on. (We will consider this method at length in the next chapter.) The interpretation also fits well with his general characterization of the search for explanatory knowledge. For this is a search that starts from what is more clear and better known to us, i.e. what is closer to sense perception, and moves towards what is more clear and better known on account of its nature, i.e. what is further removed from sense perception (see *Posterior Analytics*, 71ᵇ33–72ª4). Notable here is his use of the grammatical comparative, i.e. what is 'closer' to sense perception, and what is 'further' removed from sense perception. This suggests that not all searching for explanations needs to start directly from sense perception. It also fits well with his saying that metaphysics is the science that is 'furthest removed from the senses' (982ª25). So, on this interpretation, metaphysics is furthest removed from the senses because it starts not directly from the senses, but rather from presuppositions which originate in other sciences – sciences which, basically, start from the senses – and in general originate in the search for explanatory knowledge.

4 The theory of the four basic explanations and causes of changing things

i A summary of the theory

Having argued (in I. 1–2) that metaphysics is the science of the first explanations of all things, Aristotle (at the opening of I. 3) reminds the reader of the theory of the four explanations and causes, which he had developed in the *Physics*, books I–II (*aitiai*, which we generally translate as 'explanations', also means 'causes'):

(1) the essence (*to ti estin, to ti ēn einai*) and the form (*hē morphē, to eidos*) of a thing;
(2) the matter (*hulē*) of the thing;
(3) the source of the change and especially of the generation of the thing (*to kinoun*); and
(4) the end (*telos*) at which the change and especially the generation of the thing is directed.

He immediately points out why this theory is relevant here:

> So evidently we must apprehend the science of the fundamental explanations [*ex archēs aitiai*]; . . . But explanations are spoken of in four ways [he goes on to mention the four explanations].
>
> (983ª24–27)

'The science of the fundamental explanations' is, of course, a reference to metaphysics, the science which he has so far (in I. 1–2) been at pains to characterize. But the theory of the four explanations and causes is, precisely, a theory of certain fundamental explanations and causes of things, especially changing things. So let us first consider this theory. We will first give a general summary of the theory. Then concentrate on Aristotle's puzzling conception of matter. Finally, we will consider Aristotle's review of earlier philosophers' conception of explanation and causation, and his view that his own theory of the four basic causes is anticipated by earlier thinkers.

Aristotle's theory of the four explanations and causes, which he develops in the *Physics*, is a theory of change and changing things; it is a theory of changing things in so far as they are changing things. He thinks that such a theory is needed, for two reasons especially. First, Parmenides (sixth–fifth century BC) denies the reality of change and argues that change is only apparent, not real; only what is changeless is real. Aristotle thinks that this view is unacceptable. For it is evident to sense perception that there is change and changing things, and in general he argues that the search for explanations and scientific knowledge must start with what is evident to us and to our senses (see opening of *Physics*, discussed earlier). But he also thinks that Parmenides' challenge needs to be answered. So he thinks that even if it is evident that change is real, it still needs to be shown how it can be real; and to show this is part of his aim in developing the theory of the four explanations and causes of changing things.

Second, Plato argues that changing things, even if they are real somehow, do not have an essence; i.e. there is nothing that changing things are in virtue of themselves, and by themselves changing things are indeterminate. He concludes that only changeless forms, which are separate and distinct from changing things, have an essence. And only changeless forms are perfectly real, since he thinks that the mark of a thing's being real is its having a firm and changeless essence. So changing things, to the extent that they have determinate properties (e.g. large or small, hot or cold), depend for their determinate properties, and in general for their determination, on their relation to changeless forms. Plato's argument for the claim that changing things do not have an essence is basically this: essences are changeless; so changing things, precisely because they are changing, cannot have an essence. (We will consider this argument in Chapter 9.)

But Aristotle rejects Plato's view of essences as separate forms, and he argues against Plato's motivation for this view; for he argues that changing things, even though they are changing, have a changeless essence (see VII. 8). For example, a particular human being, although it is a changing thing, will have the same changeless essence for as long as it exists. (We will later, in Chapter 7§5vi, return to how Aristotle argues that the essence and form of changing things is itself changeless.) It is above all to defend the view that changing things have changeless essences that Aristotle develops the theory of the four explanations and causes of changing things.

The theory of the four explanations and causes basically argues that each changing thing is a composite whole (*sunholon*) resulting from two things: its essence (or form) and its matter. (We will consider in a moment to what extent and in what sense these two elements of a changing thing are components or parts of the thing.) These two elements of changing things depend on each other for their existence: the essence (or form) of a particular changing thing, such as, for instance, a particular animal, cannot exist independently of its matter; and the matter of a particular changing thing cannot exist independently of its form. The matter of a changing thing explains how the thing can change in the first place, and especially how it can be generated and come to be; for example, how a particular animal can be generated and come to be. The form of a changing thing, on the other hand, explains how the thing, although it is changing, can have the same changeless essence for as long as it exists.

Let us begin with a brief review of each of the four explanations and causes of changing things.

(1) THE ESSENCE OF A THING (*TO TI ESTIN, TO TI ĒN EINAI*) AND THE FORM OF A THING (*HĒ MORPHĒ, TO EIDOS*)

This is now commonly referred to as 'the formal cause'. In general, the essence of a thing is what the thing is in virtue of being the very thing it is; and the essence determines to what general kind the thing belongs. But Aristotle argues that the essence of a changing, material thing is its form (as opposed to its matter or to a combination of its form and its matter). By the form of a changing, material thing, such as, for instance, a particular human being, he means that which explains why the matter (e.g. the flesh and bones) of this particular thing, the human being, constitutes the thing that it constitutes: a particular human being. To take one of his illustrative examples, the form of a particular bronze sphere is that which explains why the matter (the bronze) of this particular thing, the sphere, makes up this particular thing, a bronze sphere. So the form of a changing, material thing is an explanation and cause: it explains why the matter of that particular thing constitutes – or forms – that very thing. We should also note that the form of a changing, material thing, just as the essence of such a thing, is the same changeless form for as long as the thing exists; for example, a particular human being has the same changeless form for as long as he or she exists.

(2) THE MATTER (*HULĒ*) OF A THING

This is commonly referred to as 'the material cause'. The matter of a changing, material thing, such as, for instance, a particular human being, is that which explains how the thing can change and especially how it can be generated and come to be. In Aristotle's standard terminology, the matter is 'that out of which a thing comes to be' (*to ex hou gignetai hekaston*). We can imagine matter as a certain material, e.g. bronze, in so far as this material does not, or not yet, form any particular material thing of a certain form, e.g. a bronze sphere. And we can imagine the particular thing that is of a certain form, e.g. the bronze sphere, as the thing that is generated and comes to be out of this matter. But it is important to recognize that Aristotle argues that matter cannot exist independently of particular material things of a certain form. So it is not right to imagine that matter is simply a certain material, e.g. bronze; for this may suggest that matter can exist independently of particular material things of a certain form: can exist simply as, for example, bronze that is not formed into any particular thing that is made of bronze. Aristotle emphasizes that matter cannot exist on its own when he argues that matter is not a thing in its own right, but is that which is potentially (*dunamei*) a particular material thing of a certain form. This means that matter is that which has the capacity to become a particular material thing of a certain form. (We will return in a moment to Aristotle's peculiar and puzzling conception of matter as potentiality.)

(3) THE SOURCE OF THE CHANGE AND ESPECIALLY OF THE GENERATION OF A THING (*TO KINOUN*)

This is commonly referred to as 'the moving cause' or 'the efficient cause'. We saw that a particular thing, e.g. a human being, is generated out of its matter. But what generates a particular thing, e.g. a human being, in the first place? Aristotle argues that what generates a particular thing is an already generated thing that belongs to the same general kind, e.g. an already generated human being. So an adult human being, the 'parent', generates a new human being, the 'offspring'. In particular, he argues that it is the form of an already generated thing, e.g. the form of an adult human being, that generates a new thing of the same kind, e.g. a new human being. In this way he argues that forms are changeless not only with regard to each particular thing, but also with regard to all things. On the one hand, a particular human being has the same unchanging form for as long as it exists; on the other hand, this form is passed down from parent to offspring in a series of generations which he thinks is infinite both forwards and backwards in time. But it is especially important to emphasize Aristotle's view that it is not simply the parent that generates the offspring (so much is stating what is evident), but the form of the parent; i.e. it is the form of an already formed thing that explains why a new thing is generated. This also shows that it is misleading to associate Aristotle's conception of the 'moving' or 'generating' cause with a modern conception of an 'efficient' cause. For the modern conception of an efficient cause does not involve the supposition that it is the form of a thing that is such a cause.

(4) THE END (*TELOS*) AT WHICH THE GENERATION OF A THING IS DIRECTED

This is commonly referred to as the final cause. The end (*telos*) at which the generation of a particular thing, e.g. a particular human being, is directed is evidently that particular thing. But why does Aristotle think that this end is an explanation and cause of something? It is because he argues that a particular process of generation, e.g. the process of generation of a particular human being, can be explained only by reference to its end-state (*telos*): the thing that is generated. So he thinks that the end-state of a process of generation is part of what explains why this process is as it is and takes place as it does. But we should note that Aristotle also thinks that the end (*telos*) at which a particular process of generation is directed is not simply the thing that is generated (so much is stating what is evident), but the form of that thing. He argues that the thing that is generated is a whole that results from form and matter (a *sunholon* in this sense). And the form of a thing that is generated (rather than its matter or a combination of its form and its matter) is what explains why the thing that is generated is the thing it is (see Chapter 7§5vii). So he concludes that the end-state at which a process of generation is directed, and which explains why this process is as it is and takes place as it does, is primarily the form of the thing that is generated.

ii Aristotle's conception of matter as potentiality

It would take us too far to consider in detail how Aristotle develops and defends the theory of the four causes. (He develops and defends this theory in *Physics*, books I–II. See also *Metaphysics* VII. 7–9, discussed in Chapter 7§5vi. He gives a good succinct summary of the theory in *Metaphysics* XII. 1, 1069^{b}3–7 and XII. 2.) But some understanding of his argument is necessary if we are to understand this theory and especially its most puzzling aspect: Aristotle's conception of matter (*hulē*) as potentiality. (The crucial other elements, essence and form, we will consider at length in Chapter 7.) In general, Aristotle's theory of the four causes is motivated by the question 'What is change?', and the four causes make up four integral explanatory elements in a general account of change. Aristotle begins with a basic claim. He argues that there are two fundamentally different kinds of change:

(1) a particular thing's changing from having one feature to having a different feature, e.g. a rosebush's changing from being in bloom to not being in bloom; and

(2) the coming into being (and passing away) of a particular thing, e.g. the coming into being of a rosebush.

We may refer to the former kind of change as feature-change (it is also referred to as 'accidental change') and to the latter kind of change as generation and destruction. We will see that Aristotle's notion of matter (and of form) is a crucial element in an account of generation and destruction whose aim is to establish a fundamental distinction between this kind of change and feature-change. Evidently the basic difference between the two kinds of change is this: in the case of feature-change, there is a single particular thing that endures throughout the change, e.g. the rosebush; but in the case of generation and destruction that very thing itself comes to be and passes away, and there is not a particular thing that endures in the process of generation and destruction.

First a word about Aristotle's account of feature-change, since this is important in order to understand the contrast that he draws between feature-change and generation; and this contrast is important in order to understand his conception of matter. With regard to feature-change, he argues that to make such change intelligible we need to think of each feature of things as having one or more opposite features (*enantia*). For example, to the feature *red* is opposed the features *green, yellow*, etc.; and to the feature *blooming* is opposed the feature *not-blooming*. The point here is that change in features is not simply change from one feature (e.g. *green*) to a different feature (e.g. *round*); rather, it is change from one feature (e.g. *green*, or *not-blooming*) to a different *and opposite* feature (e.g. *red*, or *blooming*). This may appear obvious; but it serves to introduce a general notion of opposites (*enantia*), and to account for this general notion is not easy. Thus to explain what in general it is for two features to be not merely different, but opposite, we may need to appeal to nothing less than a version of the principle of non-contradiction: two features are opposite if, and only if, it is impossible for one and the same thing to have both features at the same time and in the same respect. (See later and especially Chapter 5, for Aristotle's investigation of the principle of non-contradiction. At the end of this investigation he argues that it is precisely because of the principle of non-contradiction that opposites cannot, in virtue of being opposites, belong to the same thing at the same time and in the same respect; see 1011^b15–22.) So considerations which, as we would say, belong to logic, such as the investigation of the notion of opposites and of the principle of non-contradiction, may be directly relevant to the account of change and changing things – an account which otherwise belongs to physics.

But Aristotle argues further that to distinguish features into opposites, and to introduce the general notion of opposites, is only a necessary condition for giving a general account of feature-change; it is not a sufficient condition. For he argues that it is not the features themselves that change one into the other. The features themselves cannot, he argues, change into one another, precisely because they are opposite to one another. What changes is not the features themselves, but something that has them; he calls this 'the underlying thing' (*to hupokeimenon*). It is the underlying thing, e.g. the rosebush, that changes from having one feature to having a different and opposite feature. So a general account of feature-change requires the introduction of two central general notions: the notion of opposites or opposite features; and the notion of an underlying thing having such features.

But let us turn to Aristotle's special concern, which is to account for generation and destruction as opposed to feature-change. Here we find that the following principle plays a central role in his argument: a thing cannot be generated out of nothing or pass away into nothing. He concludes that a thing is generated out of something; and what a thing is generated out of is, precisely, what he calls its matter (*hulē*). It is worth asking why he thinks that a thing cannot be generated out of nothing. Presumably, the point is, ultimately, that so-called generation out of nothing would not amount to generation at all, or even to change in general. All it would amount to is: the state of there not being such and such a thing followed by the state of there being such and such a thing. But if we want in general to understand the process of generation, i.e. of how in general a thing comes to be, it is evidently not an answer to be told: first the thing does not exist; later it does. No doubt much more needs to be said about Aristotle's reasons for thinking that a thing cannot be generated out of nothing or pass away into nothing. But for now what matters is the conclusion that he draws from this view; for he argues that there is in general something that a thing is generated out of, and this is precisely what matter is (or its matter, i.e. the matter of the thing that is generated).

So Aristotle thinks that the process in general of the generation of a thing must be understood as a process out of something, namely the matter of the thing generated, and into something, namely the thing generated. To illustrate this he offers a helpful, but also misleading, analogy: a bronze sphere is generated out of bronze. Here the bronze is the matter out of which the sphere is generated; and the sphere is that into which this matter, the bronze, is generated. But this view gives rise to a central question and problem, of which Aristotle is acutely aware. Matter is characterized as that out of which a thing is generated. But is this characterization essential or not essential to a certain matter's being what it is, for example the bronze of the sphere being what it is, bronze? In the case of the bronze of the sphere, apparently the answer is that it is not essential. For apparently it is not essential to bronze that it should be that which, potentially, forms a sphere. To be bronze is rather to be a certain kind of material stuff, defined, for example, by its internal constitution. Although some properties of bronze will enable it to be formed into spheres and similar things, it is, apparently, not part of what it is to be bronze that it should be that out of which spheres and similar things can be generated. Apparently, it is its internal constitution, its material structure, that defines what bronze is. But Aristotle requires, precisely, that it should be essential to the matter of a generated thing to be that out of which such things can be generated. This shows that his illustration that appeals to bronze and the bronze sphere is misleading. More generally, it shows that his notion of matter is not simply the notion of a certain kind of material stuff. For it is essential to Aristotle's notion of matter, but apparently not to the notion of a certain kind of material stuff, to be that out of which things of a certain kind can be generated. But, most important, it shows that Aristotle has a process-based notion of matter: to be matter is to be an explanatory element in the process of the generation of things.

Why does Aristotle think that to be matter is to be that out of which a thing can be generated? Consider bronze, and suppose that although bronze can be formed into a bronze sphere, this is not part of what it is to be bronze. Suppose further that we deny Aristotle's claim that to be matter is to be that out of which something can be generated, and we suppose instead that matter is rather like bronze. In that case, the change from a lump of bronze to a bronze sphere will not be an example of a process of generation at all. It will rather be an example of feature-change: a single underlying subject, the lump of bronze, changes from having one feature (*not-spherical*) to having a different and opposite feature (*spherical*). This shows that if, *contra* Aristotle, matter is what it is independently of its being involved in processes of generation, i.e. if matter is rather like bronze, then his attempt to appeal to matter to account for generation will immediately fail. For it will imply that there really is no such thing as generation and that all change is feature-change. But Aristotle thinks that there is a fundamental distinction between generation and feature-change. So he concludes that it is part of what it is to be matter to be that out of which something can be generated. In other words, he concludes that matter can only be understood as an integral part of a process of generation; it cannot be understood independently of such processes – as bronze apparently can.

If we look to familiar processes in nature, and, in particular, biological processes, we may apparently find direct support for Aristotle's view. For example, something is an acorn only as part of the process of the generation of a tree; or something is seed only as part of the process of generation of a plant; or something is sperm only as part of the process of the generation of an animal. These things – acorns, seed, sperm – can only be understood as integral parts involved in processes of generation of things. But we may also note that this is wholly compatible with the evident fact that such things also have properties that are, to a greater or lesser extent, independent of their being parts of processes of generation. We may think of the shape and consistency of acorns. So such things, rather than, for example, bronze, would seem to be adequate examples of what Aristotle means by matter. We can also see why he is especially attracted to a particular analogy: the analogy of matter to bricks and timber. For something is bricks and timber only as an element in the generation of a house, although of course bricks and timber also have properties that are independent of their function in this process.

So Aristotle argues that what it is to be matter is to be that out of which something can be generated. This view cannot be over-emphasized. He even coins a new phrase to assist in making this emphasis: matter is 'that which is potentially' (*to dunamei on*). This means that to be matter is to be something that has the power or capacity (*dunamis*, hence the adverb *dunamei*, commonly translated 'potentially') to generate a thing. So when he says that some matter is potentially a generated thing, e.g. that seed is potentially a plant, he does not mean merely that this matter has the power or capacity to generate a plant. What he means is that to be this matter is, precisely, to be that which has this power or capacity. So he thinks that different kinds of matter are, as we may say, individuated by their capacities for generating different things. We may contrast bronze, which apparently is not individuated in this way. In this sense, matter, in Aristotle's general account of matter, is directly associated with potentiality, capacity, and power (*dunamis*).

Aristotle's process-based conception of matter has a crucial consequence: the matter out of which a particular thing is generated does not endure in the course of the process of generation. For example, the seed or sperm do not endure when a plant or an animal is generated. We may contrast the case of bronze; for the bronze does, precisely, endure when the bronze sphere is generated, and it is literally present in the bronze sphere. We may say that the matter rather becomes assimilated to, or becomes entirely mixed up with, the generated thing. But even this description is misleading. For assimilation suggests that there is already a thing there into which the matter becomes taken up; and mixture is compatible with the ingredients of the mixture enduring in the mixture – as in a poorly cooked meal. The only adequate descrip-tion of what happens to the matter in the course of the process of generation of a particular thing is this: the matter becomes this partic-ular material thing. For example, the seed becomes the plant. The reason why the matter does not endure in the course of the process of gener-ation of a generated thing is simply this: if it did endure, this would not be a process of generation at all, but the process of a single underlying thing, the enduring matter, changing from having one feature (e.g. *not-spherical*) to having a different and opposite feature (e.g. *spherical*). It would be feature-change, not generation.

We may have a natural worry about Aristotle's notion of matter as potentiality, and about the argument behind this notion. The argument, we have seen, depends crucially on the view that there is a fundamental distinction between feature-change and generation. But why does Aristotle think that this is a fundamental distinction? Why does he not think instead that all change can be reduced to feature-change and in particular to change in the features of underlying materials such as bronze? His response rests ultimately on the observation that there are particular material things and not just mixtures of materials; and that particular material things are generated in regular and uniform ways. But he argues that if materials were all that is basically real, as would be the case if all change were feature-change, then there would be nothing to explain these evident facts. Bronze can after all be shaped in any variety of regular ways; and it may not be shaped in any regular or uniform way at all. So it appears that materials such as bronze cannot by themselves explain why there are the kinds of particular material things that there are, or even why there are particular material things at all.

So the matter out of which a particular material thing is generated does not endure in the course of the process of the generation of that thing – or else there would be no generation and all change would be feature-change. This has itself a crucial consequence. In general, Aristotle argues that a particular material thing is a whole that results from form and matter (a *sunholon* in this sense). The matter is that out of which the thing is generated, and it is what explains how the thing can be generated. The form is what explains what thing it is that is generated (the notion of form will occupy us at length later). But since the matter out of which a thing is generated does not endure in the course of the generation of that thing, it follows that the whole that results from form and matter, i.e. the generated material thing of a certain form (e.g. Socrates), does not contain the original matter as a constituent. This may be contrasted with the case of the bronze sphere, which contains the original bronze as a constituent. Or alternatively, if we say that the generated material thing of a certain form (e.g. Socrates) contains the original matter as a constituent, then we mean simply that this material thing (Socrates) was generated out of this original matter. In general, if we say that a particular material thing of a certain form (e.g. Socrates) 'contains' matter, we mean simply that it is a material thing, i.e. a thing that was generated and will pass away.

So when Aristotle says that particular material things are wholes that result from form and matter (*sunhola*), he does not mean that such things contain two constituents, form and matter, and neither does he mean that they contain one constituent, matter, and that the form is a feature of matter. Again, we may contrast the bronze sphere; for the spherical shape is, precisely, a feature of the bronze. What he means is that there are particular changing things that are generated and pass away. But the existence and nature of such things involves two fundamental explanatory elements:

(1) that out of which they are generated, which explains how they can be generated (he calls this explanatory element, the matter of the generated thing); and
(2) that which explains why this matter is generated into the particular material thing into which it is generated (he calls this explanatory element, the form of the generated thing).

Aristotle calls form and matter, principles (*archai*) and elements (*stoicheia*). They are principles in the sense that they are the ultimate explanatory elements of things that are subject to generation and destruction. Because they are ultimate explanatory elements, matter and form are real; for only real things can explain anything. (Compare Aristotle's general realism about explanation.) However, form and matter are not elements in the sense of ultimate constituents or parts of things.

iii Aristotle's review of his predecessors regarding the four basic causes

In the remainder of book I (I. 3–10) Aristotle considers to what extent earlier thinkers succeeded in adequately recognizing the four fundamental explanations and causes of things. He begins (in I. 3) with those earlier thinkers that, as he sees them, recognized only material causes, e.g. Thales and Anaximenes. His main objection against the materialists is that they cannot explain why things change as they do (984^{a}19f.; also I. 8, 988^{b}23–989^{a}19); for he argues that to explain this we must also appeal to efficient causes. He makes two further objections against the materialists. First, they cannot explain the beauty and goodness of things (984^{b}11f.), for to explain this we must appeal to final causes. Second, they fail to recognize that not all reality is material (988^{b}23–26).

Next (in I. 3–4) he considers those earlier thinkers that, as he sees them, recognized both material and the efficient causes, if only dimly, e.g. Empedocles and Anaxagoras. His main criticism (in I. 8) is that while the causes that they recognize are in fact either material or efficient, they fail properly to distinguish them into these two kinds and to recognize the difference between them.

Next (in I. 5) he considers the Pythagoreans, who argued that reality consists of numbers. Aristotle praises them for being the first to offer definitions, and so to recognize that the essence of things is an explanation. For he argues that an explanatory definition of a thing is what states the essence of the thing that it defines. His main criticism is that they fail to distinguish between material explanations and explanations in terms of essence. Because of this they fail to distinguish between sense-perceptible numbers and purely intelligible numbers (I. 8, 989^{b}28–990^{a}32). As we would say, they fail to distinguish between numbers as explanations of concrete changeable things and numbers as purely abstract entities.

His criticism of Plato (in I. 6 and 9, and throughout the *Metaphysics*) we will consider later (see Chapter 9). But it is striking to see the energy that he invests in this criticism. Part of the reason apparently lies in his personal relationship with Plato; for this is his teacher and his friend. But there is also a philosophical reason. Aristotle is above all concerned with developing a theory of the essence of things; but, as he understands Plato, this is also Plato's aim. But he thinks that Plato's theory of essence, the theory which claims that essences are separate and distinct forms – i.e. separate and distinct from changing things – is fundamentally mistaken. So he is at pains to distinguish his own theory of essence from Plato's. (See Chapter 9.)

In general, Aristotle's aim in this survey of the views of previous thinkers is in part to find support for his own view, i.e. for the theory of the four explanations and causes, in part to clarify and develop this theory by setting it against other views of the fundamental explanations of things. The details of his historical survey are of considerable interest, but we will have to set them aside. In general, it is striking that Aristotle thinks that a wide variety of earlier thinkers have been engaged in the investigation of being in general and as a whole (see especially I. 3, 983^{b}1–3), i.e. the investigation that he takes up in the *Metaphysics*. It is also of special interest to observe how Aristotle initiates (together with Plato) the study of the history of philosophy, and does so in a way that makes this study an integral part of the practice of philosophy itself. But especially striking is his view that previous thinkers, even if they did not adequately recognize all the four explanations and causes, were at least searching in the right direction. Indeed, Aristotle suggests that it is the truth itself that directed them in their searches:

From these observations [i.e. that certain thinkers recognized only material explanations] one may think that the only explanation is of the kind that is called the material explanation. But as people proceeded like this, the things themselves [*auto to pragma*] cleared the way for them and forced them to search [further]. (I. 3, 984ª16–19)

... After these thinkers and such principles [i.e. fundamental explanations], and because these principles are not sufficient for generating the nature of things, people were forced, again, as we said, by the truth itself [*autē hē alētheia*], to search for the next kind of principle. (984ᵇ8–11)

So Aristotle thinks that the things themselves and the truth itself help to direct our searches, and especially to indicate to us puzzles and problems (*aporiai*) arising from our search for knowledge, and, in particular, explanatory knowledge of things. We will return in the next chapter to the fascinating idea that the source of our puzzles and problems (*aporiai*) lies not only in our thinking, but in the things themselves. (We may note that book I is continued in book III, which we will turn to next. Book II is only later inserted between books I and III.)

3

ARISTOTLE'S METHOD IN METAPHYSICS

(Book III)

1 Aristotle's method of searching in metaphysics
The method based on *aporiai*

Book III is vital for the understanding of the whole of the *Metaphysics*. For here Aristotle asks what in general provides the motivation, direction and goal of metaphysical inquiry, and he argues that puzzlement (*aporia*) and particular puzzles (*aporiai*) are what motivates, directs, and provides a goal for this inquiry – the search for the nature of being. This is clearly and memorably stated in chapter 1 of book III, which contains Aristotle's central reflections on method in metaphysics – the method that he intends to follow in the remainder of the work. But to these brief but crucial methodological reflections he adds, in the remainder of book III, a list of fifteen particular *aporiai* in and about metaphysics, which it is his aim to engage with and eventually to answer. So book III contains, on the one hand, Aristotle's statement of his method in metaphysics, i.e. of what we may call the *aporia*-based method, while on the other hand it contains also a plan for how this method specifically is to be carried out.

Book III opens with the claim that the engagement with *aporiai* is essential to metaphysics and to the very characterization of metaphysics, 'the science that we are seeking' (995ᵃ24–25). This is because:

> it is productive to those who desire to make progress [in a particular search] to engage properly with *aporiai*; for the subsequent progress is the result of resolving the things that one was previously puzzled about, and there is no resolution if one fails to recognize the knot. Rather, the *aporia* in our thought indicates this [i.e. a knot] in the object. For in so far as one is in a state of *aporia*, one resembles people that are tied, since one cannot move forward either way. This, and for the sake of these things, is why we must first study all the problems.
>
> (995ᵃ27–34)

This passage offers a memorable image of what it is like to be in the mental state of puzzlement (*aporia*): it is like being tied and not being able to move this way or that. But Aristotle argues that engaging with particular *aporiai*, in the sense of particular puzzles and problems, is conducive towards good progress (*euporia*) in an inquiry. For such progress requires or even consists in resolving (*luein*, literally, 'untying') what one was previously puzzled about; and evidently there can be no resolution or untying of a 'knot' unless one first recognizes that there is a knot there to be untied. Here an *aporia*, in the sense of a puzzle and problem rather than in the sense of the mental state of puzzlement and being puzzled, is figuratively likened to a knot, i.e. the knot that one is tied up with, just as the mental state of puzzlement is likened to one's being tied up by a particular puzzle and problem.

So far, perhaps Aristotle is only saying that engaging with particular *aporiai* is useful and advisable if one wants to make progress in metaphysics, 'the science that we are seeking'. But what he goes on to say shows quite clearly that he thinks that our recognition of and engagement with particular *aporiai* is precisely what enables us to search in metaphysics:

> Those who search without first engaging with *aporiai* are like people who don't know where they need to be going; moreover, they do not even know whether or not they have found what they are searching for. For the end [of a search] is not clear to such a person, but it is clear to the person who has first raised *aporiai*.
>
> (995ᵃ34–ᵇ2)

This striking passage invites close reading. For here it is argued that our raising of and engaging with particular puzzles and problems is both a necessary and a sufficient condition for our knowing what is the end of a particular search in metaphysics, hence for our ability to begin such a search. It is a necessary condition, since without this we 'are like people who don't know where they need to be going', and so 'the end is not clear' to us; and it is a sufficient condition, since the end of a search 'is clear to the person who has first raised *aporiai*'. So wanting to search in metaphysics without first raising and engaging with *aporiai* is so aimless as not even to amount to searching at all; it is like people who walk aimlessly. But he also says that our raising of and engaging with *aporiai*, and in general our awareness of particular *aporiai*, is what enables us to recognize the end of a search if we find it, hence this is what enables us to successfully conclude a search.

So Aristotle thinks that our engaging with particular *aporiai* is necessary and sufficient both for our ability to begin a search in metaphysics and for our ability to successfully conclude such a search. This strongly suggests that he thinks that our engaging with particular *aporiai* is precisely what enables us to search in metaphysics. For in general these two things appear to be essential to searching: on the one hand, one must be able to begin searching, i.e. one's search must aim in some direction rather than being aimless; and on the other hand, one must be able to conclude searching (or at least one must be confident that one is so able), i.e. one must be able to recognize the end or goal of the search if one finds it (or at least one must be confident that one is so able). So engaging with particular *aporiai* is not only useful and advisable for searching in metaphysics; it is essential to this search, and it is what accounts for the very possibility of this search, i.e. metaphysics.

So we see that Aristotle, having sketched an initial characterization of metaphysics in book I, goes on at the opening of the next book (i.e. III) to raise what he thinks is a pressing question: how is it possible to search, and to find, in metaphysics, i.e. to search for knowledge of the nature of being in general and as a whole? In other words: how is this search, metaphysics, possible? But he immediately proposes an answer to this central question: what enables us to search for, and to find, knowledge of the nature of being, is our recognition of particular metaphysical *aporiai*, *aporiai* that in one way or another are about the nature of being and indeed about whether being has a nature in the first place.

To understand this answer, we need to consider what in general Aristotle means by *aporia* and how, in his view, particular *aporiai* enable us to search in metaphysics. But first let us note that a completely general version of this question, 'How is searching for knowledge possible?', has an important philosophical history, which Aristotle is aware of and alludes to here. For this question was raised in a forceful and radical way by Plato in the dialogue *Meno*:

[Meno asks] And how are you going to search for this [i.e. virtue, what virtue is], Socrates, when you don't know in the least what it is? Which of the things that you don't know will you suppose that it is, when you are searching for it? And even if you *do* come across it, how are you going to know that this is the thing you didn't know?

[Socrates responds] I see what you are getting at, Meno. Do you see what a contentious argument you're conjuring up, that it isn't possible for a person to search either for what he knows or for what he doesn't know? For he wouldn't search for what he knows – for he knows it, and there is no need to search for something like that; nor for what he doesn't know, for he doesn't even know what he's going to search for.

(*Meno* 80d5–e5; translation by Robert Sharples)

As raised by Plato here, this general question, 'How is searching for knowledge possible?', is today commonly referred to as the paradox of searching or the paradox of inquiry. But as Plato formulates it, especially in the words of the character Meno, the question is supposed to amount to an *aporia*: how can one search for X, if one knows *nothing at all* (*to parapan*, here translated as 'not . . . in the least') about X? For if one knows nothing at all about X, how will one know what one is searching for ('which of the things that you don't know will you suppose that it is'); and how will one recognize X even if one comes across it ('even if you do come across it, how are you going to know that this is the thing you didn't know'). Certainly as Plato formulates it in the words of the character Meno, this is a forceful *aporia*, whose deeper point appears to be this: in order to search for something, X, or for knowledge of X, one needs already to have some knowledge about X. In general, Aristotle appears to agree with this deeper point of the *aporia*: it is prior knowledge of X that enables us to search for knowledge of X. This, we should note, implies that not all possession or acquisition of knowledge can be based on searching; otherwise one would need already to have conducted an infinite number of searches in order to begin with any one search. But Aristotle disagrees with the solution to this *aporia* that Plato puts forward in the *Meno*. (See *Posterior Analytics* I. 1 and II. 19.)

As a solution to this *aporia*, Plato introduces the so-called theory of recollection: what enables us to search for knowledge of X is prior knowledge (or belief) about X, but prior knowledge (or belief) that we have in the meanwhile forgotten and that we are trying to recollect. Plato argues that such prior knowledge (or belief) is innate, i.e. it is not acquired after birth and perhaps it is not acquired at all. It is precisely such prior knowledge (or belief) about X, he argues, that enables us to search for knowledge of X; and searching for knowledge of X consists in, or at least involves, trying to recollect this prior knowledge.

Views vary about whether searching for knowledge is as paradoxical and problematical as Plato thinks, and also about whether Plato's response to the paradox of searching, i.e. his theory of recollection, is necessary or even sufficient to answer the problem. But it is Aristotle's answer to the *aporia* about searching that interests us here, especially since there can be little doubt that when he says in our passage (i.e. *Metaphysics* III. 1, 995^{a}34–^{b}1) that:

> those who search without first engaging with *aporiai* are like people who don't know where they need to be going; moreover, they do not even know whether or not they have found what they are searching for . . .

he is directly alluding to, or even paraphrasing, Meno's statement of the paradox in Plato's *Meno*. But this is not the first time that Aristotle has tried to answer the *aporia* about searching, and to do so with an allusion or even express reference to Plato's *Meno* (see especially *Posterior Analytics* I. 1 and II. 19 for earlier responses). So he takes the *aporia* about searching seriously, and he thinks that there is a genuine question and problem about what it is that enables us to search for knowledge. But he argues against Plato's view that it is innate knowledge that enables us to search for knowledge. For he argues that what enables us to search for knowledge is rather, ultimately, our capacity for sense perception, although other capacities may also become involved (see especially *Posterior Analytics* II. 19, 99^{b}25ff.). So this appears to be his answer to the completely general question, 'How is searching for knowledge possible?'

On a different reading, his answer also centrally appeals to our knowledge of the meaning of words: when the search for knowledge is motivated by the asking of a question about something, X, it is our knowledge of the meaning of words, and in particular of the words that we use to signify X, that enables us to search for knowledge about X. For example, if we ask 'What is virtue?', as Plato does in the *Meno*, or 'What is a rose?', it is our knowledge of the meaning of the words 'virtue' or 'rose' that enables us to search for knowledge about virtue or roses. This reading draws especially on *Posterior Analytics* II. 7–10.

But it is striking that this, i.e. the view that it is our capacity for sense perception that enables us to search for knowledge, does not appear to be Aristotle's answer to the more specific question, 'How is searching for knowledge *in metaphysics* possible, i.e. knowledge of the nature of being?' For he appears to think that there is a special problem about how searching in metaphysics is possible. And the answer that he proposes appeals not to our capacity for sense perception (or to our knowledge of the meaning of the relevant words, such as the verb 'to be'), but appeals rather to our recognition of particular metaphysical *aporiai*. So it is natural to ask why he thinks that his answer to the general question, 'How is searching for knowledge possible?', is not adequate to answer the more specific question, 'How is searching for knowledge *in metaphysics* possible?' Perhaps this is because, as he says early in the *Metaphysics*, this science, metaphysics, 'is furthest removed from the senses' (I. 2, 982ª25). So he appears to think that our capacity for sense perception, which is what in general enables us to search for knowledge, does not by itself enable us to search for this most general knowledge – the knowledge of the nature of all beings and of being as a whole. Rather, it is our recognition of particular metaphysical *aporiai* that enables us to search for knowledge in metaphysics.

Let us, however, stand back and consider what in general Aristotle means by *aporia*; and how, in his view, our recognition of particular *aporiai* about a particular subject area enables us to search in that area. In the *Topics* he gives a good general characterization of the very notion of *aporia*:

> *Aporia* is not a characteristic of opposite reasonings. ... Moreover, people who define [it] in this way [i.e. who define *aporia* as an equality of opposite reasonings] put effect for cause, or cause for effect.... [Rather] it would seem that the equality of opposite reasonings is the cause of *aporia*; for it is when we reason on both [sides of a question] and it appears to us that everything can come about either way, that we are in a state of *aporia* about which of the two ways to take up.
>
> (*Topics*, VI. 145ᵇ4–20)

Here we see first of all that Aristotle thinks that there is an important distinction between two senses of the term *aporia*:

(1) *aporia* in the sense of the mental state of puzzlement and perplexity; and
(2) *aporia* in the sense of particular puzzles and problems which, he says, are responsible for and the cause of the mental state of *aporia*.

It is also important to note that he argues that the first sense is primary and that the second sense is derived from it. For he argues that it is because we think that what is responsible for our mental state of puzzlement (*aporia*) is, precisely, particular problems, that we call these problems: *aporiai*. But this view, which makes particular problems central to our very conception of puzzlement, arguably goes back to Plato, indeed the early Plato and the Socratic dialogues. For it is typical of Plato's Socrates to reduce his interlocutors to a mental state of puzzlement, perplexity and even confusion, but to do so precisely by developing what he generally thinks are genuine problems about various matters.

Although clearly Aristotle is interested in *aporia* in the sense of the mental state of puzzlement, he is equally if not more interested in *aporia* in the sense of particular puzzles and problems. In the *Topics* passage just quoted, he gives a highly distinctive account of the nature of *aporia* in this sense. Evidently an *aporia*, in the sense of a particular puzzle and problem, takes the form of a question. But clearly not every question is an *aporia*. We may think of the question, 'How many chairs are there in this room?' Aristotle argues that for a question to amount to an *aporia*, it must be a question the reflection on whose answer rationally pulls us in apparently opposite and conflicting directions. So it must be a question with two sides: the question *whether or not* such and such; or the question *whether* such and such *or* such and such (in Greek: *poteron ... ē ...*). It is especially notable that the fifteen *aporiai* that he lists in book III are all of this two-sided or dilemmatic form. But perhaps every question can, by a mere grammatical transformation, be represented in this form. For example, rather than asking 'How many chairs are there in this room?', we may ask 'Are there *n* chairs in this room, or more or less than *n*?' For a question genuinely to amount to an *aporia*, there must apparently be something that compels us to ask the question in such a way that it has two sides, i.e. as a dilemma. What compels us to do this, Aristotle argues, is our impression that there really are two sides to this question – because of our impression that there are good reasons on both sides. So when we ask a question that is genuinely an *aporia*, e.g. the question 'Does being have a nature to be investigated in the first place?' (see *aporiai* 3 and 7 in book III), we must suppose that there really are good reasons on both sides of the question. But here we must also emphasize that if one thinks that a question really amounts to a genuine *aporia*, one must oneself think that there are good reasons on both sides; it is not enough that one should think that different people give different and apparently conflicting answers to the question. In other words, even if one recognizes that others disagree with the answer that one is oneself inclined to give, one must recognize their reasons as good reasons, reasons that one is directly inclined to take seriously and to engage with; otherwise there is no *aporia*. So, in sum, Aristotle thinks that a genuine *aporia*, in the sense of a particular puzzle and problem, is a question that gives rise to a dilemma, a genuinely rational pull in two apparently opposite and conflicting directions.

But how does our recognition of a particular *aporia* about a particular subject area help us to search for knowledge in that area? In general, there appear to be four ways in which our recognition of particular *aporia* helps us to search for knowledge. First, recognizing an *aporia* provides us with motivation to search. This is because recognizing a particular *aporia* causes us to be in a mental state of *aporia*; recognizing a puzzle makes us puzzle. Second, the *aporia* gives direction and aim to our search. This is because of the logical structure of the *aporia*, its dilemmatic structure. Third, the *aporia* provides us with a way of telling (a criterion) whether or not we have found what we are searching for; for we have found what we are searching for when we have adequately answered the *aporia*. But this, of course, is not a criterion that we can apply with perfect, let alone infallible, confidence; for what constitutes an adequate answer to an *aporia* may itself be unclear. Fourth, a collection of related *aporiai* may help us to circumscribe a particular subject area; it is the subject area characterized by such and such, and similar, *aporiai*. For example, Aristotle thinks that metaphysics is the subject characterized by the *aporiai* listed in book III, and similar ones.

Let us look closer at these different ways in which our recognition of particular *aporiai* contributes to our ability to search for knowledge. First, if we recognize and are struck by a particular *aporia*, this will provide motivation for our searching for knowledge; for we will naturally want to answer the *aporia* that we are struck by. An *aporia* is after all a question that one has oneself raised or become struck by; and it is a question that will appear pressing to one because of its very nature, i.e. because of the rational pull in apparently opposite and conflicting directions. It was by challenging people with such *aporiai* that Socrates tried to stimulate them – like a gadfly – to search for knowledge. In other words, it seems impossible to recognize and be struck by an *aporia* but at the same time not to have a desire to search for an answer, although of course it is possible that other desires may prove stronger. We should note here that our recognition of *aporiai* provides us with a desire to search for knowledge in a way that does not presuppose a general desire, the desire for knowledge. Rather, because the recognition of a particular *aporia* is naturally associated with a desire to search for an answer, it is naturally associated with the desire for knowledge. So the desire for knowledge is generated by, and perhaps initially simply consists in, the desire to answer the *aporia*. We should also note that to search for knowledge here is, initially at least, nothing over and above to search for an answer to the *aporia*; no more general or demanding conception of knowledge need initially be involved. We might even go as far as saying that, initially at least, to know here is simply to know the answer to a question, or how to answer a question – a question that amounts to an *aporia*.

An *aporia* provides direction and aim to a search because of its logical and dilemmatic structure, i.e. its being a question with two apparently opposite and conflicting sides, with good reasons on both sides. Consider, for example, the central question of metaphysics, 'What is being?' As stated, it is not yet an *aporia*, although it may be closely associated with *aporiai*; for it is not structured as an *aporia*, i.e. as a question that has two sides. At the same time, and apparently because it is not yet structured as an *aporia*, this question does not indicate any directions for searching, and it may even appear to be without aim. But now let us suppose that this question, 'What is being?', is associated with a particular *aporia* about the nature of being, such as: 'Is being primarily something particular or something general?' (see the last *aporia*, number 15, in book III). Suppose also that we have some initial grasp of why both answers to this question appear genuinely attractive. Then our search is provided with direction and aim. For we know what in general we have to do to answer a dilemma: *either* defend the one side; *or* the other side; *or* argue that the two sides can after all be reconciled. So we immediately have available certain paths for searching.

On the other hand, it is also worth pointing out that these paths for searching may not be as clearly and distinctly marked out as we might think. For an important part of the search for an answer to an *aporia* will involve giving an adequate account of the central concepts in the *aporia*; for example, the concepts of *particulars* and *universals*. But in giving such an account it may emerge that different answers to the *aporia* are called for, depending on how its central concepts are understood. So the paths for searching generated by an *aporia* may depend on how the central concepts in the *aporia* are understood.

But it is also important not to misunderstand this point. For it does not mean that we must first clarify the concepts and engage in what today is sometimes called conceptual analysis, before we may try to answer the *aporia*. On the contrary, the conceptual inquiry is itself an integral part of the attempt to answer the *aporia*. Indeed, it is the endeavour to answer the *aporia* that generates the need for, and gives direction to, the conceptual inquiry. Without *aporiai*, conceptual inquiries are themselves aimless – and perhaps pointless.

A particular *aporia* evidently provides us with a way of telling (a criterion) when a search has been successfully completed, that is, when the *aporia* has been adequately answered. So an *aporia* contributes not only a means of searching, but also a criterion of finding. However, this *aporia*-based criterion of finding is neither infallible nor definitive. It is not infallible, since there is nothing in Aristotle's general conception of an *aporia* that implies that we can know for certain and without room for doubt whether the *aporia* has been answered. It is not definitive, since there is nothing in his conception of an *aporia* that implies that if one answers a particular *aporia* in one way, other ways of answering it are thereby shown to be impossible or without attraction. At the same time, however, it is striking that Aristotle does appear to think, especially in book VII, that he has successfully answered the question 'What is being?' and the *aporiai* associated with this question. How can he think this, since he does not appear to think that there is a general way of telling, in a manner that is both infallible and definitive, when an *aporia* has been successfully answered? Is there not a tension here, between his eventual confidence that he has answered the *aporiai* and his apparent lack of provision of, or even concern for, a criterion of knowledge that is general, infallible and definitive? Aristotle evidently sees no tension here; and he may be right. After all, it is plausible to think that whether or not one has successfully answered a specific question depends ultimately on the particular question at hand and on the specific answer that one comes up with; not on some general criterion. So perhaps Aristotle thinks that the only way, ultimately, of being confident that we can successfully answer a metaphysical question is, well, by answering it.

We have seen how in general an *aporia*, in the sense of a particular puzzle and problem, contributes to our ability to search for knowledge. This way of contributing to searching is distinctive of all *aporiai*, irrespective of what they are about. However, we need to emphasize that, in *Metaphysics* III. 1, Aristotle makes a special claim about the role of *aporiai* in metaphysics. For he argues that our recognition of particular *aporiai* not only contributes to our ability to search in metaphysics; it is precisely what enables us to search in metaphysics. So he does not so much argue that metaphysics, the search for the nature of being, may usefully involve *aporiai* – what he argues is that the search for the nature of being is an essentially *aporia*-based search, i.e. without *aporiai* this search is impossible and with *aporiai* it is possible (see 995^{a}34–^{b}2, especialy ^{b}1–2). *Aporiai* may form an important part of other searches too. But it is also arguable that the role and relevance of *aporiai* will gradually diminish, to the extent that a search is more strictly empirical ('closer to sense perception', as he says elsewhere). For a most strictly empirical search may derive its answers directly from sense perception and may not even generate genuine *aporiai*. But metaphysics is the search that is 'furthest removed from sense perception' (982ª25); and this may be the reason why *aporiai* have a central and essential place in metaphysics.

There remains an important question: how is Aristotle's *aporia*-based method in metaphysics, and his view that metaphysics is essentially *aporia*-based, related to his view that metaphysics is a search for explanations and explanatory knowledge – a science (*epistēmē*)? How can a search for explanations be essentially *aporia*-based? To see why there is no real tension between these two views, we need to distinguish carefully between:

(1) what enables us to search for knowledge about the nature of being; and
(2) what constitutes knowledge, or finding knowledge, of the nature of being.

Aristotle's answer to the first question, we have seen, is that it is our recognition of particular *aporiai* that enables us to search here. His answer to the second question also appeals to *aporiai*; we have found what we were searching for when we can answer the *aporia* that generated the search in the first place. But we saw that, apparently, Aristotle offers no general criterion for successfully solving an *aporia*. How, then, is he confident that he can recognize the solution, if he finds it? It is arguably at this point that we must appeal to his view that knowledge in metaphysics is explanatory knowledge. For this view implies that if we resolve an *aporia*, we must be able to explain why things are as the solution says that they are; and we must be able to explain what is wrong with conflicting solutions. For example, to argue successfully that things are primarily particular, not general, we must be able to explain why this is so and not otherwise. But this explanation, Aristotle appears to think, will also offer us a way of telling when we have actually solved an *aporia*, that is, when we can adequately explain why things must be as our solution says that they are.

Perhaps this is a general criterion for successfully solving an *aporia*, so there is a general criterion after all. If so, it is important to realize that this general criterion for recognizing that we have successfully solved a particular *aporia* is not associated with a general methodology for solving an *aporia*. More importantly, it is not associated with the idea that we can know infallibly and definitively that we have found the true solution, for it is not associated with the idea that we can know infallibly and definitively that the solution that we have found is the only or the best solution.

2 The source of the *aporiai* in metaphysics

In book III, Aristotle lists some fifteen *aporiai* in and about metaphysics, which it is his aim to engage with and eventually to answer. But before we look at the individual *aporiai*, it is natural to ask, where does he get them from and what is their source? An answer that immediately suggests itself is that he gets them from his predecessors and especially from conflicts of opinion among his predecessors (including, of course, Plato). So we might expect that in each of these *aporiai* and dilemmas, each side of the dilemma represents an opinion of an earlier thinker, and, that when Aristotle presents a dilemma, it is such conflicts of opinions that he presents. This would mean that when Aristotle engages with these *aporiai* what he is doing is engaging in dialogue with those earlier thinkers who, in his view, have addressed the subject of the nature of being. So it will emerge that the *aporia*-based method is a variation of a dialectical approach (from *dialegesthai*, 'to converse' or 'discuss'). If the *aporia*-based method is indeed a variation of the dialectical approach, it will, arguably, be a variation of the so-called *endoxic* approach (from *endoxon*, 'a reputable opinion'). For Aristotle will not want to engage equally with just any opinion, but rather with reputable opinions (*endoxa*). In general, *endoxa* are opinions that enjoy at least prima facie credibility either because they are generally shared or because they are held by 'the wise', i.e. those who have given proper thought to the matter (see *Topics* I for Aristotle's appeal to *endoxa* in this sense; see e.g. *Nicomachean Ethics* VII. 1, 1145^{b}1ff. for an approach that appeals centrally to such *endoxa*). So, on this interpretation of Aristotle's method, the *aporia*-based method is a variation of a dialectical and *endoxic* approach; i.e. it is a dialogue with earlier thinkers and in particular a discussion of reputable opinions (*endoxa*) obtained from them.

There is evidently something broadly right about this interpretation. For it is true that in some of the *aporiai* that he lists in book III we may be able to associate each side of the dilemma with the opinion of an earlier thinker (in some cases this will be Plato, who is only recently dead and whom Aristotle of course knew personally and as a friend). It is also true that Aristotle thinks that all searching for knowledge starts from so-called *phainomena*: things that are apparent to us. But *phainomena* may naturally generate reputable opinions. This may suggest that the *aporia*-based method which he adopts in metaphysics is simply a variation of a dialectical and *endoxic* approach. In that case, metaphysics is an engagement with reputable opinions about the nature of being.

However, there are serious problems with this interpretation. First of all, the whole emphasis in book III is on *aporiai* and on the claim that our recognition of and engagement with *aporiai* is what enables us to search in metaphysics. There is no appeal to *endoxa*, and no claim that it is they that enable us to search in metaphysics. It is of course true that earlier thinkers generally disagree with each other, and with the opinions pre-reflectively shared by people. But it would be wrong to think that, in Aristotle's view, every conflict of opinion, or even every conflict of reputable opinions, gives rise to an *aporia*. For we need to recall that an *aporia*, in the sense of a particular puzzle and problem, is what causes puzzlement; it causes puzzlement because we are rationally pulled in apparently opposite and conflicting directions. But this means that one must oneself find that both sides are credible; it is not enough that different people should find the different sides credible. For in that case the puzzle and problem, if it is one at all, would not *necessarily* cause any puzzlement. But this strongly suggests that thinking of the *aporia*-based method as simply a variation of an endoxic method is decisively inadequate; for it does not show why it is indeed *aporiai* that are essential to the *aporia*-based method.

But there is also a clear textual problem with thinking that the *aporia*-based method is simply a variation of an endoxic method. For at the opening of book III Aristotle says something that plainly suggests that although some of the material for his *aporiai* is obtained from his predecessors, other material may so far have been overlooked by everyone and he may be the first to recognize it:

> With a view to the science that we are seeking [i.e. metaphysics], we must first turn to those things about which we need above all to raise *aporiai*, that is, the things about which certain others have held opposed views *as well as anything besides these that happens to have been overlooked.*
>
> (995ᵃ24–27)

So it is not true that each side of an *aporia* in metaphysics must represent an already held opinion; on the contrary, there may be *aporiai* that have so far been overlooked. That there is such a non-*endoxic* and non-*doxastic* (from *doxa*, 'opinion') aspect to Aristotle's metaphysical *aporiai* is further suggested when he goes on to say that:

there is no resolution [of an *aporia*] if one fails to recognize the knot [i.e. the *aporia*]. Rather, the *aporia* in our thought indicates this [i.e. a knot] in the object.

(995ᵃ29–31)

So again he emphasizes that we may fail to recognize an *aporia*. But what he means by this is surely not that we may fail to be sufficiently thorough in our review of the reputable opinions of our predecessors. What he means is rather that an *aporia* may entirely escape notice and may need to be recognized and discovered for the first time. This is also suggested by the words: 'the *aporia* in our thought indicates this [i.e. a knot, an *aporia*] in the object'.

What this suggests is that, rather than thinking that it is simply opinions held by earlier thinkers that are the source of the individual metaphysical *aporiai*, Aristotle thinks that the things themselves are the source of the *aporiai*. So the subject under investigation is itself genuinely puzzling, and this is why we, if we are sufficiently sensitive, will be puzzled. If this interpretation is correct, it follows that the *aporia*-based method is not a variation of an endoxic method. It is true that Aristotle is very much interested in the opinions of his predecessors about the nature of being, and especially in conflicts among such opinions. But he does not think that such opinions and their conflicts, as such and by themselves, give rise to *aporiai*. What he thinks is rather that the familiarity and engagement with the conflicts of opinions of one's predecessors helps to improve one's sensibility to the *aporiai* generated by the things themselves. This reading is also confirmed when he says earlier that his predecessors were guided by the things themselves in their searches (see 984ᵃ16–19 and ᵇ8–11, quoted at the end of Chapter 2).

There is also an important advantage of this upshot, i.e. the upshot that the *aporia*-based method is not a variation of an *endoxic* method. For it is difficult to see how a search that is based on reputable opinions (*endoxa*) can at the same time, i.e. to the very extent that it is simply based on reputable opinions, be a search for objective knowledge or, as Aristotle says, a search for 'the truth' (see 998ᵃ20–21). Surely, to the extent that a search is based simply on reputable opinions, it can only result in yet further reputable opinions – rather than simply in knowledge of the truth. So, if Aristotle's method in metaphysics is based in reputable opinions, either it cannot amount to a search for knowledge of the truth, or it can do so only if he provides a general argument of the following form: ultimately, it is reputable opinions that constitute knowledge of the truth. But it is hard to find such an argument in

Aristotle. (For an alternative interpretation, which argues that in general Aristotle's method is *endoxic,* see especially Nussbaum 1982.)

To us, the idea that it is the things themselves that generate *aporiai* may appear very puzzling. After all, things do not literally ask questions. But, setting aside the potent metaphor of there being 'knots in things', what Aristotle appears to mean is this: engaging with *aporiai* may be essential to understanding certain things (although not all things), and it may be essential because of the nature of those things, rather than because of confusions in our thinking or inadequacies in our knowledge. If we still find puzzling the idea that it may be the things, rather than simply our thinking, that generate *aporiai,* we may reformulate this idea as follows: engaging with *aporiai* may be essential to our understanding certain things (although not all things), and it may be essential to our understanding of certain things, irrespective or how clear our thinking may be or how generally adequate our knowledge may be. It is arguably in this sense that the things themselves are supposed to generate *aporiai.*

There is real attraction in Aristotle's *aporia*-based method in metaphysics. Aristotle thinks of metaphysics as a fundamental inquiry: a 'first philosophy' and 'first science'. But what entitles him to this view? How can he be confident that metaphysics does not rely on certain unacknowledged presuppositions? For example, how can he be confident that it does not rely on semantic or epistemological presuppositions? This question has, of course, become the bugbear of modern metaphysics, at least since Kant. So how in general can he engage in a metaphysical inquiry without begging any questions, i.e. without presupposing claims that can themselves be contested – whether these questions are metaphysical or about the very possibility of metaphysics? But it seems clear and striking that if any method has a chance of being presuppositionless and not question-begging, and if any method has a chance of providing for a genuinely fundamental inquiry – a first philosophy and first science – than it is an *aporia*-based method. For to start with *aporiai* is to start from questions, not claims. Moreover, the questions may even include the question of how the search at hand is possible. For example, we will see that some of Aristotle's metaphysical *aporiai* in book III are directly about the very possibility of metaphysics (see *aporiai* 1–4, and 7). So if we genuinely start from questions, we can perhaps avoid begging any questions; and since metaphysics is supposed to be a fundamental inquiry – a first philosophy and first science – it is crucial that it should aspire to being presuppositionless and not question-begging.

3 The list of *aporiai* and how they structure the *Metaphysics*

Book III opens with Aristotle's reflections on the method which he wants to adopt in metaphysics: the *aporia*-based method. But does he live up to these methodological reflections? Apparently it is his intention to conduct the search for the nature of being in an *aporia*-based way. For he immediately goes on to provide a list of some fifteen *aporiai* which it is his aim to engage with and eventually to answer, and we will see that these *aporiai* in a radical way inform the structure of the *Metaphysics*. But before we review the individual *aporiai*, first some general comments on the *aporiai* and on how they serve to structure the *Metaphysics*.

It is striking that all the fifteen *aporiai* are dilemmatic in structure, i.e. they are two-sided questions of the form: *whether* such and such *or* such and such (*poteron ... ē ...*). This contrasts with the overall question, 'What is being?', which is not dilemmatic and so perhaps is not itself strictly an *aporia* – although of course it is supposed to be closely associated with *aporiai*. Why does Aristotle think that fundamental questions of metaphysics take the form of dilemmas? Part of the answer appears to be that presenting metaphysical questions in the form of dilemmas will help to motivate and to direct the search for an answer (see §1 of this chapter). But perhaps there is also a deeper reason why Aristotle thinks that metaphysical questions take the form of two-sided *aporiai*. For he thinks that questions as general and fundamental as the question 'What is being?', or indeed any question of metaphysics or even philosophy in general, by their very nature pull us in apparently opposite directions when we try to answer them; and they do so not because of confusion or ignorance on our part, but because different and apparently conflicting answers genuinely have reason behind them (see this chapter, §2). So an adequate attempt to answer such questions must work itself through apparently conflicting answers, rather than look directly for an answer that will be evident and indisputable to any right-thinking person.

Another striking feature of the list of fifteen *aporiai* is that it divides naturally into two sets of *aporiai*: on the one hand, *aporiai* about metaphysics, its nature and its possibility (see *aporiai* 1–4, and 7), and on the other hand, particular *aporiai* within metaphysics. As an example of the former kind of *aporia*, we may emphasize especially the third *aporia*, which raises the radical question: is it the task of a single investigation to investigate all being or is it simply the task of fundamentally different investigations to investigate different kinds of beings? This question is evidently about the very possibility of metaphysics. For if it is simply the task of fundamentally different investigations to investigate different kinds of beings, i.e. if, for example, this is simply the task of different special sciences such as mathematics and physics, then there will be no room for metaphysics – the investigation of all beings and of being as a whole. Moreover, in the seventh *aporia* Aristotle presents a genuine reason for thinking that it is simply the task of different sciences to investigate different kinds of beings, and that there cannot be a further science of being as a whole. For he presents an argument for thinking that there is no single kind, being, over and above the different kinds of beings, e.g. the ones investigated by mathematics and physics. So he thinks that there is a genuine problem about the very possibility of metaphysics.

This shows that Aristotle, as he sees himself, is not only searching for the answer to the question, 'What is being?'; he is just as much reflecting on this question itself and on whether and how we can in principle search for an answer to it, or even suppose that it has an answer in the first place. However, it is also important not to misunderstand this point. For it would be wrong to think that, for Aristotle, there is a sharp distinction between these two kinds of *aporiai*: those that are *about* metaphysics and those that are *within* metaphysics. It would be wrong to think that he distinguishes between metaphysical questions and, as it were, meta-metaphysical questions. For this may suggest that he thinks that the former kind of *aporiai* have their source in something outside metaphysics and outside the question, 'What is being?' But this is not at all what he thinks. On the contrary, when Aristotle raises questions about the possibility of metaphysics, he does so from within metaphysics itself, i.e. because of puzzles and problems about the nature of being.

We ought to note that this approach contrasts with a typically modern approach to the question of the possibility or impossibility of metaphysics. For typically modern attempts to defend the possibility, or impossibility, of metaphysics base themselves on considerations that are supposed to be from outside metaphysics: considerations about language and meaning (logic, semantics); or about knowledge (epistemology). Perhaps the most famous example of a modern approach is the positivist line of argument: metaphysical statements are meaningless because they are not empirically verifiable. We may note also that this critique of the possibility of metaphysics starts from the assumption that metaphysics consists basically of statements; whereas metaphysics as Aristotle conceives it consists basically of questions. The positivist critique of the possibility of metaphysics may seem too quick. But it is an example of a general modern tendency to want to defend the possibility, or impossibility, of metaphysics from outside metaphysics itself. In its most subtle and profound form, this tendency goes back to Kant and to his attempt to defend the possibility of metaphysics (but a metaphysics that is subject to certain crucial qualifications and limitations) on the basis of the question: how is objective knowledge possible for creatures such as ourselves?

Perhaps Aristotle's approach to the question of the possibility or impossibility of metaphysics enjoys a particular advantage over the typically modern approach to this question. For suppose that we set out to defend the possibility (or impossibility) of metaphysics from the basis of, let us say, semantics and a theory of meaning. Then we are tacitly presupposing that this investigation, semantics, is prior to and more fundamental than metaphysics. But such an assumption will not be obviously correct, and once it is made explicit, it may be questioned. But then what investigation can we appeal to in order to defend this assumption, or its denial? Apparently it cannot be semantics that decides whether semantics is prior to metaphysics; for that would beg the question. So some more neutral investigation will be called for. But what could this investigation be? Since no answer is forthcoming, or even available, it seems no wonder that modern answers to the question whether or not metaphysics is possible, or how it is possible, have tended to become dogmatic, with little room for real engagement between different answers. But Aristotle's approach, i.e. the approach which says that questions about the possibility of metaphysics must themselves be understood as being or involving metaphysical questions, questions about the nature of being in general, does perhaps avoid such dogmatism and mutual begging of questions.

So does Aristotle live up to his methodology? Is the *Metaphysics* structured according to these fifteen *aporiai*? We can apparently find answers in the *Metaphysics* to all or most of these *aporiai*. But if the *Metaphysics* is genuinely to be structured according to these *aporiai*, it is not enough that it should provide answers to them; for it must also be the case that the answers are arrived at by working through the *aporiai*. Whether this is how Aristotle actually proceeds will have to be made out in detail.

But there is good reason to think that this is his procedure, i.e. that it is by working through the *aporiai* that he reaches the answers that he puts forward. For this is suggested by the structure of books III–IV and the central books, VII–IX. Thus in the third and seventh *aporia* listed in book III he raises a central question about the possibility of metaphysics: is there such a thing as the nature of being in general and as a whole, or is it rather the case that there are simply as many kinds of beings as are investigated by the special sciences? But in the first two chapters of book IV he offers a distinctive solution to this *aporia*: we may suppose that there is such a thing as the nature of being in general and as a whole, provided that we can draw a distinction between primary being (*prōtē ousia*, often simply *ousia*) and non-primary being; for then we can determine being as a whole by reference to this focal point – primary being. (We will consider this line of argument, and the *aporia* behind it, at length in Chapter 4§1–3.) But this of course raises the question, 'What is primary being?' And this is precisely the question that he takes up, and pursues relentlessly, in books VII–IX, and to which eventually he offers a solution. So the question, 'What is the nature of being?', which is the basic question of metaphysics, gives rise to an *aporia*: does being, in general and as opposed to the different kinds of beings, have a nature? And it is as part of the attempt to answer this *aporia* that Aristotle introduces what is the absolutely central notion in the *Metaphysics*, the notion of *primary being* (*prōtē ousia*, often simply *ousia*). So when he goes on to search for an answer, and eventually to offer an answer, to the question, 'What is being?', he does so by focusing on the question, 'What is primary being?'; and this question is rooted in an *aporia*. In this precise and radical sense the *Metaphysics* is structured according to certain fundamental *aporiai*. But we will also see that it is by working through particular *aporiai* about being and, in particular, primary being that he tries to answer these two fundamental questions of metaphysics, 'What is being?' and 'What is primary being?'

In general, we will have to look out for two things in order to determine whether Aristotle's procedure is in fact *aporia*-based. First, the *aporiai* must be independent of the answers that he gives to them. That is to say, we must be able to appreciate how one can seriously ask these questions without already being familiar with Aristotle's answers. In other words, Aristotle's questions must not be tailored to fit his answers.

Second, the answers must also in an important sense be independent of the questions. Of course, if the *Metaphysics* is structured according to these *aporiai*, we need to understand the *aporiai* in order to understand the answers to them. But we must also bear in mind that the overall aim of the *Metaphysics* is not simply to answer a set of *aporiai*, but to answer the basic question, 'What is being?' So answering the *aporiai* must be a means to answering this overall question. This is also why the *Metaphysics* provides not simply fifteen separate answers to fifteen different questions, but above all a single answer to a single basic question, 'What is being?' In other words, the answers to the different *aporiai* are intended to add up to a single unitary theory about the nature of being. In this sense, the answers are independent of the questions.

But the answers are independent of the questions also in the following important sense. For the attempt to answer these *aporiai* may require introducing distinctive concepts not already present in the *aporiai* themselves, or at least new ways of understanding old concepts. For Aristotle may think that certain *aporiai* can only be answered if we introduce new concepts or at least importantly new variations of old ones. Aristotle's concept of primary being (*prōtē ousia*, often simply *ousia*) is such a new concept, or at least a distinctive variation on an old concept, and he develops this concept by working through an *aporia*. The same can especially be said of Aristotle's concept of essence (*to ti estin, to ti ēn einai*; see Chapters 1§4 and 7§5iii–iv).

4 A brief review of the fifteen *aporiai*

After the methodological reflections, and after arguing that it is our recognition of particular *aporiai* that enables us to search in metaphysics, Aristotle sets out a list of fifteen *aporiai*, which it is his aim to engage with and eventually to answer. We will give a paraphrase of each *aporia* and a brief comment about what it says and how it arises.

First Aporia ($996^a18–^b26$)

Is it the task of a single science to investigate all the different causes and explanations of things, or is this the task of fundamentally different sciences?

This *aporia* arises because, on the one hand, there are very different kinds of explanations and causes (e.g. the formal and the material cause); but, on the other hand, metaphysics was characterized as the science of the ultimate causes and explanations of all things, hence as the science of all the different kinds of causes and explanations of things.

Second Aporia ($996^b26–997^a15$)

Is it the task of a single science to investigate both the ultimate principles of being and the basic principles of reasoning (e.g. the principle of non-contradiction)? Or is this the task of fundamentally different sciences?

The question here is how metaphysics, i.e. the science of the nature and principles of being, is related to logic, i.e. the science of the basic principles of reasoning and rational thought (e.g. the principle of non-contradiction). Does metaphysics include logic, or is logic independent of metaphysics? And, if the latter is the case, is logic perhaps more fundamental than, or even the basis of, metaphysics? We will take up this question at length in Chapters 5 and 6.

Third Aporia (997ª15–25)

Is it the task of a single science to investigate all beings, or is it the task of fundamentally different sciences to investigate different kinds of beings?

This *aporia* raises a most pressing question about the possibility of metaphysics: how is it even possible to conceive of *all* beings and of being *as a whole*? This problem is restated in a different and apparently more technical way in the seventh *aporia* (see especially 998ᵇ22–27), where Aristotle asks whether there is such a thing as a single whole or kind, *being*, and answers that there is a problem with thinking that there is. We will take up this general *aporia* at length in Chapter 4§1–3.

Fourth Aporia (997ª25–34)

Is the task of metaphysics only to investigate the (primary) beings or also to investigate the common characteristics of the (primary) beings?

For example, suppose that all beings share the characteristic of being extended. Is it, then, the task of metaphysics also to investigate things in so far as they are extended, i.e. to investigate the properties of things in so far as they are extended? For example, is it part of metaphysics to investigate the properties of lines, circles, etc? But then, apparently, metaphysics will include, or even collapse into, geometry. We will take up this *aporia* in Chapter 4§1.

Fifth Aporia (997ª34–998ª19)

Do only sense-perceptible things exist or do non-sense-perceptible things exist, too, in addition to or besides (para) sense-perceptible ones?

The first four *aporiai* were concerned with the nature and possibility of metaphysics – they were *about* metaphysics. But this and the following *aporiai* are *aporiai within* metaphysics. The present *aporia* takes up the question, What basically is there? Only sense-perceptible things, or also non-sense-perceptible things? We may note that the reality of sense-perceptible things is taken for granted here, the question being whether, 'in addition to' or 'besides' (*para*) these, we should suppose that non-sense-perceptible things are real. It is also important to note that by 'sense-perceptible things' (*aisthēta*) he means 'changing things' (*kinoumena*); and by 'non-sense-perceptible things' he means 'change-less things' (*akinēta*). The way in which the *aporia* is presented may suggest that Aristotle sides entirely with the one side (only sense-perceptible things are real), and that it is Plato and the Platonists that take up the other side (also non-sense-perceptible things are real). He may also give the impression that no reconciliation is possible between the two sides. But these impressions are misleading. For Aristotle will argue, just like Plato, that explanations and explanatory knowledge requires the reality of non-sense-perceptible and changeless things. The disagreement with Plato is rather about how the two types of things – changing and sense-perceptible things as opposed to changeless and non-sense-perceptible things – are related to each other. In particular, are they two sets of distinct things, so that it is in this sense that non-sense-perceptible things exist 'in addition to' or 'besides' (*para*) sense-perceptible ones? This is Plato's view, as Aristotle understands it. Or can a single thing be both sense-perceptible and non-sense-perceptible, both changing and changeless? This is the solution that Aristotle will defend. We will take up this *aporia* at length in in Chapters 7 and 9.

Sixth Aporia (998ᵃ20–ᵇ13)

Are the principles of a thing the kinds to which the thing belongs or are they rather the ultimate elements that are present in the thing and compose the thing?

This important *aporia* is a variation of the central *aporia* (especially the fifteenth): are the principles of things general or particular? It arises especially from the very notion of a principle: 'It is common to all principles [of a thing] to be the starting-point from which [the thing] either comes to be or is or is known' (*Metaphysics* VI. 1, 1013ᵃ17–19). For if a principle of a thing is the starting-point from which the thing is or comes to be, then this principle will apparently be the ultimate parts and elements out of which the thing is composed. But if, on the other hand, the principle of a thing is the starting-point from which the thing is known, i.e. explanatorily and scientifically known, then the principle will apparently be rather the general kind to which the thing belongs. For explanatory knowledge requires knowledge of the general kinds to which things belong. But Aristotle argues that a principle of a thing must explain both, on the one hand, what it is, and, on the other hand, how it comes to be and how it is knowable and explicable. So this is apparently how the *aporia* arises. We will take up this *aporia* in Chapter 7, especially §5vi–vii.

Seventh Aporia (998ᵇ13–999ᵃ23)

*If we suppose that the principle of a thing is the general kind to which
the thing belongs (i.e. if we take up the former side of the previous
aporia), then how general must this kind be? Is the principle of a thing
the most general kind to which the thing belongs (i.e. the genus) or the
least general kind (i.e. the species)?*

This *aporia* arises naturally if we take up the one side of the previous
aporia. If this is the side that Aristotle will defend, then he will apparently argue, against Plato and the Platonists, that species are more basic
than genera; so he will argue, for example, that there are animals because
there are dogs, cats, humans, etc., rather than vice versa. But perhaps
Aristotle will not defend this side at all, i.e. he will not argue that the
ultimate principle of a thing is the general kind to which the thing
belongs, whether this kind is conceived as the genus or as the species.
We will take up this *aporia* in Chapter 7, especially §5viii.

Eighth Aporia (999ᵃ24–ᵇ24)

*Do general kinds exist at all (whether as species or as genera) in addition
to or besides (para) sense-perceptible particulars?*

See comment under the fifth *aporia*. Again, the question is not so
much whether Aristotle thinks that there are general kinds in reality;
he clearly does think this. The question is how they are related to sense-
perceptible particulars: whether and in what sense they exist 'in addition
to' or 'besides' (*para*) sense-perceptible particulars. But apparently he is
also raising the more radical question here: are there general kinds
at all, however they are conceived? He will argue that there must be, if
things are to be intelligible and subject to explanation in the first
place. We will take up this *aporia* in Chapter 7, especially §5ix; see also
Chapter 8.

Ninth Aporia (999ᵇ24–1000ᵃ4)

Are principles one in kind or one in number?

In other words, are there as many principles as there are particular
things (so that my principle and your principle are different, although
we both belong to the same general kind), or are there as many principles as there are kinds of things (so that my principle and your principle
are the same, since we belong to the same general kind)? At first it
may seem that Aristotle thinks that we must choose between these two
sides. But eventually he may argue rather that we can, and should,

defend both sides at once. In other words, my principle is my essence, and this is different from your essence (although we are both human and belong to the same general kind); but my essence and your essence, although different in number, are one in kind (since we belong to the same kind). However, on a different interpretation of his solution to this central *aporia*, his view is rather that principles are only one in kind, not one in number: my principle is my essence, and this is simply the same as yours (since we belong to the same general kind). We will take up this *aporia* at length below, in Chapter 7, especially §5viii–ix.

Tenth Aporia (1000^{a}5–1001^{a}3)

Are the principles of perishable and imperishable things the same or different?

On Aristotle's conception of nature and the physical universe, nature consists of both perishable things, i.e. things that are subject to generation and destruction (e.g. plants and animals), and imperishable things, i.e. eternal things, things not subject to generation and destruction (e.g. the planets and the stars, as he conceives them). The question is whether there is a single explanation to account for both of these kinds of things together, and so to account for the unity of nature. We will consider the answer to this *aporia* below, in Chapter 8.

Eleventh Aporia (1001^{a}4–^{b}25)

Is primary being simply being *itself and* unity *itself or is primary being rather things that are and are one?*

In other words, suppose that *being* and *unity* are primary beings – because they are that in virtue of which any being is a being, something that is. Are they primary beings simply because they themselves are that which primarily is, or are they primary beings only because some other thing (e.g. this rose) is and is a unified thing? We may wonder how Aristotle answers this intriguing *aporia*. He will eventually argue that primary being with regard to each thing is the essence of that thing (see Chapter 7§5iv). For it is, he will argue, in virtue of having an essence that each thing is a being, something that is, in the first place. So he appears to defend the latter side of the *aporia*: essences are primary beings because other things (e.g. this rose) are beings in virtue of having essences. But he will also argue that it is precisely essences that are the primary beings. So he also appears to defend the former side: it is the essences themselves that are primary beings. He must, apparently, think that the two sides can both be true. On a different interpretation, however, he only defends the latter side: essences are primary beings only because other things (e.g. this rose) are beings in virtue of having essences. We will take up this *aporia* below, in Chapter 7§5v.

Twelfth Aporia (1001^{b}26–1002^{b}11)

Are numbers, solids, surfaces and points themselves the primary beings or are they primary beings only because other things (e.g. this horse) have such geometrical and in general mathematical properties?

See the comment on the precious *aporia*: the question here is whether things are literally constituted by mathematical properties, so that such properties are themselves the primary beings, or whether mathematical properties are primary beings only in the sense of explaining the being of other things.

Thirteenth Aporia (1002^{b}12–32)

Are there kinds (eidē) in addition to or besides (para) both sense-perceptible things and the entities postulated by mathematics?

See the comment on the fifth *aporia*. But here the question is not simply whether there are non-sense-perceptible and changeless things, but whether these include only the entities postulated by mathematics, or whether they include also other, non-mathematical entities. In general, Aristotle argues that mathematical entities, although non-sense-perceptible and changeless, must apparently be repeatable. For example, if addition is to be possible (e.g. $1 + 1 = 2$), apparently the mathematical unit (the number 1) must be repeatable (for in the addition $1 + 1 = 2$ it occurs twice). So the question is whether, in addition to changing things and changeless things that are repeatable, there must also be changeless things that are strictly non-repeatable.

Fourteenth Aporia (1002^{b}32–1003^{a}5)

Are the elements of things potentialities and capacities for causing and generating those things or are they what actually causes and generates those things?

The elements of a thing are the ultimate causes of the thing. The *aporia* arises because, on the one hand, the capacity to cause something appears to be more basic than actually causing something; but, on the other hand, if elements are simply capacities, they may not actually cause anything to be.

Fifteenth Aporia (1003ᵃ5–17)

Are the principles of things universals or particulars?

This is perhaps Aristotle's most central *aporia* in metaphysics, and it will occupy us at length in Chapter 7, especially §5v, viii, ix and x. The *aporia* is whether the principles, i.e. the ultimate explanations, for which metaphysics is searching, are universals or particulars. On the one hand, it appears that they must be universals; for explanations are universal and require the reality of universals. So reality will be intelligible and subject to explanation only if principles are universals. On the other hand, it appears that what primarily is are particulars; for universals are real only in virtue of there being particulars that they are true of. But how can primary being be one thing, i.e. the particulars, but the primary object of knowledge be a different thing, i.e. the universals? Certainly Aristotle argues that the primary object of knowledge, i.e. what is intelligible and subject to explanation, must at the same time be what primarily is – primary being.

4

METAPHYSICS AS THE SCIENCE OF BEING *QUA* BEING

Primary being *versus* non-primary being (Books IV. 1–2 and VI. 1)

1 Metaphysics as the science of being *qua* being

In the opening sentence of book IV, Aristotle states how metaphysics is to be understood: as the science of being *qua* being. He says that there really is such a science:

> There is a science which investigates being *qua* being and what belongs to this [i.e. to being] in virtue of itself [*kath' hauto*, i.e. what belongs to being essentially].

> (1003ª21–22)

The claim that there is such a science is particularly important, for it may suggest that Aristotle thinks that there is a problem about the possibility of a science of being *qua* being, but also that the problem can be answered. In fact it will emerge that the claim that there is such a science, metaphysics, is the conclusion of a defence of the possibility of metaphysics, except that he states this conclusion before he actually undertakes the defence.

There is good reason to suppose that Aristotle thinks that there is a problem about the very possibility of metaphysics, if we recall the *aporiai* in the previous book (i.e. book III). For some of these *aporiai* raised problems precisely about the possibility of metaphysics – problems originating especially in the question of how we can conceive of *all beings* and of being as a whole and *qua* being (see especially the third *aporia*, 997^{a}15–25, and part of the seventh *aporia*, especially 998^{a}22–27). Furthermore, we will see shortly that the opening of the next chapter in the present book (i.e. IV. 2) is best understood as putting forward a solution to just these *aporiai*, and hence as defending the possibility of metaphysics.

Every science investigates being; for if a science investigates something, it investigates something that is. Otherwise there is nothing there to investigate. Biology, for example, investigates beings in so far as they are living beings; botany investigates beings in so far as they are plants; arithmetic in so far as they are countable; geometry in so far as they are extended, etc. So the view that every science is of something that is – of a being – supposes that the object of knowledge, i.e. what is known, must be or exist. What distinguishes metaphysics from other sciences is not, therefore, that it investigates being; for every science does that. Rather, metaphysics, unlike other sciences, investigates being *qua being*; i.e. it investigates beings not in so far as they are this or that kind of beings (living beings, plants, countable and extended beings, etc.), but simply in so far as they are beings – things that are.

In the immediately following lines, Aristotle clarifies this characterization of metaphysics:

> Now this [i.e. metaphysics] is not identical with any of the so-called partial [i.e. specialized] sciences. For none of the other sciences treats in a general way [*katholou*] of being *qua* being; rather, they cut off some part of being and investigate what belongs to this part – as do, for example, the mathematical sciences.
>
> (1003^{a}22–26)

The image of being as a big chunk, with each specialized science cutting out a different part for its attention, is markedly metaphorical, but the point behind it is that one science, metaphysics, is unlike the rest, in that it investigates all beings. If a science investigates beings in so far as they are, for example, living beings, it will not investigate all beings, for not all beings are living beings. But if a science investigates beings simply in so far as they are, then it will investigate all beings; for evidently all beings are. Metaphysics, therefore, is distinguished by its complete generality and universality: it investigates all beings.

But metaphysics not only investigates all beings, it investigates all beings in a completely general way (*katholou*): 'For none of the other sciences treats *in a general way* (*katholou*) of being *qua* being', 1003ᵃ23–24. If we suppose that there is a definite number of specialized sciences, then perhaps the sum of the specialized sciences will also investigate all beings; but metaphysics is evidently not the mere sum of the specialized sciences. What distinguishes metaphysics, therefore, is not only what it investigates, i.e. all beings, but also how it investigates this, i.e. in a completely general way. Indeed, it is natural to think that the phrase '*qua* being', in the statement that metaphysics 'investigates being *qua* being', serves precisely to indicate how metaphysics investigates being: it investigates being *qua being*, hence in a completely general way.

This characterization of metaphysics – as the science that investigates beings in a completely general way and simply in so far as they are – also helps to answer an *aporia* that arises naturally at this point, and that Aristotle raised earlier (in book III, see the fourth *aporia*, 997ᵃ25–34). How does metaphysics, the science of all things, differ from other sciences that may apparently themselves investigate all things, e.g. mathematics or physics? For there may apparently be such sciences. For example, if we suppose that all things that basically exist are countable (mathematics) or material (physics), then mathematics and physics will investigate all things. But evidently metaphysics is not the same as, and it does not include, mathematics or physics. However, even if, for example, mathematics investigates all things (supposing that numbers are applicable to all things), it does not investigate all things in a completely general way and simply in so far as they are. For it focuses its attention on one feature of all things (e.g. their being countable) as opposed to another feature of all things (e.g. their being material, supposing that all things are material).

Metaphysics, on the other hand, investigates all beings not in a partial way, but in a completely general way and simply in so far as they are. For it focuses its attention not on one as opposed to another feature of all beings, but simply on the basic feature of all beings: their being beings, things that are. This feature – the being of all beings – is more basic than any of the partial features of all beings (e.g. their being countable or material). For only by investigating this feature of all beings, i.e. their being beings, can we adequately investigate whether all beings are, for example, countable or material, and in general investigate a universal claim about being. In general, if we can establish a universal claim about being, and do so in a way that explains why this claim is true, we can do so only by asking the basic question of metaphysics, 'What is it for something, anything, to be?', and by searching for an answer to this question.

Aristotle provides an important clarification of the phrase '*qua* being', when he says that metaphysics 'investigates being *qua* being *and what belongs to this* [i.e. to being] *in virtue of itself* [*kath' hauto*, i.e. what belongs to being essentially].' A special science such as biology investigates not only what belongs to, i.e. what is true of some beings, namely, living beings; it investigates what is true of living beings in virtue of the fact that they are living beings. In other words, biology investigates what it is to be a living being: the essence of living beings. (This of course is a not uncontroversial claim about the sciences; it is a consequence of Aristotle's conception of science.) Likewise, metaphysics investigates not only what is true of all beings; it investigates what is true of all beings in virtue of the fact that they are. In other words, metaphysics investigates what it is for something, anything, to be: the essence of beings. So the question distinctive of metaphysics is not so much 'What is there?', but rather 'What is being?' and 'What is it for something, anything, to be?'

We may note that Aristotle supposes that the essentialism that marks his conception of the specialized sciences can be extended to the science of the whole of being; i.e. he thinks that just as we can ask 'What is a rose?' or 'What is a plant?', we can likewise ask 'What is a being?' Perhaps we will think that this supposition is questionable. After all, we may find questions such as 'What is a rose?' or 'What is a plant?' readily familiar, pre-philosophically and perhaps even pre-scientifically (perhaps we have a passion for gardening). But if we reflect for a moment, we may come to think that such questions owe their familiarity especially to the availability of contrastive questions, of the form: how do roses differ from other plants, and how do plants differ from other living things? But we are hardly familiar, pre-philosophically or even within scientific inquiry, with the question, 'What is being?'; and this may, precisely, be because there appear to be no contrastive questions available here, of the form: how do beings differ from things that are not beings?

But we will see that Aristotle himself thinks that there is a problem with this supposition, i.e. a problem of extending essentialism and the question, 'What is X?', from different kinds of beings (living beings, plants, countable and extended beings, etc.) to the whole of being. So he thinks that there is a problem of how the whole of being can have an essence, and hence can constitute a natural kind. The cutting-up-or-leaving-whole metaphor already indicates this problem. The idea of making divisions between different kinds of beings, such as, for instance, between living beings and inanimate beings, makes good sense; for these different kinds of beings can be set against one another.

But evidently there is nothing outside the whole of being which can be set against it. For the claim that there are things that are not beings, in the sense that they are not anything and lie outside of being, apparently contains a contradiction. This fundamental difference between, on the one hand, the many kinds of beings and, on the other hand, being as a whole, threatens to undermine the supposition that, just as, for example, living beings have a common essence in so far as they are living beings, so too beings have a common essence simply in so far as they are. We will consider this problem shortly.

It is worth emphasizing the idea that there is nothing outside the whole of being which can be set against it. We may perhaps use the following catch-phrase for this idea: absolute not-being is nothing at all. This idea goes back to Plato's dialogue, the *Sophist* (236dff.), where Plato argues that the notion of *that which in no way is* (*to mēdamōs on*), i.e. the notion of absolute not-being, is utterly incoherent. He concludes that when we say of something that it is not, we do not mean that it *in no way is*; i.e. we do not mean that it is not anything. Rather we mean that it is something that is, but different from something else that is: it is one being, or one kind of being, as opposed to another. So not-being indicates only a distinction within being, a distinction between different beings; it does not indicate something outside of being as a whole. It appears that Aristotle entirely accepts this lesson from Plato's *Sophist*.

2 The problem of how there can be a science of being *qua* being; and the solution in terms of the distinction between *primary being* and *non-primary being*

At the opening of book IV, chapter 2, Aristotle introduces a distinction that will become absolutely central in the *Metaphysics*: the distinction between *primary being* (*prōtē ousia*, often simply *ousia*) and *non-primary being*. This is the distinction between:

(1) things that are beings in virtue of themselves and not in virtue of their relation to other things; and
(2) things that are beings in virtue of their relation to, and so dependent on, the primary beings.

In other words, to be a primary being is to be something that is a being in virtue of itself and not in virtue of its relation to other things; whereas to be a non-primary being is to be something that is a being in virtue of its relation to, and so dependent on, a primary being. But it is important to note straight away that when he introduces this distinction here (in IV. 2), he does so in a completely general way and without yet raising the question: 'What are the beings that are primary and what are the beings that are non-primary?' We may say that he here introduces the very notions, *primary being* and *non-primary being*, but without yet asking what, if anything, satisfies these notions. In books VII–IX, the central books of the *Metaphysics*, he will go on to raise the central question: 'What is primary being?', i.e. 'What are the things that are beings in virtue of themselves and not in virtue of their relation to other things?'

In the next section, we will consider the way in which Aristotle introduces the distinction between primary and non-primary being here (in IV. 2). But first let us ask why he introduces this distinction at all. Apparently, he does so in order to answer a problem and *aporia* about the very possibility of metaphysics as it was characterized in IV. 1, i.e. as the science that investigates all beings and investigates them simply in so far as they are beings. He stated this problem in book III – the book of *aporiai*: *Is it the task of a single science to investigate all beings or is it the task of fundamentally different sciences to investigate different kinds of beings?* (See the third *aporia*, 997^{a}15–25. An aspect of this *aporia* is taken up again in the seventh *aporia*, especially 998^{b}22–27, which we will consider in a moment.)

What is this problem? Metaphysics, as characterized in IV. 1, is the science that investigates all beings and investigates them simply in so far as they are beings. So if metaphysics is possible, it is clear enough how it differs from other sciences. But is metaphysics possible? How can there be a science that investigates all beings and investigates beings simply in so far as they are beings? One reason why there is a problem with this conception of metaphysics is that there is nothing outside all beings and nothing outside being as a whole. So we cannot conceive of all beings and of being as a whole by setting this against something outside it: things that in no way are.

Perhaps this way of stating the problem may strike us as too metaphorical, because the notion, *being as a whole*, may strike us as metaphorical. But the problem can also be stated more soberly. It is distinctive of metaphysics (as it was characterized in IV. 1) to ask, 'What is being *qua* being?', i.e. 'What it is for something, anything, to be?' This question, we may think, is just like more familiar questions such as, 'What is it for something, anything, to be a rose, or a plant?' – except, of course, that the question distinctive of metaphysics is more general. So if it is possible to ask the question, 'What is X?', of roses or plants, it must be possible to ask this question simply of beings. On reflection, however, there is a striking disanalogy between the two questions (i.e. 'What is a rose?' and 'What is a being?'). For, in the former question, one thing is distinguished from another, i.e. roses are distinguished from things and especially from plants that are not roses, but not in the latter question – since there could not possibly be things that are not, i.e. that are not anything. The claim, 'There are things that are not', if it means, 'There are things that are not anything', evidently contains a contradiction. But it is natural to think that if it is possible to ask 'What is a rose?', this is possible because here one kind of thing (roses) is distinguished from another (things, or plants, that are not roses). But then the question, 'What is a being?', will not be possible – at least not if this question depends on the analogy with more familiar questions such as, 'What is a rose?'

So we cannot, apparently, conceive of being, as a whole and *qua* being, by setting it against something outside it. Still, perhaps we can conceive of being, as a whole and *qua* being, by focusing instead on what is inside it, and on the fact that everything is inside it. For evidently being includes everything that there is. So how can we conceive of being, as a whole and *qua* being, as the sum of everything that there is? It is natural to think that we can do so in the following way: just as it is familiar that there are distinctions between different things in so far as they are all *F* (e.g. in so far as they are plants, we may think of the distinction between roses and other kinds of plants), so we may suppose that there is a distinction between different things simply in so far as they are all beings, things that are. And just as we may conceive of all plants as the sum of all the kinds of plants that there are, so we may conceive of all beings as the sum of all the kinds of beings that there are. In this way, being, as a whole and *qua* being, will, precisely, be the sum of everything that there is. We may represent this sum as follows (supposing, for the sake of the example, that the distinction between different things simply in so far as they are all beings is the distinction between changing and changeless beings):

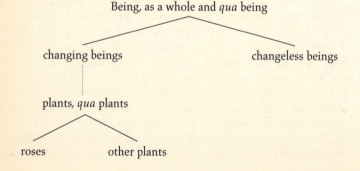

Being, as a whole and *qua* being

changing beings   changeless beings

plants, *qua* plants

roses   other plants

(This representation will lead to incoherence. We have set it out here precisely in order to show how it leads to incoherence.)

But there is a problem with this attempt to conceive of being, as a whole and *qua* being. Aristotle states this problem in book III, the book of *aporiai*; see the seventh *aporia*, especially 998ᵇ22–27. The following is an interpretation of the way in which he states the problem there. Consider, for example, the distinction of different plants into deciduous and evergreen. If this distinction is a scientific one, i.e. if it is subject to explanation, then we must suppose that there is something about deciduous plants that explains why they shed their leaves under certain environmental conditions, and something about evergreen plants that explains why they do not shed their leaves under similar conditions. We may call this feature: the distinguishing feature between these two kinds of plants ('the differentia', *hē diaphora*). But whatever this feature is, it cannot itself be a plant.

Why not? Why cannot the distinguishing feature between different things in so far as they are all plants itself be a plant? This is not so much because it sounds odd to say, or it is hard to imagine, that this distinguishing feature should itself be a plant. It is because it is incoherent to suppose that the distinguishing feature between different things in so far as they are all plants can itself be a plant. For if it is itself a plant, then further distinguishing features will be needed to distinguish it from the plants that it is supposed to distinguish from one another (e.g. the deciduous and evergreen ones); and if these further distinguishing features are themselves plants, then this will go on without end. In other words, infinitely many distinguishing features will be needed to distinguish between different things in so far as they are all plants – which is absurd. This shows that it is incoherent to suppose that the distinguishing feature between different things in so far as they are all F (e.g. in so far as they are plants) can itself be a thing that is F (e.g. a plant).

What does this conclusion show, if we apply it to the case of being, as a whole and *qua* being? The conclusion was that the distinguishing feature between different things in so far as they are all F cannot, on pain of incoherence, itself be a thing that is F. If we apply this to the case of being, as a whole and *qua* being, we get the result that the distinguishing feature between different things simply in so far as they are all beings (e.g. the distinguishing feature between changing and changeless things) cannot, on pain of incoherence, itself be a being. For if the distinguishing feature between different things simply in so far as they are all beings is itself a being, further beings are needed to distinguish the original beings from the distinguishing feature – and so on without end. But, evidently, the distinguishing feature between different beings, whether they are roses and other plants or they are changing and changeless things, is itself a being, something that is. (We will comment on this point in a moment.) It follows that the distinguishing feature between different things simply in so far as they are all beings (e.g. the distinguishing feature between changing and changeless things) is, precisely, itself a being. So, on the assumption that the distinction between, for example, changing and changeless beings, is a distinction between different things simply in so far as they are all beings, the regress and the incoherence are inescapable.

What does this show? Of course, it does not show that we cannot distinguish all beings into, for example, changing and changeless beings. We can do so, just as we can distinguish some beings, e.g. plants, into, for example, roses and other plants. For example, we can assert that all beings are either changing or changeless, and this assertion may indeed be true. What it shows is that if we distinguish all beings into, for example, changing and changeless beings, we are not, after all, distinguishing different beings simply in so far as they are all beings. If we were, then the incoherence would be inescapable. In other words, if we distinguish all beings into, for example, changing and changeless beings, we are not, after all, addressing the question, 'What is being *qua* being?', i.e. 'What is it for something to be?'; we are only addressing the question, 'What is there?' This means that the following representation is perfectly coherent:

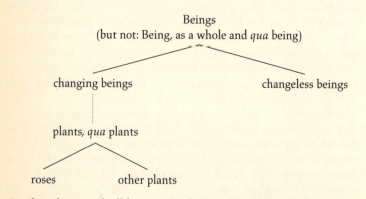

So, if we distinguish all beings into, for example, changing and changeless beings, we are no closer to conceiving of being, as a whole and *qua* being, than we were when we distinguished some beings, e.g. plants, into, for example, roses and other plants. This shows that we cannot conceive of being, as a whole and *qua* being, as the sum of all the kinds of beings that there are. For to do so we must suppose that when we distinguish all beings into certain most general kinds, e.g. changing and changeless beings, we are, precisely, distinguishing different beings simply in so far as they are all beings. But this is just what we cannot, on pain of incoherence, suppose. We may sum up this conclusion by saying that we cannot conceive of being, as a whole and *qua* being, as the sum of all the kinds of beings that there are and in general as the sum of everything that there is.

One point of clarification: why are distinguishing features ('differentiae', *diaphorai*) themselves beings, things that are? Because they are what explain why things are distinguished in the ways in which they are distinguished (e.g. why plants are distinguished into deciduous and evergreen). On Aristotle's conception of explanation, it is the features of the things themselves that explain why the things are as they are, and to explain anything, a feature has itself to be real – to be a being, something that is. Here we have of course to remember that, on Aristotle's conception of science, when we ask why things are distinguished in the ways in which they are distinguished, we are assuming that there are distinctions in reality – natural kinds – and that there are explanations in reality that explain these real distinctions. So we are not simply concerned with how we distinguish things and how we explain the distinctions that we make; we are concerned with how the things themselves are distinguished and with features of things that themselves explain why things are distinguished as they are.

So there appears to be a problem about whether it is possible to conceive of being as whole, and so about the very possibility of metaphysics. For on the one hand, we cannot conceive of being, as a whole and *qua* being, by distinguishing it from something outside it; but, on the other hand, neither can we conceive of being, as a whole and *qua* being, by distinguishing it from what is inside it, i.e. by conceiving of it as the sum of everything that there is and of all the kinds of beings that there are.

It is for the sake of answering this problem, and so defending the possibility of metaphysics (as metaphysics was characterized in IV. 1), that Aristotle introduces (in IV. 2) a general distinction between primary being (*prōtē ousia*, often simply *ousia*) and non-primary being. This is the distinction between:

(1) things that are beings in virtue of themselves and not in virtue of their relation to other things; and
(2) things that are beings in virtue of their relation to, and so dependent on, the primary beings.

But before we consider how Aristotle introduces the distinction between primary and non-primary being, let us ask how in general this distinction answers the problem of how we can conceive of being, as a whole and *qua* being. Suppose that we cannot conceive of being, as a whole and *qua* being, either by distinguishing it from something outside it or by distinguishing it from what is inside it. Perhaps we can still conceive of being, as a whole and *qua* being, if we suppose that there is a distinction between things that are beings in virtue of themselves (i.e. primary beings) and things that are beings in virtue of their relation to those things (i.e. non-primary beings). For then we can, apparently, conceive of being, as a whole and *qua* being, in the following way: by supposing that anything that is, i.e. any being, is a being *either* in virtue of itself and not in virtue of its relation to other things (in which case it is a primary being) *or* in virtue of its relation to a primary being (in which case it is a non-primary being).

This will enable us to conceive of being, as a whole and *qua* being, not because we will be able to distinguish being from something outside it or from what is inside it, but because it will enable us to point directly to, as it were, the source of all beings: that which explains what it is for something, anything, to be. (We should remember that this was precisely the question distinctive to metaphysics as characterized in IV. 1: 'What is it for something, anything, to be?') For now we can say the following. A primary being is something that is a being simply in virtue of itself and not in virtue of its relation to other things; and this is because a primary being explains directly what it is for it itself to be. A non-primary being, on the other hand, is something that is a being in virtue of its relation to, and so dependent on, a primary being; and this is because a primary being indirectly explains also what it is for other things (the non-primary beings) to be, i.e. things that are beings in virtue of their relation to, and so dependent on, the primary beings.

It is worth emphasizing that this way of conceiving of being, as a whole and *qua* being, is not subject to the previous incoherence. For the distinction of beings into primary beings and non-primary beings is, precisely, *not* a distinction between different things simply in so far as they are all beings. If it were, then the previous incoherence would re-emerge. So the distinction of beings into primary beings and non-primary beings is not at all like the attempt, previously, to distinguish beings simply in so far as they are beings into, for example, changing and changeless beings – the attempt that led to incoherence.

Let us look closer at why the incoherence does not re-emerge. If we distinguish beings simply in so far as they are beings into, for example, changing and changeless beings, we are thereby supposing two things.

First, there is something that constitutes what it is to be a being, and this belongs equally to changing and changeless beings. Second, there is something that distinguishes changing from changeless beings, such that this distinguishing feature, precisely, distinguishes different things in so far as they are all beings. This is just as if we distinguish things in so far as they are plants into e.g. roses and other plants, we are thereby supposing two things. First, there is something that constitutes what it is to be a plant, and this belongs equally to roses and other plants. Second, there is something that distinguishes roses from other plants, such that this distinguishing feature, precisely, distinguishes different things in so far as they are all plants. However, if we distinguish beings into primary beings and non-primary beings, we are supposing that there is something that constitutes what it is to be a being, but that this, precisely, does *not* belong equally to primary beings and non-primary beings. On the contrary, it is the primary beings themselves that constitute what it is to be a being; and the non-primary beings have a share in what it is to be a being only because they depend, for their being beings, on the primary beings. So, although of course there is something that distinguishes primary beings from non-primary beings, this distinguishing feature does not at all serve to distinguish different things in so far as they are all beings – and this is why the incoherence does not re-emerge.

Hopefully, this notion of primary being will become more clear and better understood as we go along. But in order initially to understand this notion, it is important to emphasize the following points. First, the notion of primary being is introduced (in IV. 2) precisely in order to explain how we can even conceive of being, as a whole and *qua* being, and how we can even ask the question, 'What is being *qua* being?', i.e. 'What is it for something, anything, to be?' – the question distinctive to metaphysics as characterized in IV. 1. Second, the notion of primary being is introduced precisely as the notion: *that which ultimately explains what it is for something, anything, to be.* At the end of book VII, the central book of the *Metaphysics*, Aristotle says that primary being is, precisely, the ultimate explanation of the being of each thing, i.e. that which ultimately explains what it is for each thing to be (see VII. 17, 1041^{b}27–28: *ousia* is the 'ultimate explanation of the being of each thing', *prōton aition tou einai [hekastou]*). But by considering why he introduces the notion of primary being in IV. 2, we have seen that this is also what he means by primary being as soon as he introduces this notion: *primary being is that which ultimately explains what it is for something, anything, to be.* Third, when he introduces this notion here, Aristotle is not yet raising the question, 'What is primary being?', i.e. 'What is it that ultimately explains what it is for something, anything, to be?' All that he has done is argue that this explanation, whatever it turns out to be, will have the following form: there is something, primary being, which explains directly what it is for it itself to be and indirectly explains what it is for anything else to be.

Alternative interpretation

There is an alternative, and very common, interpretation of why Aristotle introduces the distinction between primary and non-primary being in IV. 2 (see, for example, Bolton 1996). On this interpretation, he introduces this distinction because he is already committed to a particular view about what things are primary beings and what things are non-primary beings. For, in the earlier work, the *Categories*, he argued that there are two fundamentally different kinds of beings: beings that are true of other beings and beings that are not true of other beings. (For example, being snub-nosed or being human are things that are true of other things, e.g. of Socrates; but a particular thing such as Socrates is not true of other things.) But he also argued, in the *Categories*, that the beings that are not true of other beings are primary beings, whereas the beings that are true of other beings are dependent on the beings of which they are true, i.e. on the primary beings. (We will consider the theory of the *Categories* in §4 of this chapter.) So, on this interpretation, the reason why he introduces the distinction between primary being and non-primary being in IV. 2 is that he is already committed to a particular view about what things are primary beings and what things are non-primary beings.

But there are problems with this interpretation. First, as we have understood Aristotle's introduction of the distinction between primary being and non-primary being in IV. 2, this distinction is entirely general and it does not commit one to any view about what things are primary beings and what things are non-primary beings. This accords with the way in which he proceeds later (especially in book VII); for in book VII he asks 'What is primary being?', and he points out that this question can be answered in very different and apparently conflicting ways (see opening of VII. 3; we will return to this important point later). But only one of the different possible answers that he distinguishes in VII. 3 is the answer that he defended in the *Categories*. Moreover, we will see that it is not clear that he will defend the same answer in the *Metaphysics*. So it is not plausible to think that the way in which he distinguishes between primary being and non-primary being in

IV. 2, i.e. when he first introduces this distinction in the *Metaphysics*, is supposed straight away to be understood in terms of the view of the *Categories*.

Second, we have seen that the way in which Aristotle characterizes metaphysics in IV. 1 gives rise to a problem and *aporia* about the possibility of metaphysics, an *aporia* which he himself raised in book III, the book of *aporiai*; and that the general distinction between primary being and non-primary being which he introduces in IV. 2 is naturally understood as an answer to this *aporia*. So Aristotle's method is, apparently, to start with a problem or *aporia* and then to search for a solution to it. But this method evidently requires that the problems that he wants to answer should be capable of being understood independently of understanding the answers that he gives to them. But if the distinction between primary being and non-primary being as introduced in IV. 2 is straight away understood in terms of a particular view about what primary being is (i.e. the view that he defended in the *Categories*), then it appears that we cannot understand what problem he wants to answer here, unless we already understand his answer to it (i.e. the answer that he defended in the *Categories*; for we must not assume that this is also the answer that he defends here, in the *Metaphysics*). But this is to tailor Aristotle's questions to fit his answers.

3 How Aristotle introduces the distinction between *primary being* and *non-primary being*

At the opening of IV. 2 Aristotle makes a central claim about being:

> Being is said [i.e. what is, is said to be] in several ways, but with reference to one thing [*pros hen*], i.e. one particular nature, and not homonymously [i.e. simply ambiguously].

> (1003ᵃ33–34)

This passage appears to be the exact point in the *Metaphysics* at which he introduces the distinction between primary being and non-primary being – which gradually emerges as the absolutely central distinction in the *Metaphysics*. So Aristotle claims that 'being is said in several ways', but there is 'one thing' with reference to which these ways are said. This 'one thing' he will later call 'primary being' (*prōtē ousia*, often simply *ousia*; see also *to prōton* later in IV. 2, 1003ᵇ16). We may refer to this claim as Aristotle's focal theory of being; for primary being is like a focal point with reference to which the other ways of being, the non-primary ways, are said to be.

We should above all recognize the aim of Aristotle's focal theory of being. For the aim is to answer a problem and *aporia* about how it is possible to conceive of being, as a whole and *qua* being, and to ask 'What is being *qua* being?', i.e. 'What is it for something, anything, to be?' – the question distinctive of metaphysics as it was characterized in IV. 1. In other words, how is it possible to conceive of a single kind, being, just as it is possible to conceive of other kinds of beings, e.g. plants or roses. Thus he concludes later in IV. 2:

> For it is not only in the case in which things are said in respect of a single thing [*kath' hen*, i.e. the case in which there is evidently a single kind, e.g. plants] that there is a single science whose task it is to consider those things, but also in the case in which things are said with reference to a single nature [*pros mian phusin*, i.e. focally; later called *pros hen*]. For even these things are in a way said in respect of a single thing [i.e. even in this case there is a single kind]. So it is evident that there is also a single science whose task it is to consider the beings *qua* beings [i.e. the science which is metaphysics]. But it is true quite generally that science is above all about that which is primary [*tou prōtou*] and which the other things depend on [*ērtētai*] and in virtue of which they are said [i.e. are said to be what they are]. So if this [i.e. that which is primary without qualification and on which other things depend simply for being things that are] is primary being [*ousia*], it will be necessary for the philosopher to grasp the principles and explanations of the primary beings [*ousiai*].
>
> (1003ᵇ12–19)

This is a complex and difficult passage. The first point that Aristotle makes here is that there is indeed a way in which being is a single kind, namely, 'with reference to a single nature' (*pros mian phusin*, later called *pros hen*), i.e. with reference to primary being (*ousia*). But this is so although being is not a single kind in the way in which the other kinds are single kinds, i.e. 'in respect of a single thing' (*kath' hen*; see 1003ᵇ12–15). He then goes on to draw the central conclusion from this point: 'it is evident that there is also a single science whose task it is to consider the beings *qua* beings' (1003ᵇ15–16). This conclusion is precisely a response to the third *aporia* in book III, the book of *aporiai*: *Is it the task of a single science to investigate all beings or is it the task of fundamentally different sciences to investigate different kinds of beings?* (see 997ᵃ15–25) In particular, it is a response to the question of how metaphysics as characterized in IV. 1, i.e. as the science that considers being *qua* being, is possible. The response relies on drawing a distinction between, on the one hand, primary being (*ousia*), i.e. that which is primary without qualification and simply in respect of its being a being, and, on the other hand, non-primary being, i.e. that which depends on, and which is a being in virtue of its relation to primary being.

The claim that being is said in several ways is sometimes referred to as the theory of focal meaning: the verb 'to be' has several meanings or senses, but they all refer to a single sense – which is as it were their focal point. But it is better to avoid the label 'focal meaning' and to speak rather of focal structure. For we must not suppose that Aristotle's claim is about the word 'to be', and its meaning or sense, as opposed to being itself, what the word signifies. In fact it is questionable whether his claim is at all that the verb 'to be' has several meanings or senses. If this were his claim, it ought, presumably, to be a claim whose correctness or incorrectness we can assess simply in virtue of being able to use the verb 'to be', i.e. in virtue of our being speakers of Greek, English or any other language that uses this verb. But evidently we cannot at all assess his claim in this way; we can assess it only by considering what problem or *aporia* it is an answer to, whether it is an adequate answer to this *aporia*, and whether there may perhaps be different and perhaps better answers.

The claim that being is said in several ways is not the obvious claim that very different things, such as concrete particulars (e.g. this rose) and qualities (the colour of this rose), can all be said to be. It is the interesting and substantive claim that if the things that are said to be are sufficiently and appropriately different, then different things are signified by saying that they are. But why is this a substantive and disputable claim? To deny this claim is to suppose that, however different two beings may be, they are identical in respect of their being beings and in so far as they are. In other words, it is to think that being is a kind that is like the other kinds. (For example, all things that are roses, or plants, however different they may be otherwise, are identical in respect of their being roses, or plants.) But this is just what Aristotle is denying when he claims that being is said in several ways. This too shows that his claim that being is said in several ways is motivated, precisely, by his view that being is not a kind that is like the other kinds: it is a kind, but not in the way in which the other kinds are kinds. (See the previous section for crucial disanalogies between being and other kinds of things.)

The focal theory of being says that there are different ways in which something can be said to be, but that ultimately they refer to and depend on a single way and a single kind of being, primary being – which is, as it were, their focal point. Here we have, in a nutshell, Aristotle's notion of primary being (*prōtē ousia*, often simply *ousia*), which gradually emerges as the absolutely central notion in the *Metaphysics*. We must, of course, ask how the different ways in which something can be said to be ultimately 'refer to' and 'depend on' a single way and a single kind of being – primary being. Apparently, the point is that something is a primary being if, and only if, it is a being in virtue of itself and not in virtue of its relation to other things; on the other hand, something is a non-primary being if, and only if, it is a being that 'refers to' and 'depends on' a primary being, i.e. it is a being in virtue of its relation to a primary being.

The focal structure of being implies that although being is said in several ways, depending on what is said to be, this does not render the word 'to be' simply ambiguous ('homonymous'). For example, we may say that *bank* is said in several ways, depending on whether what is called a bank is a river bank or a financial bank. But this only means that the word 'bank' is ambiguous, and there is no reason why we should use the same word, 'bank', in the two cases. But because the different ways in which something can be said to be ultimately depend on a single way and a single kind of being, the word 'to be' is not simply ambiguous. (However, we must also recall that Aristotle's point is not ultimately about the word 'to be', but about what it is for something to be. We will return to this point in a moment.)

How in general does Aristotle determine whether, when two different things are said to be F, F is said in the same way or in different ways of each thing? He provides a general criterion at the opening of the *Categories*: if two different things are both said to be F, then F is said in the same way of both things if, and only if, the account or definition (*logos*) of what it is to be F applies (and applies in the same way) to both things. For example, if a cat and a dog are both said to be animals, *animal* is said in the same way of both; for the definition of what it is to be an animal applies (and applies in the same way) to both cats and dogs. At the opposite extreme, if a river bank and a financial bank are both said to be banks, *bank* is not said in the same way of these two things; for there is no single definition of what it is to be a bank that applies to both these things.

As it stands, however, this criterion does not determine whether, if F is said in two different ways of two things, these ways are entirely unrelated, in which case we are dealing with simple ambiguity (as in the meaning of 'bank'), or they are somehow related, perhaps by one way being the central or focal way and the other way being dependent on it (as in the meaning of 'being'). To distinguish a case of simple ambiguity from a case where there are different but related meanings, we need to distinguish two cases:

(1) a single definition of F does not in any way apply to both things; and

(2) a single definition of F applies to both things, but in different ways.

In the first case we have simple ambiguity, but in the second case we have different but related ways of saying something, F, of something (we may call this 'complex ambiguity'). Both cases contrast with the case in which

(3) a single definition applies to both things, and does so in the same way (as in the meaning of 'animal').

We may call this case 'strict synonymy'.

To clarify the claim that *being* is a focal concept, Aristotle invokes an analogy with the concept of health, which apparently is also a focal concept but in which the focal structure is more readily evident:

> Just as that which is healthy all has reference to health – either because it preserves health, or because it produces it, or because it is a sign of health, or because it is capable of receiving health – . . ., so too that which *is* is said in several ways, but all with reference to a single principle.
>
> (1003ª34–b6)

The claim that *health* is a focal concept involves three claims. First, very different things can all truly be said to be healthy: a living organism; a diet (it preserves health in a living organism); a medical remedy (it produces health in a living organism); a certain kind of complexion (it is a sign of health in a living organism). Second, health is said in different ways depending on which of these things it is said of. Third, one of these ways is central and focal, and the other ways must be understood by reference to it. The central way signifies the primary case of something being healthy, and the other ways signify cases of something being healthy that are non-primary and dependent on the primary way. Aristotle refers to this primary case simply as *health*, but what he has in mind is the general condition of a living organism that constitutes its being healthy; and this is the condition that a definition of health seeks to define.

Let us, therefore, apply his general criterion of synonymy, simple ambiguity and complex ambiguity, to his example of health. Clearly, this is not a case of simple ambiguity; for the same definition of health applies, in some way, to all the cases. However, Aristotle thinks that health is said in different ways in the different cases, hence this definition does not apply to all the cases in the same way. Suppose the definition of health is something like this: 'health is the condition of an organism that allows its parts to function properly so as to preserve the good of the organism as a whole'. Clearly, this definition does not apply to the non-primary cases directly; for it would be absurd to think that a healthy diet consists of food that is in 'a condition that allows its parts to function properly together so as to preserve the good of the food as a whole.' But the definition does apply to the non-primary cases in a way, namely, indirectly; for the non-primary cases can be said to be cases of something healthy only because they are related in certain ways to the primary case: a healthy diet is a diet that preserves health, i.e. preserves the ingesting organism in a condition that allows its parts to function properly together so as to preserve the good of the organism as a whole; a healthy drug is a drug that produces health, i.e. produces in the drug-taking organism a condition . . . (same as before), etc. But the primary case is primary precisely because the definition of health applies to it directly.

How is this analogy supposed to clarify the focal theory of being? The point is that something like food or drugs or skin complexions can be described as healthy only in relation to something else being described as healthy: an organism. Independently of this relation, these things cannot be described as healthy at all, truly or falsely. But the point is equally that the converse does not hold; for, in describing an organism as healthy, there is no need to refer to these other things as healthy. Analogously, the focal theory of being says, for example (this example is based on the *Categories*), that a quality (e.g. white) can be said to be, only in relation to something else's being said to be: a concrete particular (e.g. a white swan). On the other hand, in saying of a concrete particular that it is, there is no need to refer to other things, e.g. qualities, as being. So being is said in the primary way of concrete particulars, and they are the primary beings; but being is said only in a derivative way of things that are not concrete particulars, and they are beings only because concrete particulars are beings.

We have seen that whether F is said in the same or different ways of different things depends on whether a single definition of what it is to be F applies to the different things. But it is important to recognise that Aristotle is concerned here with definitions of what it is for a thing to be F and with the essence of things in so far as they are F; he is not concerned with definitions of what we ordinarily mean by the word that we use to signify F. The task of establishing such definitions, which we may call 'real' as opposed to 'linguistic' definitions, belongs to science, in the broad sense of the search for explanatory knowledge; it does not belong to the analysis of words or concepts. But metaphysics – the science of what it is for something to be, is characterized (at the opening of the *Metaphysics* and again at the opening of book IV) as the most general science. This also confirms that his claim is not so much about the verb 'to be', and it is not that the verb 'to be' is subject to complex ambiguity.

Furthermore, Aristotle supposes that if being is said in several ways, then this creates a problem for how there can be a single science of being; he argues that nevertheless there can be a single science of being, provided that these ways are not unrelated but are focally structured. But if the claim that *F* is said in several ways is based on linguistic considerations about the sense of the word we use to signify F, it does not really give rise to such a problem. For science, i.e. the search for explanatory knowledge, may ignore linguistic distinctions. For example, 'water', 'ice' and 'steam' may have different senses, but they all signify the same thing, which is investigated by a single science. This again confirms that his claim is not that the verb 'to be' is subject to complex ambiguity. In general, his claim is not so much about the verb 'to be', but about what it is for something to be.

We may summarize Aristotle's focal theory of being as follows:

1. *Being is said in several ways*
    What it is for something to be will differ depending on what kind of thing is said to be – provided that the kinds of things are sufficiently and appropriately different. So the real definition of what it is for something to be will differ depending on what kind of thing is said to be – provided that the kinds of things are sufficiently and appropriately different.

2. *But being is nevertheless said with reference to a single thing*
    But there is one kind of being, primary being, such that (a) the real definition of what it is for *it* to be will refer only to this kind of being, primary being; and (b) the real definition of what it is for any other kind of being to be will refer also to what it is for a primary being to be.

So something is a primary being if, and only if, it is a being simply in virtue of itself (i.e. the real definition of what it is for it to be will refer only to it); and something is a non-primary being if, and only if, it is a being in virtue of its relation to something else, a primary being (i.e. the real definition of what it is for it to be will refer also to something else, a primary being). But we cannot consider Aristotle's theory of the focal structure of being much further, until he asks (especially in books VII–IX) what things are primary beings and what things are non-primary beings.

4 Primary being as the ultimate subject of predication: the theory of the *Categories*

The central question in the *Metaphysics* is the question 'What is being (*to on*)?', i.e. 'What is it for something to be?' But Aristotle argues that this question must be addressed by addressing the question 'What is primary being (*prōtē ousia*, often simply *ousia*)?' and 'What is it for something to be in the primary way?' At the same time he wants to make a fresh start and address this question without straight away assuming an answer to it. Thus he will later (in book VII, especially VII. 3) begin by distinguishing three very different answers to the question 'What is primary being?', before he goes on to consider which is the correct answer:

(1) the universals (this, he thinks, is Plato's answer);
(2) the ultimate subject of predication (this was his own answer in the *Categories*); and
(3) the essence (this is the answer that he will defend in the *Metaphysics*).

So, in the *Metaphysics* he is not committed to his earlier view about primary being, the view that he defends in the *Categories*. Let us, therefore, consider the theory of primary being that he defends in his earlier work: the *Categories*, and let us consider also a central problem with this theory, a problem that leads Aristotle, in the *Metaphysics*, to abandon or seriously revise his own earlier theory of primary being.

The theory of primary being in Aristotle's earlier work: the Categories

In the *Categories*, Aristotle argues that primary being (*prōtē ousia*, often simply *ousia*) with regard to each thing is the ultimate subject of predication (*to hupokeimenon*) with regard to that thing. Today this is commonly referred to as the view that primary being, according to the *Categories*, is 'particular substance'. The Greek noun *to hupokeimenon* means 'that which lies under', from the verb *hupokeisthai*, 'to lie under'. The noun 'substance' is derived from the Latin verb '*substare*': 'to lie under'.

The source of and underlying motivation for this view – the view which says that primary being with regard to each thing is the ultimate subject of predication with regard to that thing – is a very general conception of the structure of things: things are distinguished into, on the one hand, things, and, on the other hand, things that are true of things (i.e. properties of things, as we may say). So the general structure of things is of the form: *x is true of y*, where x and y are both real things – beings. But now suppose that we ask, against the background of this general conception of things, 'What is it for something to be?' Then it may appear natural to answer as follows: if this question is asked of a thing that is true of another thing, then we must say that to be, for such a thing, is, precisely, for it to be true of another thing. In other words, we must say that for a property to be real is for it to be true of something. For example (based on *Metaphysics* VII. 1, 1028^{a}20–25), if we ask what it is for such things as *walking* or *being healthy* to be, and if we are puzzled about whether such things are beings at all, it may appear natural to answer that they are beings only because there is something else that they are true of (i.e. the particular thing, e.g. a human being, that is walking or healthy). But then we will naturally arrive at the conclusion that such things, i.e. things that are true of other things, are beings not in virtue of themselves (*kath' hauta*), but only in virtue of their relation to other things, i.e. the beings of which they are ultimately true (i.e. the particular thing, e.g. a human being, that is walking or healthy). We may then sum up this conclusion by saying that the things that are true of other things are not primary beings, but are rather dependent beings; for they are beings, things that are, only in virtue of their relation to, and so dependent on, the things of which they are true. But once we have reached this conclusion, it may seem only a small step to conclude, further, that if there is anything that is a being in virtue of itself and not in virtue of its relation to other things, this will be, precisely: something that is not true of something else – and this is what we may call 'the ultimate subject of predication' (*to hupokeimenon*). So in this way we reach the conclusion that primary being is the ultimate subject of predication.

But, to understand this view better, we need to consider what Aristotle means by 'the ultimate subject of predication' (*to hupokeimenon*, literally: 'that which lies under'). By the ultimate subject of predication he means that of which other things are predicated, but which is not itself predicated of other things. By 'x is predicated of y', he means 'x is true of y', where x is not identical with y. We should note that the relation of predication, as he understands it here, is primarily a relation between things, not primarily a relation between thoughts or words: it is the relation of one thing being true of another. The thing that is predicated he calls *to katēgoroumenon*; and the ultimate thing of which it is predicated he calls *to hupokeimenon*. But he thinks that these two things are correlative and depend on each other: if something (a *katēgoroumenon*) is predicated of something else, then there is an ultimate subject of predication (a *hupokeimenon*) of which it is ultimately predicated; and if there is an ultimate subject of predication (a *hupokeimenon*), then there are things (*katēgoroumena*) that are predicated of it.

So, by the term 'the ultimate subject of predication' Aristotle means: that of which other things are predicated (i.e. are true), but which is not itself predicated of (i.e. true of) other things. But although in general the meaning of this term is clear enough, it is not so clear how it should be applied to particular cases: how it should be established what is the ultimate subject of predication with regard to a particular thing, such as, for instance, Socrates.

Consider, for example, a particular human being, Socrates, and suppose that he is snub-nosed. Evidently being snub-nosed is not the ultimate subject of predication with regard to Socrates, for it is something other than Socrates and something that is predicated of him. In particular, being snub-nosed is true of Socrates, but it is true of him only accidentally (*kata sumbebēkos*), not essentially (*kath' hauto*). That is to say, being snub-nosed is true of Socrates not in virtue of his being the very thing he is (*kath' hauto*), but in virtue of something else, namely, *snub-nosedness*, being true of him. In general, by the 'accidental properties' (*ta sumbebēkota*) of a thing Aristotle means those properties which the thing has not in virtue of its being the very thing it is (*kath' hauto*), but in virtue of something else being true of it. So, in general, the accidental properties of a thing are not the ultimate subjects of predication with regard to that thing, for they each are something other than the thing and something that is predicated of it and true of it.

But what about the essence of a thing – is this perhaps the ultimate subject of predication with regard to the thing? For example, let us suppose that Socrates' essence is being human or his being human. (We will see in a moment that it makes a crucial difference whether his essence is being human, i.e. something that he shares with other human beings, or it is his being human, i.e. something that he does not share with other human beings. But let us set aside this point for a moment.) Is Socrates' essence the ultimate subject of predication with regard to Socrates? This question is central to understanding Aristotle's metaphysics. For in the *Categories* he argues that the essence of a thing is not the ultimate subject of predication with regard to that thing; but in the *Metaphysics* he argues, on the contrary, that the essence of a thing is precisely the ultimate subject of predication with regard to that thing. This is a fundamental change of mind, and it is of central importance to understanding Aristotle's metaphysics.

In the *Categories* Aristotle argues that the ultimate subject of predication with regard to a thing cannot be the essence of the thing. For he argues that the essence of a thing is a universal, and evidently a universal is predicated of something, it is not that of which something is predicated (see e.g. *Categories* 2^b29f.). For example, let us suppose that Socrates' essence is being human, and let us suppose (as Aristotle does in the *Categories*) that this essence is a universal: being human. Then evidently the essence of Socrates cannot be the ultimate subject of predication with regard to Socrates; for evidently the universal, being human, is something other than Socrates and something that is predicated of Socrates. (We recall that the ultimate subject of predication is that of which other things are predicated but which is not itself predicated of other things.) So, if we suppose (as he does in the *Categories*) that essences are universals, then we must conclude that the ultimate subject of predication cannot be the essence. It is also important to note that when, in the *Metaphysics*, Aristotle changes his mind and argues that the essence is the ultimate subject of predication, he can do so only because he no longer thinks that essences are universals. (But we must note again that this interpretation is controversial. For an alternative interpretation, see Chapter 7, especially §5viii)

But let us consider for a moment how there may be room for thinking that the ultimate subject of predication is the essence (as Aristotle does in the *Metaphysics*, but not the *Categories*). For, at first sight, it may seem that this view is obviously absurd. Let us suppose that Socrates' essence is being human (or his being human), and let us consider the true sentence: 'Socrates is human'. Surely, we may think, this already shows that the ultimate subject of predication cannot be the essence; for evidently 'human' is grammatically predicated of 'Socrates', so apparently being human (or his being human) cannot be the ultimate subject of predication with regard to Socrates.

But this objection against the idea that the ultimate subject of predication may be the essence is superficial. It overlooks two important features of what Aristotle means by 'the ultimate subject of predication' (*to hupokeimenon*) and 'that which is predicated' (*to katēgoroumenon*). First, he means a relation between things: the relation of one thing (that which is predicated) being true of another thing (the ultimate subject of predication). He does not mean a relation between words, or parts of a sentence. So to appeal to the fact that the word 'human' is grammatically predicated of the word 'Socrates' is not sufficient to show that one thing, being human (or his being human), is different from and predicated of another thing, Socrates. Grammar is not always a good guide to reality.

Second, Aristotle thinks that the relation between the ultimate subject of predication and something predicated of it is a relation between two things: one thing being true of another – not a relation between a thing and itself. (In general, examples of a thing's being related, in a particular way, to itself are readily available: one is one's own best friend, or one is one's own worst enemy.) For he wants to set the things that are predicated (*ta katēgoroumena*) against the thing of which they are ultimately predicated (*to hupokeimenon*). But the fact that we may truly say of something, e.g. of Socrates, that he is human, evidently does not show that what is said (being human, or his being human) and that of which it is said (Socrates) are two things, not one. To see this, we may consider a sentence such as 'This (pointing to an infant) is my daughter'. Our aim in using such a sentence is evidently not to say that one thing ('my daughter') is true of *another* thing ('this'); it is rather, we may suppose, to specify more fully ('my daughter') something that one has referred to and is already familiar with ('this'). But perhaps we may suppose that this is also a function of a sentence such as 'Socrates is human': to specify more fully ('a human thing') something that one has referred to and is already familiar with ('Socrates'). But in that case this sentence will not express a relation between two things: Socrates and a human thing, just as the sentence 'this is my daughter' does not express a relation between two things. So we cannot argue that because being human (or his being human) is truly said of Socrates, therefore one thing, being human (or his being human), is predicated of another thing, Socrates. Of course, when we know the essence of a thing, we know more about the thing than before we know its essence. But this does not show that what we know when we know the essence of a thing is something other than the thing itself; all it shows is that when we know the essence of a thing, we know the thing itself more fully and more properly than before.

Let us above all recall what Aristotle means by 'the essence' of a thing (*to ti estin, to ti ēn einai*): the essence of a thing is that which is true of the thing in virtue of the thing's being the very thing that it is. This may already suggest that the relation between a thing and its essence is not a relation between two things, but rather a fundamental relation between a thing and itself. It is true that the relation between a thing and the general kind to which it belongs is a relation between two things, one being true of another; for example, Socrates is one thing, and being human – the general kind to which he belongs – another; and being human is true of Socrates. But we must not suppose that the essence of a thing simply is the general kind to which the thing belongs; all that we may suppose is that the essence of a thing determines the general kind to which the thing belongs. In Chapter 7 (especially §5viii–ix) we will ask: which view does Aristotle ultimately defend:

(1) the view that the essence of a thing simply is the general kind to which the thing belongs; or
(2) the view that the essence of a thing determines the general kind to which the thing belongs, but without the essence being itself a general kind?

However, to make further progress with this fundamental question, i.e. the question whether the essence of a thing can be the ultimate subject of predication with regard to that thing, we really have to face up to the following question: is Socrates' essence simply being human, i.e. is it something that he shares with other things of the same general kind, or is Socrates' essence rather his being human, i.e. something that he does not share with other things of the same general kind? If Socrates' essence is something that he shares with other things of the same general kind, e.g. with Plato, then it is hard to see how Socrates' essence can be the ultimate subject of predication with regard to him. For the ultimate subject of predication with regard to any one particular thing is not shared with other particular things of the same general kind. For example, the ultimate subject of predication with regard to Socrates, i.e. that of which all the things that are said of Socrates are ultimately said of, is, precisely, this particular thing, Socrates; it is not also any other particular thing of the same general kind, e.g. Plato. So if we are to suppose that Socrates' essence can somehow be the ultimate subject of predication with regard to him, we must suppose that Socrates' essence is not simply being human, but rather his being human, i.e. something that he does not share with other things of the same general kind.

We will see later (in Chapter 7§5viii) that it is controversial whether Aristotle thinks that a thing's essence is something that it shares with other things of the same general kind or whether he thinks that a thing's essence is something that it does not share with other things of the same general kind. (We will argue for the latter interpretation, but the former interpretation is also common.) But let us note straight away that Aristotle himself raises this question: is a thing's essence something that it shares, or is it something that it does not share with other things of the same general kind? For in book III, the book of problems or *aporiai*, he asks: *Are principles one in kind or one in number?* (see the ninth *aporia*, 999ᵇ24–100ᵃ4) In other words, are there as many principles as there are particular things (so that my principle and your principle are different, although we belong to the same general kind) or are there as many principles as there are general kinds of things (so that my principle and your principle are the same)? But it has emerged in the meanwhile that the essence of things is a fundamental principle, i.e. an ultimate explanation of why things are as they are. So the question that Aristotle raises in the ninth *aporia* is a more general version of precisely this question: is a thing's essence something that it shares, or is it something that it does not share with other things of the same general kind? So we must not begin by prejudging this question, either by assuming that he thinks that a thing's essence is something that it shares, or by assuming that he thinks that a thing's essence is something that it does not share, with other things of the same general kind.

So what does Aristotle, in the *Categories*, think is the ultimate subject of predication with regard to each thing, since he thinks that it is neither the essence of the thing nor the accidental properties of the thing? He answers that the ultimate subject of predication with regard to each thing is the particular (*to kath' hekaston*) which this thing is; for example, the ultimate subject of predication with regard to Socrates is the particular thing which Socrates is. In general, Aristotle uses the term 'particular' (*to kath' hekaston*) in contrast to the term 'universal' (*katholou*): a universal is something that can be predicated of (i.e. be true of) other things, and many things; but a particular is something that is not capable of being predicated of other things. So evidently a particular is an ultimate subject of predication.

Aristotle's theory in the *Categories* can be summarized as follows:

CAT1. The ultimate subject of predication with regard to each thing is a particular.

CAT2. The essence with regard to each thing is a universal, namely, the general kind to which the thing belongs. (He rejects this view in the *Metaphysics*.)

Therefore,

> CAT3. The ultimate subject of predication with regard to
>   each thing is different from the essence of the thing.
>   (He rejects this view in the *Metaphysics*, where he argues
>   that the essence and the ultimate subject of predication
>   are one thing, not two different things.)

But the theory of the *Categories*, just as that of the *Metaphysics*, is a
theory about primary being (*prōtē ousia*, often simply *ousia*); and the
main claim in the *Categories* is that:

> CAT4. Primary being with regard to each thing is the ultimate
>   subject of predication with regard to that thing.

But since he thinks that the ultimate subject of predication is different
from the essence (i.e. CAT3), he concludes that:

> CAT5. Primary being with regard to each thing is not the essence
>   of the thing. (He rejects this view in the *Metaphysics*,
>   where he argues that primary being with regard to each
>   thing is, precisely, the essence of the thing.)

A central problem with Aristotle's theory of the Categories

However, Aristotle's theory in the *Categories* leads to a particular and
central problem, a problem that he points out in the *Metaphysics* (see
especially VII. 3; we will consider this problem, and his response to it,
more fully later). For suppose that (CAT1) the ultimate subject of predication with regard to a thing is a particular, whereas (CAT2) the essence
of a thing is a universal; hence (CAT3), the ultimate subject of predication with regard to a thing is different from the essence of the thing.
Then it follows that there is nothing that the ultimate subject of predication (and the particular) is essentially and in virtue of itself (*kath'
hauto*). Rather, the ultimate subject of predication (and the particular)
depends for its essence on its relation to something other than itself,
namely, a universal. But this means that, in virtue of itself, the ultimate
subject of predication (and the particular) is indeterminate. But this
result may well appear unacceptable.

Why is it unacceptable to think that, in virtue of itself, the ultimate
subject of predication and the particular is indeterminate? On its own,
perhaps, this view may not be unacceptable. Plato, for example, thinks

that sense-perceptible, changing particulars are indeterminate in virtue of themselves and depend for their determination on their relation to something other than themselves, namely, the 'ideas' or 'forms'. But the view that, in virtue of itself, the ultimate subject of predication and the particular is indeterminate certainly appears unacceptable, if it is combined with the view that (CAT4) primary being with regard to each thing is the ultimate subject of predication with regard to that thing. (Plato rejects this view, so his position may not be unacceptable.) For it is natural to think that primary being, whatever it turns out to be, cannot be something that, in virtue of itself, is indeterminate. In general, a primary being cannot depend on something else for its being something determinate, for then it would not be primary without qualification. We recall that primary being is, precisely, what does not depend on other things for its being a being, something that is. But if a primary being does not depend on other things for its being a being, then it is natural to think that neither does it depend on other things for its being something determinate. For it is natural to think that something cannot be a being, unless it is something determinate, and that its being something determinate is at least part of the explanation of what it is for it to be a being. (We will see in Chapter 7§5iv that this is precisely Aristotle's view: something cannot be a being, unless it is something determinate; and its being something determinate is a central element in the explanation of what it is for it to be a being.) In the *Metaphysics*, Aristotle recognizes and points out this problem with the theory of primary being of the *Categories*; and this leads him to abandon, or seriously revise, his own earlier theory of primary being. (We will return to this point later.)

5 Is metaphysics about all things, about primary being, or about God?

What is metaphysics, as characterized by Aristotle, about? Is it about all being, or is it only about a special kind of being – primary being? As we have understood Aristotle, the answer is that metaphysics is both about all being and about primary being. He thinks that the fundamental question of metaphysics is the question: 'What is being (*to on*)?'; so in this sense metaphysics is primarily about all being. But he also argues that the question 'What is being?' must be addressed by addressing the question 'What is primary being (*prōte ousia*, often simply *ousia*)?', so in this sense metaphysics is primarily about primary being. So Aristotle thinks that, on the one hand, what we are searching for in metaphysics is the essence of being in general, so in this sense metaphysics is primarily about all being; but, on the other hand, the essence of being in general depends on the essence of primary being, so in this sense metaphysics is primarily about primary being. There is no tension here between his claim that metaphysics is primarily about all things and his claim that it is primarily about primary being; on the contrary, these two claims are complementary sides of a single overall project: to examine what is it for something, anything, to be.

But there is a complication. For Aristotle characterizes metaphysics not only as ontology (the theory of being in general and of all things) and as ousiology (the theory of primary being, *ousia*); he also (especially in book VI. 1, see later in this chapter) characterizes metaphysics as theology (the theory of divine being – God; he defends this view of metaphysics in book XII). This is because he argues that what is primary being most strictly and absolutely, is, precisely, divine being or God. So we must ask whether metaphysics, as characterized by Aristotle, is about all things, or about primary being, or about divine being and God.

We will consider Aristotle's general theory of primary being at length later (in Chapter 7) and his theory of divine being, or God, later again (in Chapter 8). The point here is that he characterizes metaphysics, on the one hand, as ontology (the theory of being in general and of all things), but also, on the other hand, as ousiology (the theory of primary being, *ousia*) and ultimately as theology (the theory of divine being, God, which is primary being most strictly). But there is no tension between Aristotle's different characterizations of metaphysics, and we do not have to choose between them or even to suppose that one of them is the central one. On the contrary, he thinks that all the characterizations are equally important. For he thinks that what we are searching for in metaphysics is what it is for something, anything, to be; so in this sense metaphysics is primarily ontology (about all things). But he also argues that what it is for things in general to be depends on what it is for primary being to be, so in this sense metaphysics is primarily ousiology (about primary being, *ousia*). But since he eventually argues that divine being and God are primary being most strictly and absolutely, he concludes that ultimately metaphysics is primarily theology (about divine being or God).

At the end of book VI. 1, Aristotle directly addresses the question of whether metaphysics is about all being (ontology) or about God (theology):

> So if there is something that is everlasting, changeless and separate [i.e. God, it will emerge], evidently knowing this is the task of a theoretical science. However, this science is not physics (for physics is

about certain changing things), and not mathematics either [since Aristotle thinks that mathematics is not about separate things]; rather it is prior to both physics and mathematics. ... For the primary science [i.e. metaphysics] is about things that are both separate and changeless [i.e. about God]. ... There will, then, be three theoretical philosophies: mathematics, physics, and theology [*theologikē*]. For it is only natural that if what is divine is to be found anywhere, it is to be found in this kind of thing [i.e. in things that are changeless and separate], and that the most worthy science should be about the most worthy kind [i.e. the most worthy kind of being, namely, God].

(1026ª10–21)

So here he appears to argue that metaphysics, or what he calls 'primary philosophy' (*prōtē philosophia*, 1026a24) and 'primary science' (*prōtē epistēmē*, 1026a29), is exclusively about divine being and God. But when he continues, it emerges that he thinks that there is a problem and *aporia* with this view:

But one may, precisely, raise the question [*aporein*: 'to raise a problem and puzzle']: is the primary philosophy [i.e. metaphysics] universal [i.e. about all things] or is it about some one kind and some one nature of thing?

(1026ª23–25)

He answers this *aporia* as follows:

So if, on the one hand, there is not some other primary being [*tis hetera ousia*] in addition to [or 'besides', *para*] those that are formed by nature, then physics [i.e. the science of changing and material things, things in nature] will be the primary science. But if, on the other hand, there is a changeless primary being [*tis ousia akinētos*, i.e. divine being and God], then this will be prior [i.e. prior to primary being with regard to changing things], and [the philosophy of this] will be primary philosophy; and *this will be universal [katholou] precisely because it is primary*. So it will be the task of primary philosophy to consider being *qua* being – both what being is and what belongs to it *qua* being.

(1026ª27–32)

So Aristotle concludes that metaphysics, or what he calls 'primary philosophy' and 'primary science', is the science that is universal (*katholou*, literally 'of the whole'); it is about *all* things, for it is the science of being *qua* being. This, we recall, is precisely how he began (at the opening of book IV) by characterizing metaphysics: as the science of being *qua* being (1003ª21–22) and about being 'as a whole' (*katholou*, 1003ª23–26). But, at the same time, he argues that, if there is a primary being that is changeless and separate, namely, divine being and God (and he will argue in book XII that there is such a thing), then metaphysics will be the science of this kind of being.

So Aristotle argues that metaphysics is, on the one hand, about all things (ontology) and, on the other hand, about divine being and God (theology). But how can he combine these views? He says how: '*this [metaphysics] will be universal [i.e. about all being] precisely because it is primary [i.e. because it is about divine being and God, the most primary being]*' (1026ª30–31). This combination of views should no longer seem puzzling to us. For we have seen that Aristotle thinks that the fundamental question of metaphysics is the question 'What is being?', so metaphysics is about all things (ontology). But he also thinks that the question 'What is being?' must be addressed by addressing the question 'What is primary being?'; and since he eventually (in book XII) argues that what is primary being most strictly and absolutely is, precisely, divine being and God, he concludes that metaphysics is both ontology and theology.

5

THE DEFENCE OF
THE PRINCIPLE OF
NON-CONTRADICTION

(Book IV.3–6, especially 3–4)

1 Aristotle's characterization of the principle of non-contradiction (PNC)

Here (in IV.3–6) Aristotle considers the principle of non-contradiction (PNC). This principle states that:

> PNC. It is not possible for one and the same thing both to have and not to have one and the same property.

This can also be expressed in a more formal way: $\forall x \forall F \neg \Diamond$ (Fx & $\neg$ Fx); meaning 'for any object x, and any property F, it is not possibly the case that x is both F and not-F'. Or alternatively: $\forall x \forall F \Box \neg$ (Fx & $\neg$ Fx); meaning 'for any object x, and any property F, it is necessarily not the case that x is both F and not-F'.

Aristotle formulates PNC in a number of ways:

> [1] It is impossible for the same thing both to belong and not to belong to the same thing at the same time and in the same respect.
>
> (1005^b19–20)

For example, it is impossible for motion both to belong and not to belong to one and the same spinning-top, at the same time and in the same respect; i.e. one and the same spinning-top cannot at the same time and in the same respect be both in motion and not in motion.

> [2] It is impossible for contrary things [e.g. motion and rest] to belong to the same thing [e.g. the same spinning-top] at the same time.
>
> $(1005^b26\text{–}27)$

> [3] It is impossible for something to be [here 'to be' is used as an abbreviation of 'to be F'] and not to be [i.e. not to be F] at the same time.
>
> $(1006^a3\text{–}4)$

> [4] It is impossible that it should at the same time be true to say of the same thing both that it is human and that it is not human.
>
> $(1006^b33\text{–}34)$

The first formulation appears to express most carefully how Aristotle conceives of PNC. The second is significantly different from the first, since it appeals to contrary properties, such as motion and rest, rather than contradictory properties, such as the presence of motion and the absence of motion. But he is not concerned with contrary properties in particular, but with contradictory properties in general, i.e. with a property's being true of an object and the property's not being true of an object. The third formulation is simply an abbreviation of the first two. The last formulation is clearly different from the first three. For while the first three formulations mention not statements, but things, the last mentions statements. We will see later that it is important to distinguish the question whether PNC is true with regard to statements (or only with regard to statements, or primarily with regard to statements) from the question whether PNC is true with regard to things. Evidently Aristotle thinks that PNC is true both with regard to statements and with regard to things. But he appears to be especially interested in the question of whether PNC is true with regard to things.

We should especially note a particular feature of Aristotle's formulation of PNC. For in the main formulation he makes a very important point:

> [1] It is impossible for the same thing both to belong and not to belong to the same thing at the same time and in the same respect – *and one may add any further qualification with a view to [answering] the dialectical difficulties*.
>
> (1005^{b}19–20; see also 1011^{a}34–^{b}1)

If we do not add such qualifications as 'at the same time', 'in the same respect', and any further qualifications that may be required, then PNC will evidently be open to various objections. For example, one and the same tomato can be both green (at one time) and not green (at a different time); or, one and the same shirt can at the same time be both red (in one respect) and not red (in a different respect), if, for example, it is checkered. Aristotle invites us to search for whatever further qualifications are required to avoid such objections. This introduction of relevant qualifications, it is natural to suppose, is also meant to recall Plato's formulation of PNC (in *Republic* IV. 436b–437a); for Plato takes particular care to introduce similar qualifications. Plato's purpose is to consider various ways in which a thing may or may not be unitary. For example, he points out that a spinning-top may at the same time be both in motion and at rest. But he argues that this is because a spinning-top is not something perfectly unitary. For it is not a single unitary thing, as a whole, that is at the same time both in motion and at rest; rather, it is the circumference of the spinning-top that is in motion and it is its axis that is at rest.

As Aristotle clearly recognizes, we must immediately add such qualifications to PNC, if we at all want to argue that PNC is true of things and of all things. Here we may note that a recent critic of the truth of PNC at one point argues against PNC precisely by ignoring such qualifications, for he objects to PNC by appealing to the following situation:

> If a duly constituted legislature passes legislation which makes it illegal for a certain person to do something (*under one description*) and makes it legally required of that person (*under another [description]*), this determines a true contradiction.
>
> (Graham Priest 2000: 310; emphasis added)

This legal situation is, of course, perfectly possible; but it is not at all an objection to PNC as characterized by Aristotle. For Aristotle emphasizes that if we want to argue that PNC is true of things, then we must immediately add the relevant qualifications to PNC, i.e. we must consider things in just one respect and under just one description. So he would respond that although the above legal situation is perfectly possible (probably it is quite common), it does not at all 'determine a true contradiction'. To show that such a situation can determine a true contradiction, we would need to show that it can be both legally required of a certain person to perform a certain action and legally required of such a person not to perform such an action, even if we add the relevant qualifications, i.e. even if we consider the person, the action, and indeed the legislature *in just one respect and under just one description*. But it is evidently far from easy to show this – perhaps it is impossible.

But we may note that apparently Priest ignores these qualifications, and does so deliberately, because his primary aim here is to argue that PNC is not *obviously* true, and that, if it is true at all, this has to be shown. If this is indeed Priest's primary aim, it is one which Aristotle wholly shares. We will see (in this chapter and Chapter 6) that Aristotle goes to great length to defend PNC. He does not at all think that PNC is *obviously* true.

But there may also be a deeper point behind the need to add such qualifications. If PNC is to be true, it must be understood to say not only that a property (e.g. *redness* or *motion*) cannot be both true of and not true of a single thing, in a loose sense of 'a single thing'. For the tomato is a single thing in spite of the various times of its existence, and it can be both red and not red; the shirt is a single thing in spite of its various patterns, and it can be both red and not red; the spinning-top is a single thing in spite of its various geometrical parts, and it can be both in motion and not in motion. Rather, if PNC is to be true, it must be understood to say that a property (e.g. *redness* or *motion*) cannot be both true of and not true of a single thing, in a more strict sense of 'single' or 'unitary' thing. For example, if PNC is to be true of the spinning-top, it must be understood to say that *motion* cannot at any particular time be both true of and not true of the very same aspect or part of the spinning-top, e.g. its circumference or its axis.

So Aristotle, like Plato, argues that, if we at all want to defend the proposition that PNC is true of things and of all things, we need to investigate with particular care various ways in which things may or may not be unitary. This point is extremely important. For it suggests that he thinks that, if we at all want to defend that PNC is true of things and of all things, we need to engage in metaphysics and to ask the question, 'What is it for something, anything, to be a being, something that is?' Indeed, in IV. 2 he argues that to investigate what it is for something, anything, to be a being, is to investigate what it is for something, anything, to be *one* thing. In general this is because metaphysics is centrally concerned with the individuation of things, i.e. with the question of what it is for a thing to be one or many; and to this issue belongs the examination of how things may or may not be unitary. So the investigation into various ways in which things may or may not be unitary, which is also necessary in order to defend PNC, belongs at the core of metaphysics.

2 Aristotle's overall aim in considering PNC

Why, in general, does Aristotle consider PNC here (in IV. 3–6)? What is his overall aim? At the end of the investigation of PNC (i.e. at the end of IV. 6), he gives a good summary of his main aims:

> Let this, then, suffice to show that [A] the claim that contradictory statements cannot at once be true [i.e. PNC] is the most secure [*bebaion*] of all claims; and [B] what consequences are incurred by those who deny this claim; and [C] why those who deny it do so.
>
> $(1011^b13–15)$

So the investigation of PNC has three main aims. First [A], Aristotle wants to argue that PNC is 'the most secure (or 'firm', *bebaion*) of all claims'. He will defend this view (in IV. 3) by arguing that the truth of PNC must be presupposed in all reasoning and rational thought, or certainly in all rational thought that involves deductive reasoning (see later in this chapter, §3).

Second [B], he wants to consider 'what consequences are incurred by those who deny this claim', PNC. He will argue (especially in IV. 4) that if one denies PNC, and in particular if one argues that PNC is not true of things, then one incurs the consequence that it is impossible to think and speak about things.

Third [C], he wants to consider 'why those who deny it [PNC] do so', i.e. to diagnose the source of the denial of PNC. His strategy here (especially in IV. 5–6) is to ask what is the best line of reasoning that one may set out if one wants to deny PNC.

It will emerge that the best line of reasoning in support of the denial of PNC relies above all on the following views:

(1) the things themselves are radically indeterminate.
(2) Because the things themselves are radically indeterminate, PNC is not true of them.
(3) Because PNC is not true of the things themselves, it is impossible to think or speak of the things themselves.

(4) But it is nevertheless possible for us to think and speak of things, even though it is impossible to think or speak of the things themselves; for we can still think and speak of things as they appear to us and as we conceive them.

So he argues that these are the views that one must defend if one wants to deny PNC. But he thinks that there are thinkers – in particular Protagoras, Heracleitus and their followers – who defend these views, and so deny PNC. We may call these thinkers, as Aristotle characterizes them: phenomenalists and relativists. (But we will need to consider the exact sense of 'phenomenalism' and 'relativism' here.) The ultimate challenge that Aristotle sets himself is, therefore, to respond to these thinkers and these views (i.e. 1–4). For he will argue (in IV. 5–6) that PNC is indeed true of the things themselves and of things *without qualification*; it is not only true of things as they appear to us and as we conceive them.

We will consider Aristotle's first two aims (i.e. A and B) in this chapter; and his third aim (C), i.e. the response to phenomenalism and relativism, in the next chapter.

There is, however, also a single overall aim to Aristotle's defence of PNC. In book III, the book of *aporiai*, he raised the following *aporia*: *Is it the task of a single science to investigate both the ultimate principles of being and the basic principles of reasoning (e.g. the principle of non-contradiction)? Or is this the task of fundamentally different sciences?* (see the second *aporia*, 996^{b}26–997^{a}15). The question in this *aporia* is how metaphysics, i.e. the science of the nature of being, is related to logic, i.e. the science of the basic principles of reasoning and rational thought (e.g. the principle of non-contradiction). Does metaphysics include logic or is logic independent of metaphysics? And, if the latter is the case, is logic perhaps more fundamental than metaphysics? But Aristotle will argue (in IV. 3) that metaphysics as it was characterized at the opening of book IV, i.e. as the science of all beings and of beings simply in so far as they are beings, includes logic, i.e. the science of the basic principles of reasoning and rational thought. For he will argue that in particular PNC, which is a central principle of reasoning and rational thought, is true of things, and it is true of things simply in so far as they are beings – things that are. So this is how he answers this fundamental *aporia* about the relation between metaphysics and logic.

It is important from the start to emphasize this central overall aim of Aristotle's defence of PNC, i.e. the aim of arguing that PNC is true not only and not primarily with regard to reasoning and rational thought (i.e. PNC is not only and not primarily a logical principle), but is true with regard to things and things simply in so far as they are beings (i.e. PNC is a metaphysical principle). A large part of his defence of PNC may suggest that he wants to defend PNC only, or primarily, as a logical principle, i.e. a principle that is only, or primarily, about the nature of reasoning and rational thought. This may be suggested by his aim of arguing (in IV. 3) that PNC must be presupposed in all reasoning and rational thought; and it may especially be suggested by his aim in arguing (in IV. 4) that to deny PNC is to be committed to the view that thought and language are impossible. But we must resist the impression that Aristotle defends PNC only or primarily as a logical principle. For he argues that PNC is a metaphysical principle, i.e. a principle about beings, and about beings simply in so far as they are beings. He defends this view in IV. 3, when he argues that presuppositions of reasoning, such as PNC, are true of beings simply in so far as beings are beings. But he defends this view more radically in IV. 5–6, when he argues against those – phenomenalists and relativists – who argue that PNC is true only of things as they appear to us and as we conceive them, and not true of the things themselves and of things *without qualification*. For he will argue (in IV. 5–6) that PNC is indeed true of the things themselves and of things *without qualification*; it is not only true of things as they appear to us and as we conceive them.

Aristotle's examination and defence of PNC occupies a pivotal position in the *Metaphysics*. He argues, on the one hand, that PNC is a necessary condition for the possibility of thought and language; but, on the other hand, that PNC is true of the things themselves and of things *without qualification*, it is not only and not primarily true of things in so far as we can think and speak of things. But it will emerge that the upshot of his overall argument is this: we must engage in metaphysics, i.e. in the project of asking 'What is being?' and 'What is primary being?', and we must search for an answer to these questions, if we at all want to consider how thought and language are possible. So, ultimately, the aim of the examination of PNC is to provide vital motivation for engaging in his own overall project, i.e. metaphysics as he conceives it – indeed to show that this project is, in a way, inescapable.

3 Why PNC cannot itself be demonstrated

In IV. 3 Aristotle argues that PNC is the most 'secure' or 'firm' (*bebaion*) of all claims, and that this is because its truth must be presupposed in all reasoning and rational thought. So PNC is a fundamental principle of reasoning and rational thought; and this is why there is nothing more firm or secure than it. He concludes that because PNC is a fundamental principle of reasoning and rational thought, it cannot be demonstrated or proved to be true; i.e. it cannot be deductively derived from something more firm or secure. For its truth must be presupposed in all reasoning, and, in particular, in all deductive reasoning.

Aristotle characterizes PNC as a 'principle of reasoning' (*sullogistikē archē*, 1005^{b}7) and as an 'axiom' in just the sense of a 'principle of reasoning' (see 1005^{a}20). He argues that PNC is true of all things, and that everyone and all sciences make use of it. So he thinks that PNC is a principle of all reasoning. But an axiom, as he uses the term 'axiom', is something that one must presuppose if one is to learn anything (see *Posterior Analytics* I. 2, 72^{a}16–17). Hence PNC is a principle of all reasoning in the sense that if one is to reason at all about anything, and so learn anything in a way that involves reasoning, one must presuppose PNC. Unfortunately, he does not spell out how we presuppose PNC in all reasoning. In the *Prior Analytics* he uses the term 'reasoning' (*sullogismos*) in particular to mean 'deductive argument' (I. 1, 24^{b}18–20). So apparently his view is that we presuppose PNC in all deductive argument. But he does not say how we do this.

Here is an attempt to show how we presuppose PNC in all deductive argument. A deductively valid argument is an argument in which, if the premises are true, then necessarily the conclusion is also true:

> A deduction [*sullogismos*] is an argument in which, if certain things are supposed [i.e. the truth of the premises], then something other than the things supposed [i.e. the conclusion and its truth] follows of necessity from their being true [i.e. from the premises being true].
> (*Prior Analytics*, I. 1, 24^{b}18–20)

In short, a deductively valid argument is an argument in which the premises entail the conclusion. But this means that, in a deductively valid argument, to assert the premises and deny the conclusion is to assert a contradiction. This shows that the principle that it is impossible to assert a contradiction, i.e. the principle of non-contradiction in one of its formulations, is part of the definition of a deductively valid argument. For the impossibility, in a deductively valid argument, of asserting the premises but denying the conclusion, is precisely the impossibility of asserting a contradiction. So, if we think that some arguments are deductively valid, we must think that it is impossible to assert a contradiction. In short, PNC is part of the concept of deductive validity, and it is in this way that we presuppose PNC in all deductive argument.

However, to conclude that we presuppose PNC in all reasoning, and not just in all deductive reasoning and deductive argument, we must suppose that Aristotle thinks that deductive argument is central to all reasoning and rational thought, and that there would be no reasoning or rational thought if there were no deductive argument. Or at least we must suppose that he thinks that deductive reasoning is central to the reasoning that is distinctive of us humans, and perhaps especially to the reasoning of those of us who engage in science and the search for explanations. For, in general, he argues that we must engage in deductive argument in order to establish an explanatory relation between explanations and what they explain.

So is this what Aristotle has in mind when he argues (in IV. 3) that PNC is a principle of all reasoning? Probably. It makes good sense of his view that PNC is a principle of all reasoning and is presupposed in all reasoning. But perhaps there is a further aspect to his view. For when he says that everyone makes use of PNC whatever they are reasoning about, he appears to think of PNC not only as a principle of reasoning, but as a metaphysical principle – a principle about things. Thus, when he says that 'everyone uses them [the principles of reasoning]' (1005^{a}23–24), he appears to have in mind all the sciences. For he goes on to say:

> But they use them [the principles of reasoning] just so far as is suffi-
> cient for them, that is, so far as the kind extends about which they
> are carrying out demonstrations.
>
> (1005^{a}25–27)

Here he is evidently thinking of scientists – those who set out to demonstrate truths about some particular kind of beings. But in general he thinks that a special science is concerned with the nature of some things, but not all things, and that metaphysics is the science that is concerned with the nature of all things. So this suggests that he conceives of PNC as a metaphysical principle, i.e. as a principle of reasoning, and in particular of demonstration, about each and every thing.

Here it is important to draw attention to Aristotle's general distinction between, on the one hand, 'reasoning' and in particular 'deductive reasoning' (*sullogismos*) and, on the other hand, 'demonstration' (*apodeixis*; he introduces this distinction in *Posterior Analytics* I. 2). All demonstration is deductive reasoning, but not all deductive reasoning is demonstration. For a piece of deductive reasoning to constitute a demonstration, it must be a scientific or explanatory deductive reasoning (*sullogismos epistēmonikos*, see *Posterior Analytics* I. 2, 71^{b}17–19). This means that the truth of the premises in the deductive reasoning must not only entail *that* the conclusion is true, it must also explain *why* the conclusion is true. To do so, the premises must in general be more explanatory than the conclusion. Aristotle argues that explanatory knowledge (*epistēmē*) is aimed at demonstrations, i.e. at using deductive reasoning to derive explanatory conclusions from more explanatory premises. As he conceives of PNC, it is evidently a principle of deductive reasoning (*sullogismos*); but it is also, and perhaps especially, a principle of demonstration (*apodeixis*).

So Aristotle argues that PNC is a principle of all deductive reasoning and demonstration, and that PNC is presupposed in all deductive reasoning and demonstration. But he also argues that PNC is indemonstrable, i.e. it is a claim whose truth is presupposed in demonstrating other claims but which cannot itself be demonstrated. In general, he argues that not every claim can be demonstrated; for if every claim could be demonstrated, then a demonstration of a particular claim would go on forever: each premise in the demonstration would be derivable from a further premise or set of premises, and each of these premises would in turn be derivable from another premise or set of premises, and so on without end. But that would undermine the very possibility of demonstrating any claim. Thus he says:

> For it is a lack of education not to recognise of which things demonstration ought to be sought, and of which not. For in general it is impossible that there should be demonstration of everything (for in that case demonstration would proceed to infinity, and so there would be no demonstration). But if there are some things of which demonstration ought not to be sought, they [i.e. those who deny PNC and who require a demonstration in order to be convinced otherwise] could not say what they regard as a principle more fully of that kind [i.e. even less capable of demonstration].
>
> (1006^a6-11)

So some claims cannot be demonstrated; and he thinks that PNC is one of them (see 1006^a5-11). To say that PNC cannot be demonstrated is to say that there is no claim that is more secure or firm (*bebaion*) than PNC and from which PNC can be deductively derived (1005^b8f.). In this sense, PNC is a claim that is fundamental and 'presuppositionless' (*anhupotheton*, 1005^b14): it is a 'first' principle of reasoning.

Aristotle argues that there are claims that cannot be demonstrated, and that PNC is one of them. But why does he think that PNC in particular cannot be demonstrated? This is because he thinks that we must presuppose the truth of PNC when we demonstrate, and in general deductively argue for, any claim. From this, he argues, it follows that

PNC cannot itself be demonstrated. For if the truth of PNC could be demonstrated, then we would have to presuppose its truth in trying to demonstrate its truth; but then our demonstration of PNC would be circular and would 'beg the question' (see 1006ª15–18). But he thinks that no genuine demonstration can be circular. So he concludes that PNC contributes to the possibility of demonstrating the truth of any claim, and in general of arguing deductively for the truth of any claim, but it is not itself a claim whose truth can be demonstrated.

Aristotle's view that PNC cannot be demonstrated is important not least because it is associated with his view that PNC is fundamental to all deductive reasoning and in general to all reasoning and rational thought. But it is crucial not to misunderstand his view that PNC cannot be demonstrated. For this view does not mean that PNC is self-evident or obviously true, i.e. that anyone who considers it will immediately recognize that it is true. First, Aristotle does not at all think that it is self-evident or obvious that PNC is a presupposition of all reasoning and rational thought; on the contrary, he is at pains to argue this point. Second, even if one accepts that PNC is a presupposition of all reasoning and rational thought, one may still ask why we should think that PNC is true and even whether PNC is true in the first place. Of course, if one accepts that PNC is a presupposition of all reasoning and rational thought, one will readily conclude that PNC is true of things in so far as we can rationally think of things. But one may still ask why we should think that PNC is true of the things themselves and of things *without qualification*. We will see that Aristotle is acutely aware of these questions; and he does not at all think that arguing that PNC cannot itself be demonstrated is sufficient to answer them.

4 Aristotle's conception of PNC as a metaphysical principle

The question whether Aristotle thinks that PNC is a logical or a metaphysical principle is central to understanding his examination of this principle. He begins by arguing that the examination of PNC belongs to metaphysics: the science of being *qua* being (see opening of IV. 3; we will consider this argument in a moment). But if he has the logical conception in mind, then this is very puzzling. For if we conceive of PNC as a logical principle, then this principle does not at all appear to be about being *qua* being, i.e. about things simply in so far as they are beings; it appears rather to be about statements, and about things only or primarily in so far as they can be the subject of statements. This is a central point about the logical conception of PNC. It allows a philosopher like Russell, who is otherwise thoroughly a metaphysician, to claim that PNC is a logical and not a metaphysical principle:

> It is of *propositions* [i.e. meaningful statements] . . ., not of subjects [i.e. things talked about], that the law of contradiction [i.e. PNC] is asserted. To suppose that two contradictory propositions can both be true seems equally inadmissible whatever their subjects may be [hence whatever the nature of things may be].
>
> (Russell 1973: 92–93)

This also allows less metaphysically minded philosophers, or those who deny the possibility of metaphysics altogether, readily to accept PNC conceived as a logical principle. The point is simply this: apparently, in order to examine PNC as a logical principle, one need not engage in metaphysics, the science of being *qua* being, or even believe in the possibility of metaphysics. So, if we suppose that Aristotle conceives of PNC as a logical principle, then we will have a serious problem of reconciling this with his claim that the examination of PNC belongs to metaphysics. If, on the other hand, we suppose that from the start he conceives of PNC as a metaphysical principle, then there is no such problem. Today philosophers are perhaps more readily inclined to conceive of PNC as a logical than as a metaphysical principle; but the same may not be true of Aristotle.

Aristotle begins the examination of PNC (in IV. 3) by arguing that this examination belongs to metaphysics – the science of being *qua* being. He argues that the examination of all 'principles of reasoning', which he also calls 'axioms', belongs to metaphysics, and he argues that PNC is a fundamental principle of reasoning:

> We must state whether it belongs to a single science or different sciences to consider both what in the mathematics are called axioms [i.e. principles of reasoning] and primary being [*ousia*]. Now it is obvious that the examination of these [the axioms], too, belongs to a single science, namely that of the philosopher [i.e. metaphysics]. For they [the axioms] belong to all beings and not to some peculiar kind distinct from the other kinds. Moreover, everyone makes use of them, because they are about being *qua* being, and each kind is something that is.
>
> (IV. 3, 1005ª19–25)

We may note that the question that he asks, and answers, here is the question of the second *aporia* in book III, the book of *aporiai*; see

996^{b}26–997^{a}15. This argument seems straightforward: the examination of a principle of reasoning, such as PNC, belongs *either* to a specialized science, i.e. a science of one kind of beings as opposed to another, *or* it belongs to metaphysics – the science of all beings and of being *qua* being; but the examination of a principle of reasoning, such as PNC, does not belong to a specialized science; therefore, it belongs to metaphysics. The grounds for thinking that the examination does not belong to a specialized science, is that principles of reasoning, such as PNC, are true of all things, not just some things; and this is confirmed by the fact that everyone and all sciences make use of them.

But this argument is deceptively simple; for its conclusion is striking and puzzling. It says that the examination of principles of reasoning belongs to metaphysics, the science of being *qua* being. But a principle of reasoning is evidently a logical principle – a principle about what it is to reason and think rationally. But why should the examination of a logical principle belong to metaphysics? Why should a principle of reasoning, which is apparently about thought, be 'about being *qua* being'? (1005^{a}24) The claim that a principle is about being *qua* being presumably implies that the principle is true because of the nature of things. But how can a principle of reasoning, which is apparently about thought, be true not so much because of the nature of thought, but because of the nature of things?

Let us anticipate Aristotle's solution to this striking puzzle. PNC is true of things as things appear to us and as we conceive them; for PNC is a necessary condition for the possibility of thought and language. But PNC is true of things as things appear to us and as we conceive them because it is true of the things themselves and of things *without qualification*. So PNC is primarily true of the things themselves and of things *without qualification*; and because of this, it is true of things as they appear to us and as we conceive them. In other words, PNC is a necessary condition for the possibility of thought and language; but what explains why thought and language is possible is, precisely, the things themselves and *without qualification*, and in particular that PNC is true of them. We will consider this defence of PNC conceived as a metaphysical principle, especially in Chapter 6.

So we can see why Aristotle's initial argument for the view that the examination of PNC belongs to metaphysics is too simplistic (i.e. the argument at the opening of IV. 3). It assumes that PNC is true of the things themselves: either of some of them or of all of them. If we assume that PNC is true of the things themselves, then it is perhaps plausible to conclude that PNC is true of all of them, not just some of them. But the assumption that PNC is true of the things themselves is questionable and, Aristotle recognizes, it has been questioned. He thinks that it is questioned by Protagoras, Heracleitus and their followers. For one may think that PNC is true because of the nature of statements, or thoughts expressible in statements, rather than because of the nature of things. If so, PNC will be true of things as they appear to us and as we conceive them, and in general it will be true of things in so far as we can think and speak of things; but it may not be true of the things themselves and of things *without qualification*. To avoid this objection, Aristotle will argue that thought and thoughtful speech is possible only because of the nature of the things themselves, and in particular because PNC is true of the things themselves. But so far he has not even suggested this crucial argument. He develops this argument especially in IV. 5–6 (see Chapter 6).

5 Is PNC transcendental, i.e. is it true of things because it is true of thought?

Aristotle argues (in IV. 4) that if PNC were not true of things, then we could not use thoughts and words to signify things, and in general we could not think and speak about things. He concludes that if PNC were not true of things, then thought and language about things would be impossible. So the consequences of denying PNC are evidently difficult to accept. We will consider this argument in a moment, but first there is a particular and important problem about what Aristotle thinks is the aim of this argument. On one interpretation, the aim is to show why PNC is true of things: PNC is true of things because it is a necessary condition for the possibility of thought and language about things. On a different interpretation, the aim is not to show why PNC is true of things, but only to show what the consequences are of denying that it is true of things. Certainly, if a consequence of denying that PNC is true of things is that thought and language about things is impossible, then the consequences of denying that PNC is true of things are difficult and apparently impossible to accept. So the aim of the argument is a refutation (*elenchos*, 1006^{a}11–12) of those who deny PNC. On the former interpretation, this will also show why PNC is true of things: PNC is true of things because it is a necessary condition for the possibility of thought and language about things. But, on the latter interpretation, the aim of this refutation is not to show why PNC is true of things, but only to show what the consequences are of denying that it is true of things.

Something crucial hangs on the difference between the two interpretations. On the former interpretation, Aristotle's conclusion is that

PNC is true of things because it is a necessary condition for the possibility of thought and language about things. But this is to conceive of PNC as a transcendental principle, in a Kantian sense of the term 'transcendental'; i.e. it is a principle about what things must be like for thought and language about things to be possible. On the latter interpretation, PNC is true of things, and it is a necessary condition for the possibility of thought and language about things; but it is not the case that PNC is true of things because it is a necessary condition for the possibility of thought and language about things. PNC is not, therefore, a transcendental principle, a principle about what things must be like for thought and language about things to be possible. Rather, PNC is a metaphysical principle, a principle about what things must be like simply in order to be; i.e. it is about things, and it is about things simply in so far as they are beings, things that are. So the two interpretations differ over whether PNC is a transcendental or a metaphysical principle.

Why cannot PNC be both a transcendental and a metaphysical principle? In a sense, it can. That is to say, in so far as PNC, in its metaphysical formulation, is true simply about things, it is a metaphysical principle; and in so far as PNC is a necessary condition for the possibility of thought and language about things, it can in a loose sense be called a transcendental principle. The question, however, is whether PNC is true of things *because* it is a necessary condition for the possibility of thought and language about things. Only then is PNC a transcendental principle in a distinctively Kantian sense; i.e. it is *primarily* about thought and language about things, and only *as a consequence* is it about things. The question is whether, according to Aristotle, PNC is in this sense a transcendental principle.

It appears that Aristotle does not think that PNC is a transcendental principle; i.e. a principle that is primarily about thought and language about things, and only as a consequence about things. In other words, although he thinks that PNC's being true of things is a necessary condition for the possibility of thought and language about things, he does not think that PNC is true of things because it is a necessary condition for the possibility of thought and language about things. In other words, Aristotle distinguishes sharply between the logical question, 'What role does PNC play in thought and language?', and the question, 'What is PNC about?' and 'Of what is PNC true?' Kant, of course, argued that logic and epistemology are prior to, and the key to, metaphysics. But there is no such transcendental turn in Aristotle, whether in general or with regard to PNC in particular. We may get the impression that, especially in his defence of PNC, Aristotle came close to such a transcendental turn – but he steered clear.

One reason for denying that Aristotle thinks that PNC is a transcendental principle is that he thinks that it is impossible to demonstrate PNC, i.e. to show why it is true. It follows that even if PNC is a necessary condition for the possibility of thought and language about things, this does not show why PNC is true of things, or in general why it is true. For nothing can show why PNC is true.

Aristotle argues that PNC cannot be demonstrated, but he also says that PNC can be demonstrated 'in the manner of refutation' (*elenktikōs*, 1006ª11–12). What does this mean? Does it mean that there is after all a way of demonstrating PNC, i.e. of showing why it is true? In that case, this would, presumably, be the transcendental way, i.e. by arguing that PNC is a necessary condition for the possibility of thought and language. But this interpretation is implausible. For he has just argued that it is not possible to demonstrate PNC, i.e. to show why it is true. The claim that PNC can be demonstrated 'in the manner of refutation' means, therefore, that it is possible to refute those who deny PNC, but that this will be a demonstration of PNC only in a sense that does not amount to showing why PNC is true (see 1006ª15–18). So this appears to be the aim of Aristotle's argument for the claim that PNC is a necessary condition for the possibility of thought and language about things. He wants to establish the consequences of denying PNC, and, by so doing, to refute those who deny PNC; but he does not want to show why PNC is true of things, or why in general it is true.

So Aristotle argues that we have good and even decisive reasons to believe that PNC is true. For he argues that PNC is a necessary condition for the possibility of thought and language about things. However, he does not think that this shows why PNC is true; for he argues that nothing can show why PNC is true. In general, Aristotle argues that not all reasons for believing that a proposition is true are reasons which show why the proposition is true. A reason which shows why a proposition is true must explain why it is true, or contribute to the explanation, but not all reasons for believing that a proposition is true do that. For example, one may have reason to believe that grass is green, for grass visually appears green, but this is not a reason which explains why grass is green, or even contributes to the explanation.

We may conclude that Aristotle does not think that the reason why PNC is true of things is because it is a necessary condition for the possibility of thought and language about things. So he does not think that PNC is a transcendental principle, i.e. a principle that is primarily about thought and language about things and only as a consequence about things. Indeed, it will emerge that Aristotle thinks that the relation is the reverse, i.e. PNC is primarily about things and only as a consequence about thought and language about things. This accords with the analogy: it is because grass is green that it can visually appear green to creatures with certain cognitive capacities; it is not because grass can visually appear green to creatures with certain cognitive capacities that it is green. In general, it will emerge that Aristotle thinks that what explains why it is possible to think and speak about things is the nature of the things themselves (see Chapter 6).

6 How can one deny PNC?

Aristotle argues that PNC is true, and that it is impossible to deny it. It is impossible to deny it in the sense that it is impossible to accept the consequences of denying it. But he also thinks that there are thinkers who deny PNC. So he thinks that those who deny PNC do not recognize what the consequences are of denying it, or they do not recognize why it is impossible to accept these consequences. He does not find it at all surprising that some thinkers deny PNC. For he does not think that it is obvious what the consequences are of denying PNC, or that they include ones that it is impossible to accept. However, he thinks that it is possible to show what the consequences are of denying PNC, and this is what he sets out to do in the defence of PNC. The overall conclusion of the defence is that if PNC were not true of things, then it would be impossible to use thoughts or words to signify things, so it would be impossible to think or speak about things.

Aristotle thinks that different thinkers have wanted to deny PNC, such as Heracleitus (1005^b25), Protagoras (1007^b21), and some of the 'natural philosophers' (*hoi peri phuseōs*, 1006^a2). But he also thinks that some of those who argue against PNC do so fallaciously; i.e. they assert something which they think implies the falsity of PNC, but which does not really have this implication. For example (see 1009^a22–38), some natural philosophers, such as Anaxagoras and Democritus, argue that in order to understand the nature of change, we need to suppose that something can at the same time be in opposite states (e.g. both green and red), which implies the denial of PNC. But Aristotle responds that it is possible to understand the nature of change without denying PNC, and he tries to explain how this is possible.

However, Aristotle also thinks that there are philosophers who deny PNC and do so without arguing fallaciously. In other words, they defend views that they think imply the falsity of PNC, and he agrees that their views do indeed have this implication. As we will see, it is the following view in particular which both those who deny PNC and Aristotle think directly implies the falsity of PNC:

Things are radically indeterminate (*aorista*).

So both according to those who deny PNC and according to Aristotle, if things are radically indeterminate, then PNC will not be true of things – and in this sense PNC will be false. The difference between Aristotle and those who deny PNC, therefore, is over whether things really are radically indeterminate. Those who deny PNC think so, but Aristotle thinks not – he argues, on the contrary, that things are determinate (*hōrismena*). So the task that Aristotle sets himself is to argue against those who think that things are radically indeterminate, and so to defend PNC against those who want to deny it.

We will later consider this fundamental dispute between Aristotle and those who in this way deny PNC (see §§7–9 of this chapter, and also Chapter 6). But let us begin by considering how in general he understands those who in this way deny PNC. As he sees them, they claim not only that it is possible that there are things that are both F and not-F. Rather, they claim that there actually are things that are both F and not-F; and they are ready to give examples of such things (see 1006^{b}33–34). Even more radically, they claim that all things are both F and not-F:

> The same view [i.e. that all things are both F and not-F] is also the source of Protagoras' view. . . . For if [as Protagoras thinks] all beliefs and appearances are true, it is necessary that everything should be at once true and false.
>
> (IV. 5, 1009^{a}6–9)

> Heracleitus' view, which says that all things are and are not [i.e. are F and are not-F], makes everything true.
>
> (IV. 7, 1012^{a}24–26)

It appears that Aristotle clearly distinguishes between the view that *some* things are both F and not-F and the view that *all* things are both F and not-F (see 1008^{a}7–12). So he must be thinking deliberately that those who in this way deny PNC generally assert not only that some things are both F and not-F, but that all things are both F and not-F.

It is crucial to emphasize here the distinction between the view that *some* things are both F and not-F and the view that *all* things are both F and not-F. In its original formulations, and as Aristotle sets out to defend it, PNC says that *no* things can be both F and not-F. Indeed it says that *no* things, with regard to *any* property F, can be both F and not-F. So to deny PNC, one need only argue that *some* things, with regard to *some* property F, are both F and not-F. One may go further, and argue that *all* things, with regard to *some* property F, are both F and not-F, or even that *all* things, with regard to *every* property F, are both F and not-F. But evidently one need not.

It is, therefore, especially striking and puzzling that when Aristotle defends PNC against those who deny it, he concentrates largely on the most radical denial: *all* things, with regard to *every* property F, are both F and not-F. This also immediately gives rise to a problem about his defence. For suppose that he succeeds in his response to the radical denial of PNC, i.e. in showing that *some* things, with regard to *some* property F, cannot be both F and not-F; or even that *all* things, with regard to *some* property F (their essence, it will emerge), cannot be both F and not-F. Still, this will not by itself show that *all* things, with regard to *any* property F, cannot be both F and not-F. So it will not show what Aristotle originally sets out to show (we will also return to this problem later in this chapter, §9).

Aristotle is clearly aware of the distinction between the view that *some* things are both F and not-F and the view that *all* things are both F and not-F (see especially 1008^{a}7–12). In particular, when he diagnoses what leads Anaxagoras and Democritus to deny PNC (1009^{a}22f.), he argues that they deny PNC only with regard to changing things, not with regard to all things. In other words, they argue that changing things are both F and not-F, not that all things are both F and not-F. Indeed, they argue that a thing is both F and not-F precisely if F is a property that the thing has in so far as it is involved in change, i.e. in so far as it changes from having to not having this property. That this is how Aristotle understands the way in which they deny PNC is especially clear from his response to them (1009^{a}30–38). For he responds that, on the one hand (1009^{a}30–36), their argument for denying PNC with regard to changing things is fallacious, but also, on the other hand (1009^{a}36–38), that there may be things that are not subject to change, and to generation and destruction, in any way.

It is sometimes thought that Aristotle does not at all clearly distinguish between the view that *some* contradictions are true and the view that *all* contradictions are true; and that this spoils his defence of PNC. Thus Priest writes: 'Aristotle, in fact, slides back and forth between 'all' and 'some' with gay abandon. His defence of the LNC [i.e. PNC] is therefore of little help.' (Priest 1998: 417.) But it appears that the truth is rather that Aristotle does clearly distinguish between the view that *some* contradictions are true and the view that *all* contradictions are true, and that he deliberately chooses to concentrate primarily on the latter view, in his defence of PNC. So the question is, why does Aristotle deliberately choose to concentrate on the radical view that *all* contradictions are true, in his defence of PNC? And how, in Aristotle's view, will the response to the radical denial of PNC, i.e. to the view that *all* contradictions are true, contribute to the response to the moderate denial of PNC, i.e. to the view that *some* contradictions are true? (We will return to this question later, in §9 of this chapter.)

In general, Aristotle's strategy here (in IV. 4–6) appears to be diagnostic: he wants to trace the denial of PNC back to its root source, i.e. to trace the line of reasoning – the best line of reasoning – that the disputant of PNC can set out in support of the denial of PNC. He wants to do this in order that he may then direct his examination and response at this root source of the denial of PNC. But he thinks that an important line of reasoning for the denial of PNC is the view that things are radically indeterminate (*aorista*). So he directs his examination above all at this view.

However, it will emerge that this view, i.e. the view that things are radically indeterminate, has an inherent tendency towards being a global and not just a local view. That is to say, it is hard to think that *some* things are radically indeterminate, without thinking that *all* things are radically indeterminate. Aristotle himself makes this important point (see 1008^{a}11–12). For suppose that only some things are radically indeterminate. But then we must ask, which things are they? Suppose that we identify something radically indeterminate, e.g. clouds or sub-atomic particles. Evidently, even if these things are not wholly determinate, they are not radically indeterminate; for they differ and can be distinguished from other things. We have, after all, just distinguished them from other things, i.e. from things that are not clouds or sub-atomic particles. Indeed, Aristotle will argue that a thing, unless it is radically indeterminate, differs and can be distinguished from other things above all because it is the determinate and well-defined thing that it is – because it has an essence – or because it depends on something that is a determinate and well-defined thing and has an essence.

So, if this argument succeeds, it will establish not only that *some* things are determinate, but that *all* things are determinate. In other words, it will establish that, with regard to each and every thing, x, there is at least one property, F, such that x cannot be both F and not-F. This property, F, it will emerge, is the essence of x, i.e. that in virtue of which x is a determinate and well-defined thing in the first place.

Of course, there will still remain a problem. For Aristotle's original aim was to establish that *all* things, with regard to *any* property F, cannot be both F and not-F. But if his argument succeeds, it will, in the first instance at least, establish only that *all* things, with regard to *some* property F (namely, their essence), cannot be both F and not-F. We will return to this problem later (in §9 of this chapter).

To us, Aristotle's strategy may appear very puzzling. We tend to find it hard enough to imagine someone asserting that it is possible for something to be both F and not-F; let alone asserting that something is actually both F and not-F; not to speak of asserting that all things are, for any property F, both F and not-F. So, to us, Aristotle's familiarity with those who in this way deny PNC, and his radical characterization of their denial, may appear very puzzling. It is worth concentrating for a moment on how we tend to conceive of PNC, since this may indicate how, and how very differently, Aristotle conceives of PNC and of those who deny it. Incidentally, it is also worth emphasizing that there are notable exceptions to this modern tendency. Graham Priest is an exception, for he finds it all too easy to imagine true contradictions, i.e. some true contradictions. Apparently, Priest is closer to Aristotle than to the modern tendency. We should also note that Priest is a clear exception to the following diagnosis of the modern tendency.

We tend to conceive of PNC as the principle which says that no statement can be both true and not true. And we tend to think that PNC is a logical principle, both in the sense that it is about statements and in the sense that, if it is true, it is true because of the nature of statements. We also tend to think that PNC is a perfect candidate for a principle whose truth is a priori and even analytical. We tend to think that PNC is a priori and analytical in the sense that its truth is independent of what things are like. But, if a statement is analytical, then it is impossible to imagine or conceive of what things must be like for the statement to be false. It is generally because we consider PNC to be an a priori and analytic truth that we consider it to be a necessary truth: for any statement, it is necessarily not the case that both it and its negation are true ($\forall p \; \Box \; \neg(p \; \& \; \neg p)$).

There is, it is true, a relatively recent debate about whether PNC is really an a priori and analytical truth, or whether, on the contrary, it is possible to deny PNC and to do so for a reason. But this debate confirms that we find it difficult to imagine a denial of PNC. For the recent debate about whether PNC is a priori and analytical is largely about whether PNC is revisable, i.e. whether, granted that we actually accept PNC, we could have reason to cease to accept it. (See, for example, Hilary Putnam 1983.) The question in this debate is whether we could have reason to think that *some* contradictions are true. But this debate assumes that, actually, we do accept PNC, i.e. we think that *no* contradictions are true, and that, actually, we have no reason not to accept

PNC. The recent debate is between those who think PNC is unrevisable, hence a priori and analytical, and those who think that it is in principle revisable. But this debate is evidently very different from the debate between Aristotle and those whom he thinks deny PNC. For those whom he thinks deny PNC are not concerned with whether we might in the future come to have reason to revise and give up PNC, i.e. to think that *some* contradictions are true. Rather, they refuse to accept PNC here and now, and they argue that *all* contradictions are true.

So why are we inclined to accept PNC, i.e. to think that no contradictions are true, and why are we inclined to be confident that there is no reason against accepting PNC? Apparently, this is precisely because we conceive of PNC as a logical principle, i.e. a principle that is about statements and whose truth is based on the nature of statements. For we are perhaps inclined to reason along the following lines. Consider any statement, p. How could one assert that p is both true and not true? If one asserts that p is both true and not true, one asserts that p is true and one asserts that p is not true. But to assert that p is true is to assert p, and to assert that p is not true is to deny p. Hence one both asserts and denies p. Now, there are various ways in which one may both assert and deny p. Perhaps one does so unwittingly and without realizing what one is doing. Or perhaps one is using p ambiguously in the assertion and the denial. Or perhaps one is asserting that there is good reason for asserting p and that there is equally good reason for denying p. But we may be inclined to think that, once we take into account such qualifications, it is part of the nature of statements, and in particular of asserting and denying a statement, that one cannot both assert and deny one and the same statement. For both to assert and deny one and the same statement is to say nothing at all – it is like taking back with one hand what one gives with the other.

But let us note how very differently Aristotle understands those whom he thinks deny PNC. For, as he sees them, they think that there is reason to deny PNC and to assert its very opposite, i.e. that all things, and with regard to any property, are both F and not-F. This suggests that they do not conceive of PNC as a logical principle. So perhaps we may understand better the readiness with which they deny PNC, and the radical way in which they deny it, if we suppose rather that they conceive of PNC as a metaphysical principle.

We may, however, wonder how one can deny PNC even with regard to a single thing, let alone all things. How can one think, with regard to even a single thing, that it is both F and not-F, at the same time and in the same respect? To address this question, let us in general distinguish between two very different ways in which one may deny a statement: an 'ordinary' way and an 'extra-ordinary' way. Ordinarily, to deny a statement (e.g. the statement that grass is green) is to accept the concepts in that statement (e.g. the concepts *grass* and *green*), and to accept that in general these concepts are applicable to reality, but deny that the things referred to in the statement are as the statement says that they are (e.g. to deny that grass *is* green). Extra-ordinarily, however, to deny a statement is to deny that the concepts in it apply to reality at all. For example, one may deny that things are really coloured, or that grass is a real thing any more than lawns are. Extra-ordinary denials appear distinctively metaphysical; for they are completely general and they deny that certain concepts apply to anything at all.

Certainly an ordinary denial of PNC may be difficult to imagine, especially if we add Aristotle's qualification to PNC, i.e. the qualification *in one and the same respect*. In other words, once it is granted that the concepts in PNC apply to things, PNC may well be true of things. However, it is perhaps not so hard to imagine an extra-ordinary denial of PNC. As Aristotle formulates PNC, it says that one and the same property cannot both be true of and not be true of one and the same thing, at the same time *and in the same respect*. But now suppose that all things are so radically indeterminate that it is not possible to distinguish a particular respect in which a thing may be either F or not-F but not both F and not-F. To illustrate this, we may think of, for example, clouds. For a cloud may at the same time look both round and not round, and it may not be possible to distinguish a particular respect in which it is round and a different particular respect in which it is not round. But if all things are so radically indeterminate that it is not possible to distinguish a particular respect in which a thing may be either F or not-F but not both F and not-F, then PNC will not apply to anything, and in this sense PNC will not be true: it will not be true of any thing.

It is worth emphasizing this central idea, i.e. that PNC may not be true of a thing precisely because the thing may be so radically indeterminate that it is not possible to distinguish a particular respect in which it may be either F or not-F but not both F and not-F. Graham Priest offers the following argument against PNC and in favour of thinking that there are true contradictions:

> Another example: I walk out of the room; for an instant, I am symmetrically poised, one foot in, one foot out, my center of gravity lying on the vertical plane containing the center of gravity of the door. Am I in or not in the room? By symmetry, I am neither in rather than not in, nor not in rather than in. The pure light of reason therefore

countenances only two answers to the question: I am both in and not in, or neither in nor not in. . . . But wait a minute. If I am neither in nor not in, then I am not (in) and not (not in). By the law of double negation, I am both in and not in. (Even without it, I am both not in and not not in, which is still a contradiction.)

(Priest 1998: 415)

But there is a very natural objection to this argument against PNC. For even if it shows that I can be both in the room and not in the room, indeed even if it shows that I can be just as much in the room as not in the room (and it is natural to think that it shows this much), evidently it does not show that I can, *in one and the same respect*, be both in the room and not in the room. On the contrary, as Priest describes the case, it is in respect of the one side of my centre of gravity, i.e. of my centre of gravity that for an instant lies on the vertical plane containing the centre of gravity of the door, that I am in the room, but in respect of the other side of my same centre of gravity that I am not in the room. And this centre of gravity is, precisely, what distinguishes these two respects of mine. So, as Priest describes the case, it is, precisely, possible to distinguish a particular respect in which a thing may be either F or not-F but not both F and not-F. Because of this possibility, Priest's argument against PNC fails. Certainly it fails against PNC as defended by Aristotle. For Aristotle emphasizes that PNC is true of a thing only if we consider the thing *in one and the same respect*. This also shows something crucial, namely that to deny that PNC is true of a thing, one must argue that it is not possible to consider the thing *in one and the same respect* – just as, apparently, it is not possible to consider a cloud in the single respect of its determinate shape.

We have seen that it is one thing to deny PNC conceived as a logical principle, but something very different to deny PNC conceived as a metaphysical principle. But Aristotle is above all concerned with responding to the latter kind of denial. So he conceives of the debate between himself and those who deny PNC as a metaphysical debate, i.e. a debate about what things in general must be like for PNC to apply to them. And he argues that for PNC to apply to things, things must be strictly determinate. This sets Aristotle's debate very much apart from the modern, logical debate. The modern debate starts with a logical question: is PNC an analytical truth, i.e. a truth independent of what things are like? Or else it starts with an epistemological question: is PNC an a priori truth, i.e. a truth independent of all sense-experience? It relies on these questions to establish whether PNC is a necessary truth: PNC will be a necessary truth if it is a priori or if it is analytical. Aristotle certainly thinks that PNC is a necessary truth. But he does not base this on logical or epistemological considerations. His notion of necessity here is rather that of directly metaphysical necessity.

If we turn to our notions of a priori truth and analytical truth, it is notable that nothing like them is prominent in Aristotle's examination and defence of PNC. So does he think that PNC is analytical? Since he thinks that PNC depends on a particular conception of reality, i.e. the view that things are strictly determinate, and since he thinks that there are thinkers that deny this conception of reality, and do so without obvious absurdity, he evidently does not think that PNC is analytical. Does he think that PNC is a priori? Again, it appears that he does not. At the beginning of the *Metaphysics* he claims that metaphysical principles are 'furthest removed from the senses' (982ª25). But this suggests that sense perception plays some role in establishing metaphysical principles, even if a lesser role than in establishing other things. So Aristotle appears to think that sense perception and experience in general contribute to the belief that things are strictly determinate, hence to the belief that PNC is true of things.

7 The consequences of denying PNC: It is impossible to think and speak about things

In IV. 4 (especially 1006ª11–ᵇ34, summarized in ª11–28) Aristotle argues that PNC is true of things. He does so by arguing that if PNC were not true of things, then thought and language about things would be impossible. In particular, he argues that whether PNC is or is not true of things depends on whether things are determinate (*hōrismena*) or indeterminate (*aorista*). This, above all, is the question that divides Aristotle from those who deny PNC.

Aristotle uses a variety of ways to indicate the contrast between the two views – the view that things are determinate and the view that things are indeterminate. For example, he also describes the disputant's view as being that things are not unitary (1007ᵇ26), whereas his own view is that things are unitary (1006ª31–4, ᵇ7–10); or as the view that things do not have an essence (1007ª20–21), whereas his own view is that things have an essence (1006ª32–34); or as the view that things are not definable, whereas his own view is that things are definable (1012ª21f.; in general a definition of a thing is a true statement of its essence). So those who deny PNC think that the truth of PNC stands and falls with the view that things are determinate, unitary, in possession of an essence and definable; but what they think is just that things are not like that.

Aristotle agrees that the truth of PNC stands and falls with the view that things are determinate, unitary, in possession of an essence and definable. But he argues that the consequences of denying this view are unacceptable. For he argues that if things are not determinate, not unitary, not in possession of an essence and not definable, then it is impossible to signify (*sēmainein*) things, i.e. to think and speak about things (1006ᵃ18–ᵇ34). He also thinks that this is evidently an unacceptable consequence; for he argues that to say something at all is to signify something, i.e. to think and speak about something (1006ᵃ21–22).

So Aristotle's argument against those who deny PNC can be summarized as follows (1006ᵇ18–34):

P1. PNC is not true of things if, and only if, things are indeterminate.

P2. If things are indeterminate, then it is impossible to think and speak about things.

P3. It is possible to think and speak about things.

Therefore,

C. It is not the case that PNC is not true of things; i.e. PNC *is* true of things.

Perhaps this argument looks simple (certainly it is valid). But it raises fundamental and difficult questions. In particular, the third premise (P3 'It is possible to think and speak about things'), which may appear unobjectionable, can be understood in two very different ways. Aristotle, it appears, understands it to mean that we can think and speak about the things themselves, not just about things as they appear to us and as we conceive of them. But if this is what he means, then this premise is not so unobjectionable after all, and the disputant may want to deny it (we will take up this important issue in Chapter 6).

Here it is important to emphasize that Aristotle wants the premises to be acceptable to the disputant. For he thinks that when the disputant denies PNC, it is first of all he, the disputant, that is committed to unacceptable consequences, and in particular to the view that thought and language about things is impossible. In fact, Aristotle says that the person who denies PNC somehow refutes himself (see 1006ᵃ26, 1008ᵇ2f.). So he thinks that his refutation of the person who denies PNC amounts to what is now sometimes called a 'self-refutation', i.e.

the disputant's refuting themselves. But then it is especially important that we should understand the premises in such a way that they are acceptable not only to Aristotle, but also to the disputant.

In general, the structure of the refutation of those who deny PNC is as follows. The disputant denies PNC and claims that PNC is not true of things. Aristotle argues that if PNC is not true of things, then thought and language about things are impossible. But naturally the disputant believes that thought and language about things are possible. So they are committed to a contradiction. In ordinary circumstances, this would force them to give up one of these two beliefs. And since it is difficult to give up the belief that thought and language about things is possible, they would rather give up the denial of PNC. The disputant, however, is prepared to accept contradictions, so they cannot be refuted in this usual way. But Aristotle thinks that they can still be refuted, in a striking way:

> If he [the disputant] says nothing [i.e. if he really accepts that language is impossible], it is ridiculous to try to say something against one who does not have a statement to make about anything, in so far as he is like that; for such a person is to that extent already like a vegetable.
>
> (1006ª13–15)

So what is intended to disturb the disputant is not so much that denying PNC commits them to a contradiction; for they are prepared to accept contradictions. What is intended to disturb the disputant is rather that denying PNC commits them to the impossibility of thought and language about things. The disputant cannot seriously accept this commitment, any more than they can seriously think of themselves as being as mindless and dumb as a vegetable.

The first premise (P1 'PNC is not true of things if, and only if, things are indeterminate') we have already considered at some length (see §6 of this chapter). We will return to it later (§§8–9 of this chapter) and in Chapter 6.

The second premise (P2) says that 'If things are indeterminate, then it is impossible to think and speak about things'. This central premise means that if we are to think and speak about things at all, things must be determinate. Thus Aristotle says:

> For not to signify *one* thing [*hen*, a unitary thing, a determinate thing] amounts to not signifying anything at all.
>
> (1006ᵇ7)

In other words, to signify something at all, i.e. to think and speak about something at all, we must signify one thing as opposed to another: we must signify something determinate. But what does Aristotle mean when he says that if we are to think and speak about something at all, then we must think and speak of it as something determinate? He means that we must think and speak of it as being, simply in virtue of being the very thing it is, F as opposed to not-F. For example, to think that clouds are something determinate is to think that a cloud, simply in virtue of being the very thing it is, namely, a cloud, is condensed vaporous water, as opposed to something else. Or, in Aristotle's example, to think that a human being is something determinate is to think that a human being, simply in virtue of being the very thing it is, namely, a human being, is a two-footed animal, as opposed to something else (see 1006ᵃ31–34 and ᵇ13–14; we may note that the content of the particular example does not appear to matter to him, for he hardly thinks that this, a two-footed animal, is what a human being essentially is). This is also what he means when he says that to think and speak of something is to think and speak of something as having an essence (see 1006ᵇ32–34); for in general when he says that the essence (*to ti ēn einai*) of a thing, x, is F, he means that the thing, x, is, simply in virtue of being the very thing it is, F. (We will consider his conception of essence in a moment; see §8 of this chapter.)

If we ask why Aristotle thinks that to think and speak about something is to think and speak about something determinate, the reason is, apparently, that he thinks that to think and speak about something is to think and speak about one thing as opposed to another. In other words, when we think and speak about something (e.g. Socrates, which is Aristotle's example, see 1007ᵇ5f.), we think and speak about *it* as opposed to anything else. So we must be able to indicate, or at least we must be willing to try to indicate, what distinguishes the thing that we are thinking and speaking about from other things. But to indicate this is, exactly, to indicate how the thing that we are thinking and speaking about is the determinate thing that it is.

So Aristotle thinks that if we are to think and speak about something at all, then we must think and speak of it as something determinate. He concludes that if we are to think and speak about something at all, then we must suppose that PNC is true of it (see 1006ᵇ28–34). The reasoning behind this conclusion is as follows. Suppose that we are thinking and speaking about a cloud. Perhaps we will think that a cloud can be both round and not round; for it looks both round and not round, and there may not be a respect in which it is round and a different respect in which it is not round. But the question is this: can what we are thinking and speaking about be at the same time both a cloud and not a cloud? We have supposed that if we are to think and speak about a cloud at all, then we must think and speak about it as something determinate, for example, as condensed vaporous water. But then *it*, the very thing that we are thinking and speaking about, cannot at the same time not be condensed vaporous water; or else it would not be something determinate after all: it would not be *it* as opposed to something else. (Aristotle's reasoning, at 1006ᵇ28–34 is about human beings, not clouds, but otherwise it runs along these exact lines.) So, on the supposition that to think and speak about things is to think and speak about determinate things, Aristotle concludes that PNC is true of things. But this argument gives rise to fundamental and difficult questions (see later in this chapter, §§8–9 and in Chapter 6).

8 The defence of PNC and the defence of the view that things have an essence

Aristotle has argued that we can think and speak about a thing, x, only if PNC is true of this thing, x. In particular, he has argued that we can think and speak about a thing, x, only if there is some property, F, such that x is F and x cannot at once be not-F. For it is in virtue of there being such a property that the thing, x, is a determinate thing in the first place; and if it were not a determinate thing, then we could not think or speak about it – for we would not think or speak about *it* as opposed to any other thing. Let us suppose that this argument succeeds. What does it establish? It is crucial to recognize that Aristotle thinks that it has established that we can think and speak about a thing, x, only if this thing, x, has an essence (or at least if it depends on a thing that has an essence – we will not repeat this qualification, although it is important). For it is in virtue of having an essence that a thing, x, is a determinate thing in the first place; i.e. it is in virtue of having an essence that a thing is the very thing that it is, as opposed to any other thing. This means that Aristotle thinks that the defence of the view that PNC is true of things is at the same time a defence of the view that things have an essence. And this defence of the view that things have an essence is a truly radical defence. For it argues that unless things have an essence, we cannot think or speak about things. For this reason above all, Aristotle's defence of PNC occupies a pivotal position in the *Metaphysics*. For it will emerge that the view that things have an essence is vital in Aristotle's attempt to answer the basic question of metaphysics, 'What is it for a thing to be a being, something that is?' (see Chapter 7§5iv).

This defence of the view that things have an essence gives rise to difficult questions. One question is this. Suppose that the defence succeeds. Does it establish that the things themselves and without qualification have an essence or only that things as we conceive them have an essence? We will take up this central question in the next chapter.

Another question is this. Suppose that the defence succeeds. Of what things does it establish that they have an essence? Does it establish that particulars have an essence, or only that the properties that are true of particulars have an essence? Here it is important to recognize that Aristotle thinks that the defence has established that particulars have an essence. This is above all because it was crucial in the defence that we can think and speak about a thing, x, only if x has an essence; for it is in virtue of having an essence that this thing, x, is the very thing that it is, as opposed to any other thing. But the things about which we think and speak are, evidently, particulars, e.g. a particular human being (see 1006^{b}28–34, later he chooses Socrates as example, 1007^{b}5f.). So if the defence succeeds, it establishes that particulars have an essence.

That this is the conclusion of the defence is also clear in the following way. It was crucial in the defence that we can think and speak about a thing, x, only if PNC is true of this thing, x. In particular, we can think and speak about a thing, x, only if there is some property, F, such that x is F and x cannot at once be not-F. So the conclusion is that, for any thing, x, there is a property, F, such that x is F and x cannot at once be not-F. This property, it emerges, is the essence of this thing, x, i.e. it is that which determines what this very thing, x, is. But the disputant of PNC, against whom this defence is directed, has no problem with assuming from the start that the property, F, is a single, determinate, well-defined property, i.e. it is this very property, F, as opposed to any other property. For his point is that this very property, F, can be at once true and not true of one and the same particular thing, x. So to argue that this property, F, is the very property that it is, and not any other property, would be to argue what the disputant is already happy to assume.

It is important to emphasize that Aristotle thinks that the defence establishes that it is particulars, not just properties, that have an essence. For it will emerge that the view that precisely particulars have an essence is vital in Aristotle's attempt to answer the basic question of metaphysics, 'What is it for a thing to be a being, something that is?' (see later in this chapter and Chapter 7§§3 and 5v).

How are we to assess this defence, i.e. the defence of the view that we can think and speak about a particular thing, x (e.g. Socrates), only if this particular thing, x, has an essence (or at least if it depends on a thing that has an essence)? Let us set aside the question of whether this essence will belong to the particulars themselves and without quali- fication or it will belong only to particulars as we conceive them (see Chapter 6 for this question). Still, the defence gives rise to a number of questions.

First, does the defence establish that each thing has a single, unitary essence, or may the essence of each thing be complex and manifold? Aristotle is aware of this question. He argues that what has been estab- lished is only that the essence of each thing cannot be indefinitely complex and manifold, but must contain a determinate number of parts (cf. *hōrismenoi ton arithmon*, 1006^{b}4). For if it is indefinitely complex and manifold, it may after all contain contradictory properties (see 1006^{a}34–^{b}11, translating *apeiron* as 'indefinite').

Second, even if the defence establishes that particulars have an essence, of what particulars does it establish this? Does it establish this of the particulars with which we are directly familiar from sense percep- tion and experience, e.g. Socrates (see 1007^{b}5f. for Aristotle's use of Socrates as an example)? Perhaps the particulars that have an essence will rather be the ultimate parts of the particulars with which we are directly familiar. We might even wonder whether the argument estab- lishes that particulars (in the plural) have an essence. For perhaps it may establish rather that there is some one particular, such as the universe as a whole, that has an essence.

Third, does the argument establish that a particular has an essence simply in virtue of itself and not in virtue of its relation to other partic- ulars, or may a particular have an essence only in relation to other particulars – perhaps even to all other particulars? In other words, does the argument establish a non-relational conception of essence or it is compatible with a relation conception? Apparently, Aristotle thinks that it has established a non-relational conception of essence. Certainly he speaks as if the property that constitutes the essence of a particular thing, x, is that which determines what this very thing, x, is simply in virtue of itself and not in virtue of its relation to other things. Perhaps his reasoning here is as follows: the essence of a particular thing, x, is that which determines why this particular thing, x, is the very thing it is *as opposed to any other particular thing*; therefore, the essence of this particular thing, x, belongs to x simply in virtue of itself and not in virtue of its relation to any other particular thing. This reasoning may be attractive, but it is not evidently cogent.

These are difficult questions, but we cannot take them up here. Perhaps we may conclude that Aristotle's defence here (in VI. 4) of the view that particulars have an essence serves above all to introduce an initial and rough conception of essence – a proto-conception – which is both striking and attractive. For, on this proto-conception of essence, a particular is the very particular that it is, as opposed to any other particular, precisely in virtue of having an essence. And this, we may think, is just what we need in order to distinguish one particular from any other particular, and thus to think and speak about *it*, as opposed to any other particular, in the first place. This proto-conception of essence Aristotle will develop later (especially in book VII), and, in so doing he may also begin to answer some of the questions to which the idea of essence gives rise.

9 Does Aristotle succeed in showing that there are *no* true contradictions?

Aristotle has argued that, with regard to each thing, x, there is a property, E (i.e. the essence of x), such that x is E and x cannot at once be not-E. But his original aim was to argue that, with regard to each thing, x, and each property, F, that x cannot be at once F and not-F. How, if at all, does his argument contribute to this original aim? Of course, if he simply moves from, 'Some contradictions cannot be true', to, 'No contradictions can be true', then he is simply arguing fallaciously. But there is a reason against this verdict. For we saw that Aristotle is careful to distinguish the view that all contradictions are true from the view that some contradictions are true (see §6 of this chapter). Furthermore, while evidently the claim that 'Some contradictions cannot be true' does not entail the claim that 'No contradictions can be true', perhaps Aristotle thinks, without obvious fallacy, that the claim that 'Some contradictions, namely those involving the essence of a thing, cannot be true' entails, or at least provides reason for thinking, that 'No contradictions can be true'.

How can the claim that 'With regard to its essence, E, a thing cannot be both E and not-E' provide reason for thinking, as in Aristotle's original aim, that 'With regard to any property, F, a thing cannot be both F and not-F'? Here we need to recall that Aristotle's original aim was rather to defend the claim that 'With regard to any property, F, a thing cannot be both F and not-F *at the same time and in one and the same respect.*' He emphasizes this qualification, and we have seen that it is crucial (see §§1 and 6 of this chapter). But we have also seen that, apparently, Aristotle thinks that in order to deny that PNC is true of a thing, x, i.e. in order to argue that there are true contradictions with regard to a thing, x, one must argue that this thing, x, is so radically indeterminate that it is not possible to distinguish a particular respect in which it may be either F or not-F but not both F and not-F.

This, if anything, provides the key to Aristotle's strategy. For he appears to think that if a thing, x, has an essence, then, if it is this very thing, x, that is both F and not-F, it is possible to distinguish a particular respect in which it is either F or not-F but not both F and not-F. In other words, Aristotle thinks that we are entitled to be confident that, when it appears that a single thing, x, is at once F and not-F, then, if it is this very thing, x, that is both F and not-F, we can distinguish a respect in which it is F and a different respect in which it is not-F. And he thinks that what entitles us to this confidence is, precisely, the view that x is a determinate and well-defined thing – a thing that has an essence.

Perhaps the cloud example may help to illustrate this strategy. Evidently, a particular cloud may look both round and not-round, and it may be difficult or impossible to distinguish a respect in which it is round and a respect in which it is not-round. Must we conclude that the cloud is at once round and not-round, and that this is a true contradiction? We cannot directly conclude this. We can conclude this only if we argue that *either* (option 1) the cloud is both round and not-round *in one and the same respect*; or (option 2) although it is this very cloud that is both round and not-round, still it is not possible to distinguish a respect in which it is round and a different respect in which it is not round. Evidently the former option will not be at all attractive. For it is difficult to see how one and the same thing can be both F and not-F *in one and the same respect*. What about the latter option? Aristotle argues that if we can think and speak about this cloud, then it has an essence, i.e. there is something that it is to be this very cloud, as opposed to any other thing. Now suppose, on the one hand, that what it is to be a particular cloud involves its being something that has a particular shape. For example, suppose that to be a particular cloud is to be a particular set of water molecules arranged in a particular way in space. Then evidently one and the same cloud cannot be both round and not-round – for then the cloud would not have a particular shape and so it would not be a cloud at all. So suppose, on the other hand, that what it is to be a particular cloud does not involve its being something that has a particular shape. In that case, we need not at all say that it is this very cloud that is both round and not-round. For we may say, instead, that there is something that is round here (e.g. there is roundly shaped material within the confines of this particular space) and there is something that is not-round here (e.g. there is not-roundly shaped material within the confines of the same particular space). But evidently this is not even the whiff of a contradiction.

Hopefully, the above illustration will carry some conviction on its own merits and on account of its details, not merely as an illustration of a general strategy. For suppose that Aristotle's general strategy is indeed to argue that the view that a thing, x, has an essence, E, entitles us to be confident that, when it appears that a single thing, x, is at once F and not-F, *either*:

(1) we may distinguish a respect in which x is F and a different respect in which x is not-F; *or*
(2) we may say that it is not this very thing, x, that is both F and not-F, but rather there is something in the area of x that is F and that there is something in the area of x that is not-F.

If this strategy is to convince, then it must convince not only as a general strategy, but also from case to case. In other words, it will be a task to show, from case to case, *either*:

(1) what the respect is in which a particular thing, x, is F and what the different respect is in which this same thing, x, is not-F; *or*
(2) it is not this very thing, x, that is both F and not-F, rather there is something in the area of x that is F and there is something in the area of x that is not-F.

For example, suppose that we today think that light manifests at once the behaviour of waves and the behaviour of particles. And suppose that we think that light has an essence, i.e. there is something that it is to be this very thing – light. Perhaps we think that this essence is what the science, physics, is searching for. It may then appear that we have a true contradiction: one and the same emission of light is at once an emission of waves and an emission of particles. To show that this is not really a true contradiction, we will need to consider what the essence of light is; and by doing so we will need to show *either*:

(1) what the respect is in which light is the emission of waves and what the different respect is in which light is the emission of particles; *or*:
(2) it is not this very thing, light, that is both the emission of waves and the emission of particles, rather, for example, the presence of light within a particular confines of space implies that there is within these confines of space both wave-activity and particle-activity – which evidently is not even the whiff of a contradiction.

6

THE RESPONSE TO PHENOMENALISM AND RELATIVISM

(Book IV. 5–6)

1 How phenomenalism and relativism present a challenge to Aristotle's defence of the principle of non-contradiction conceived as a metaphysical principle

In book IV, chapters 5–6, Aristotle considers and responds to the following two views:

> (PHEN) Anything that appears thus and so to someone, and anything that someone believes to be thus and so, is thus and so (i.e. all appearances and all beliefs are true);

and:

> (REL) Anything that appears thus and so to someone, and anything that someone believes to be thus and so, is thus and so *for him* (i.e. all appearances and all beliefs are true *relative to the one who has them*).

We may call the first view 'phenomenalism' and the second 'relativism'. By these terms we will mean just these views. (In the next section we will see that Aristotle distinguishes precisely these two views – regardless of how they are labelled.) This must not be confused with a wider use of these terms, for today they are obviously used in a variety of ways. In particular, we must be careful to bear in mind that phenomenalism, as this view is characterized by Aristotle here (in IV. 5–6), is the view that all appearances (*phainomena*) and all beliefs *are true*. This must not be confused with a more familiar modern use of the term 'phenomenalism', to mean that all knowledge (or, alternatively, all meaning) is based in and constructed out of appearances, i.e. how things directly appear to our senses.

Indeed, there is a very important difference between using the term 'phenomenalism' to mean that all appearances and all beliefs *are true*, and using this term in its more modern epistemological or semantic senses. For we will see that the view that all appearances and all beliefs *are true* directly entails a radical denial of the principle of non-contradiction. (Aristotle carefully argues for this point at the opening of IV. 5.) But phenomenalism in the modern senses of the term is usually thought to be perfectly compatible with the truth of PNC. Aristotle tends to associate the first view with Protagoras, and the second with Heracleitus; so we might simply use these names as labels for these views. But this would be misleading and confusing. For we, if anything, are accustomed to associate the name of Protagoras with relativism, not with phenomenalism in the above sense. Indeed, the direct association of Protagoras with relativism goes back to Plato's dialogue, the *Theaetetus*, a dialogue to which Aristotle refers here (see 1010^{b}11–14) and which is very much in the background of his present investigation (i.e. in IV. 5–6). This suggests that he is not so much concerned with who exactly held these two views, or how they held them; he is, we will see, rather concerned with arguing that these two views, phenomenalism and relativism, are the root source of the denial of PNC. We will return at length to Aristotle's diagnosis of the source of the denial of PNC.

But what is Aristotle's aim in considering phenomenalism and relativism here (in IV. 5–6), and why does he consider these views at all? It will emerge that he is not so much concerned with these views in their own right, and neither is it his aim directly to argue against them. Rather, he is concerned with phenomenalism and relativism because they present a serious challenge to his defence of PNC and to his defence of the view that things are determinate and well-defined (i.e. the defence that he developed in IV. 3–4, which we considered in the previous chapter). So his response to phenomenalism and relativism must be understood as a central part of his defence of PNC.

We may recall that Aristotle's defence of PNC (especially in IV. 4) was basically this:

(P1) Only if PNC is true of things can we think and speak about things;

but evidently,

(P2) We can think and speak about things;

Therefore,

(C1) PNC is true of things.

Further, he diagnosed the source of the denial of PNC, and in particular of the radical view that PNC is not true of anything, as the view that things are radically indeterminate, i.e.:

(P3) PNC is not true of anything if, and only if, things are radically indeterminate.

But since he argues that (C1) PNC is true of things, he also concludes that:

(C2) It is not the case that things are radically indeterminate.

But now (in IV. 5–6) it emerges that there is a serious challenge to this argument. For one may think that the things themselves are radically indeterminate and that PNC is not true of them; so one may deny his conclusions, C1 and C2. And one may think that if the things themselves are radically indeterminate and PNC is not true of them, then it is impossible to think or speak of the things themselves; so one may accept his premise P1, on one understanding of this premise. But one may nonetheless argue that we can still think and speak about things, namely things as they appear to us and as we conceive them; so one may also accept his premise P2, on one understanding of it. This shows that there is a way of accepting the premises in Aristotle's argument (i.e. P1, P2 and P3) while at the same time rejecting its conclusions (i.e. C1 and C2). So Aristotle's argument may not be valid after all – it all depends on how we understand its premises and especially the premise which says that (P2) we can think and speak about things.

This is precisely the challenge that phenomenalism and relativism, as Aristotle understands these views, present to his defence of PNC and to his defence of the view that things are determinate and well-defined. The challenge is that, apparently, we can think and speak about things even if PNC is not true of things and things are radically indeterminate; for although PNC may not be true of the things themselves, and even though the things themselves may be radically indeterminate, we can still think and speak about things as they appear to us and as we conceive them. This, the phenomenalist and relativist will argue, is because there is a sharp distinction between, on the one hand, things as they appear to us and as we conceive them and, on the other hand, the things themselves. So even if it is impossible to think or speak of the things themselves, we can still think and speak about things; for we can think and speak about things as they appear to us and in general as we conceive them.

This is evidently not a minor challenge to Aristotle's defence of PNC and to his defence of the view that things are determinate and well-defined; on the contrary, it threatens entirely to undermine his defence. For it was his original aim to defend PNC as a metaphysical principle (PNC-M): a principle which is true of all beings, and which is true of all beings for no other reason, ultimately, than that all beings are beings – things that are (see, for example, 1005ª27–29, where he says that principles such as PNC are true of being *qua* being). So his aim was to show that:

(PNC-M) PNC is true of the things themselves and of things *without qualification*.

It was not his aim to defend PNC only as a logical principle (PNC-L), i.e. to show that:

(PNC-L) PNC is true of things *in so far as we can think and speak about things*.

So his aim was to defend not only PNC-L but also, and primarily, PNC-M. (But we may note also here that his aim included defending PNC-L.) But now it emerges that he may after all have succeeded in defending PNC at most as a logical principle and not also as a metaphysical principle: not as a principle that is true of the things themselves and of things *without qualification*, but at most as a principle that is true of things *in so far as we can think and speak about things*.

Aristotle's engagement with phenomenalism and relativism shows that he is acutely aware of this challenge to his defence of PNC. Indeed, this engagement serves precisely to point out this challenge and, at least to some extent, to respond to it. For what is distinctive of phenomenalism and relativism, as he characterizes these positions here, is that they draw a sharp distinction between, on the one hand, things as they appear to us and as we conceive them and, on the other hand, the things themselves. But it is precisely this sharp distinction that ultimately threatens entirely to undermine Aristotle's defence of PNC conceived as a metaphysical principle (i.e. PNC-M).

Let us focus for a moment on how drawing a sharp distinction between appearances and the things themselves threatens to undermine Aristotle's defence of PNC-M. The defence was as follows: (P1/P3) Only if PNC is true of things, and things are not radically indeterminate, can we think and speak about things; but evidently, (P2) we can think and speak about things; therefore, (C1/C2) PNC is true of things, and things are not radically indeterminate. (Here P1/P3 and C1/C2 are simply the result of conjoining, for the sake of brevity, P1 with P3 and C1 with C2.) But now suppose that one draws a sharp distinction between appearances, i.e. things as they appear to us and in general as we conceive them, and the things themselves. Then one may argue that it is evident that (P2) we can think and speak about things, only if this means that:

> (P2-REL) We can think and speak of appearances, i.e. of things as they appear to us and as we conceive them.

For it is not evident, one may argue, that (P2) we can think and speak about things, if this means that:

> (P2-M) We can think and speak of the things themselves and of things *without qualification*.

But this shows that Aristotle's argument, if it succeeds at all, establishes only that:

> (C-REL) PNC is true of appearances, i.e. of things as they appear to us and as we conceive them.

(The argument will succeed in showing this, if we also introduce the same notion of things, i.e. things as they appear to us and as we conceive them, in its major premise, P1/P3.) But of course, Aristotle's real aim was to defend not (C-REL), but rather:

> (C-M) PNC is true of the things themselves and of things *without qualification*. (= PNC-M)

So if, as does phenomenalism and relativism, we draw a sufficiently sharp distinction between appearances and the things themselves, we may entirely undermine Aristotle's argument in defence of PNC-M and of the claim that the things themselves are determinate and well-defined.

Before we turn to Aristotle's response to this challenge, it is important to emphasize that he may not want to conduct the response on terms that phenomenalism and relativism accept. In particular, he may not think that there is such a sharp distinction between, on the one hand, things as they appear to us and as we conceive them and, on the other hand, the things themselves. That is to say, he may think that this distinction is not so sharp as to allow one to argue that although it may not be possible to think and speak of the things themselves, and although PNC may not be true of the things themselves, still we can think and speak about things as they appear to us and as we conceive them, and PNC may be true of them. So he may, ultimately, think that the distinction between the things themselves, or things *without qualification*, and things as they appear to us and as we conceive them, is such that if we can think and speak about things as they appear to us and as we conceive them, then we can also think and speak of the things themselves; i.e. we can think and speak about things *without qualification*.

2 The characterization of phenomenalism and relativism

Aristotle distinguishes carefully between phenomenalism and relativism. He characterizes phenomenalism as the claim that:

(PHEN)   Anything that appears thus and so to someone, and anything that someone believes to be thus and so, is thus and so (i.e. all appearances and all beliefs are true).

At the opening of IV. 5 he refers to 'the view of Protagoras' (1009^{a}6) as the view that 'all things believed [*ta dokounta panta*] and [all] appearances [*ta phainomena*] are true' (1009^{a}8). Later, when he distinguishes relativism from phenomenalism and considers how they are related (IV. 6, 1011^{a}17ff.), he refers to phenomenalism simply as the view that 'all appearances are true' (*pan to phainomenon alēthes* and *hapanta ta phainomena alēthē*, see 1011^{a}18 and ^{a}19–20).

Relativism, on the other hand, he characterizes as the view that:

(REL)   Anything that appears thus and so to someone, and anything that someone believes to be thus and so, is thus and so *for him* (i.e. all appearances and all beliefs are true *relative to the one who has them*).

It is important to distinguish, as Aristotle does here, between the claim that 'All appearances and all beliefs are true' (phenomenalism) and the claim that 'All appearances and all beliefs are true *relative to the person who has them*' (relativism). This is important especially since his aim here (in IV. 5–6) is above all to consider how phenomenalism and relativism are related to the denial of PNC and especially PNC-M (i.e. PNC conceived as a metaphysical principle). It is obvious that phenomenalism implies the falsity of PNC, at least if we add the evident fact that people contradict each other and hold contrary beliefs. For if all beliefs are true (i.e. phenomenalism) and if, as they do, people contradict each other and hold contrary beliefs, then any two contrary beliefs will both be true; so PNC will be false, and it will be false with regard to any two contrary beliefs. (Aristotle makes this point at the opening of IV. 5, 1009ª7–12.) On the other hand, it is not so obvious that relativism implies the falsity of PNC. It is even arguable that the two assertions, 'It is true *for N* that p' and 'It is true *for M* that q' (where N and M are different people, and p and q are the contents of their beliefs), cannot contradict each other at all. But if two assertions do not contradict each other, then they may both be true, and they may both be true even if PNC is true. In general, it is arguable that if the truth of a belief is relative to the person who holds the belief, then a belief of one person cannot contradict a belief of another person. But then no seeming conflict of belief between people can pose a threat to the truth of PNC. So it is obvious that phenomenalism implies the denial of PNC; but it is not at all obvious that relativism implies the denial of PNC. For this reason alone, it is important to distinguish between phenomenalism and relativism. We will consider later how exactly Aristotle thinks that phenomenalism and relativism are related to each other and to the denial of PNC and especially PNC-M. For he argues that those who think carefully about the source of phenomenalism, i.e. about the best line of reasoning in support of this view, will recognize that what this line of reasoning ultimately supports is, rather, relativism (see IV. 6, 1011ª22–24).

But it is also important to note that Aristotle distinguishes phenomenalism ('All appearances and all beliefs are true'), which is a primarily epistemological claim, from a version of phenomenalism that combines this epistemological claim with a metaphysical claim, a claim about all things. This claim says that:

1.   What there is includes only sense-perceptible beings, things that can appear to our senses.

(See 1010ª2–3: 'But they [the followers of Heracleitus, and in general some of those who defend phenomenalism] supposed that the beings include only the sense-perceptible beings.') So he thinks that some phenomenalists combine their view with the metaphysical claim that what there is includes only sense-perceptible things, i.e. they argue that:

2. (i) All our appearances and all our beliefs are true; and (ii) what there is includes only sense-perceptible beings – things that can appear to our senses.

But Aristotle also draws an important distinction between two different versions of relativism: an epistemological and a metaphysical version. For he distinguishes relativism, in the sense of the claim that all appearances and all beliefs are true relative to the person who has them, from relativism in the sense of the claim that:

(REL-M)   All things are what they are relative to other things, and nothing is what it is simply in virtue of itself.

(See 1011ª17). But relativism as he characterizes it here, i.e. as the view that 'all things are relative', is evidently a metaphysical claim, a claim about all things: all things are what they are relative to other things (*pros ti*), and nothing is what it is simply in virtue of itself (*auto kath' hauto*). This must be distinguished from relativism in the sense of the primarily epistemological claim that 'All appearances and all beliefs are true relative to the one who has them', i.e. a claim which limits the scope and the object of our sense perceptions and our beliefs to things as they appear to us and as we conceive them.

But we will see that he also distinguishes relativism in the sense of the primarily epistemological claim that 'All appearances and all beliefs are true relative to the one who has them' from relativism in the sense of a claim that combines this primarily epistemological claim with the metaphysical claim that 'All things are what they are relative to other things, and nothing is what it is simply in virtue of itself'. This combination results in the view that:

(REL-EP/M)   Anything that appears thus and so to someone, and anything that someone believes to be thus and so, is thus and so *for him*; and for something to appear thus and so *for someone*, and to be thus and so *for him*, is for it to be something that is thus and so *in relation to him, and especially in relation to his senses and his mind*.

Thus understood, relativism is at once an epistemological claim (which limits the scope and the object of our sense perceptions and our beliefs to things as they appear to us and as we conceive them) and a metaphysical claim (which says that the things that we sense and hold beliefs about are what they are only relative to our senses, and in general to our mind).

Why, in general, is Aristotle concerned not only with epistemological versions of phenomenalism and relativism, but also with versions that involve metaphysical claims? The reason is that, apparently, his aim here is above all to consider how phenomenalism and relativism are related to the denial of PNC-M (i.e. PNC conceived as a metaphysical principle). For his fundamental aim is to defend PNC conceived as a metaphysical principle: a principle that is true not only and not primarily of things as they appear to us and as we conceive them, but is true of the things themselves and of things *without qualification*.

Finally, it is important to emphasize a particular feature of Aristotle's characterization of both phenomenalism and relativism: the distinction which he draws between 'the things that appear to us' (or simply, 'appearances', *ta phainomena*) and 'the things that we believe' (*ta dokounta*, see esp. 1009ª8). By 'the things that appear to us' (*ta phainomena*), he means, in particular, things as they appear to our senses, i.e. the contents of our sense perceptions; whereas by 'the things that we believe' (*ta dokounta*) he means in general things as we believe them to be, i.e. the contents of our beliefs in general. So there may be things that we believe (*dokounta*), but which are not things that appear to us (*phainomena*); for perhaps not all our beliefs are based on what we perceive through the senses, or based directly in what we perceive through the senses. But may there, likewise, be things that appear to us, but which are not things that we believe? Evidently, there may. For example, the tower may appear round to one's sight, but one may not believe that it is round – if, for example, one is looking at it from a distance and one knows from experience that even square things may look round from a distance. So not all *phainomena* are *dokounta*.

But are at least some *phainomena* (i.e. things as they appear to our senses) *dokounta* (i.e. things as we believe them to be)? This depends on what exactly Aristotle means by a *phainomenon* here. Does he mean 'a thing's appearing, on the basis of sense perception, *to be* thus and so' or does he mean merely 'a thing's appearing, to one's senses, thus and so'? In other words, does a *phainomenon* involve the thought, 'perhaps what I am sensing *is* thus and so', or does a *phainomenon* not involve any such thought? For example, if a coin looks round to one, does this already involve the thought that perhaps it *is* round, or does it not involve any such thought? We can also formulate this question as follows: as Aristotle is using the term *phainomenon* here, do *phainomena* involve predicative or judgemental thought, i.e. thought of the form, 'perhaps what I am sensing *is* thus and so; or do *phainomena* not involve any predicative or judgemental thought? Apparently, Aristotle uses the term *phainomenon* in such a way that *phainomena* are ways in which things appear to us, on the basis of sense perception, *to be.* So *phainomena*, as he uses the term here, involve predicative or judgemental thought, i.e. thought of the form: 'perhaps what I am sensing *is* thus and so'. For only if he uses the term in this predication-involving or judgement-involving way can he assume, as he evidently does, that *phainomena* are true or false (or even merely: true or false relative to the one who has them). This is because the content of our mental states can be true or false only if this content involves a predicative or judgemental structure, i.e. a structure of the form: 'things *are* thus and so' or 'things *are not* thus and so'.

3 The aim of considering phenomenalism and relativism

Aristotle intends the examination of phenomenalism and relativism to contribute directly to the defence of PNC. For when (at the end of IV. 6) he concludes and summarizes the overall defence of PNC, he presents this conclusion as being at the same time the conclusion of his examination of phenomenalism and relativism. He summarizes the overall defence of PNC as follows:

> Let this, then, suffice to show [A] that the claim that contradictory statements cannot at once be true [i.e. PNC] is the most secure [*bebaion*] of all claims; and [B] what consequences are incurred by those who deny this claim; and [C] why those who deny it do so.
>
> (1011^{b}13–15)

(See Chapter 5§2 for these aims.) But the reference to [C] why those who deny PNC do so concludes, precisely, the examination (in IV. 5–6) of phenomenalism, relativism and their relation to the denial of PNC.

Evidently Aristotle does not accept phenomenalism or relativism, and he offers various objections to these views here (in IV. 5–6). So we may easily form the impression that his aim is directly to argue against these views. It emerges, however, that this is not really his aim; his aim is rather to trace the source of the denial of PNC and especially PNC-M, and in this way to defend PNC and PNC-M against those who deny them. In his words, the aim is 'to show . . . why those who deny this [i.e. PNC] do so' (1011^{b}13–15). For he will argue that the source of the denial of PNC and PNC-M, i.e. the best line of reasoning in support of the denial of PNC and PNC-M, is phenomenalism, relativism and certain other views that are themselves the sources of phenomenalism and relativism. (We will consider this argument in a moment.) We may say that his aim here is not so much directly to argue against certain views, as diagnostic, i.e. to trace the source of certain views and the best line of reasoning that can be set out in support of them – and especially of the denial of PNC and PNC-M.

It is important to recognize that although Aristotle offers various objections to phenomenalism and relativism, they are not really intended as direct arguments against these views. For his objections largely pre-suppose a number of his opposing views; indeed they largely amount to no more than a short summary statement of his opposing views. So if his aim were directly to argue against phenomenalism and relativism, he would manifestly have begged the question against them. But we have seen that, in his defence of PNC, he is especially concerned not to beg the question against those who deny PNC; he wants, on the contrary, to conduct the argument against those who deny PNC by relying as far as possible on shared assumptions.

His response to phenomenalism is conducted not by concentrating directly on the statement and formulation of this view, but by concen-trating rather on the source of this view, i.e. the best line of reasoning in its defence. But he will argue that an important part of the source of phenomenalism is a certain extreme view about the nature of all things: all things change always and in every way, and nothing is constant about anything (see 1010^{a}7ff.; we will return to this shortly). So it is in this way, apparently, that things are radically indeterminate; they are radically indeterminate because they change always and in every way and nothing is constant about them. But his response here (in IV. 5–6) to phenomenalism, and in particular to the view that all things are radically changing and radically indeterminate, consists largely in his stating his opposing views about all things and about changing things in particular (see 1010^{a}15–35). For he asserts that a process of change presupposes that there is something constant that underlies the change (1010^{a}16–22), and that although things may constantly change in virtually every way, there is a crucial way in which they are changeless: things are changeless in respect of their form (*eidos*, 1010^{a}22–25).

We may wonder what the point is of his stating his opposing account of change and changing things, if it is not directly to argue against phenomenalism, relativism and their source or sources. But here we should note how he concludes this response to phenomenalism and to the conception of change that leads to phenomenalism:

> We must show to them and convince them [i.e. the phenomenalists and those who defend this radical view about change] that there is a nature that is changeless [*akinētos tis phusis*].
>
> (1010ª33–35)

So Aristotle himself points out that it is not adequate simply to state his opposing account of change; rather, this account must itself be defended, and especially its most central claim must be defended, i.e. the commitment to something changeless. (It is plausible to think that here he is referring to his general view that changeless things are changeless in respect of their form. But he may also be referring to his more specific view that there is an absolutely primary being – a divine being, God – which is the ultimate explanation of all intelligible change, and that this absolutely primary being is in every respect changeless.) He does not undertake this defence here (in IV. 5–6), i.e. the defence of the claim that there are changeless things; rather this defence is a central part of the *Metaphysics* as a whole (especially books VII–IX and XII).

This suggests that there is an important programmatic and antici-patory side to his response to phenomenalism and relativism, and in general to his response to the denial of PNC and especially PNC-M. He wants to set out a programme of systematically developing an account of the nature of things in such a way that there is something funda-mentally changeless about changing things; for he wants to argue that only if there is something fundamentally changeless about changing things can changing things be not radically indeterminate, but deter-minate and well-defined. So, far from its being his aim in a few lines to refute phenomenalism, relativism and other views that lead to the denial of PNC and PNC-M, he thinks rather that an adequate response is really the task of metaphysics – and the *Metaphysics* – in general. In other words, the quick objections to phenomenalism, relativism and to other views that lead to the denial of PNC and PNC-M, which may at first strike us as question-begging and dogmatic, are best under-stood as programmatic and anticipatory. These objections set out an overall task, and they anticipate how, in broad outline, this task is to be carried out and what overall conclusions it is directed towards.

So it appears that Aristotle's aim here (in IV. 5–6) is not directly to argue against phenomenalism and relativism, but rather to trace the source of the denial of PNC and especially PNC-M. For he will argue that this source can be traced back to phenomenalism, relativism and further back to certain other views. (We will consider this argument in the following section.) But how can such a diagnostic examination contribute to the defence of PNC and PNC-M? Here we have above all to recall that his overall aim (in book IV. 3–6) is not to demonstrate the truth of PNC; on the contrary, he argues that PNC is such a basic and secure principle that its truth cannot be demonstrated. His aim is rather, as he said earlier, to defend PNC in an elenctic way (*elenktikōs*, see 1006ᵃ11f.), i.e. by responding to the arguments against PNC put forward by those who deny PNC. So what he wants to do here (in IV. 5–6) is to show that the denial of PNC and PNC-M has its source in phenomenalism, relativism and certain other views that are themselves the source of phenomenalism and relativism. But he is concerned with such a diagnosis of the source of the denial of PNC and PNC-M because he wants to argue that the views that lead to the denial of PNC and PNC-M do not in the end succeed in their aim – the aim of undermining PNC and PNC-M. But evidently, to argue that a certain view, V, does not succeed in undermining a certain other view, W, it is not necessary to argue directly against V; all that is required is to show that V does not entail the denial of W, or that those who argue that V entails the denial of W in the end find themselves in too much difficulty.

4 The relation between phenomenalism, relativism and the denial of PNC

i General

In general, Aristotle's examination of phenomenalism and relativism (in IV. 5–6) is diagnostic: he wants to trace these positions back to their source, i.e. to trace the line of reasoning – the best line of reasoning – that a defender of these positions can set out in support of them. But he will argue that, ultimately, the source of phenomenalism and relativism is the same as the source of the denial of PNC and especially the denial of PNC-M (i.e. PNC conceived as a metaphysical principle, i.e. a principle that is true not only and not primarily of things as they appear to us, but is true of the things themselves and of things *without qualification*). This root source, he will argue, is the view that things are radically indeterminate. So his general conclusion here is that the denial of PNC-M stands and falls with phenomenalism and relativism; for they all stand and fall with the view that things are radically indeterminate. We may also set out more rigorously the way in which Aristotle thinks that the denial of PNC-M is related to phenomenalism and relativism:

(P1) PNC is not true of the things themselves if, and only if, the things themselves are radically indeterminate.

(P2) The things themselves are radically indeterminate if, and only if, *either* all appearances and all beliefs are true (i.e. phenomenalism) *or* all appearances and all beliefs are true relative to the one who has them (i.e. relativism).

Therefore,

(C) PNC is not true of the things themselves if, and only if, *either* phenomenalism is true *or* relativism is true.

Earlier (in Chapter 5) we looked at length at premise P1, which he defends in IV. 4. Here (in IV. 5–6) Aristotle will defend premise P2, and we will concentrate on this defence now. The defence of premise P2 involves considerable complexity, but it can also be understood in a more general and informal way. (The following is an overall interpretation of IV. 5, 1009ª38–b15 and IV. 6, 1011ª17–b6. We will first present the argument in a general and informal way, then concentrate on its complex individual steps.) Suppose that we believe that the things themselves are radically indeterminate. Then it is natural to reason as follows: if the things themselves are radically indeterminate, then it is impossible to think or speak of the things themselves; so we can, at best, think and speak about things as they appear to us and as we conceive them. Kratylus, whom Aristotle presents as having ended up merely moving his finger, reasons in just this way (1010ª7–13): all things are always changing in every way, and there is nothing constant about anything, so in this way things are radically indeterminate; but then it is impossible to think or speak about anything at all – which is why he ended up merely moving his finger. Kratylus evidently takes this reasoning to an extreme and perhaps unnecessary conclusion: it is impossible to think or speak of anything at all.

But this extreme conclusion may be avoidable; for if we draw a sufficiently sharp distinction between the things themselves and things as they appear to us, then we may rather conclude that although it is impossible to think or speak of the things themselves (since they are radically indeterminate), we can still think and speak about things as they appear to us and as we conceive them. But this conclusion, apparently, is distinctive of phenomenalism and relativism. This is because it is distinctive of phenomenalism and especially of relativism to draw a sharp distinction between things as they appear to us and the things themselves, and to argue that we can only think and speak about how things appear to us, not about the things themselves. So the view that things are radically indeterminate leads naturally to phenomenalism and relativism. Of course, Aristotle does not himself defend the view that things are radically indeterminate – it is the disputant of PNC-M that defends this view. But Aristotle thinks that this view leads naturally to phenomenalism and relativism; for, like the disputant, he thinks that if things are radically indeterminate, then it is impossible to think or speak about things. In this way he traces phenomenalism and relativism back to an important source, i.e. he traces an important line of reasoning in support of these views. This reasoning starts from the supposition that things are radically indeterminate and concludes that we can think and speak about things only as they appear to us and as we conceive them – a conclusion distinctive of phenomenalism and especially of relativism.

But apparently Aristotle argues not only that the view that things are radically indeterminate leads naturally to phenomenalism and especially relativism; he also argues that, conversely, in particular phenomenalism leads naturally to the view that things are radically indeterminate. So he argues that the view that things are radically indeterminate is not only *a* source of phenomenalism and relativism; it is *the only* source, or *the best* source. This claim may strike us as implausible. After all, we are accustomed to philosophers urging that it is perfectly possible for us to make epistemological claims (phenomenalism and relativism, as they stand, are epistemological claims) without making any metaphysical claims (the view that things are radically indeterminate is evidently a metaphysical claim). Moreover, the relativist Protagoras, as Plato presents him in the dialogue *Theaetetus* (166e–167d), appears to emphasize that an important source of relativism is not metaphysical, but ethical or pragmatic. For Protagoras, as Plato presents him here, argues that to possess knowledge is not at all a matter of knowing objective truths; it is simply a matter of knowing how to persuade people to believe things, and to do things, that are beneficial to them, and not to believe things, or do things, that are harmful to them. (Here we may note that Aristotle is thoroughly familiar with Plato's dialogue, the *Theaetetus*, indeed he refers to it here; see 1010^b11–14, which refers to *Theaetetus* 178c and 171e. In general, there are strikingly close parallels between Aristotle's diagnosis of the source of phenomenalism and relativism in *Metaphysics* IV. 5–6 and Plato's diagnosis of the source of the view that knowledge is perception in *Theaetetus* 151d–184b.) But perhaps it would be wrong to make too much of this general objection to Aristotle here, i.e. the objection which says that the source of phenomenalism and relativism may be ethical or pragmatic, not metaphysical. For if we bear in mind that his overall aim here is to defend PNC conceived as a metaphysical principle, then we can appreciate why he concentrates in particular on metaphysical sources of phenomenalism and relativism.

But Aristotle's approach here, and especially his response to phenomenalism and relativism, may also stimulate us to examine our own confidence that epistemological claims can be entirely divorced from metaphysical claims. For we will see that he has what appears to be a forceful and non-dogmatic response to a radical dissociation of epistemology from metaphysics; for, in his response to phenomenalism and relativism, he argues that there is not a sharp distinction between, on the one hand, how things appear to us and how we conceive them (hence things considered from the point of view of our natural search for knowledge, which starts with how things appear to us) and, on the other hand, the things themselves. On the contrary, he argues that, on the one hand, our natural search for knowledge must start with things as they appear to us and as we conceive them; but that, on the other hand, it is precisely the things themselves that we are investigating in this search for knowledge. So, if we find this view attractive, i.e. the view which says that there is a seamless continuum between appearances and the things themselves, we may ourselves be less inclined to assume that epistemological claims, i.e. claims about things as they appear to us and from the standpoint of our natural search for knowledge, can be readily divorced from metaphysical claims, i.e. claims about the things themselves.

So we can see why, in general, Aristotle thinks that the view that things are radically indeterminate, and hence the radical denial of PNC, stands and falls with phenomenalism and relativism. But he presents a complex argument for this conclusion, which we will consider next.

ii Tracing the source of phenomenalism and of the denial of PNC

STEP 1

At the opening of IV. 5, Aristotle states that the source of the radical denial of PNC is, precisely, phenomenalism, and that these two views stand and fall together (see 1009a6–7). In other words:

1. PNC is not true of anything if, and only if, all appearances and all beliefs are true.

Here the radical denial of PNC is the claim that any thing is at once thus and so (i.e. F) and not thus and so (i.e. not-F), and that this is so with regard to any property or quality F. (See 1009ª11–12. He also states the radical denial of PNC by saying that all things are at once true and false; see 1009ª9. For if it is true that a thing is F, it is also false that it is F, since it is at once not-F; and if it is true that a thing is not-F, then it is also false that it is not-F, since it is at once F.) The argument for this claim (i.e. claim 1) is relatively straightforward (see 1009ª8–16). Suppose, on the one hand (1009ª8–12), that all appearances and all beliefs are true, i.e. suppose phenomenalism. Since people generally contradict each other and hold contrary beliefs, contradictory beliefs will at once be true. So PNC will be false. (Strictly, to obtain the result that PNC will not be true *of anything*, we need to add that people can have beliefs, and indeed contradictory beliefs, *about anything*.) Suppose, on the other hand (1009ª12–15), that any thing is at once thus and so (i.e. F) and not thus and so (i.e. not-F), and that this is so with regard to any quality F, i.e. suppose the radical denial of PNC. Then the belief that a thing is F will be true (since the thing is F) and likewise the belief that a thing is not-F will be true (since the thing is at once not-F). So contradictory beliefs will at once be true. But if we suppose, further, that to believe something about something is *either* to believe that it is thus and so (i.e. F) *or* to believe that it is not thus and so (i.e. not-F), then we may conclude that all beliefs will at once be true. So, in general, phenomenalism is the source of the radical denial of PNC, and the two views stand and fall together (i.e. claim 1 is true).

STEP 2

Aristotle's next step is to ask: what is the source of phenomenalism itself, i.e. what is the best line of reasoning that a defender of phenomenalism can set out in support of their position? (see 1009ª38–ᵇ2) Since they have just argued that phenomenalism stands and falls with the radical denial of PNC, the quest for the source of phenomenalism is at the same time a quest for the source of the radical denial of PNC. It emerges that the line of reasoning in support of phenomenalism involves considerable complexity and needs to be traced with particular care (see 1009ᵇ2–1010ª15). First, part of the source of phenomenalism is, apparently, the observation that there is conflict among the sense perceptions of different people – and indeed of the same person at different times, or the same person at the same time but in respect of different senses (e.g. sight and touch). For example, the wine that tastes sweet to the healthy person tastes bitter to a person that is ill (see 1009ᵇ3–5; it is interesting to compare Plato's *Theaetetus*, e.g. 166e1–4). Indeed, there is conflict in general among the beliefs of different people. For example, people that are mad, or temporarily beside themselves, think thoughts and hold beliefs different from and conflicting with those of sane people (see 1009^{b}4–6, ^{b}28–33). In short:

2. Sense perceptions, and beliefs in general, conflict with each other.

STEP 3
The fact that sense perceptions, and beliefs in general, conflict with each other may be part of the source of phenomenalism, but evidently it is not sufficient to generate phenomenalism. For perhaps there is a way, or ways, of determining which sense perceptions and beliefs are true and which are false. If there is such a way, or ways, we evidently need not conclude that all sense perceptions (or all appearances based on sense perceptions) and all beliefs are true. So we need not conclude that phenomenalism is true. But perhaps phenomenalism will emerge, if we think not only that sense perceptions and beliefs conflict, but that there is no adequate way of determining which sense perceptions and beliefs are true and which false, i.e. if we think that there is no criterion of truth with regard to sense perceptions and in general with regard to beliefs. So, in order to generate phenomenalism, we need to add:

3. It is apparently impossible to resolve conflicts among sense perceptions and in general among beliefs.

In this way Aristotle points out that this claim (i.e. 3) is an important part of a line of reasoning in support of phenomenalism (see 1009^{b}2f.).

STEP 4
But will phenomenalism emerge, even if we suppose that sense perceptions and beliefs conflict (i.e. 2) and that apparently it is impossible adequately to resolve such conflict (i.e. 3)? Aristotle points out an important reason for thinking that the combination of these two views (i.e. 2 and 3) is still not sufficient to generate phenomenalism. For even if, for example, some wine appears to some people to be sweet, but appears to other people not to be sweet, and even if apparently such conflict cannot be resolved, i.e. even if apparently we cannot know whether the wine itself really is sweet or not sweet, still we need not conclude that the wine is at once sweet and not sweet (i.e. the conclusion required by phenomenalism). For we may instead conclude that the wine itself is either sweet or not sweet, but not both; but that apparently we cannot know which it is. In general, suppose we think that sense perceptions and beliefs conflict, and that apparently we cannot

resolve such conflicts. From these two claims we may conclude not that all sense perceptions and all beliefs are true (i.e. phenomenalism), but rather that although, at most, some sense perceptions and beliefs are true, apparently we cannot know which are true and which are not. So we may rather conclude that:

4.   The truth is hidden from us or not evident to us.

(See 1009^{b}9–12 for this claim. The term *adēlon* here may mean either 'hidden' or, what is more likely, 'not evident'.) We may naturally call this claim 'scepticism', i.e. the claim that:

5.   Things have certain qualities as opposed to others (they are thus and so, as opposed to not thus and so), but apparently we cannot know what qualities they have. (= scepticism)

So the point is that claims 2 and 3 need not generate phenomenalism, for they may instead generate scepticism. In other words:

6.   (2 and 3) entails *either* phenomenalism *or* scepticism.

This line of argument in support of scepticism, we may note, became especially prominent much later in ancient scepticism, and in particular in the synthesis and summary of scepticism that we find in the sceptic Sextus Empiricus (second century AD). For it became standard for the ancient sceptics to argue that because appearances and beliefs conflict, and because apparently there is no way of resolving such conflict, we should cease making claims about how things really are and should limit ourselves to reporting how things appear to us – we should suspend judgement about the things themselves (*epechein*, hence *epochē*, 'to suspend judgement'). (See Annas and Barnes 1985 for a good introduction to ancient scepticism, and especially for this argument in support of scepticism: the argument from conflicting appearances and in general conflicting beliefs.)

For our present purpose, however, it is important carefully to distinguish scepticism from phenomenalism and relativism. Scepticism argues that apparently we cannot know what the things themselves are really like; but it assumes that the things themselves really are thus and so as opposed to not thus and so, and that we can think about and make claims about how the things themselves may really be. Phenomenalism, on the other hand, argues that things are both thus and so and not thus and so; and relativism argues that it is impossible – in principle and not just for us – even to think about or make claims about how things may really be, it is only possible to think about and make claims about how things are relative to us, our appearances and our conception of things.

STEP 5

So what must the defender of phenomenalism add to claims 2 and 3 in order to generate precisely phenomenalism as opposed to scepticism? Evidently, they must add something that will serve to undermine the view that the truth is hidden from us or not evident to us (i.e. claim 4) – the view behind scepticism. They may naturally do so by defending the following claim:

> 7. Our sense perceptions and beliefs are only of things as they appear to us and as we conceive them; they are not about the things themselves.

For example, if some wine appears sweet to one, and if one goes on on this basis to believe that the wine is sweet, then this belief is not (according to claim 7) at all about the wine itself, it is only about the wine as it appears to one and to one's taste. This claim (i.e. 7) serves naturally to undermine the option of scepticism and the view that the truth is hidden from us or not evident to us; for although the things themselves may be hidden from us or not evident to us, it is not plausible to think that how things appear to our senses, or, in general, things as we conceive them, may be hidden from us or not evident to us. On the contrary, if there is anything that is not hidden from us and that is evident to us, it is how things appear to our senses, and, in general, how we conceive things. So if we argue that what we perceive with our senses, and, in general, what we believe, is not the things themselves, but only things as they appear to our senses, and, in general, as we conceive them, then we may undermine the option of scepticism. (The above is an interpretation especially of Aristotle's highly compressed argument in 1009^{b}9–15.)

But we must note an important presupposition of claim 7. For this claim presupposes that:

> 8. There is a sharp distinction between, on the one hand, things as they appear to us and in general things as we conceive them and, on the other hand, the things themselves; indeed, this distinction is so sharp that we can think and speak about appearances even if it is impossible to think and speak about the things themselves.

We will see later that Aristotle's response to phenomenalism and relativism is especially directed against this presupposition of phenomenalism and relativism.

STEP 6
This goes a long way towards tracing the source of phenomenalism, i.e. tracing the best line of reasoning available to the defender of phenomenalism. Still, we have not yet succeeded in generating phenomenalism. For the combination of claims 2, 3 and 7 still does not entail phenomenalism. Phenomenalism claims that:

9. All our appearances and all our beliefs are true.
    (= phenomenalism)

But claims 2, 3 and 7 entail at most that:

10. All our appearances and all our beliefs are true *of things as they appear to us and as we conceive them*.

But we cannot simply assume that for a belief to be true of things as they appear to us and as we conceive them is the same as for a belief to be, simply, true. We can see that it would be wrong to assume this, if we suppose that:

11. It may be possible *in principle* to think and speak of the things themselves, even if it is not possible *for us* to think and speak of the things themselves (hence even if *we* can only think and speak about things as they appear to us and in general as we conceive them).

As we might say, it may be possible for God, or in general for a being whose knowledge does not at all depend on sense perception and on appearances based on sense perception, to think and speak of the things themselves, even if this is not possible for us, or, in general, for a being whose knowledge depends on sense perception and on appearances based on sense perception. According to claim 11, there may be true and false statements about the things themselves, i.e. statements that truly or falsely state what the things themselves are like, even if we cannot entertain such statements – perhaps God alone can entertain such statements. We cannot entertain such statements because, according to claim 7, we can only think and speak about things as they appear to us and as we conceive them; we cannot think or speak of the things themselves.

So what must we add to claims 2, 3 and 7 in order to ensure that the combination of these claims entails not only that all our appearances and all our beliefs are true of things as they appear to us and as we conceive them (i.e. claim 10), but that all our appearances and all our beliefs are, simply, true (i.e. phenomenalism)? Evidently, we must add that:

12. It is impossible to think or speak of the things themselves; and this is impossible *in principle*, not just *for us*.

But, apparently, the best way of defending claim 12 is, precisely to claim that:

13. The things themselves are so radically indeterminate that it is impossible to think and speak of them (i.e. this is impossible *in principle*, not just *for us*).

This is precisely the claim that Kratylus, and in general the followers of Heracleitus as Aristotle understands them, defend (see 1010^{a}7–15). In particular, they defend this claim by arguing that:

14. All things change always and in every way, and there is nothing constant about anything.

So they argue that things are radically indeterminate because things change always and in every way and nothing is constant about anything; and they conclude that it is impossible to think and speak about things (i.e. this is impossible *in principle*, not just *for us*). But, as Aristotle understands them, they defend these claims (i.e. 13 and 14) in order to defend phenomenalism and the radical denial of PNC (we recall that the radical denial of PNC stands and falls with phenomenalism; see claim 1 above). Here Aristotle also makes a penetrating observation: this way of defending phenomenalism and the radical denial of PNC amounts, in effect, to reducing reality to reality as it appears to us and especially to our senses ('they [i.e. the followers of Heracleitus] supposed that the beings include only the sense-perceptible beings', 1010^{a}2–3).

In this way, Aristotle traces phenomenalism, and the radical denial of PNC, back to their root source: claims 2, 3, 7, 8, 13 and 14. So we see that, central to the source of phenomenalism, and of the radical denial of PNC, is the view that the things themselves are radically indeterminate (i.e. 13); but also the view that there is a sharp distinction between, on the one hand, things as they appear to us and in general

things as we conceive them and, on the other hand, the things themselves (i.e. 8). For if the things themselves are radically indeterminate,
then it is impossible (in principle and not just for us) to think and speak
about the things themselves; but if there is a sharp distinction between
appearances and the things themselves, then it may still be possible for
us to think and speak about how things appear to us and in general
about things as we conceive them.

So, if we take account of the best line of reasoning in support of
phenomenalism, we see that phenomenalism leads to the view that, on
the one hand, PNC is not true of the things themselves, i.e. it leads to
the radical denial of PNC conceived as a metaphysical principle; but that,
on the other hand, it may still be possible for us to think and speak
about things, namely of things as they appear to us and in general as
we conceive them. But evidently this presents a serious challenge to
Aristotle's overall aim; for his aim was to defend PNC as a metaphysical principle, i.e. a principle that is true of the things themselves and
of things *without qualification*; and to do so by arguing that we can
think and speak about things only if PNC is true of things. So Aristotle
has set himself the highest challenge: to argue, against phenomenalism
and relativism, that PNC is true not only and not primarily of things
as they appear to us and as we conceive them, but of the things themselves and of things *without qualification*.

iii A central consequence of phenomenalism and the denial of PNC: relativism

Before we turn to Aristotle's response to this challenge, we should note
that, so far (i.e. in IV. 5), he has been concerned with diagnosing the
source of phenomenalism; he has not yet introduced relativism. He
introduces relativism (in IV. 6) as follows:

[1011ª17–20] But if it is not the case that all things are relative [*pros
ti*], but there are also some things that are themselves by themselves
[*auta kath' hauta*, i.e. if some things are what they are not in virtue
of their relation to other things, but simply in virtue of themselves],
then it will not be the case that all appearance is true [i.e. phenomenalism will be false]. For an appearance is an appearance *for someone*
[i.e. relative to someone]. So those who claim that all appearances
are true make all beings relative [*pros ti*].

[ª21–24] For this reason, too, those who want to trace the force of
the argument, and who at the same time are prepared to submit to

argument, must take care to assert not that appearance is true [i.e. phenomenalism], but rather that appearance is true *to the one to whom it appears, and at the time when it appears, and in the respect in which it appears, and in the way in which it appears* [i.e. relativism].

(1011ª17–24)

Here Aristotle makes two claims: first (1011ª17–20), phenomenalism, i.e. the view that all appearances (and all beliefs) are true, entails metaphysical relativism, i.e. it entails the view that:

(REL-M)   All things are what they are relative to other things, and nothing is what it is simply in virtue of itself.

Second (1011ª21–24), if we observe that phenomenalism entails metaphysical relativism, and if at the same time we take account of the best line of reasoning in support of phenomenalism (i.e. the reasoning set out in IV. 5, which we have traced above), then we will recognize that this line of reasoning leads not so much to phenomenalism, but to relativism, i.e. it leads to the view that:

(REL)   Anything that appears thus and so to someone, and anything that someone believes to be thus and so, is thus and so *for him* (i.e. all appearances and all beliefs are true *relative to the one who has them*).

His argument for these two claims is highly compressed, but perhaps it can be understood as follows. First, why does he think that phenomenalism entails metaphysical relativism? Suppose that there is a thing that is F not in virtue of its relation to any other thing, but simply in virtue of itself (i.e. suppose that metaphysical relativism is false). It follows immediately that it is not the case that this thing is F in virtue of its relation to our senses. If it were F in virtue of its relation to our senses, then it would not be F simply in virtue of itself. But if the thing is F not in virtue of its relation to our senses, but simply in virtue of itself, i.e. if the thing is F independently of us and our senses, then, presumably, we can be mistaken in our beliefs about it; i.e. we may believe, perhaps on the basis of how this thing appears to our senses under certain conditions, that the thing is G (where G is different from and contrary to F). But then it will not be the case that all our sense perceptions, and in general all our beliefs about this thing, will be true. So, if we suppose that metaphysical relativism is false, then it follows that phenomenalism is false. In other words, phenomenalism entails metaphysical relativism.

Second, why does he think that if we observe that phenomenalism entails metaphysical relativism, and if at the same time we take account of the best line of reasoning in support of phenomenalism (i.e. the reasoning set out in IV. 5), then we will recognize that this line of reasoning leads not so much to phenomenalism, but to epistemological relativism? To understand this argument we need (as Aristotle indeed indicates here) to recall the reasoning behind phenomenalism, and in particular the claim that:

1. Our sense perceptions, and in general our beliefs, are only about things as they appear to us and as we conceive them; they are not about the things themselves. (= claim 7 in the previous subsection)

But it is perhaps natural to understand this claim to mean that:

2. Our sense perceptions, and in general our beliefs, are only of things that are what they are only relative to our senses, and in general to our minds; they are not about things that are what they are simply in virtue of themselves.

The difference between 1 and 2 is that claim 1 is a primarily epistemological claim, which limits the scope and the object of our sense perceptions and our beliefs to things as they appear to us and as we conceive them. Claim 2, on the other hand, contains also a metaphysical claim, namely, the claim that the things that we sense and hold beliefs about are what they are only relative to our senses, and in general to our mind.

Evidently, 1 does not directly entail 2. But 1 does entail 2 if we add metaphysical relativism. So we can see why Aristotle thinks that the line of reasoning in support of the view that all perceptions and all beliefs are true (i.e. phenomenalism) is really a line of reasoning in support of the view that all perceptions and all beliefs are true *relative to the one who has them* (i.e. relativism). Now we can also see more clearly what this relativism amounts to; for it amounts to the claim that:

(REL-EP/M) Anything that appears thus and so to someone, and anything that someone believes to be thus and so, is thus and so *for him*; and for something to appear thus and so *for someone*, and to be thus and so *for him*, is for it to be something that is thus in so *in relation to him, and especially in relation to his senses and his mind*.

Thus understood, relativism is evidently at once an epistemological claim (which limits the scope and the object of our sense perceptions and our beliefs to things as they appear to us and as we conceive them) and a metaphysical claim (which says that the things that we sense and hold beliefs about are what they are only relative to our senses, and in general to our mind).

So here (in IV. 6) Aristotle argues that, if we take account of the best line of reasoning in support of phenomenalism, we will, ultimately, recognize that this line of reasoning leads to relativism – relativism in precisely this sense (i.e. REL-EP/M). But previously (in IV. 5) he argued that phenomenalism stands and falls with the radical denial of PNC, and that to defend phenomenalism one must, in particular, deny PNC-M (i.e. PNC conceived as a metaphysical principle – a principle that is true of the things themselves and of things *without qualification*). So his overall conclusion (in IV. 5–6) is that the denial of PNC-M stands and falls with relativism. Since the denial of PNC-M stands and falls with the view that the things themselves are radically indeterminate, his overall conclusion is that:

(C) PNC is not true of the things themselves, and the things themselves are radically indeterminate, if, and only if, relativism is true (i.e. REL-EP/M).

So it is precisely relativism (in the sense of REL-EP/M) that he must respond to in order to defend PNC conceived as a metaphysical principle. This completes Aristotle's diagnosis of the source of the denial of PNC and PNC-M – the diagnosis that appeals to phenomenalism, relativism and to their sources in turn – and so his diagnosis of the challenge that he has to answer in order to defend PNC-M.

5 How far does Aristotle succeed in defending PNC conceived as a metaphysical principle?

Aristotle's defence of PNC-M (i.e. PNC conceived as a metaphysical principle – a principle that is true of the things themselves and of things *without qualification*) is not a direct defence; it is rather an indirect defence, which consists of responding to those who deny PNC-M. But he wants to respond to those who deny PNC-M by tracing their denial to its root source, i.e. by tracing the best line of reasoning in support of the denial of PNC-M, and by responding to this line of reasoning. We have seen that an important part in the reasoning for the denial of PNC-M involves the views that:

1.   Our sense perceptions and beliefs are only of things as they appear to us and as we conceive them; they are not about the things themselves; and

2.   There is a sharp distinction between, on the one hand, things as they appear to us and in general things as we conceive them and, on the other hand, the things themselves; indeed, this distinction is so sharp that we can think and speak about appearances even if it is impossible to think and speak about the things themselves.

It is above all these views that Aristotle responds to in order to respond to the reasoning behind the denial of PNC-M. Thus in an important and striking passage (at the end of IV. 5) he directly argues against the view that our perceptions are only of things as they appear to us:

> [1010^{b}30–35] But in general, if only what is sense-perceptible exists, then nothing would exist if there were no minds [*empsucha*, i.e. things that have senses and in general souls or minds]; for there would be no sense perception. Now, the view that neither sense-perceptible things nor sense perceptions exist may perhaps be true; for sense perception is an affection of a thing that has sense perception. But the view that the underlying things, which produce the sense perception [in a thing that has sense perception], do not exist without the sense perception – this view is impossible.
>
> [1010^{b}35–1011^{a}2] For sense perception is not simply directed at itself, rather there is also something other than [*heteron*] and distinct from [*para*] the sense perception, which is necessarily prior to the sense perception. This is because that which causes change [*to kinoun*] is naturally prior to that which is caused to change [*to kinoumenon*] – and this is so even if these are said to be correlative.
>
> (1010^{b}30–1011^{a}2)

In this striking passage (and especially 1010^{b}35–1011^{a}1), Aristotle makes three fundamental and closely related claims: first (^{b}35–36), what we perceive with our senses are objects other than and distinct from our sense perceptions; second (^{b}34 and ^{b}37–1011^{a}1), the objects that we perceive are the objects that cause our sense perceptions; and third (^{b}36–37), the objects that we perceive are essentially prior to our sense perceptions, i.e. they are independent of and causally explanatory of our sense perceptions. We may call this, 'a causal realist theory of sense perception'. It is a causal theory because it argues that the objects that we perceive are the objects that cause our sense perceptions. It is a realist theory because it argues, first, that what we perceive with our senses are objects other than and distinct from our sense perceptions and, second, that the objects that we perceive are essentially prior to our sense perceptions, i.e. they are independent of and causally explanatory of our sense perceptions.

What is especially striking, and fascinating, about this whole passage is that the causal realist theory of sense perception (in 1010^{b}35–1011^{a}1) is set against a theory of sense perception which we, following Berkeley, may not hesitate to call, 'subjective idealism' (see 1010^{b}30–35). For the causal realist theory of sense perception is set against a view which claims that 'nothing would exist if there were no minds' (1010^{b}30–31). But if we read the passage in its context, we see that this view, i.e. the view which says that 'nothing would exist if there were no minds', is rather an extreme form of metaphysical relativism; it is a view that makes all reality relative to us and to our senses. But Aristotle (in 1010^{b}31–35: the lines italicized) directly rejects this extreme form of relativism; and he rejects it precisely by defending a causal realist theory of sense perception.

For our purpose, what matters especially in this passage is that Aristotle, by defending a causal realist theory of sense perception, rejects the view that our sense perceptions and beliefs are only of things as they appear to us and as we conceive them, and not about the things themselves (i.e. he rejects claim 1 above). And he rejects the view that there is a sharp distinction between the things themselves and things as they appear to us and especially our senses (i.e. he rejects claim 2 above). For he argues that what appears to our senses is, precisely, the things themselves, i.e. things that are different from (*hetera*), distinct from (*para*), and prior to (*protera*) our perceptions of them; and he argues that there is a direct relation between the things themselves and our perceptions of them – a causal relation.

So Aristotle rejects a central part in the reasoning in support of the denial of PNC-M. More positively, however, his causal realist theory of sense perception allows him to argue that if we can think and speak about things as they appear to us, and in particular to our senses, then we can also think and speak of the things themselves. For our sense perceptions are caused by the things themselves and, as a consequence, they are of the things themselves. We recall that those who deny PNC-M do so by arguing that the things themselves are radically indeterminate, hence PNC is not true of them and it is impossible to think or speak of them. But they conclude that things as they appear to us may be sufficiently determinate for PNC to be true of them and for us to be able to think and speak of them. But now Aristotle argues that how things appear to us and especially to our senses is the product of how the things themselves act on our senses; and that it is this causal relation between the things themselves and our senses that explains how we can perceive things in the first place. So it emerges that the only or the best explanation of why things as they appear to us and to our senses are sufficiently determinate for PNC to be true of them and for us to be able to think and speak of them is, precisely, that the things themselves are determinate and that PNC is true of them. So we see that Aristotle argues that the only or the best explanation of why things appear determinate to us and our senses, and that PNC is true of them, is that the things themselves are determinate and PNC is true of them. But this shows that if we can think and speak about things as they appear to us, which evidently we can, then we can also think and speak of the things themselves. In this way Aristotle defends PNC as true not only and not primarily of things as they appear to us and in general as we conceive them, but as true also of the things themselves and of things *without qualification*. This completes an important part of his defence of PNC-M.

This is a penetrating and highly interesting defence of PNC-M. However, there is an obvious problem with it, for the disputant of PNC-M will evidently not want to accept the causal realist theory of sense perception, on which the defence is based. So has Aristotle perhaps begged the question against the disputant of PNC-M? To consider this, it may help to remind ourselves that these lines (at the end of *Metaphysics* IV. 5), which merely state the causal realist theory of sense perception, are only a summary statement of Aristotle's theory of sense perception, which he defends carefully and at length, especially in the *De Anima*. So these few lines are evidently not supposed to be the last word.

But if we look a little further (than the end of IV. 5), we see that it may not after all be Aristotle's aim to base the defence of PNC-M solely on the causal realist theory of sense perception. Rather, his aim is to present the disputant of PNC-M with the following challenge: how will *he*, the disputant, want to explain why PNC is true at least of things as they appear to us, and why at least things as they appear to us are determinate? How will he do this, if not by arguing that PNC is true of the things themselves and that the things themselves are determinate? The latter explanation is, of course, Aristotle's, and it relies on the causal realist theory of sense perception. So the challenge is this: does the disputant have a better explanation of why PNC is true of things as they appear to us, and why things as they appear to us are determinate?

Thus shortly after the passage at the end of IV. 5 (i.e. in IV. 6, 1011ᵃ31–ᵇ1) Aristotle emphasizes that even those who argue that the things themselves are radically indeterminate, and that PNC is not true of them and it is not possible to think or speak of them, must admit that PNC is at least true of things as they appear to us and our senses, and that at least appearances are not radically indeterminate; and they must admit this even if they defend an extreme form of relativism. For example, they must admit that if something, at a particular time, appears red to one's sight, or to one's sight in a certain respect (e.g. to one's left eye), then it does not, at that particular time, appear not-red to one's sight, or to one's sight in that particular respect (e.g. to one's left eye). But how will those who deny PNC-M, and who claim that the things themselves are radically indeterminate, explain why PNC is true at least of things as they appear to us, and that at least things as they appear to us are not radically indeterminate? Aristotle provides an explanation: it is because the things themselves are determinate, and PNC is true of them, that the things as they appear to us are determinate and PNC is true of them. But evidently this explanation will be not acceptable to the disputant of PNC-M. So it appears that the disputant of PNC-M must argue, on the one hand, that things as they appear to us are determinate and that PNC is true of them but, on the other hand, that this determinacy does not require further explanation, i.e. it does not require an explanation that appeals to anything other than the things as they appear to us. But this, in effect, amounts to thinking that the things as they appear to us are determinate *in virtue of themselves and not in virtue of their relation to other things – and in particular not in virtue of their relation to the things themselves* (See 1011ᵇ1: 'But then this [i.e. things as they appear to us, to the extent that these things are determinate and PNC is true of them] will be [what is] true'. Note especially that he does not say 'true *for someone*', but simply 'true'.)

This challenge to the disputant of PNC-M begins to look like a promising defence of PNC-M, and a defence that is not dogmatic or question-begging. But it is at the same time a defence that is to a large extent programmatic and anticipatory. For it will emerge later in the *Metaphysics* that precisely the appeal to determinacy is a candidate answer to the question, 'What is primary being (*prōtē ousia*, often simply *ousia*)?' and 'What is it for something to be a primary being?' So ultimately the appeal to determinacy is a candidate answer to the question, 'What is being?' and 'What is it for something, anything, to be?' Thus Aristotle has already argued (in IV. 1–2, which we discussed in Chapter 4) that the answer to the question 'What is being?' must, in general, take the following form: for something, anything, to be a being, something that is, is for it to be *either* a primary being *or* a being that depends for its being a being, something that is, on its relation to a primary being. But he will argue later (especially in book VII, the central book of the *Metaphysics*) that a candidate answer to the question 'What is primary being?' is, precisely, this: for something to be a primary being is for it to be something determinate (i.e. something that is F, for some specific F) in virtue of itself and not in virtue of its relation to other things. Indeed, we will see that this candidate answer to the question, 'What is primary being?', is precisely the answer that Aristotle will defend.

So it emerges that, apparently, the disputants of PNC-M are in effect conceiving of the things as they appear to us, i.e. of appearances, as if they were primary beings. For they think that the things as they appear to us are determinate in virtue of themselves and not in virtue of their relation to other things – and in particular not in virtue of their relation to what they themselves, the disputants, conceive as the things themselves. But to be something determinate in virtue of itself is, precisely, a good candidate answer to the question: 'What is it for something to be a primary being?'

Clearly, this begins to look like a formidable challenge to the disputants of PNC-M. For suppose, on the one hand, that the disputants simply accept that it is the appearances that are the primary beings. Then it will be difficult for them at all to distinguish appearances from the things themselves. We may recall that they want to distinguish appearances from the things themselves, since their whole point against PNC-M is that PNC may be true only of appearances and not of the things themselves. For surely, if something is a primary being, then *it*, precisely, is one of the things themselves – it is a being *without qualification*. After all, if the notion of *the things themselves* has any meaning, it means, presumably, *things that are beings without qualification*; and it contrasts with the notion of *things that are beings only in virtue of their relation to other things* (e.g. their relation to us and our senses). So the disputant cannot simply accept that it is the appearances that are primary beings.

So let us suppose, on the other hand, that the disputant of PNC-M does not want to accept that it is the appearances that are primary beings. Then he must argue that appearances are not primary beings even though they are something determinate in virtue of themselves. But to argue this, he must, ultimately, ask: 'What is primary being?' and 'What is it for something to be a primary being?' So he must engage in Aristotle's own project: metaphysics.

At the end of the day, this may be just what Aristotle wants when (in IV. 5–6) he defends PNC-M against those who deny it. He wants to show that those who deny PNC-M *either* fail successfully to defend the denial of PNC-M *or* they can begin to argue for the denial of PNC-M only by engaging in metaphysics – the project of asking 'What is being?' and 'What is primary being?' This is a formidable defence of PNC-M, and in general of PNC, especially because Aristotle has argued (in IV. 4) that PNC-M, and in general PNC, is a necessary condition for the possibility of thought and language. So it emerges that Aristotle's response to those who deny PNC-M is simply this: *either* you make thought and language impossible *or*, if you want even to begin arguing that thought and language is possible while PNC-M is false, you must engage in metaphysics – the project of asking 'What is being?' and 'What is primary being?'

In sum, Aristotle has argued that we must engage in metaphysics, i.e. in the project of asking 'What is being?' and 'What is primary being?', and we must search for an answer to these questions, if we at all want to consider how thought and language is possible. In other words, metaphysics is fundamental even to logic. So we cannot escape metaphysics simply by having recourse to logic. This shows that, ultimately, the aim of the examination of PNC is to provide vital motivation for engaging in Aristotle's overall project, metaphysics – indeed to show that this project is, in a way, inescapable. In this way, the examination of PNC occupies a pivotal position in the *Metaphysics*.

We may also recall that this was one of the first *aporiai* that he raised in book III, the book of *aporiai*: *Is it the task of a single science to investigate both the ultimate principles of being and the basic principles of reasoning (e.g. the principle of non-contradiction)? Or is this the task of fundamentally different sciences?* (see the second *aporia*, 996^{b}26–997^{a}15) The question in this *aporia* was how metaphysics, i.e. the science of the nature of being, is related to logic, i.e. the science of the basic principles of reasoning and rational thought (e.g. the principle of non-contradiction). Does metaphysics include logic, or is logic independent of metaphysics? And if the latter is the case, is logic perhaps more fundamental than metaphysics? Aristotle has now (at the end of IV. 6 and in general at the end of book IV) defended an answer to this fundamental *aporia*: logic is not independent of metaphysics; on the contrary, logic requires metaphysics.

7

THE SEARCH
FOR PRIMARY BEING

(Book VII)

1 The question at the centre of the *Metaphysics:* 'What is primary being?' (*prōtē ousia*, often simply *ousia*) (VII. 1–2)

In a striking and memorable statement at the end of the first chapter of book VII, Aristotle indicates his overall aim in these central books of the *Metaphysics* (i.e. books VII–IX):

> Indeed, that which is always, both now and long ago, sought after and which is always a source of puzzlement, i.e. the question, *What is being?*, is really the question, *What is primary being?* [*ousia*]. . . . So we too must, most of all, primarily, and so to speak exclusively, investigate about that which is being in this way [i.e. that which is being in the primary way]: what is it?
>
> (1028^{b}2–7)

As he has earlier (in IV. 1–2) characterized metaphysics, the basic question of metaphysics is the question, 'What is being?' But this question, as he emphasizes here, is far from his own invention. On the contrary, it is as old as the trees, never ceasing to be 'that which is sought after' (*to zētoumenon*) and 'a source of puzzlement' (*to aporoumenon*, i.e.

something that puzzles us and that we puzzle about). So, having raised this basic question of metaphysics, 'What is being?', at the opening of book IV, he now wants to take it up and search for an answer to it. But he says that we must address this question, 'What is being?', by directly associating it with another question: 'What is primary being?' (We will return in a moment to the translation of *prōtē ousia*, and in general *ousia*, as 'primary being'.) For he says: 'the question, *What is being?*, is really the question: *What is primary being (ousia)?*' It will emerge that to search for an answer to the question 'What is primary being?', and so to search in just this way for an answer to the basic question, 'What is being?', is Aristotle's overall aim in the central books of the *Metaphysics* (VII–IX).

Why does Aristotle directly associate the basic question of metaphysics, 'What is being?', with the question, 'What is primary being?'? And how are we to understand this peculiar question, 'What is primary being?'? To consider this, we need to go back to his original introduction (in IV. 1) of the question 'What is being?', and to his original introduction (in IV. 2) of the general notion, *primary being (prōtē ousia, often simply ousia)*. (We discussed this at length earlier, in Chapter 4, §§1–3; the following is a recapitulation.) We recall that the basic question of metaphysics, 'What is being?', and in particular 'What is being *qua* being?', gave rise to a fundamental *aporia* about the very possibility of metaphysics: how is it possible even to conceive of being *qua* being and meaningfully to ask, 'What is being *qua* being?' and 'What is it for something, anything, to be?'? Aristotle himself raised this *aporia* in book III, the book of *aporiai* (see the third *aporia*, 997^{a}15–25, and part of the seventh *aporia*, 998^{b}22–27). Summarily, the *aporia* was this: we cannot conceive of being *qua* being, i.e. of what it is for something, anything, to be, by distinguishing this from not-being; but neither can we conceive of being *qua* being as the sum of all the kinds of beings that there are. So, apparently, we cannot conceive of being *qua* being at all, either by distinguishing it from something outside it, i.e. from not-being, or by distinguishing it from what is inside it, i.e. by conceiving of it as the sum of all the kinds of beings that there are and in general as the sum of everything that there is.

When (in IV. 2) Aristotle introduced the general notion, *primary being*, and the general distinction between *primary being* and *non-primary being*, he did so precisely in order to answer this *aporia* about the very possibility of meaningfully asking: 'What is being *qua* being?' Summarily, the answer to the *aporia* was this. Suppose that we cannot conceive of being as a whole either by distinguishing it from something outside it or by distinguishing it from what is inside it. Perhaps we can still conceive of being as a whole, if we suppose that there is a distinction between things that are beings simply in virtue of themselves (i.e. primary beings) and things that are beings in virtue of their relation to those things (i.e. non-primary beings). For then we can conceive of being as a whole in the following way: by supposing that anything that is, i.e. any being, is a being *either* simply in virtue of itself and not in virtue of its relation to other things (in which case it is a primary being) *or* in virtue of its relation to a primary being (in which case it is a non-primary being).

The aim of Aristotle's distinctive answer to this *aporia* is to show that we can ask the basic question of metaphysics, 'What is being?', only if we do so by asking, 'What is primary being?' In other words, if we are at all to search for an answer to the question: 'What is being?' and 'What is it for something, anything, to be?', we must from the start suppose that the answer must take the following form: for something to be a being, something that is, is for it *either* to be a primary being, i.e. something that is a being simply in virtue of itself, *or* to be a non-primary being, i.e. something that is a being in virtue of its relation to a primary being. So if we are at all to ask the basic question of metaphysics, 'What is being?', we must above all ask: 'What is primary being?' This is just what Aristotle says at the end of VII. 1: 'So we too [i.e. like other thinkers that have asked the basic question, 'What is being?'] must, most of all, primarily, and so to speak exclusively, investigate about that which is being in this way [i.e. that which is being in the primary way]: what is it?' (1028^{b}6–7).

So we see that Aristotle's direct association here (in VII. 1) of the basic question of metaphysics, 'What is being?', with the peculiar question, 'What is primary being?', is the consequence of his raising and answering, earlier in the *Metaphysics*, an *aporia* about the very notion, *being*, and the very question, 'What is being?' We also see how the peculiar notion, *primary being*, is to be understood. In general, to be a primary being is to be something that is a being simply in virtue of itself and not in virtue of its relation to other things, whereas to be a non-primary being is to be something that is a being in virtue of its relation to a primary being. In other words, to be a primary being is to be something that directly explains what it is for itself to be, i.e. for a primary being to be, and explains indirectly also what it is for non-primary beings to be, i.e. things that are beings in virtue of their relation to a primary being. In sum, this notion, *primary being*, is the notion: *that which ultimately explains what it is for something, anything, to be*. Aristotle will make explicit this characterization of primary being at the end of book VII, when he says that *ousia* is the 'ultimate explanation of the being of each thing (*prōton aition tou einai* [*hekastou*])' (VII. 17, 1041^{b}27–28). But this is the notion of primary being that he is working with from the start of book VII, and indeed since IV. 2, when he says that to answer the question, 'What is being?', the basic question of metaphysics, is really to answer the question, 'What is primary being?' For to answer the question, 'What is being?', is to determine *in virtue of what* something, anything, is a being; i.e. to determine *what explains why* something, anything, is a being. But it has emerged that such an explanation must crucially appeal to primary being, and it must take the following form: for something to be a being is for it *either* to be a primary being, i.e. something that is a being simply in virtue of itself, *or* to be a non-primary being, i.e. something that is a being in virtue of its relation to a primary being (see also this chapter, §4).

So the central question in the central books of the *Metaphysics* is, 'What is primary being (*ousia*)?' And addressing this question serves above all to address the basic question of metaphysics, 'What is being?' It is interesting to note (both from the passage at the end of VII. 1 and especially from what he says in VII. 2) that Aristotle thinks that different thinkers argue for very different answers to just this question: 'What is primary being?' For example, materialists argue that it is above all the basic material elements of physical bodies, such as the elements fire, water and earth, that are primary beings (see VII. 2, 1028^{b}8f.). But Plato and the Platonists argue that what is primary being above all is certain everlasting beings that are distinct from (*para*) the sense-perceptible and physical things; i.e. they argue that the forms (*eidē*) are the primary beings (see 1028^{b}18f.). This, we may note, is nicely summed up also at the beginning of book XII:

> The present-day thinkers hold that the universals are more properly primary beings. . . . But the past thinkers hold that the particulars are more properly primary beings, such as fire and earth, but not what is common to both, i.e. *body*.
>
> (XII. 1, 1069^{a}26–30)

So Aristotle thinks that just as he shares the basic question, 'What is being?', with other thinkers, so the question, 'What is primary being?', is a shared one. His view here, apparently, is that other thinkers, too, want to explain in virtue of what something, anything, is a being, and that they, too, argue that this explanation will take the following form: for something to be a being is for it *either* to be something that is a being simply in virtue of itself *or* to be something that is a being in virtue of its relation to a primary being. Platonists, for example, argue

that the forms are beings simply in virtue of themselves (*auta kath'
hauta*, which is Plato's standard phrase for the forms) whereas sense-
perceptible things are beings only in virtue of their relation to the forms
– the relation to which he variously refers as 'participation' and 'communion' (see, for example, *Phaedo* 100d). But materialists argue that
the basic material elements of physical bodies, such as the elements fire,
water and earth, are beings simply in virtue of themselves, whereas
the physical bodies that are composed out of these elements are beings
only in virtue of their relation to the elements in them, i.e. the relation
of physical composition.

So Aristotle thinks that the question, 'What is primary being?', is
common to very different thinkers, and that very different answers can
be defended in response to it. This has two important consequences.
First, he does not immediately (in book VII) associate this question with
any one particular answer. In particular, he does not associate it with
his own earlier answer – the one that he defended in the *Categories*.
In the *Categories* he argued that primary being with regard to each
thing is simply the ultimate subject of predication (*to hupokeimenon*)
with regard to that thing; i.e. primary being is simply that of which
other things are true but which is not itself true of other things. (See
Chapter 4§4 for the theory of the *Categories*.) We will see shortly that
here (in VII. 3) he will argue that although being an ultimate subject
of predication may be a necessary condition of primary being, it is not
a sufficient condition. At the opening of VII. 3 he will set out three very
different candidates for primary being: the ultimate subject; the universals; and the essence. (We will consider these candidates in a moment.)
This also confirms that he does not immediately associate the question,
'What is primary being?', with any one particular answer.

Second, it is wrong to translate *ousia* as 'substance', or *prōtē ousia*
as 'primary substance'. For the claim that *prōtē ousia* is substance is a
particular answer to the question, 'What is *prōtē ousia*?' It is not what
the term *prōtē ousia* means in the question, 'What is *prōtē ousia*?' The
Latin term *substantia*, which literally means 'that which lies under',
translates Aristotle's term *to hupokeimenon*, i.e. 'that which lies under'
(from *hupokeisthai*, 'to lie under'). It is true that in his earlier work,
the *Categories*, he argues that *prōtē ousia* is simply *to hupokeimenon*.
But this is a particular view about what *prōtē ousia* is, i.e. a particular
answer to the question, 'What is *prōtē ousia*?' It is not what the term
prōtē ousia means or what the question 'What is *prōtē ousia*?' is asking.
We have chosen to use the term 'primary being' for *prōtē ousia* and in
general for *ousia*.

We have focused on how (at the beginning of books VII–IX, the central books of the *Metaphysics*) Aristotle understands the question, 'What is primary being?', and its relation to the basic question of metaphysics, 'What is being?' But this has also indicated something of Aristotle's distinctive method in these central books of the *Metaphysics*. For it has suggested that the method is dialectical and above all *aporia*-based. It is dialectical in so far as the search for an answer to the two central questions of metaphysics, 'What is being?' and 'What is primary being?', is to be conducted by investigating very different and apparently conflicting answers, answers that are, in one way or another, defended by different thinkers. It is *aporia*-based at least in so far as the very question, 'What is primary being?', and the very notion, *primary being*, are directly associated with certain fundamental *aporiai* and largely originate in such *aporiai*.

This raises an intriguing general question: is Aristotle's aim here, in the central books of the *Metaphysics*, to defend a single overall answer to the question, 'What is primary being?', i.e. to defend a systematic theory of primary being, or is his aim rather to show that different answers may be required in response to this question, 'What is primary being?', depending on what *aporia* associated with this question we are addressing? It will emerge (at least on our reading, for this issue is controversial) that he does indeed want to defend a single overall answer, i.e. a systematic theory of primary being. At the same time, this theory is developed largely by engaging with *aporiai* associated with the question, 'What is primary being?' And in general Aristotle recognizes that if something is a genuine *aporia*, then, even once one has answered it to one's satisfaction, and perhaps done so by developing a systematic theory, still it will not cease to puzzle one, and competing answers will not cease to exercise their attraction on one. Perhaps this is what he means when he says memorably, at the end of VII. 1, that the question, 'What is being?', is *always* a source of searching and *always* a source of puzzlement and *aporia*: 'that which is always, both now and long ago, sought after and which is always a source of puzzlement, i.e. the question, *What is being?*, is really the question, *What is primary being? . . .*' (1028b2–4).

2 Initial suggestions and candidates for what primary being may turn out to be (VII. 1)

At the opening of book VII, Aristotle introduces two initial suggestions and candidates for what primary being may turn out to be.

These suggestions and candidates are supposed to be at least initially plausible as answers, or partial answers, to the question, 'What is primary being?'

First suggestion

Primary being with regard to each thing is the essence (*to ti estin*) of that thing (see VII. 1, 1028ª13–20, especially 13–15). For example (1028ª15–18), suppose that we are thinking about a particular thing, and suppose that we think that it is a human being, and pale, and warm, and five foot tall, etc. If we ask what is primary being with regard to this thing, we will naturally answer not that primary being with regard to it is for it to be pale, or warm, or five foot tall, even if all these things are true of it, but rather that primary being with regard to it is for it to be, precisely, human. Here Aristotle assumes that to be human is the essence of the thing about which we are thinking – the particular human being.

The reasoning in this example appears to be this. Even if the thing about which we are thinking, the particular human being, is in fact pale, or warm, or five foot tall, it is not a being, something that is, in virtue of being pale, or warm, or five foot tall. For it is not its being pale, or warm, or five foot tall that ultimately explains why this thing is a being, something that is. This is because such things as being pale, warm or five foot tall are themselves beings only in virtue of their relation to, precisely, such things as a particular human being (see 1028ª18–20). Rather, the thing that we are thinking about is, apparently, a being, something that is, precisely in virtue of being human, i.e. in virtue of its essence. For, apparently, it is its being human, and in general its essence, that ultimately explains why it is a being, something that is. This last point in particular, although it may appear plausible, will need especially to be defended.

Second suggestion

Primary being with regard to each thing is the ultimate subject of predication (*to hupokeimenon*) with regard to that thing and the particular (*to kath' hekaston*) that this thing is (see 1028ª25–27). For example (1028ª20–31), if we are puzzled about whether such things as walking, sitting or being healthy are beings at all, then we may naturally argue that such things are not beings in virtue of themselves (*kath' hauta*), but rather, if anything, it is a particular human being, i.e. one that is walking, sitting or healthy, and of which these things, walking, sitting and being healthy, are true, that is a being in virtue of itself. We recall that, in general, to be a primary being is to be something that is a being in virtue of itself and not in virtue of its relation to other things. So we will naturally conclude that such things as walking, sitting or being healthy are beings only in virtue of their relation to other things, i.e. the relation, *being true of another thing*; and that primary being is rather, if anything, that of which such things as walking, sitting or being healthy are ultimately true. In general, we may conclude that primary being with regard to each thing is, if anything, the ultimate subject of predication with regard to that thing and the particular thing that this is.

We may summarize these initial candidates for primary being and non-primary being as follows. Primary being with regard to each thing (e.g. Socrates) is either the essence of that thing (e.g. being human) or the ultimate subject of predication with regard to that thing (e.g. the particular thing that Socrates is); and non-primary being with regard to each thing is the qualities that are true of that thing (e.g. being pale or healthy), and the quantities that are true of that thing (e.g. being five foot tall), and in general the things that are different from and true of the ultimate subject of predication.

This is exactly how Aristotle, at the opening lines of book VII, indicates that the distinction between primary being and non-primary being is to be filled in:

> Being is said in many ways . . .; for it signifies, on the one hand, *what something is* [*ti esti*, i.e. the essence of something] and *a this-such* [*tode ti*, i.e. the ultimate subject of predication] and, on the other hand, a quality, or quantity, or each of the other things that are said [i.e. said of a thing and in general true of a thing] in this way.
>
> (1028ª10–13)

Here he indicates, 'on the one hand', the two initial candidates for primary being, i.e. the essence and the ultimate subject of predication, and 'on the other hand', the initial candidate for non-primary being, i.e. the things that are different from and true of the ultimate subject of predication. So a good way of understanding these first lines of book VII, which may otherwise seem abrupt and unprepared, is as serving above all to introduce an initially plausible way of filling in the distinction between primary being and non-primary being, i.e. to introduce some initial suggestions and candidates for what primary being and non-primary being may turn out to be. We will consider in a moment the important term here, *a this-such* (*tode ti*), and why he uses this term for what is, apparently, a reference to the ultimate subject of predication (*to hupokeimenon*; see 1028ª26 for this term in VII. 1). It is also important to note that he says that primary being is the essence '*and*' (*kai*) the ultimate subject of predication; for this suggests that these two candidates are supposed to be conjoined and to add up to a single unitary answer to the question, 'What is primary being?'

What, in general, is Aristotle's aim in straight away (at the opening of book VII) setting out these two candidates for primary being, i.e. the essence and the ultimate subject of predication? Apparently his aim is above all simply to get the search for primary being started. It is important not to suppose that his aim, at this early stage, is more ambitious. It is true, and very important, that these two candidates indicate something of his own answer to the question, 'What is primary being?', i.e. the answer that he will defend in the course of book VII. For Aristotle will eventually argue that:

> Primary being with regard to each thing is the essence of that thing; and the essence of each thing is identical with the ultimate subject of predication with regard to that thing.

(We will consider this at length later.) So his aim in immediately setting out these two candidates for primary being is to a large extent programmatic and anticipatory. But his main aim here is more limited: it is simply to get the search for primary being started. First of all, the arguments that he gives here in defence of each of these two candidates (see 1028ª13–31; i.e. the arguments that we have just considered) are evidently far from conclusive or even generally persuasive. So it is natural to think that their aim is only a limited one, i.e. to provide some initial plausibility for some initial suggestions and candidates for primary being, and so to get the search for primary being started.

Finally, what does Aristotle mean by the phrase 'a this-such' (*tode ti*), and why does he use this phrase to refer to the ultimate subject of predication? Apparently, the demonstrative expression, 'this' (*tode*), serves to refer to an ultimate subject of predication as such, i.e. simply as an ultimate subject; for example, it may refer to this thing, Socrates (here one points to Socrates). The expression, 'such' (*ti*), on the other hand, serves to signify the essence of the ultimate subject to which one is pointing; for example, it may signify the fact that this thing, Socrates, is essentially a human being. So the whole phrase, 'a this-such', signifies an ultimate subject together with its essence; for example, 'this human being'. If we ask why Aristotle uses this phrase to refer to the ultimate subject of predication, then it may well be because he wants to indicate by its use that (as he will argue later, see below, §5v of this chapter) the relation between an ultimate subject and its essence is not a relation between two things, but a relation between a thing (the *this*) and itself (the *such*).

3 Three main candidates for primary being: the ultimate subject of predication; the universals; and the essence (VII. 3)

So far (in VII. 1), Aristotle has introduced two main candidates for primary being: the essence and the ultimate subject of predication. But at the opening of VII. 3 he introduces a third: the universals. He says that:

> Primary being [*ousia*] is spoken of, if not in even more ways, then certainly in four main ways. For [1] the essence, [2a] the universal and [2b] the genus are thought to be primary being with regard to each thing, and also, fourthly, [3] that which underlies these.
>
> (VII. 3, 1028^{b}33–36)

The genus of a thing is itself a universal: it is the most general kind to which the thing belongs. So we may here ignore the distinction between universals that are genera and universals in general, and we may consider the two under the single heading, i.e. the universals. We may also note that in the book of *aporiai*, book III, Aristotle himself distinguishes the most general question, whether primary being is the universals (see the fifteenth *aporia*, 1003^{a}5–17), from the more particular questions: whether primary being is the kinds to which a thing belongs and, if so, how general these kinds will be (see the sixth and seventh *aporiai*, 998^{a}20–999^{a}23).

Apparently, Aristotle introduces this candidate for primary being, i.e. the universals, because he has just mentioned (in VII. 2) that certain thinkers, i.e. Plato and the Platonists, argue that primary being is the changeless forms, which exist 'apart from' or 'besides' or 'over and above' (*para*) sense-perceptible and in general changing things; i.e. they exist distinct from changing things. But, in general, Plato's forms, certainly as Aristotle understands them, are universals, i.e. things that are true of other things and of many things. For example, the one thing, *being human*, is true of other things and of many things: Socrates, Plato, etc. So we may associate the view that primary being is the universals with Plato and the Platonists, as Aristotle understands them. And we may associate the view that primary being is simply the ultimate subject of predication with his own earlier view, in the *Categories* (see Chapter 4§4, for this view). The view that primary being is the essence is the view that he will defend here, in the central books of the *Metaphysics*. But he will argue that the essence, once it has been properly understood, is identical with the ultimate subject of predication, once *it* has been properly understood.

So these, it emerges, are the main candidates for primary being:

(1) the ultimate subject of predication;
(2) the universals; and
(3) the essence.

Can we perhaps stand back and in some way see why Aristotle thinks that just these are the main candidates for primary being? An attempt to do so is offered in Chapter 1§4.

4 Primary being and separation (ontological independence) (VII. 1)

Early in book VII Aristotle says that primary being is separate being (*chōriston*, 'separate'):

> For none of the other things that are said [i.e. the non-primary beings] are separate; but primary being [*ousia*] alone is separate.
>
> (VII. 1, 1028ª33–34)

(See also XII. 1, 1069ª24–30 for this same claim, and for the view that many and various philosophers have, both now and in the past, committed themselves to it.) So the claim is that primary being is separate being, whereas non-primary being is not separate being. This claim is evidently also about Aristotle's preferred candidates for primary being, i.e. the essence and the ultimate subject of predication (we will return to this point below, in §5iv of this chapter). But it is above all about primary being in general and the very notion of primary being, hence about any candidate for primary being. So he thinks that any philosopher that raises the question, 'What is primary being?', will naturally think of primary being as separate being, i.e. separate from non-primary being; for to think of primary being as separate being is part of the very notion of primary being.

But what does Aristotle mean by 'separate' (*chōriston*) when he says that primary being is separate being? This claim means, apparently, that primary being is independent of non-primary being, whereas non-primary being is dependent on primary being. We may also refer to this claim as the claim that primary being is ontologically independent of non-primary being, whereas non-primary being is ontologically dependent on primary being. For it is natural to use the term 'ontology' for the theory of what it is for something, anything, to be; and we will see that the claim that primary being is separate being is a central ontological claim. But what kind of dependence and independence does Aristotle have in mind? Apparently, he has in mind a very particular kind of explanatory independence and dependence. For the claim that primary being is separate being is about the very notion of primary being. But this notion is, precisely, the notion: that which ultimately explains what it is for something, anything, to be; and which does so by directly explaining what it is for itself (i.e. for primary being) to be and indirectly explaining also what it is for anything else (i.e. for non-primary being) to be. (See §1 of this chapter for this point, also Chapter 4§§1–3.) In general, primary being is separate from non-primary being in just this sense: it does not depend for its being a being on its relation to anything else (i.e. to non-primary being). And non-primary being is not separate from primary being in just this sense: it depends for its being a being on its relation to primary being. This, we recall, is the fundamental distinction between primary beings and non-primary being as introduced already in book IV. 2: for something to be a primary being is for it to be a being simply in virtue of itself (*kath' hauto*) and not in virtue of its relation to other things; and for something to be a non-primary being is for it to be a being only in virtue of its relation to other things (*pros ti*). So the claim that primary being is separate being (in VII. 1) does not introduce a new idea; it simply serves to capture the original characterization of the very notion of primary being.

It is crucial to recognize also what kind of separation Aristotle does not have in mind when he says that primary being is separate being. This is crucial especially because, in his criticism of Plato in particular, he tends to use the term 'separate' in a different sense or senses.

First, when he says that primary being is separate from non-primary being, he does not mean that primary beings and non-primary beings are distinct from one another, e.g. that they exist in different places. Here we may also note that the notion of distinctness is symmetrical: if x is distinct from y, then y is distinct from x. But the notion of primary being is, precisely, asymmetrical: primary being is separate from non-primary being, but non-primary being is, precisely, not separate from primary being. We recall that when he initially (here, in VII. 1) set out to make plausible the two suggestions and candidates for primary being, i.e. the essence and the ultimate subject of predication, he said that a primary being is, for example, a human being, i.e. the ultimate subject and the particular; or it is what it is to be human, i.e. the essence of the ultimate subject and of the particular. And he set these primary beings against, for example, being pale, or five foot tall, or healthy, or walking or sitting, etc., which are each of them non-primary beings. But evidently he does not think that a human being, or what it is to be human, on the one hand, and being pale, five foot tall, etc., on the other hand, are two sets of distinct things, e.g. things that exist in different places. This is evident from his examples, but especially from his criticism of Plato's view that universals are distinct from sense-perceptible and in general changing particulars. Being pale, for example, is a universal, since it is true of other things and many things; and a human being is a sense-perceptible and changing particular. In general, Aristotle tends to use the word *para* ('in addition to', 'besides') when he wants to consider whether two things are distinct from one another. When this is his concern, he will generally ask whether the one thing exists 'in addition to' or 'besides' (*para*) the other. But he criticizes Plato for thinking that universals are distinct from sense-perceptible and in general changing particulars (see Chapter 9, especially §4).

Second, when he says that primary being is separate from non-primary being, he does not mean that a primary being can exist without non-primary beings existing in relation to it. None of the candidates for primary being that he mentions (e.g. in VII. 1–2), whether they are his own or those that he attributes to other thinkers, imply that a primary being can exist without a non-primary being existing in relation to it. Consider, for example, a particular human being, or its essence, i.e. Aristotle's own preferred candidates for primary being. Evidently they cannot exist without non-primary beings, such as being pale, healthy, etc., being true of them and so existing in relation to them. In particular, it does not follow from the claim that a particular human being, or its essence, are primary beings, i.e. that they are beings simply in virtue of themselves and not in virtue of their relation to other things, e.g. to things such as being pale, healthy, etc., that they can exist without such things as being pale, healthy, etc., also existing in relation to them and being true of them.

Or consider the materialists' candidate for primary being, i.e. the material elements of things, e.g. the elements fire, earth or water, from which all things are composed. One may think that all other things are beings because they are composed of the material elements, but also at the same time think that the elements can exist only as part of compound material things that are composed out of them.

Or consider the Platonic candidate for primary being, i.e. the universals. One may think that the universals are the primary beings; and one may think that this is because the particulars are, in virtue of themselves, completely indeterminate and depend, for their determination, on their relation to the universals. (See §3 of this chapter for this point.) But one may at the same time think that universals cannot exist without being true of particulars – they cannot exist without being instantiated in particulars. So one may, without contradiction, think both that the universals are the primary beings and that they cannot exist without particulars also existing in relation to them. Here we need to remember that, on this view, the particulars are non-primary beings, since they depend on universals for their determination. It is true that, as Aristotle understands him, Plato thinks that universals can exist separately from particulars, in the sense of 'separate' in which this means that universals can exist without being true of particulars, hence without particulars existing in relation to them. But this is not, we should note, simply a consequence of Plato's thinking that universals are separate, in the sense of 'separate' in which this means that universals do not depend for their being beings, things that are, on their being true of particulars, hence on particulars existing in relation to them.

In general, it is crucial to recognize that we cannot infer from the claim that one thing, x, is ontologically independent of another thing, y, that x can exist without y existing (or, without y existing in relation to x). In other words, we cannot infer from:

P.   x is a being simply in virtue of itself and not in virtue of its relation to any other thing, y,

that

Q.   x can exist without y existing (or, without y existing in relation to x).

P asserts that something, x, does not depend on anything else, y, for its being a being, something that is. But Q asserts that x can exist without y existing (or, without y existing in relation to x). To see that P does not entail Q, let us recall what it means to say that something, x, does not depend on anything else, y, for its being a being, something that is. This means that it is not the case that x is a being in virtue of its relation to anything else, y; i.e. what explains what it is for x to be a being, or why x is a being, is not its relation to anything else, y. But from this we cannot infer that x can exist without anything else, y, existing in relation to it. In general, we cannot infer from:

P*. What explains what it is for x to be a being, or why x is a being, is not its relation to any other thing, y,

that:

Q. x can exist without y existing (or, without y existing in relation to x).

This is because quite generally we cannot infer from:

P**. What explains what it is for x to be F, or why x is F, is not its relation to y,

that:

Q. x can exist without y existing (or, without y existing in relation to x).

In other words, we cannot infer an existential independence from an explanatory independence.

The distinction between these two kinds of independence – explanatory and existential independence – is very important. It was clearly articulated by Plato in the dialogue *Euthyphro* (9–11). Plato asks us to consider the relation between two sets of things: the things that are holy (or, in general, good); and the things that are loved by perfect beings such as the gods. He further asks us to consider that these two sets of things may coincide: all things that are good are loved by the gods, and all things that are loved by the gods are things that are good. Indeed, he suggests that this coincidence may even be necessary. The gods are, after all, perfect beings, so they will love good things and good things only; and if, as befits gods, they also know all things, then they will love all good things. Still, Plato argues, there remains the question of explanatory priority: are good things good because they are loved by the gods, or do the gods love good things because they, the good things, are good?

In general, Aristotle apparently uses the term 'separate' in three ways:

Separation 1. A thing, x, is a separate being if, and only if, x is a being simply in virtue of itself and not in virtue of its relation to anything else, y. (= ontological independence)

Separation 2. A thing, x, is separate from another thing, y, if, and only if, x and y are distinct from one another. (= distinctness)

Separation 3. A thing, x, is separate from another thing, y, if, and only if, x can exist without y existing (or, without y existing in relation to x). (= separable existence)

We have seen that separation 1 does not entail separation 3; i.e. a thing, x, may be ontologically independent of another thing, y, without being capable of existing without y existing (or without y existing in relation to x). The relation between separation 2 and separation 3 is less clear, and we will return to it later (in Chapter 9§4).

5 Aristotle's answer: primary being is the essence of each thing

i A summary of Aristotle's account of primary being

In book VII, Aristotle sets out to answer the question, 'What is primary being?' This project will occupy us at length in what follows, but an initial synoptic summary of his conclusions may be useful. Above all, he argues that:

A. Primary being with regard to each thing is the essence of that thing.

But he also argues that:

B. The essence of each changing, material thing is the form of that thing.
   So the essence of each changing, material thing is neither simply the matter of that thing nor a combination of its form and its matter.

From these two claims he concludes that:

C. Primary being with regard to each changing, material thing is the form of that thing.
   So primary being with regard to each changing, material thing is neither simply the matter of that thing nor a combination of its form and its matter.

He summarizes claims A, B and C when he says that:

> By form [*eidos*] I mean the essence [*to ti ēn einai*] of each thing and
> its primary being [*prōtē ousia*].
>> (VII. 7, 1032ᵇ1–2; see also 1032ᵇ14 and 1037ª29–30)

By 'I mean' (*legō*) here, he does not mean that this is simply what the
words 'form' (*eidos*), 'essence' (*to ti ēn einai*) and 'primary being' (*prōtē
ousia*) mean. Rather, he is summarizing here the meaning of his own
distinctive view, which is that the essence of each changing, material
thing is its form, and that the essence and the form of each changing,
material thing is exactly what primary being is with regard to that thing.

But he argues further that there is an important sense in which:

D. The essence of each thing, on the one hand, and the ultimate
    subject of predication with regard to each thing, on the other
    hand, are not two different things, but one and the same
    thing. In short, the essence is identical with the ultimate
    subject of predication.

This allows him to conclude that:

E. Primary being with regard to each thing is both (1) the
    essence of that thing and (2) the ultimate subject of
    predication with regard to that thing.

He summarizes claims D and E when, at the end of a difficult argument
in VII. 6, he concludes that:

> Thus it is clear that, with regard to primary things [*ta prōta*] . . ., the
> essence of each thing and each thing are one and the same.
>> (VII. 6, 1032ª4–6; see also 1031ᵇ11–14,
>> 18–20 and VII. 11, 1037ª33–ᵇ4)

(We will return to this argument later, see Chapter 9§§5–6.) For when
he says here that each thing is identical with its essence, he means by
'each thing' the ultimate subject of predication. So it is the ultimate
subject of predication, on the one hand, and the essence, on the other
hand, that he claims are really one and the same.

In this way Aristotle defends the view which he put forward to begin
with (at the opening of book VII; see §2 of this chapter). There he stated
that primary being with regard to each thing is both:

(1) the essence of each thing, and
(2) the ultimate subject of predication with regard to each thing.

For, to defend this view, one must argue that the two candidates for primary being, i.e. the essence and the ultimate subject of predication, necessarily pick out one and the same set of things, i.e. they pick out precisely the primary beings. But this is just what he defends when he argues that (D) the essence of each thing, on the one hand, and the ultimate subject of predication with regard to each thing, on the other hand, are not two different things, but one and the same thing.

Since he argues that (C) primary being with regard to each changing, material thing is the form of that thing, he concludes that:

F.   The essence and the form of each changing, material thing, on the one hand, and the ultimate subject of predication with regard to each changing, material thing, on the other hand, are not two different things, but one and the same thing. In short, the essence and the form is identical with the ultimate subject of predication.

This allows him to conclude that:

G.   Primary being with regard to each changing, material thing is both (1) the essence and the form of that thing, and (2) the ultimate subject of predication with regard to that thing.

These claims (i.e. A–G) summarize most of Aristotle's account of primary being, which he develops in the course of book VII. In what follows, we will examine them one by one. We will also consider what he means by *the essence of a thing* (*to ti ēn einai, to ti estin*), since his main claim is that (A) primary being with regard to each thing is the essence of that thing. This also reflects the structure of the first chapters of book VII. For, after having introduced the search for primary being (in VII. 1–2), he sets out on this search by first clarifying what he means by *essence* and what things have an essence (VII. 4–5).

However, before Aristotle turns (in VII. 4–5) to the notion of essence, and (in VII. 6) to the claim that primary being with regard to each thing is the essence of that thing, he begins (in VII. 3) with an argument for an important negative conclusion:

H.   Primary being with regard to each changing, material thing is not simply the ultimate subject of predication with regard to that thing.

We should also note that he will later (in VII. 13–16) defend a further very important negative conclusion:

I. Primary being with regard to each changing, material thing is not the universals that are true of that thing.

So let us begin with the claim that (H) primary being with regard to each thing is not simply the ultimate subject of predication with regard to that thing.

But first, one important point of clarification is necessary. Aristotle clearly distinguishes between the question, 'What is primary being with regard to each thing?' and the question, 'What is primary being with regard to each changing, material thing?' In particular, the claim that (A) primary being with regard to each thing is the essence of that thing, is about all things, not just changing, material things. By contrast, the claim that (C) primary being with regard to each changing, material thing is the form of that thing, is not about all things, but only about changing, material things. For it is changing, material things that Aristotle conceives as things that result from form and matter. Indeed, the notion of *form* is correlative to the notion of *matter*, and both notions are elements in an account of changing things, and, in particular, things that are subject to generation and destruction. (See Chapter 2§4.) In book VII, and in general in the central books of the *Metaphysics* (i.e. VII–IX), Aristotle does not assume that all things are changing, material things. But neither does he assume that some things are changeless, immaterial and distinct from changing, material things. He appears deliberately to leave open the question whether all things are changing and material or there are some things that are changeless, immaterial and distinct from changing, material things. In general, it appears that in the central books of the *Metaphysics* Aristotle is searching for primary being exclusively by considering changing, material things and without raising the question whether this is all that there is. We may, therefore, speak somewhat loosely of his views in book VII about 'each thing', when really we mean 'each changing, material thing'. This will not cause misunderstanding, provided that we also bear in mind that there are a number of references in the central books of the *Metaphysics* which indicate that while in these books he is searching for primary being exclusively by considering changing, material things, there is still a further project to be undertaken in order fully to answer the question, 'What is primary being?' – and so answer the basic question of metaphysics: 'What is being?' (For such references, see 1028^{b}13–15; 1028^{b}28–31; 1037^{a}10–14; 1041^{a}7–9; and 1050^{b}3–8.)

For it still needs to be considered whether there are also things that are changeless, immaterial and distinct from changing, material things. This question he will take up in book XII (see Chapter 8).

ii Primary being is not simply the ultimate subject of predication (VII. 3)

So far (in VII. 1–VII. 3, 1029ª9) Aristotle has introduced and clarified the very concept, *primary being*, and the question, 'What is primary being?' Further, he has indicated how this question is related to the basic question of metaphysics: 'What is being and what is it for something, anything, to be?' Finally, he has introduced three main candidates for primary being:

(1) the ultimate subject of predication;
(2) the universals; and
(3) the essence.

Now (in VII. 3, 1029ª9ff.), finally, he sets out to answer the question, 'What is primary being?' – a project that will occupy the remainder of book VII (or books VII–IX). He begins (in the remainder of VII. 3) by arguing that primary being is not simply the ultimate subject of predication. In other words, primary being is not simply substance (*to hupokeimenon*), which had been his view in the *Categories* (see above, Chapter 4§4). For he argues that the view that primary being is simply the ultimate subject of predication has the unwelcome consequence that primary being is, in virtue of itself, something indeterminate. He concludes that being an ultimate subject of predication is a necessary, but not a sufficient, condition for primary being. A further necessary condition is that primary being should be something determinate and well-defined, something having an essence or indeed being an essence. The essence of a thing, let us recall, is what is stated in the definition of that thing, and it is what makes the thing the determinate and well-defined thing that it is. The wider upshot is that the ultimate subject of predication and the essence must be inseparably connected, must unite into a single thing, indeed must be a single thing.

He begins with a reminder of what he means by the ultimate subject of predication, 'the underlying thing' (*to hupokeimenon*):

> By the underlying thing [*to hupokeimenon*] I mean the thing of which the other things are said [or predicated, i.e. true of], but which itself is not further said of [or predicated, i.e. true of] another thing.
>
> (1028ᵇ36–37)

But he argues that this is not a sufficient condition for primary being. For if primary being were simply the ultimate subject of predication, then it would follow that matter (*hulē*), which, in virtue of itself, is something indeterminate, is primary being:

> We have now said in rough outline what *ousia* [i.e. primary being] might be, namely, what is not itself said of an underlying thing [*hupokeimenon*] but of which the other things are said. But we ought not to speak in this way alone; for it is not sufficient. For this is itself unclear, and it also follows that matter [*hulē*] would be *ousia*.
>
> (1029ᵃ7–10)

But it emerges that the reason why primary being cannot be matter is, exactly, that matter is, in virtue of itself, something indeterminate:

> By matter I mean that which, in virtue of itself [*kath' hautēn*], is said to be neither a *what* [*ti*, probably short for *tode ti*, i.e. particular with a certain essence], nor a quantity, nor any other thing through which being [*to on*] is determined [*hōristai*]. For it [i.e. matter] is something of which of all these are said, but whose mode of being is different from each of the kinds of things that are said.
>
> (1029ᵃ20–21)

To understand why Aristotle thinks that matter is, in virtue of itself, something indeterminate, we must recall that, in his view, matter is always to be understood in relation to form, i.e. the form which makes the material thing into the determinate and well-defined thing that it is (see above, Chapter 2§4, especially ii, i.e. the conception of matter as potentiality). For example, the bricks and timber of a particular house are the matter of the house only in relation to the form of the house, the structural principle which, when combined with the bricks and timber, results in the house. By themselves, the bricks and timber are not the matter of the house; for they might not have been formed into a house, but into a different kind of material thing, and perhaps they might even have been left unformed into any material thing. So the account of the matter of a material thing, e.g. of a house, must always mention the form of the material thing whose matter it is. In other words, matter can be understood only in relation to the form of the material thing whose matter it is. This is why matter is, in virtue of itself, something indeterminate.

We should note, by the way, that here (in VII. 3), Aristotle assumes that the essence of something (*to ti estin, to ti ēn einai*) is identical with its form (*eidos, morphē*). This is something that he will defend later in book VII, along the following lines. The essence of a thing is what makes it the determinate and well-defined thing that it is. But when we are considering material things, things that are subject to change and in particular generation and destruction, it is the form that makes the thing into the determinate and well-defined thing that it is. So, in the case of material things, form and essence are the same.

But why cannot something which is in virtue of itself indeterminate, be primary being? To see this, we have only to recall the main requirement for primary being: primary beings are separate from non-primary beings, 'separate' in the sense of ontologically independent of non-primary beings. This means that a primary being is a being, something that is, simply in virtue of itself (*kath' hauto*) whereas a non-primary being is a being only in virtue of its relation to something else (*pros ti*). (See §4 of this chapter.) But matter is, on the contrary, ontologically dependent on form: it is a being not in virtue of itself, but in virtue of its relation to something other than itself, namely, its relation to form. Aristotle emphasizes this when he concludes that the reason why primary being cannot be matter is, exactly, that matter is not separate:

> But it is impossible that matter should be *ousia* [primary being]. For it appears that *ousia* is above all characterized by the fact that it is separate [*chōriston*] and *a this such* [*tode ti*]. For this reason form, or the thing that is the product of both form and matter [*to ex amphoin*, literally, 'that which is out of both', i.e. the particular material thing of a certain form], would appear to be *ousia*, rather than matter.
>
> (1029ª27–30)

That matter is, in virtue of itself, something indeterminate, and that it is not separate, amounts to the same thing. It means that matter is a being, something that is, only in virtue of its relation to something else, namely, form.

But why does Aristotle think that the ultimate subject of predication, taken in virtue of itself and in isolation from the essence and form, is matter? He invites us to focus our attention on a material thing, e.g. a bronze statue, and then to 'strip off' (*aphairein*) its features one by one. If we do this, he thinks that we will recognize that what we are left with at the end, when we have stripped off every feature that can be stripped off, is the matter of the material thing, in this case a shapeless lump of bronze. For every feature other than the matter can be stripped off and still there is something left which has the feature; and it is only when we try to strip off matter that nothing is left. Hence matter alone cannot be stripped off, and so it is what ultimately underlies the features of the material thing, i.e. it is the ultimate subject of predication. For example (see 1029ª11–19), the variety of features (*pathē*) of the statue, e.g. its colour, can be stripped off and still there is something left which has them. Even its particular spatial dimensions, the particular length, breadth and depth that determine the particular shape of the statue, can be stripped off and still there is something left which has them, namely, something whose shape is determined by these dimensions, i.e. a shape-less lump of bronze. But this shows that the thing whose shape is determined by these spatial dimensions will in virtue of itself be some-thing shapeless and indeterminate, but capable of being given a shape and made determinate. So it will be matter, or just like matter.

So if a feature of a material thing can be stripped off that thing and still there is something left which has the feature, then the feature is not the ultimate subject of predication. But if stripping off the feature leaves nothing behind, then this feature is, exactly, the ultimate subject of predication. The stripping off of features is an act of our intellect, prompted by our search for the ultimate subject of predication. We may, it is true, wonder whether this mental process of stripping off provides a genuine test of whether something is or is not the ultimate subject of predication. But perhaps Aristotle does not intend it as a strict test, but only as a helpful way of illustrating what is the ultimate subject of pred-ication with regard to a material thing, namely, its matter.

So we must still ask why it is matter, which in virtue of itself is something indeterminate, that is the ultimate subject of predication. Let us distinguish the features of a thing into its accidental features, on the one hand, and its essence, on the other (as Aristotle does here, 1029ª23–24). The accidental features are obviously predicated of some-thing else, namely, a thing which is, in virtue of its essence, already determinate and well-defined. For example, the colour red is true of, for example, this tomato; and the tomato is, in virtue of its essence, already something determinate and well-defined. But what about the essence itself? Is this also predicated of something else? If the essence is predicated of something else, then it is certainly plausible to think that what it is predicated of should be something that is, in virtue of itself, indeterminate, hence something like matter. For it is the essence of a thing that makes the thing into something determinate and well-defined in the first place. But why is the essence predicated of anything? This is not so obvious. For the essence might not be predicated of anything at all, hence it, rather than matter, might be the ultimate subject of predication.

In fact Aristotle will argue, later in book VII, that the essence is precisely the ultimate subject of predication. So why does he think here that the essence is also predicated of something else, i.e. of matter? There are two possibilities. He may have in mind a peculiar sense of predication, such that the fact that the essence is predicated of matter is compatible with, and perhaps part and parcel of, the view that the essence is itself the ultimate subject of predication. For suppose that the essence is predicated of the matter only in the following sense: the essence is the form; and the form is that in virtue of which the matter constitutes the material thing that it constitutes. In that case, the claim that the essence is predicated of the matter, which means that the essence and form is that in virtue of which the matter constitutes the material thing that it constitutes, may go together with the claim that the essence and form is itself the ultimate subject of predication. For the ultimate subject of predication is a determinate and well-defined thing only in virtue of its relation to its essence and form, but Aristotle will argue that this relation is not a relation between two things, but a relation between a thing and itself. (For this point, see §5v&viii of this chapter; see also Chapter 2§4.)

Alternatively, when Aristotle says here (in VII. 3) that the essence is predicated of matter, he may mean only that this is what follows if one thinks that primary being is simply the ultimate subject of predication, hence that primary being is matter. But since he, precisely, argues against this view, he may think that he is not himself committed to the view that essence is predicated of matter.

So far Aristotle's argument has been largely negative, for he has argued that we must not think that primary being is simply the ultimate subject of predication. For the ultimate subject of predication, taken in virtue of itself and in isolation from the essence, is matter. But matter, since it is in virtue of itself something indeterminate, cannot be primary being. However, he draws a positive conclusion when he concludes that primary being is not matter, but rather that which results from both form and matter (*to ex amphoin*, literally, 'that which is out of both [the form and the matter]'), i.e. a particular material thing of a certain form (1029^{a}29–30). Indeed, he concludes that if primary being is essence and form rather than matter, then primary being will be essence and form rather than that which results from both form and matter (*to ex amphoin*, see 1029^{a}5–7). This anticipates the claim that he will defend later: primary being with regard to each changing, material thing is the essence and the form of that thing.

Does the positive conclusion that primary being is above all form follow from the negative conclusion that primary being is not matter?

We saw that the reason why primary being is not matter is that the matter of a material thing is a being not in virtue of itself, but in virtue of its relation to something else, form. So it appears that form is a better candidate for primary being than matter; i.e. it is the form of a material thing, rather than its matter, that ultimately explains why the thing is a being, something that is, in the first place. Strictly, however, this does not follow. For the form and the matter might have an equal share in this explanation; i.e. the explanation of why a particular material thing is a being, something that is, might need to appeal equally to the form and the matter of that thing (we will return to this issue later, §5vii of this chapter).

Finally, Aristotle's argument against the view that primary being is simply the ultimate subject of predication may remind us of Locke's memorable attack on the concept of substance, 'substance' precisely in the sense of the ultimate subject of predication. Locke mocks this concept for signifying something wholly indeterminate, hence 'something we know not what' and 'children's talk'. And he appears to discard this concept of substance altogether, for signifying something utterly inconceivable (*Essay Concerning Human Understanding*, 2. 23. 2). But it would be a mistake to read Aristotle's argument through the eyes of Locke. First, Aristotle's aim is not to discard the concept of the ultimate subject of predication, or substance. His aim is rather to argue that this concept, although it is a necessary condition, is not a sufficient condition for primary being. Second, he does not argue that the concept of the ultimate subject of predication, or substance, signifies something *wholly* indeterminate; he argues rather that it signifies something *in virtue of itself* indeterminate. For matter, which in Aristotle's argument is what the ultimate subject of predication turns out to be, is not something *wholly* indeterminate; it is something *in virtue of itself* indeterminate. This makes all the difference. Consider, for instance, the matter of a particular house, the bricks and timber. When he says that the matter of a house is in virtue of itself indeterminate, he means that it is the matter of the house only in relation to the form of the house, the structural principle which, when combined with the bricks and timber, results in a house. This is plausible enough; for the bricks and timber are not by themselves the matter of a house, since they might not have been formed into a house, but into a different kind of material thing, and perhaps they might even have been left unformed into any material thing. But of course it does not follow that the bricks and timber are something wholly indeterminate; clearly they are not. Aristotle nowhere in this argument introduces the concept of something *wholly* indeterminate, and we must not suppose that his argument commits him to this concept.

iii What in general is the essence of each thing, and what things have an essence? (VII. 4–5)

Aristotle characterizes the concept of essence in two ways here (in VII. 4–5). First, he says that:

> The essence [*to ti ēn einai*] of each thing is what the thing is said [to be] *in virtue of itself* [*kath' hauto*].
>
> (1029ᵇ13–14)

Second, he says that the essence of each thing is what is defined in the definition (*horismos*) of that thing (1030ᵃ6–7; see VII. 5, 1031ᵃ12: 'clearly, then, a definition is an account of the essence').

When he says that the essence of a thing is what the thing is *in virtue of itself*, he means that the essence of a thing is what is true of the thing simply in virtue of its being the thing that it is and not in virtue of how it is related to other things. So, in other words, the essence of a thing is the properties it must have if it is to be the thing that it is. This really is a basic characterization of the concept of essence. It is only natural that Aristotle cannot go much further in explaining in general terms what he means by *essence*, but can only illustrate this through particular examples. Thus he says that *your* essence (he is pointing to the reader, or to a member of the audience to which he is speaking) does not consist in your being educated, even if you are in fact educated; for it is not simply in virtue of your being yourself (*kata sauton*) that you are educated (1029ᵇ14–16). Presumably, this is because your being educated depends not just on yourself and who you are, but also on your circumstances and how they affect you. So, even if you are in fact educated, being educated is not one of the properties that you must have if you are to be the very thing that you are. He does not say here what is your essence, but presumably he thinks it is your being human and rational; for it is simply in virtue of being yourself that you are human and rational, and these are properties that you must have if you are to be the very thing that you are.

When he adds that the essence of a thing is what is defined in the definition (*horismos*) of that thing, he is first of all reminding us of what is meant by 'definition': a definition is an account of 'what precisely' (*hoper*) something is, i.e. what it is 'in virtue of itself' (*kath' hauto*). For example, even if water is a particular kind of liquid, this is not what precisely water is and what it is in virtue of itself; hence 'a particular kind of liquid' is not the definition of water. For water's being a particular kind of liquid depends on other things and in general on those circumstances that determine in what state the water is in. If anything, the definition of water, as we now know, is H_2O, and this is what precisely water is and what it is in virtue of itself, and not in virtue of its relation to other things.

Evidently, Aristotle is assuming here that it is possible to define things, not just words, and that, with regard to each thing, there is indeed precisely something that it is and that it is in virtue of itself. He is assuming that things have essences. So the kind of definitions that he has in mind are real, not nominal definitions: definitions of things, not words.

However, even if we are satisfied with this general characterization of the concept of essence, there is a striking problem about how to apply it to particular cases. This is a problem that Aristotle recognizes and tries to answer here (in VII. 4–5). The problem is whether each thing has just a single essence or, on the contrary, indefinitely many essences. This is a problem, especially if one argues, as Aristotle does, that changing, material things (e.g. Socrates) have an essence. For a changing, material thing has indefinitely many properties and indefinitely many things are true of it. So why should just one of its properties have a decisive claim to being its essence, i.e. the very thing that the thing is?

It is worth emphasizing here Aristotle's view that changing, material things have an essence. Indeed, he thinks that, primarily and above all, it is changing, material things, when conceived as ultimate subjects of predication, that have an essence. Thus he will argue that primary being with regard to each changing, material thing is both the essence and the form of that thing, on the one hand, and the ultimate subject of predication with regard to that thing, on the other hand. For he will argue that the essence and the form of a changing, material thing is, precisely, the ultimate subject of predication with regard to that thing (see §5v in this chapter).

But each changing, material thing (e.g. Socrates) has many properties, indeed indefinitely many. So why does it not have just as many essences, depending on which of its properties we have in mind when we ask, 'What is its essence?'? For example, Socrates is a human being, but he is also snub-nosed, pale, five foot tall, the mentor of Plato, etc. So we may ask, 'What is the essence of this human being, Socrates?', or 'What is the essence of this snub-nosed thing, Socrates?', etc. And each question will apparently demand a different answer. This is a problem because Aristotle supposes that each thing has just one essence, not many, let alone indefinitely many. But he is right to suppose this. For if a thing has as many essences as it has properties, then we can forget about the concept of essence altogether, and we need only retain the general concept of a property, i.e. of what is true of a thing. After all, the essence of a thing is *the* identity of that thing, not its indefinitely multiple identities. It is *what precisely (hoper)* the thing is, not just anything that it is. It is what the thing is simply in virtue of being *the very thing it is (kath' hauto)*, not in virtue of being any of the indefinitely many things that it is.

By making (in IV. 4–5) a move that may by now strike us as familiar and unsurprising, Aristotle wants to answer this problem and to argue that, in spite of the indefinitely many properties of each changing, material thing, its essence is only one. The move that he makes is to argue that the indefinitely many things that a changing, material thing, such as Socrates, is (e.g. a human being, a snub-nosed being, a pale being, etc.) can be distinguished into just two things: a single primary being (e.g. a particular human being), on the one hand, and an indefinite number of non-primary beings (e.g. a particular snub-nosed being, a particular pale being, etc.), on the other hand. The primary being is the ultimate subject of predication, and the indefinitely many non-primary beings are things that are different from and true of this subject. He argues that this will ensure that each thing has only one essence, if we suppose that it is only or primarily the primary being, which is one rather than many, that has an essence. So he concludes that we really must make this supposition, i.e. the supposition that it is only or primarily the primary being and the ultimate subject of predication that has an essence, if we want to ensure that each thing has only one essence. Non-primary beings, he argues, either do not have an essence at all, or they have an essence only in a derived way. That is to say, non-primary beings have an essence only because primary beings have an essence and because non-primary beings depend for their being beings, things that are, on their relation to the primary beings.

So Aristotle answers the problem of whether each changing, material thing (e.g. Socrates) has only one essence or it has indefinitely many essences in the following distinctive way. He argues that in general each thing has only one essence. He does so by, first, distinguishing between primary being and non-primary being with regard to each thing. Second, he argues that primary being with regard to each thing is the ultimate subject of predication with regard to that thing. Third, he argues that it is only or primarily the primary beings that have an essence.

But it is important to emphasize what motivates Aristotle to argue that each changing, material thing has only one essence. For he wants, precisely, to argue that changing, material things, and not only the universals that are true of them, have an essence. And he wants to argue that a changing, material thing has an essence in virtue of itself, i.e. in virtue of being the particular thing that it is, and not only in virtue of the universals that are true of it having an essence. For example, the particular thing, Socrates, and not only universals such as being human, snub-nosed, five foot tall, etc., have an essence. And this particular thing, Socrates, has an essence in virtue of being the particular thing that it is, and not only in virtue of each of the universals that are true of it having an essence.

This view is directly opposed to Plato's view, which is that it is only or primarily universals that have an essence, and that changing, material particulars have an essence, if at all, only in virtue of each of the universals that are true of them having an essence (see also Chapter 9). In response to the same question, i.e. whether each thing has only one essence or it has indefinitely many essences, Plato agues that it is only or primarily universals that have an essence, and that each universal has just one essence – otherwise it would not be the determinate and well-defined universal that it is. So if indefinitely many universals are true of a changing, material thing, and if none of these have a decisive claim to being *the* essence of the thing, then Plato will simply conclude that changing, material things do not have an essence at all and that only universals have an essence. This will be in tune with his general conclusion that changing, material things are, in virtue of themselves, indeterminate and depend on their relation to universals for their determination.

So it emerges that Aristotle's distinctive answer to the question whether each changing, material thing (e.g. Socrates) has only one essence or it has indefinitely many essences is really part of his attempt to argue that changing, material things are determinate simply in virtue of themselves and not in virtue of their relation to universals (see also §3 of this chapter).

But why does Aristotle argue that each changing, material thing (e.g. Socrates) has only one essence, not indefinitely many essences, i.e. as many essences as it has properties? Why, in other words, does he want to argue that a changing, material thing has an essence in virtue of itself, i.e. in virtue of being the particular thing that it is, and not only in virtue of the universals that are true of it having an essence? Suppose that a thing, x, has indefinitely many essences, i.e. as many essences as it has properties. What this means is that there is no one thing, E, that this very thing, x, is; on the contrary, what this very thing, x, is is indefinitely many things, E1, E2, etc. But what this means, apparently, is that the thing, x, which we perhaps call by a single name, e.g. 'Socrates', is really simply an aggregate and compound thing that is made up of indefinitely many things: Socrates the human thing,

Socrates the snub-nosed thing, Socrates the pale thing, etc. It is precisely in order to avoid this result that Aristotle argues that each changing, material thing (e.g. Socrates) has only one essence, not indefinitely many essences.

This also shows something especially important. For it shows that Aristotle's claim that each particular thing has only one essence, and not indefinitely many essences, is directly associated with the view that each particular thing is not merely an aggregate or compound of indefinitely many things (e.g. Socrates the human thing, Socrates the snub-nosed thing, Socrates the pale thing, etc.). Rather, each particular thing is a single unitary thing. And its unique and unitary identity is provided for, precisely, by its single essence.

iv Primary being with regard to each thing is the essence of that thing (VII. 1, 6 and 17)

This is Aristotle's most central claim about primary being in the *Metaphysics*:

> Primary being with regard to each thing is the essence
> (*to ti ēn einai*) of that thing.

(For this claim, see also e.g. VII. 6, 1032ª4–6; also 1031ᵇ11–14, 18–20 and VII. 11, 1037ª33–ᵇ4.) This claim goes to the heart of the *Metaphysics*. To begin with, it can be grasped in a relatively informal way. The essence of a thing is what explains what it is for that thing to be the very thing it is. But the essence is also what is stated in the definition of a thing. So we may also say that the essence of a thing is what explains what it is for that thing to be the determinate and well-defined thing that it is. So far, this is simply what Aristotle means by essence. But now he argues that primary being with regard to each thing is, exactly, the essence of that thing. So he evidently thinks that:

> What explains what it is for something to be the determinate and
> well-defined thing it is is also what explains what it is for that
> thing to be a being, a thing that is, in the first place. In other
> words, something is a being at all, something that is, precisely in
> virtue of its being a determinate and well-defined thing.

So this view, together with his conception of essence, is what leads him to the view that primary being with regard to each thing is the essence of that thing. If we ask, further, why he argues that something is a being at all precisely in virtue of its being a determinate and well-defined thing, the answer, apparently, is that he thinks that:

> If something is not a determinate and well-defined thing, or if it does not depend on something which is a determinate and well-defined thing, then it is not a being, a thing that is, at all, but is as good as nothing. Conversely, if something is a determinate and well-defined thing, or if it depends on something which is a determinate and well-defined thing, then it is a thing that is, a being.

So it is, apparently, along these lines that Aristotle arrives at the view that primary being with regard to each thing is the essence of that thing.

Aristotle introduces the view that primary being with regard to each thing is the essence of that thing at the very opening of book VII, when he immediately states that a good candidate for primary being is, precisely, the essence (*to ti estin*, see especially 1028ª13–15, discussed in §2 of this chapter). It is also worth noting that at the opening of VII. 6, when he begins to develop his own positive account of primary being and to search for an answer to the question, 'What is primary being?', he simply states that: 'it is also true that the essence is said to be the primary being [*ousia*] of each thing' (1031ª18).

However, if we look closer at the beginning of book VII, we can perhaps identify a particular argument that helps considerably to generate the view that primary being with regard to each thing is the essence of that thing. He began (in VII. 1, 1028ª33–34) by characterizing a primary being as a being that is separate (*chōriston*). Primary being is 'separate' being in the sense that it is a being, something that is, simply in virtue of itself (*kath' hauto*) and not in virtue of its relation to other things (*pros ti*). This, we saw, is part of the very notion, *primary being* (see §4 of this chapter). But this evidently implies that primary being with regard to each thing is something that we grasp when we grasp the thing in its own right and when we set aside its relations to other things; i.e. when we grasp the thing, as it were, in isolation – in this sense, when we grasp it 'separately' (*chōris*). But what is it that we grasp when we grasp a thing in its own right and when we set aside its relations to other things? Evidently, what we grasp in this way is, precisely, the essence of the thing. For the essence of a thing is, exactly, what the thing is simply in virtue of itself (*kath' hauto*) and not in virtue of its relation to other things (*pros ti*). So it emerges that what we grasp when we grasp what is primary being with regard to each thing is exactly what we grasp when we grasp the essence of each thing. It is only a small step to conclude that primary being with regard to each thing is the essence of that thing.

The above argument, for thinking that primary being with regard to each thing is the essence of that thing, is a natural way of understanding what Aristotle says in VII. 1, 1028^{a}31–^{b}2, when he argues that both primary being (*ousia*) and essence (*to ti estin*) are primary 'with respect to knowledge' (*gnōsei*). For, in VII. 1, 1028^{a}31–^{b}2, he puts forward an argument that appears to be of the following form. Both primary being and essence have an equal claim to being 'that which is primary with respect to knowledge' (*to prōton gnōsei*); i.e. they both have an equal claim to being what we need to know in order to know a thing most strictly and most properly (*malista*, 1028^{a}36). But then it is natural to conclude that primary being and essence are one and the same; i.e. that primary being with regard to each thing is, precisely, the essence of that thing.

We may perhaps also restate this argument in the following way. The essence of each thing is the primary object of knowledge with regard to that thing. For it is when we know the essence of a thing that we know that thing most strictly and most properly (*malista*, see VII. 1, 1028^{a}36–^{b}2; this is of course also a general view in Aristotle's theory of knowledge and science, see Chapter 2§3). But the primary object of knowledge must at the same time be primary being. That is to say, what is primary with respect to knowledge must at the same time be primary with respect to being (we will return to this point §5x of this chapter). Therefore, the essence of each thing is, precisely, primary being with regard to that thing.

This is perhaps the closest that Aristotle comes to providing an explicit and succinct argument for the absolutely central claim that primary being with regard to each thing is the essence of that thing. There are of course more elaborate arguments in book VII, but they are concerned with drawing out the consequences of this account of primary being, i.e. the account that argues that primary being is the essence, and with responding to competing accounts. Thus he will argue that the essence of each changing, material thing is the form of that thing. So the essence of each changing, material thing is neither simply the matter nor a combination of the form and the matter of that thing. This will allow him to conclude that primary being with regard to each changing, material thing is the form of that thing. He will further argue that there is an important sense in which the essence and the form, on the one hand, and the ultimate subject of predication, on the other hand, coincide and designate a single thing. So he will conclude that primary being with regard to each changing, material thing is both:

(1) the essence and the form of that thing, and
(2) the ultimate subject of predication with regard to that thing.

Finally, he will conclude that primary being with regard to each thing is *not* the universals that are true of that thing and that determine what the thing is like.

Let us focus once again on Aristotle's basic reasoning for the view that primary being with regard to each thing is the essence of that thing. The reasoning is that the essence of a thing is what explains what it is for that thing to be the determinate and well-defined thing it is. But Aristotle argues that by explaining what it is for a thing to be the determinate and well-defined thing it is, the essence also explains what it is for that thing to be a being, something that is, in the first place. This reasoning becomes fully explicit only at the end of book VII (in VII. 17). The argument in VII. 17 is along the following lines. First, Aristotle clarifies that 'primary being [*ousia*] is a principle and a certain kind of explanation [or cause, *aitia*]' (1041^{a}9–10). For it is the explanation of why a thing is a being, something that is. Second, he argues that this explanation is provided by the essence of each thing (*to ti ēn einai*, 1041^{a}28). For the essence of each thing is what explains why the thing is the very thing it is; and, by doing so, the essence explains also why the thing is a being, something that is. Third, he argues that the essence of each thing, and in particular each changing, material thing, explains why the thing is the very thing it is in the following way: it explains why the matter of a particular material thing, e.g. a human being, constitutes the very thing that it constitutes, e.g. a particular human being (1041^{b}4–9). This argument evidently assumes what was argued for earlier (in VII. 10–12), namely, that the essence of a changing, material thing is the form of that thing. Fourth, he repeats that this explanation, the essence, is primary being, *ousia* (104^{b}8–9). Finally, and strikingly, he concludes: 'this [the essence] is the primary being of each thing; *for this [the primary being, and the essence] is the ultimate explanation [aition prōton] of its being* [i.e. *of why the thing is a being, something that is, in the first place*]' (1041^{b}27–28).

This brings out most clearly that Aristotle's basic argument for the view that primary being with regard to each thing is the essence of that thing is of the following form: the essence of a thing is what explains what it is for that thing to be the determinate and well-defined thing that it is; but by explaining what it is for a thing to be the determinate and well-defined thing that it is, the essence also explains what it is for that thing to be a being, something that is, in the first place.

How, in general, are we to respond to Aristotle's basic claim that primary being with regard to each thing is the essence of that thing? We may find the claim attractive, but the reasoning behind it may also strike us as, at best, inconclusive. In particular, is the claim not open to an obvious objection, namely that it assumes that things have essences in the first place? And even if we grant Aristotle the view that things have essences, we may still object that it is surely not credible to argue that things could not exist unless they had essences. But this is precisely what he argues when he argues that primary being with regard to each thing is the essence of that thing.

This objection may have considerable force. But it is crucial to recognize that Aristotle does himself address it. He does so not here, in book VII, but earlier, in book IV (especially IV. 4–6), when he examined and defended the principle of non-contradiction. For there he argued, in general, that for a thing to have an essence is for it to be a determinate and well-defined thing. But he argued that unless we think of things as determinate and well-defined, we cannot at all think or speak of things. Indeed, he argued that unless the things themselves are determinate and well-defined, it is impossible to think or speak of the things themselves, i.e. this is impossible in principle and not just for us. (See Chapters 5 and 6.) So he has argued that the view that things have essences really is inescapable, i.e. the view which says that, with regard to each real thing, there is something, E, that the thing is simply in virtue of itself and not in virtue of its relation to other things.

v Primary being with regard to each thing is both (1) the essence of that thing and (2) the ultimate subject of predication with regard to that thing (VII. 6)

At the opening of VII. 6 Aristotle argues that:

> With regard to those things that in the strict sense have an essence, namely primary beings, the essence of a thing is identical with the thing itself, i.e. with the ultimate subject of predication.

It emerges that by 'the thing itself' here, he means, precisely, the ultimate subject of predication. This is also clear from what follows. For in what follows (1031^b15–18) he takes this argument to have shown that primary being is indeed the ultimate subject of predication (see also VII. 3, 1029^a2–3 and VIII. 1, 1042^a28–29, where he says that the form, which he argues is the essence of a changing, material thing, is an ultimate subject of predication). But, since he has argued that primary being with regard to each thing is the essence of that thing, he directly concludes that:

> Primary being with regard to each thing is both (1) the essence of that thing and (2) the ultimate subject of predication with regard to that thing.

It is also worth noting straight away that he will go on to argue that:

> The essence of a changing, material thing is the form of that thing.

So he concludes that:

> The essence and the form of a changing, material thing is identical with the thing itself, i.e. with the ultimate subject of predication.

And hence:

> Primary being with regard to each changing, material thing is both (1) the essence and the form of that thing and (2) the ultimate subject of predication with regard to that thing.

Let us concentrate on Aristotle's central view that, with regard to those things that in the strict sense have an essence, namely primary beings, the essence of a thing is identical with the thing itself, i.e. with the ultimate subject of predication. This view, we recall, was anticipated at the opening of book VII, when he said that primary being with regard to each thing is both the essence of that thing (*to ti estin*, 1028ª14) and the ultimate subject of predication with regard to that thing (*to hupokeimenon*, 1028ª26). In particular, what he said there (102811–12) was that primary being is both the essence (*to ti estin*) and something having an essence (*tode ti*). So when he argues now (in VII. 6) that the essence of a thing is identical with that thing itself, in the sense of the ultimate subject of predication, he is arguing that these two things, the essence of something (*to ti estin*) and the thing having an essence (*tode ti*), coincide and are identical.

Aristotle asserts (at the opening of VII. 1) that a thing is identical with its essence:

But we must examine whether the essence and each thing are the same [*tauton*] or different [*heteron*]. For this will indeed further the task of examining primary being [*ousia*]. For it appears that each thing is not different [*ouk allo*] from its own primary being [*ousia*]; and indeed that the essence [*to ti ēn einai*] is said to be the primary being of each thing.

(1031ª17–18)

But in the case of things that are said [to be] in virtue of themselves [*ta kath' hauta legomena*], they [i.e. the essence and the thing whose essence it is] are necessarily the same [*tauto*].

(1031ª28–29)

Here we also see that he immediately (1031ª28f.) argues that the claim that a thing is identical with its essence is true only of things that in the strict sense have an essence, namely, primary beings. In other words, it is true only of things that are the very things they are, and indeed are beings, simply in virtue of themselves and not in virtue of their relation to other things. He calls these things 'the things that are said [i.e. said to be] in virtue of themselves' (*ta kath' hauta legomena*, 1031ª28). This is a crucial qualification, especially if we recall the problem that Aristotle raised, and answered, earlier (in VII. 4). The problem was whether each particular thing (e.g. Socrates) has only one essence or it has indefinitely many essences, i.e. as many essences as it has properties (see §5iii of this chapter). Apparently, each particular thing, e.g. Socrates, has indefinitely many properties, e.g. it will be pale, human, etc. So, apparently, each particular thing, e.g. Socrates, will be at once indefinitely many things, i.e. Socrates the pale thing, Socrates the human thing, etc. But Aristotle argues here (1031ª20–24) that Socrates the pale thing cannot be the same as his essence, i.e. as what it is to be a pale thing. For Socrates the pale thing is, after all, the very same thing as Socrates the human thing; for there is just a single thing that is both pale and human. But evidently what it is to be a pale thing and what it is to be a human thing are not the same.

This argument may not immediately convince. For perhaps Socrates the pale thing is only in a loose sense the same thing as Socrates the human thing; i.e. perhaps there really are two things here, Socrates the pale thing and Socrates the human thing, that merely happen to form an aggregate and compound thing. In that case, even if Socrates the pale thing is identical with what it is to be a pale thing, and Socrates the human thing is identical with what it is to be a human thing, it does not follow that, absurdly, what it is to be a pale thing and what it is to be a human thing are the same.

But we know what Aristotle would respond. For he denies that Socrates the pale thing is only in a loose sense the same thing as Socrates the human thing; i.e. he denies that there are two things here that merely happen to form an aggregate and compound thing. He denies this precisely because he argues that a thing, such as Socrates, has only one essence, not indefinitely many essences or as many essences as it has properties. For if Socrates the pale thing were only in a loose sense the same thing as Socrates the human thing, i.e. if there were two things here that merely happened to form an aggregate and compound thing, then the thing that we call by one name, 'Socrates', would really be indefinitely many things: Socrates the pale thing, Socrates the human thing, etc. So it would have indefinitely many essences, i.e. as many essences as it has properties (see §5iii of this chapter).

So we can now see why Aristotle limits the claim that each thing is identical with its essence to things that strictly have an essence and are primary beings; i.e. to things that are the very things they are, and indeed are beings, simply in virtue of themselves (*ta kath' hauta legomena*). For suppose that a thing such as Socrates the pale thing was identical with its essence, i.e. with what it is to be a pale thing, and likewise with Socrates the human thing, etc. In general, suppose that the claim that each thing is identical with its essence was not limited to some things, but was intended to be true of all things. Then it would follow that, absurdly, what it is to be a pale thing and what it is to be a human thing are the same. This would follow unless Socrates were merely an aggregate and compound thing that is made up of indefinitely many things, i.e. of Socrates the pale thing, Socrates the human thing, etc. So, in order to ensure that Socrates is not merely an aggregate of indefinitely many things, and at same time to ensure that there is something with regard to Socrates that is identical with his essence, Aristotle argues that just one of the things that Socrates is is identical with his essence. This one thing that Socrates is and that is identical with his essence is, precisely, the ultimate subject of predication with regard to Socrates. For the ultimate subject of predication with regard to Socrates is just one thing, not indefinitely many things. And each of the things that are different from and true of this subject, e.g. being pale, snub-nosed, five foot tall, etc., are things that are true of Socrates not in virtue of himself (*kath' hauton*), but only in virtue of his relation to these things or properties. Aristotle also calls the things that Socrates is in virtue of his having such properties, e.g. Socrates the pale thing, the snub-nosed thing, etc., 'the things that are said [i.e. said to be] by accident' or 'by circumstance' (*ta legomena kata sumbebēkos*, 1031ª19). For it is only by accident and by circumstance that Socrates is, for example, pale, snub-nosed, five foot tall, etc. But the crucial point is that the ultimate subject of predication is the very thing that it is (e.g. a particular human being) not in virtue of its relation to something else, but simply in virtue of itself. As he says, it is a *kath' hauto legomenon*. And the reason why the ultimate subject of predication is the very thing that it is simply in virtue of itself is, precisely, that it is identical with its essence.

So Aristotle argues that a thing, in the sense of an ultimate subject of predication, is identical with its essence. This is a striking, but also a puzzling view. But it is also clear why in general he wants to defend this view. For suppose that the ultimate subject of predication and the essence are not identical. Then the ultimate subject of predication will, in virtue of itself, be something indeterminate. For it is in virtue of its essence that it is the determinate and well-defined thing that it is. But something which is, in virtue of itself, indeterminate, cannot be primary being. So the ultimate subject of predication will no longer be primary being. Only the essence, when set against the ultimate subject of predication, will be primary being. But this, Aristotle thinks, is an unacceptable result. This also appears to be the thrust of the difficult argument in VII. 6, 1031^{a}31f, especially ^{a}31–^{b}3 and ^{b}15–18 (we will return to this argument later, see Chapter 9§§5–6).

But what does Aristotle think is unacceptable about the view that only the essence of things, and not those things themselves, i.e. the ultimate subjects of predication, are primary beings? We should note that this is precisely the view that he here ascribes to Plato (see especially 1031^{b}15–18). And he criticizes this view at length, both here and elsewhere. So we may set aside for later, when we consider his critique of Plato, his objections to the view that only the essence of things, and not those things themselves, are primary beings (see Chapter 9). Still, we can see what in general he finds objectionable about this view. For the things that he is considering here (in books VII–IX) are material things – things that are subject to change and especially generation and destruction. But if these things are not primary beings, and if primary beings are rather some other things – namely essences as opposed to ultimate subjects – then this means that material things do not have an essence, i.e. they are not, in virtue of themselves and in virtue of being things that are subject to change and especially generation and destruction, something determinate and well-defined. Plato is happy to accept this result. But Aristotle finds it unacceptable.

But Aristotle's view that a thing, in the sense of an ultimate subject of predication, is identical with its essence may still strike us as puzzling. Surely, we may object, a thing, in the sense of an ultimate subject of predication, cannot be identical with its essence; for the essence of a thing is rather something that the thing has, something that is predicated of it and true of it. So the essence, since it is something predicated of and true of something, cannot be identical with that of which it is predicated, i.e. the ultimate subject of predication. This is a natural objection, but Aristotle's response is familiar (see also Chaper 4§4). He argues that the essence is not at all true of and predicated of the thing whose essence it is, for it is in virtue of its essence that a thing is a determinate and well-defined thing in the first place. It is true that the essence and the form of a material thing, e.g. a particular human being, is what explains why the matter of that thing constitutes the very thing that it constitutes, e.g. a human being. But this is not a case of predication, i.e. of one thing being true of another thing. For the matter of a material thing is not, in virtue of itself, a thing at all. Rather, the matter of a particular material thing, e.g. a particular human being, is the matter it is only because it can constitute such a material thing, e.g. a human being. (See above, Chapter 2§4ii for Aristotle's conception of matter as potentiality.)

But we may still find puzzling the view that a thing, in the sense of an ultimate subject of predication, is identical with its essence. For we may find it natural to think that an ultimate subject of predication, such as Socrates, evidently includes more than its essence, hence it cannot be identical with its essence. We may even think that Aristotle invites this objection by suggesting that a material thing, such as Socrates, is a compound (*sunholon*) of its essence and form, on the one hand, and its matter, on the other hand. For how can a compound of two things be identical with one of its parts? How can a thing that includes two things be identical with just one of them? Surely this is impossible. But Aristotle's response will by now be familiar. First of all, when he says that a particular material thing is a whole that results from form and matter, i.e. a *sunholon* in this sense, he does not mean that a material thing is a compound of two parts, its form and its matter. Indeed, neither the form nor the matter of a thing are parts of or constituents in that thing. The form is evidently not a part of or constituent in the thing whose form it is; it is rather that which explains why the thing is the very thing that it is and why the matter constitutes the very thing that it does. But the matter can be said to be part of the thing whose matter it is only in the sense that it is 'that out of which' (*to ex hou*) the thing is generated. For the matter does not endure in this process of generation; it is not like bronze, which endures in the process of the generation of, for example, a bronze sphere (see Chapter 2§4ii).

It is true that a thing, in a wide and loose sense of 'thing', can be said to include its accidental properties. For example, Socrates, as we encounter him in experience, is not just the human being, but also the snub-nosed thing, the five foot tall thing, etc. But a thing, in the sense of the ultimate subject of predication, can still be identical with its essence. For the ultimate subject of predication evidently does not include the accidental properties. For an accidental property, e.g. being snub-nosed, is something predicated of and true of something that is already a determinate and well-defined thing, e.g. a human being. So an accidental property belongs not to the ultimate subject of predication, but to what is predicated of and true of this subject. In general it is important to emphasize that to speak of a thing in the sense of an ultimate subject of predication is not to speak of a thing as we encounter it in experience, and in general it is not to speak of a thing in a wide and loose sense of 'thing'. So a thing in the sense of an ultimate subject of predication can be identical with its essence, even though the thing in a wider and looser sense will evidently include more than its essence.

However, it may still be an open question whether, at the end of the day, Aristotle succeeds in defending the view that a thing, in the sense of an ultimate subject of predication, is identical with its essence. For there remains the following problem. Of what are the things that are predicated of a material thing, and in particular the accidental properties of the material thing, ultimately predicated? Are the accidental properties ultimately predicated of the whole that results from both form and matter, i.e. are they predicated of the *sunholon*, or are they rather ultimately predicated only of the form and the essence? To defend the view that a thing, in the sense of an ultimate subject of predication, is identical with its essence, Aristotle must evidently argue that the latter is the case, i.e. it is the essence and the form that is the ultimate subject of predication, not the whole that results from both form and matter (the *sunholon*). For his claim is, precisely, that the essence and the form are identical with the ultimate subject of predication. But how can he argue that the accidental properties are ultimately predicated of the essence and form, and not of the whole that results from both the form and the matter (the *sunholon*)? To argue this, he will no doubt once again invoke the claim that the whole that results from form and matter (the *sunholon*) is a determinate and well-defined thing, hence a being in the first place, only because of its essence and form. And it is of a thing that is already determinate and well-defined that the accidental properties are true; for example, being pale or snub-nosed are true of a thing that is already determinate and well-defined, e.g. a particular human being.

Alternative interpretation

On any interpretation, Aristotle argues that primary being with regard to each thing (e.g. Socrates) is both the essence of that thing and the ultimate subject of predication with regard to that thing (e.g. this particular thing, Socrates). As we have understood this claim, it means that strictly one and the same thing is both an essence and an ultimate subject of predication. For they are both, precisely, primary being. But there is a very different interpretation of Aristotle's claim. (This interpretation is defended by, for example, Woods 1967, 1991, and in general by critics who argue that Aristotle conceives of essences as universals.) On this interpretation, it is not at all one and the same thing that is both an essence and an ultimate subject of predication; on the contrary, the essence and the ultimate subject of predication are different things. So how, on this interpretation, can Aristotle at the same time argue that primary being is both the essence and the ultimate subject of predication? He can do so, it is said, because he distinguishes two different senses of the term *ousia* or 'substance' (i.e. what we have generally translated as 'primary being'). For in *Metaphysics* V. 8 he distinguishes between *ousia* in the sense of 'the ultimate subject of predication' (*hupokeimenon*, $1017^{b}13$–14) and *ousia* in the sense of 'essence' (*to ti ēn einai*, $1017^{b}21$–23). So the reasoning of this alternative interpretation is this: Aristotle distinguishes two senses of *ousia* (primary being), *ousia* in the sense of 'the ultimate subject of predication' and *ousia* in the sense of 'essence'; therefore, when he argues that *ousia* is both the essence and the ultimate subject of predication, he need not think that it is strictly one and the same thing that is both an essence and an ultimate subject of predication. On the contrary, since different senses are involved, it is natural to think that different things are involved.

What is the motivation for this interpretation? Basically, the motivation is that it is simply not credible that Aristotle should think that strictly one and the same thing is both an essence and an ultimate subject of predication. For one cannot, it will be said, coherently think this. After all, the ultimate subject of predication is a particular (e.g. this particular thing, Socrates), but the essence (it will be said) is a universal (e.g. being human). In general, the essence of a particular thing (e.g. of Socrates) is that in virtue of which this thing is the determinate and well-defined thing that it is (e.g. a human being); i.e. the essence is a cause or explanation. So how can the essence be the same thing as the particular thing whose essence it is? Apparently, it cannot. But since the ultimate subject of predication is, precisely, the particular (e.g. this particular thing, Socrates), the essence cannot, apparently, be the same thing as the ultimate subject of predication.

Our response to the motivation for this alternative interpretation is as follows. Aristotle may, without obvious incoherence, argue that strictly one and the same thing is both an essence and an ultimate subject of predication, provided that he does not think that the essence is a universal (see Chapter 4§4 for this response). Indeed, since at the beginning (in book III, the book of *aporiai*) he himself raises the question and *aporia* whether principles are universal or particular (see ninth *aporia*, 999^{b}24–1000^{a}4), we must not simply assume that he thinks of essences – which, it has emerged, are the fundamental principles – as universals. In general, it is true that the essence of a particular thing (e.g. of Socrates), i.e. the essence of an ultimate subject of predication, is that in virtue of which the thing is the determinate and well-defined thing that it is (e.g. a human being). But this is compatible with thinking that the essence is identical with the ultimate subject of predication and the particular. For Aristotle may think, and indeed he appears to argue, that the ultimate subject of predication and the particular is what it is, and in general it is a determinate and well-defined thing, simply in virtue of itself.

Our response to the reasoning in the alternative interpretation is as follows. It is of course true that, in V. 8, Aristotle distinguishes two senses of *ousia* (primary being): *ousia* in the sense of 'the ultimate subject of predication' and *ousia* in the sense of 'essence'. But this is no reason at all for thinking that it is not strictly one and the same thing that is *ousia* in both senses, i.e. that it is not strictly one and the same thing that is both an essence and an ultimate subject of predication.

In general, it does not follow from the claim that a term, n, has two different senses that what is strictly one and the same thing cannot at once satisfy both senses. On the contrary, one may think that a term, n, has two senses, but at the same time one may argue that if something satisfies the one sense, then it (the very same thing) must also satisfy the other sense, and conversely. For example, one may think that we need to distinguish two senses of the term 'human being': 'human being' in the sense of a thing that belongs to a certain biological species (e.g. one that has evolved through a certain natural selection); and 'human being' in the sense of a thing that possesses certain distinctive abilities (e.g. the ability to use language, etc.). But at the same time one may argue that if something is a human being in the first sense, then it (the very same thing) must also be a human being in the second sense, and conversely. In other words, one may argue that only things that belong to this biological species can develop, and can possess, these distinctive abilities, and conversely.

This may be just how Aristotle proceeds. He begins (in V. 8) by arguing that we need to distinguish two senses of the term *ousia*: *ousia* in the sense of 'the ultimate subject of predication' and *ousia* in the sense of 'essence'. But he goes on (in book VII) to argue that if something is an *ousia* (a primary being) in the sense of an ultimate subject of predication, then it (the very same thing) must also be an *ousia* (a primary being) in the sense of an essence, and conversely.

It may certainly be true that if two senses of a term, n, are wholly unrelated, or if they are related in a particular way, namely, as a primary sense and a non-primary sense, then what is strictly one and the same thing cannot at once satisfy both senses. For example, one and the same thing cannot be both a river bank and a financial bank; for these two senses of the term 'bank' are wholly unrelated. Or, one and the same thing (e.g. an apple) cannot, in the same respect, be both healthy in the sense of 'conducive to the health of the organism that eats it' and healthy in the sense of 'a healthy organism'. Of course, the apple that is conducive to the health of the organism that eats it may itself be a healthy organism. The point is that its being conducive to the health of the organism that eats it and its being itself a healthy organism will be different properties of the apple or will depend on different properties of the apple. In general, it certainly appears true to say that if a term, n, has both a primary and a non-primary sense, then what is strictly one and the same thing cannot at once satisfy both senses.

But what is noteworthy is that neither of these conditions, i.e. conditions for arguing that if a term, n, has two different senses, then what is strictly one and the same thing cannot at once satisfy both senses, applies to Aristotle's two senses of *ousia*. Evidently the two senses of *ousia* are not wholly unrelated. But just as evidently, they are not a primary sense and a non-primary sense; on the contrary, they are both senses of primary being – *ousia*. But then the fact that Aristotle distinguishes two senses of *ousia* goes no way towards showing that he thinks that it is not strictly one and the same thing that is *ousia* in both senses, i.e. that it is not strictly one and the same thing that is both an essence and an ultimate subject of predication.

vi Primary being is changeless being (VII. 7–9)

Aristotle's main aim here (in VII. 7–9) is to argue that the form of a changing, material thing (e.g. Socrates) is itself changeless, and in particular it is not subject to generation and destruction. So a changing, material thing, which is subject to generation and destruction, is a thing of a certain form; but this form is not itself subject to generation and destruction, and in general it is changeless. But Aristotle also argues, both in general and here (VII. 8, 1033^{b}19ff.), that the form of a changing, material thing is not separable, or distinct (*para*), from the thing whose form it is. In general, he criticizes Plato and the Platonists for separating forms from changing, material things. So he concludes that the form of a changing, material thing is itself changeless, but it does not, in general, exist prior to the generation or survive the destruction of the thing whose form it is: for to do so it would have to be distinct from or separable from the changing, material thing whose form it is. This means that Aristotle argues that although the form of a changing, material thing is changeless, it is not, unlike in the view of Plato and the Platonists, everlasting (*aïdion*, see also VII. 15, 1039^{b}23–26). So the claim that the form of a changing, material thing is itself changeless means that, for any time or duration in which this form exists, it is not subject to change, and in particular it is not subject to generation and destruction. But the times in which this form exists include only the duration of the existence of the changing, material thing whose form it is, e.g. the duration of the life of Socrates, i.e. some eighty years.

The view that the form of a changing, material thing is itself changeless is an important part of the argument for the view that primary being with regard to each changing, material thing is the essence and the form of that thing. We can see this in the following way. The essence of a changing, material thing, or indeed of any thing, is evidently something changeless. So if the essence of a changing, material thing is the form of that thing, then the form of a changing, material thing will be changeless. But while it is evident that essences are changeless, it is far from evident that forms are changeless. Indeed it is difficult to see how forms can be changeless, and in particular how they can be free from generation and destruction, if they are not distinct from or separable from changing, material things, which are subject to generation and destruction. So this is something that needs to be shown, and this is what Aristotle attempts to do in VII. 7–9. In other words, what has to be shown is how the essence of a changing, material thing can be, precisely, the form of that thing. And this has to be shown especially in view of the following *aporia*: if the essence of a changing, material thing is, precisely, the form of that thing, then the form, like the essence, will be changeless; but how can the form be changeless, and in particular free from generation and destruction, if it is inseparable from the changing, material thing whose form it is, and this thing is subject to generation and destruction?

It is worth emphasizing this *aporia*. For let us recall what Aristotle in general means by the form (*eidos, morphē*) of a changing, material thing: the form of a changing, material thing is that in virtue of which the thing is the very thing it is; and it is that in virtue of which the matter of the material thing constitutes the very thing that it constitutes. If we bear in mind this notion of form, then it will perhaps be directly evident that the form of a changing, material thing is changeless. For in this notion it is assumed that the form of a changing, material thing is the essence of that thing. After all, the essence of a changing, material thing is that in virtue of which the thing is the very thing it is. Once we assume that the form is the essence, it follows directly that the form is changeless, because the essence is changeless. But the question and *aporia* is how the form of a changing, material thing, which is subject to generation and destruction, can be changeless, and in particular how it can be free from generation and destruction.

Let us first note that it is indeed evident that the essence of any thing is something changeless, i.e. this is part of the very notion of essence. In general, the essence of a thing, x, is what we search for when we ask, 'What is this thing, x?', i.e. when we search for the definition of this thing, x. But suppose that x has an essence, i.e. there is something, E, that it is to be this thing, x. In Aristotle's words, suppose that there is something, E, that x is simply in virtue of itself (*kath' hauto*), i.e. in virtue of being the very thing it is. Then evidently x will be E for as long as x exists. For example, suppose that the essence of Socrates is being human, then evidently Socrates will be human for as long as he exists. Or suppose that the essence of water is H_2O; then evidently water will be H_2O for as long as it exists. So, in general, if E is the essence of a thing, x, then x will be, without change or variation, E for as long as it exists. It is in just this sense that the essence of a thing is something changeless. But note also that this can be understood in two ways. It may be understood to mean that the essence, E, is changeless and everlasting. This will be the natural way to understand it, if one thinks, as does Plato, that the essence is separable and distinct from changing, material things. On the other hand, it may be understood to mean that the essence, E, is changeless but not everlasting. This will be the natural way to understand it, if one thinks, as does Aristotle, that the essence is inseparable from the changing, material thing whose essence it is.

While it is evident that essences are changeless, it is far from evident that the inseparable form of a changing, material thing, i.e. a thing which is subject to generation and destruction, can be free from generation and destruction. And this is a problem for Aristotle, because he argues that the essence of a changing, material thing is, precisely, its form. To illustrate the problem further, suppose that we conceive of the form of a material thing as something like the shape or arrangement of that thing, and in particular as the shape or arrangement of its matter. Then it is natural to think that the process of generation of a particular material thing of a certain shape and arrangement involves a process of generation of a certain particular shape and arrangement, i.e. the shape and arrangement of the particular thing that is generated. Indeed, we may even think, quite naturally, that in some cases we can literally see the generation not only of the particular material thing, but also of its shape and arrangement, its form. So there is nothing obvious about the view that the form of a changing, material thing, i.e. a thing which is subject to generation and destruction, is not itself subject to generation and destruction.

It is worth noting that this is a problem for Aristotle, who argues that the essence of a changing, material thing is inseparable from that thing. It is not a problem for Plato, who argues that essences and forms are separable and distinct from changing, material things. This also indicates why here (in VII. 7–9) he not only argues that the form of a changing, material thing is changeless and free from generation and destruction, but also argues against Plato's view that the form of a changing, material thing is something distinct from (*para*) that thing (see VII. 8, 1033^{b}19ff.)

Aristotle argues (especially in VII. 8) that the process of generation of a particular material thing (e.g. Socrates, when Socrates is generated in his mother's womb) does not involve a process of generation of the form of that thing. He concludes that the form of a changing, material thing is not subject to generation and destruction, and in general it is changeless. Evidently, the process of generation of a particular material thing involves change and something changing. In general, Aristotle argues that it involves something changing into something else, i.e. the matter changing into a generated material thing (e.g. into Socrates; for this argument in general, see Chapter 2§4i and ii). In other words, he argues that the generation of a particular material thing must be understood as the generation of something, i.e. the particular material thing, out of something (*ek tinos*), i.e. out of its matter. He also recalls this argument at the opening of both VII. 7 and VII. 8. But what he argues here (especially in VII. 8, 1033^{a}24–^{b}16) is that, in the process of generation of a particular material thing of a certain form, e.g. of a particular human being, Socrates, the matter is *the only* thing that is involved in change; the form is not itself involved in change. So, for a particular material thing of a certain form, e.g. a particular human being, Socrates, to be generated is for some matter to become a particular material thing of that form. But Aristotle argues that the only thing that is generated here is, precisely, the particular material thing of a certain form, e.g. Socrates. The form, or indeed the matter, is not itself generated in this process. In particular, the form is not involved in change in this process; only the matter is involved in change in the process of generation of a particular material thing.

Aristotle's argument is highly formal and compressed. It goes like this: if the form were itself generated, then a single process of generation would involve an infinite number of processes of generation – which is absurd (see VII. 8, 1033ª32–ᵇ7). The reasoning in this exceedingly formal and compressed argument is along the following lines. For a particular material thing, x, of a certain form, f, to be generated is for something else, i.e. some matter, m, to become that particular thing, x, of that form, f. In general, for something, x, to be generated is for something else, y, to become x. But suppose that the form, f, were itself generated in this process. Then the process would involve the generation not of one thing, x, but of two things, x and f; i.e. it would involve the generation both of a particular material thing of a certain form, f, and of that form itself, f. But if the form, f, as opposed to the particular material thing, x, were itself generated in this process, then (by the general principle that for something, x, to be generated is for something else, y, to become x) a further thing, u, would be involved, i.e. a thing that comes to be f and out of which f comes to be. Evidently, u will not be the same as the matter m; for what the matter m comes to be is evidently not the form, f, as opposed to the material thing, x, rather it comes to be simply the material thing, x, of this form, f. So the question is whether u will itself be generated when f is generated out of u. If so, then the regress that Aristotle envisages will directly emerge, and so a single process of generation will directly involve infinitely many processes of generation – which is absurd. Evidently Aristotle thinks that u will itself be generated, if f is generated out of u. He does so, apparently, because he thinks that if one argues, instead, that u is not generated when f is generated out of u, then really there is no need to introduce u at all; rather one may simply conclude that f is not generated in the first place.

This argument deserves close examination. But let us suppose that it works, i.e. that it establishes that, in the process of generation of a particular material thing of a certain form (e.g. a particular human being, Socrates), the form is not itself generated. Let us also suppose that if the form is not generated in this process, then it is not at all involved in change in this process. We may still wonder how this can be so; i.e. how can the inseparable form of a particular material thing not be generated when that thing is generated?

It is, apparently, in order to make this exceedingly compressed and formal argument more intuitively convincing that Aristotle directly associates it with a different argument. This argument compares the generation, out of some matter, of a particular material thing of a certain form with a craftsman's producing, out of some matter, a particular material thing of a certain shape; e.g. the sculptor's making, out of some bronze, a particular bronze sphere (see opening of VII. 8). The argument is this. When sculptors make a bronze sphere, they do so by making some bronze come to be a particular bronze sphere; but they do not, apparently, make the spherical shape of the particular sphere that they make. Analogously, when a particular material thing is generated, it is generated by some matter coming to be a particular material thing of a certain form; but, apparently, the form of the particular material thing is not itself generated in this process.

Unfortunately, this argument, although less formal and abstract, also may not convince. The sculptors already have in mind the spherical shape, i.e. what it is for something to be a spherical shape, when they make the bronze sphere. So in making the bronze sphere, evidently they do not make the spherical shape that they already have in mind. So much may be clear. But it is not clear why they do not make the particular spherical shape of the bronze sphere that they make. Consider, for example, someone who draws a circle in the sand. Apparently, what they make is not only a thing with a certain shape or pattern, i.e. some sand with a certain pattern; they also make that particular pattern or shape, i.e. the particular circle in the sand. If, for example, they are interrupted while having drawn only part of this circle, it is natural to think that this particular shape has not been fully drawn or generated. It is indeed also natural to think that, even if they are interrupted, still some sand with a certain pattern, e.g. some sand with a half-circle, has been fully generated. So it is natural to think that it is precisely the particular shape that they set out to draw in the sand that has not been fully generated, as opposed to some sand with some pattern, which has been fully generated.

So we need, apparently, to look further than the argument at the opening of VII. 8 to see why Aristotle is confident that when a particular material thing of a certain form is generated, the form is not itself generated or involved in change. But it is also clear where in general we need to look; namely, to his general conception of matter as potentiality, i.e. to his process-based conception of matter (see Chapter 2§4ii for this conception). For suppose that we press the crucial question here, i.e. why is Aristotle confident that, when some matter changes into a particular material thing of a certain form, it is *only* the matter, and not the form, that changes? He is confident about this, because, in general, he argues that matter is potentiality, i.e. that to be some particular matter is, precisely, to be the starting-point of a process of generation that, provided that the appropriate external circumstances are present, will generate a particular material thing of a certain form. For example, the matter that actually generates Socrates is the matter that it is precisely because it is the matter that will, provided that the appropriate external circumstances are present, come to be a particular human being.

Now we can begin to see why, when some matter, m, changes into a particular material thing of a certain form, f (e.g. a particular human being), only the matter, m, and not the form, f, is involved in change. For, at any state in this process of generation, the matter involved is the matter it is precisely because it will, provided that the appropriate external circumstances are present, come to be a particular material thing of precisely this form, f. But this means that at every stage in this process of generation, there is a form involved, and there is just a single form, f, involved. For it is precisely because a single form is involved that a single process of generation is involved. So the form, f, cannot itself change in this process of generation, i.e. the generation of a particular material thing of this form, f. For if the form did change in this process, then this process would not be the process it is and perhaps it would not be a determinate and well-defined process at all. In general, Aristotle's reason for thinking that the form of a particular material thing is not involved in change, or generated, when that thing is itself generated, is ultimately to be found in his view that a process of generation is the determinate and well-defined process it is only with reference to a single form, i.e. the form of the particular material thing that is generated.

How, then, does this answer our initial *aporia*? The *aporia* was this: how can the inseparable form of a material thing fail to be generated when that thing itself is generated? Suppose that matter is potentiality, i.e. that for some matter to be the matter that it is is for it to be capable of generating a particular material thing of a certain form. This will mean that the matter of a particular material thing is not a constituent in or part of the thing whose matter it is. Alternatively, if we say that it is a constituent or part, we mean only that it is that out of which (*to ex hou*) this thing was generated (see also Chapter 2§4ii for this point). Likewise, the form of a particular material thing is not a constituent in or part of the thing whose form it is. Rather, it emerges, the form is what that very thing, the generated material thing, is – its essence. This form, or essence, is the very same one for as long as the thing exists. Indeed, we have seen that it is the very same one also in the duration of the process of generation of the thing whose form or essence it is. For otherwise neither the thing itself, once generated, nor the process of its generation, would be the very thing and the very process they are.

The *aporia* arose because, naturally enough, we thought of the form and the matter of a particular thing as inseparable constituents in or inseparable parts of that thing. If we think this, then it is hard to see how, when the particular thing is generated, its form and matter can be free from generation. For in general it is natural to think that the constituents in or the parts of a thing must be generated when that thing is generated, unless they are separable from that thing. For example, when we make soup out of beans and water, the reason why the beans and the water are not produced when the soup is produced is simply that they are separable from the soup, indeed they exist prior to the soup. Aristotle is happy to think that there is something that exists prior to the generation of a particular material thing of a certain form; what exists prior to the generated thing is its matter. At the same time, of course, he argues that the matter exists prior to the generated thing whose matter it is, not as an independent thing, but only as what potentially is a generated thing of that form. But he argues, especially against Plato and the Platonists, that the form does not exist prior to the generation of the particular material thing whose form it is, and in general it is not separable or distinct from the thing whose form it is. So, in order at the same time to argue that the form is not generated, and is not involved in change, when the particular material thing whose form it is is generated, he needs to argue that the form is not a constituent in or part of the particular material thing whose form it is. This in general is just what he argues. The form of a particular material thing is not a constituent in or part of that thing. Rather it is the essence of that thing; i.e. it is that in virtue of which the thing is the very thing it is, and in particular it is that in virtue of which the matter constitutes, and is generated into, the very thing that it constitutes and into which it is generated.

vii Primary being with regard to each changing thing is its essence and its form (VII. 10–12)

Above all, Aristotle argues that primary being with regard to each thing is the essence of that thing. This claim is intended to be true of all things, not just changing, material things. But books VII–IX are limited in their consideration of changing, material things. Only in book XII will Aristotle consider whether there are also things that are immaterial, changeless and distinct from changing, material things. With regard to changing, material things, Aristotle argues that the essence of each thing is the form of that thing. So he concludes that primary being with regard to each thing is the form of that thing. The things that he is considering here are material things, and material things, according to his general view, are things that come to be and pass away. But, in general, he argues that such things must be understood as wholes or units that result from form and matter (as *sunhola*). In particular, the matter of a material thing is that out of which (*to ex hou*) the material thing comes to be and into which it passes away. In general, matter is what explains how the thing can come to be and pass away, how it can be subject to generation and destruction (see §5vi of this chapter, and Chapter 2§4). On the other hand, the form of a material thing is what explains why the thing is the very thing that it is. In particular, the form of a particular material thing, e.g. of a particular human being, is what explains why the matter of that thing constitutes the very thing which it constitutes, e.g. a human being.

If we focus on this account of what form is, i.e. that it is what explains why a particular thing is the very thing it is, it is striking that this is also Aristotle's account of what essence is, i.e. essence with regard to changing, material things (see especially VII. 17). So evidently he thinks that the essence of a material thing and the form of that thing are identical. But why does he think this? Certainly, he does not think that the word 'essence' and the word 'form', as he uses these words, mean the same. On the contrary, he thinks that there is a real issue about what the essence of a material thing is. Is it only the matter of the thing, or only the form of the thing, or a combination of its form and its matter? He argues that primary being with regard to each thing is not simply the matter of that thing (in VII. 3; see §5ii of this chapter). So when he claims that primary being with regard to each thing is the essence of that thing, he evidently thinks that the essence of a thing is not simply the matter of that thing. But this still leaves the following choice: is the essence of each thing only the form of that thing or is it a combination of its form and its matter? So when he argues that primary being with regard to each thing is the form of that thing, he is arguing against the latter option. In other words, he argues that the matter of a material thing is simply not part of its essence. Only the form is part of the essence of a changing, material thing; and the form of a changing, material thing is the essence of that thing.

He argues for this view in VII. 10–11, and it is summed up in the very useful summary at the end of VII. 11:

> So then, in general and with regard to all things, it has been said what the essence [*to ti ēn einai*] is and how it is [what a thing is] simply in virtue of itself [*auto kath' hauto*] . . . and [it has been said] that the material parts [of a thing] are *not* included in the account of primary being.

(1037ª21–25)

So primary being with regard to each changing, material thing, and indeed with regard to all things, is the essence of that thing. But, with regard to changing, material things in particular, the essence of a thing does not include the material parts or the matter of that thing. Rather, primary being with regard to each changing, material thing is simply the form of that thing. As he says:

> For primary being [*ousia*] is the form that is present [in each material thing]; and that which results out of this [i.e. out of the form] and the matter is called the primary being that is the resulting whole [*hē sunholos ousia*, often translated as 'the concrete substance'].

(1037ª29–30)

In other words, it is the form of each thing that is primary being with regard to that thing. But the thing that results out of form and matter, and does so as a single unitary whole (*hē sunholos ousia*, often translated as 'the concrete substance'), is a being, something that is, only or primarily because of its form.

But why does Aristotle think that the matter of a thing is not part of its essence, i.e. part of what it is for that thing to be the very thing it is? This is because in general he argues that the matter of a material thing is not the matter that it is simply in virtue of itself (*kath' hauto* and *auto kath' hauto*; see 1037ª21–22); it is the matter it is only in virtue of its relation to the form of the material thing whose matter it is. Indeed, he argues that the matter of a material thing is not a being at all, something that is, simply in virtue of itself; it is a being only in virtue of its relation to the form of the material thing whose matter it is. By contrast, the form is the form it is, indeed it is a being, something that is, simply in virtue of itself and not in virtue of its relation to the matter of the material thing whose form it is. (For Aristotle's conception of matter as potentiality, see Chapter 2§4ii.)

Apparently, to say that the matter of a material thing is not part of its essence is equivalent to saying that the same particular material thing (e.g. this human being, Socrates) could have been generated out of a matter different from the matter out of which it is actually generated.

And it is equivalent to saying that the same kind of material thing (e.g. a human being) can be generated out of different matter. For the essence of a thing, x, is what this very thing, x, is. And the essence of a thing, x, either is the kind to which the thing belongs or certainly it determines the kind to which the thing belongs. Thus, at the opening of VII. 11, Aristotle points out that it is not part of the essence of a spherical material thing that is actually generated out of bronze to be generated out of bronze; for there are also spherical material things that are generated out of stone, wood, etc. (1036ᵃ31–34). He adds that even if it should happen that all spherical material things are generated out of bronze, still it would not be part of the essence of spherical material things to be generated out of bronze (1036ᵃ34–ᵇ3). Intriguingly and suggestively, he adds that although human beings are actually generated out of flesh and bones, being generated out of flesh and bones is not part of the essence of a human being (1036ᵇ3–7); for the same kind of thing, a human being, could have been generated out of a different matter. This is intriguing and suggestive, not least because Aristotle knew nothing of artificial intelligence. Evidently he thinks that this claim, i.e. the claim that human beings could have been generated out of a different matter than the matter out of which they are actually generated, is one that we will naturally find plausible. Indeed, we may find it plausible, as in fact we appear to do when we speculate whether there may be human beings on other planets, e.g. Mars, although we also think that, if there are Martians, their material constitution is likely to be different from ours. So we may well share Aristotle's intuition that it is not part of the essence of a material thing to be generated out of the matter that it is actually generated out of; and that, therefore, the matter of a material thing is not part of its essence.

Still, such intuitions can be questioned, so we may still ask why Aristotle thinks that the matter of a material thing is not part of the essence of that thing. The reason, it appears, is that he thinks that the matter of a particular material thing, e.g. a human being, contributes only to the explanation of how the thing comes to be and passes away, i.e. how it is generated and destroyed; it does not contribute to the explanation of why the thing is the very thing it is. For the matter of a material thing is, exactly, that out of which (*to ex hou*) the thing comes to be and that into which it passes away (see especially VII. 10, 1035ᵃ17f.; see also VII. 7, especially 1032ᵇ32f.). We thus saw that Aristotle argues (in VII. 8) that when a material thing, e.g. a bronze sphere, is involved in its own process of generation, the only thing that changes in this process is the matter of the material thing; for example, the bronze changes shape when it is shaped into a bronze sphere.

By contrast, the form of the thing that is generated, i.e. the principle which explains why the matter is generated into the very thing into which it is generated, e.g. into a bronze sphere, does not change in the process of generation of the bronze sphere. He even argues that the form of a changing, material thing is itself something changeless (see §5vi of this chapter).

But we may still ask why Aristotle thinks that the explanation of how a thing is generated does not contribute to the explanation of why the thing is the very thing it is. The reason, it appears, is that he thinks that a process of generation of a particular material thing, e.g. a particular human being, is a determinate and well-defined process only because, in the natural course of events, its end-result is the generation of a thing of a certain form, e.g. a human being. So a process of generation is nothing determinate and well-defined by itself, i.e. in virtue of the matter that is involved in it. Rather, a process of generation is something determinate and well-defined only in relation to, and hence dependent on, its end-result, hence in virtue of the form of the material thing which is, in the natural course of events, generated. This is why Aristotle thinks that what is involved in the process of generation of a material thing, namely, the matter of the material thing that is generated, does not contribute to the essence of the material thing itself. (For this notion of matter as potentiality, see also above, Chapter 2§4ii.)

viii No universal is a primary being (VII. 13–16)

In VII. 13, Aristotle argues against the view that primary being with regard to each particular thing (e.g. Socrates) is the universals that are true of that thing, and he concludes that no universal is a primary being:

> For it appears impossible that any of the things that are universally predicated [*ta katholou legomena*] should be a primary being [*ousia*].
> (VII. 13, 1038^{b}8–9)

That he endorses this appearance is confirmed in the summary at the end of VII. 16, when he says:

> So it is evident that none of the things that are universally predicated [*ta katholou legomena*] is a primary being.
>
> (1041^{a}3–5)

So Aristotle argues against the view that primary being with regard to a particular thing, e.g. Socrates, is the universals that are true of the thing and that determine what the thing is or is like. What this means is that no universal that is true of a particular thing, whether it is true of it accidentally, e.g. being snub-nosed with regard to Socrates, or essentially, e.g. being human with regard to Socrates, is primary being with regard to that thing. (But see below, for a very different interpretation of Aristotle's claim here. For, on a very different interpretation, he is only arguing for the claim that not all universals are primary being, and not for the claim that no universal is primary being. We will first set out our interpretation, and then consider the alternative interpretation.)

It is worth emphasizing that when Aristotle argues here (in VII. 13) that primary being with regard to a particular thing is not the universals that are true of that thing, and that no universal is a primary being, he is relying on his own view of what primary being is. In particular, he is relying on the view, which he has defended so far in the course of book VII, that the essence and the form, on the one hand, and the ultimate subject of predication, on the other hand, are strictly one and the same thing; and they are both equally primary being. Evidently the ultimate subject of predication is not a universal. So if the ultimate subject of predication is strictly the same thing as the essence and the form, and if both are equally primary being, then evidently primary being is not a universal at all, and no universal is a primary being. It is, therefore, no coincidence that the argument for the claim that no universal is a primary being comes only towards the end of book VII.

The claim that no universal is a primary being is clearly a most important claim. Aristotle argued earlier (in VII. 3) that primary being is not simply the ultimate subject of predication. But now (in VII. 13) he argues that primary being is not what is predicated of the ultimate subject either, if what is predicated is a universal. So evidently he wants to avoid the dilemma: *either* primary being is simply the ultimate subject of predication *or* it is a universal predicated of and true of this subject. But it appears particularly difficult to avoid this dilemma. (See §3 of this chapter, for the see-saw between the view that primary being is simply the ultimate subject of predication and the view that primary being is the universals that are predicated of and true of this subject.) So it is especially important that this is what Aristotle wants to do. We should also recall the basic attraction of the view that primary being with regard to a particular thing, e.g. Socrates, is the universals that determine what that thing is or is like. For it appears to be precisely the universals that are true of a particular thing, or at least some of them, that explain why this thing is a determinate and well-defined thing at all. Indeed, in virtue of itself and setting aside the universals that are true of it, a particular thing, e.g. Socrates, appears to be wholly indeterminate. But Aristotle wants to resist the attraction of the view that the universals, or even merely some of them, are primary being.

But is Aristotle making this radical claim, i.e. that no universal is a primary being? In fact he has been interpreted as denying only that primary being is the universals, as universals are understood by Plato. For it is Plato, certainly as Aristotle understands him, who believes that primary being is the universals, and his argument is certainly also directed against Plato and the Platonists. It is also true that he disagrees fundamentally with Plato about the nature of universals. (We will examine this criticism later, in Chapter 9.) But if he is only denying that primary being is the universals, as Plato understands universals, this is obviously a less radical claim. For then he could still claim that primary being is the universals, as he understands universals.

Aristotle gives the following characterization of what he means by 'a universal', when he claims that primary being is not the universals:

> For that thing is called a universal which by its nature is capable of holding good of [i.e. being true of] several things.
>
> $(1038^{b}11-12)$

In other words, something is a universal if it is the kind of thing that can be true of many things; for example, being snub-nosed and being human are universals, since many things can be snub-nosed and many things can be human. But this characterization is clearly intended to be non-contentious and to be acceptable to any thinker that is committed to the reality of universals, whether or not this thinker is a Platonist. So when he denies that primary being is the universals, he means to deny this without qualification and on any theory of universals. Platonists are mistaken to think that primary being is the universals, but this mistake does not depend on their conception of universals. Rather, it is mistaken to think that primary being is the universals, however one conceives of universals. So Aristotle is indeed making this radical claim, i.e. that no universal is a primary being. (But see below for a very different interpretation, which argues that his claim is only that not all universals are primary being, not that no universal is a primary being.)

Aristotle offers four arguments against the view that primary being is the universals. But they all rely on a central view, which stands out clearly in the first two arguments ($1038^{b}9-15$ and $1038^{b}15-23$; we will consider only these two arguments here). The view is that the relation between primary being with regard to something (e.g. Socrates) and that thing (Socrates) is not a relation between two things, one being true of the other; on the contrary, it is a relation between a thing and itself. It follows directly that no primary being is a universal. For no relation between a universal and a particular of which it is true is a relation between a thing and itself. He has already defended the view that the relation between a thing and its primary being is a relation between a thing and itself. For he has argued that a particular thing, in the sense of an ultimate subject of predication, is identical with its essence and its form, and all these are equally primary being (see §5v and vii of this chapter). So here he draws a crucial consequence from this view, namely, that no universal is a primary being.

The first argument (1038^{b}9–15) is this:

> First, [P1] the primary being [*ousia*] of each thing is peculiar to [*idion*] that thing, i.e. it does not also belong to another thing; but [P2] a universal is common to many things.
>
> (1038^{b}9–11)

It immediately follows that no universal is a primary being. P1 is a version of the central view that primary being with regard to a particular thing, e.g. Socrates, is peculiar to that thing, Socrates, and cannot also belong to another thing, e.g. Plato. So the relation between a thing and its primary being is a relation between a thing and itself. He underlines this when he says:

> For if [two] things have one primary being [*ousia*] and one essence [*to ti ēn einai*], then they are themselves one thing.
>
> (1038^{b}14–15)

In other words, if Socrates and Plato had a single primary being and a single essence, then they would be a single particular thing. But since they are evidently two particular things, they do not have a single primary being or a single essence. Rather, the primary being of each is peculiar to each and is not shared by the other. (For a very different interpretation of the claim that the primary being and the essence of a thing is 'peculiar to' (*idion*) that thing, see later in this chapter.)

The second argument (1038^{b}15–16) is this:

> Further, [P3] that thing is said to be a primary being [*ousia*] which is not said of an underlying thing [*hupokeimenon*, i.e. of the ultimate subject of predication]; but [P4] the universal is always said of an underlying thing.
>
> (1038^{b}15–16)

Again it directly follows that no universal is a primary being. P3 is, of course, based on the view, which he defended earlier, that primary being with regard to each particular thing is identical with that thing, i.e. with the ultimate subject of predication (see §5v). So primary being is not said of, i.e. it is not true of the ultimate subject of predication; for it simply is the ultimate subject of predication.

We have seen that a central assumption behind these two arguments, for the view that no universal is a primary being, is that primary being with regard to a particular (e.g. Socrates) cannot be shared by other particulars (e.g. Plato). But how is this assumption consistent with Aristotle's view that the primary being of something is its essence? He explicitly identifies primary being with essence in 1038^b14–15, quoted above, relying on what he had argued earlier in book VII. But he also thinks that Socrates and Plato belong to the same kind and species, since they are both human. So, apparently, they share the same essence. The inconsistency arises if Aristotle thinks that the essence of something (e.g. Socrates) is the kind and species to which the thing belongs (e.g. the species, being human). For then he will be holding a set of claims that are obviously inconsistent:

(1) Socrates and Plato do not share the same primary being and essence;
(2) the primary being and the essence of Socrates and Plato are the kind and the species to which they belong; and
(3) Socrates and Plato belong to the same kind and species.

Aristotle expressly makes claim 1 here (certainly he does so on the above interpretation; see below for a very different interpretation). But 3 is a general view of his. So if he is not to be inconsistent, he must deny 2, i.e. he must deny that the primary being and the essence of a particular are the kind and the species to which the particular belongs. In fact the denial of 2 follows directly from the view that no universal is a primary being; for a kind and species is evidently a universal. So when Aristotle argues that no universal is a primary being, he is immediately committed to denying that primary being is a kind or species. In other words, primary being with regard to a particular (e.g. Socrates) is not the kind or species to which the particular belongs. And since he identifies primary being with essence, it is likewise true that primary being with regard to a particular (e.g. Socrates) is not the kind or species to which the particular belongs. Aristotelian essences are not kinds or species.

Alternative interpretation

On our interpretation of Aristotle's argument in VII. 13, he argues that no universal is a primary being. For primary being with regard to each particular thing (e.g. Socrates) is peculiar (*idion*) to that thing, 'peculiar' in the sense that two distinct particulars (e.g. Socrates and Plato) do not strictly share one and the same primary being; and they do not share the same primary being even if they belong to the same kind or species (e.g. they are both human). But of course, no universal is in this sense peculiar to the particular of which it is true. On the contrary, it is part of what it is to be a universal that universals can be true of many things (e.g. many things can be human). So no universal is a primary being.

But there is a very different interpretation of Aristotle's argument in VII. 13. This is of central importance. For we will see that it makes a fundamental difference to the overall understanding of how, in book VII, Aristotle answers the question, 'What is primary being?', which of the two interpretations we adopt. On the alternative interpretation, what Aristotle argues in VII. 13 is not that no universal is a primary being, but rather that to be a primary being is not simply to be a universal. What this means is that not every universal is a primary being; but it allows that some universals, or some distinctive type of universals, are primary beings. Indeed, on this interpretation, Aristotle argues here (in VII. 13–16) that it is precisely a distinctive type of universals that are primary being with regard to each particular thing; namely, the species to which the particular belongs. For example, primary being with regard to Socrates is being human, where being human is the species to which Socrates belongs. Species-universals are peculiar (*idia*) to the particulars of which they are true, in the sense that they cannot be true of particulars that are different in kind. For example, being human cannot be true of both Socrates and the cock that, as his last wish, he asked to be sacrificed to Asclepius. For although both Socrates and the cock are animals, they are different in kind, since Socrates is a human being and the cock is a bird. Indeed, species-universals appear to be the only universals that are peculiar (*idia*) in this sense. For generic-universals, such as being an animal, can evidently be true of things that belong to different kinds, e.g. Socrates and the cock. The same is obviously true of universals that do not signify kinds at all, such as being of a particular colour, e.g. orange; for example, both the rose and the goldfish can be orange. So it is distinctive of species-universals to be peculiar (*idia*) in this sense, i.e. they cannot be shared by particulars that belong to different kinds. But obviously such universals are not peculiar in the sense that they cannot be shared by distinct particulars (e.g. Socrates and Plato). On the contrary, they can be shared by distinct particulars, provided that these belong to the same kind and species.

But what is distinctive of species-universals, on the present interpretation, is above all that a particular thing (e.g. Socrates) is the very thing that it is, i.e. it has the essence that it has, precisely in virtue of a species-universal being true of it and in virtue of its belonging to a particular species. For example, Socrates evidently is not the very thing that he is in virtue of being pale, five foot tall, educated, healthy, just, etc. But neither is he the very thing that he is in virtue of being, for example, an animal, i.e. in virtue of a generic-universal being true of him and his belonging to a particular genus. For the cock belongs just as much to this genus, but evidently Socrates is not the very thing that he is in virtue of being a particular kind of bird. Rather, on this interpretation, Socrates is the very thing that he is in virtue of being human, i.e. in virtue of a species-universal being true of him and his belonging to a particular species.

Before we consider how these two interpretations, i.e. ours and the alternative interpretation, in general compare with each other, it is natural to ask how this alternative interpretation fits the text of VII. 13. For it appears to be ruled out by what Aristotle says, especially when he says:

> For it appears impossible that any of the things that are universally predicated [*ta katholou legomena*] should be a primary being [*ousia*]. For, first, the primary being of each thing is peculiar to each thing, but the universal is common; for that thing is called a universal which by its nature is capable of holding good of [i.e. being true of] several things.
>
> (VII. 13, 1038^{b}8–12)

This certainly appears to say that no universal is a primary being; it does not appear to say only that not every universal is a primary being. This impression is confirmed when, at the end of VII. 16, Aristotle sums up the conclusion of the argument by saying: 'So it is evident that none of the things that are universally predicated [*ta katholou legomena*] is a primary being' (1041^{a}3–5).

But whether the text allows for the alternative interpretation depends on what Aristotle means by 'the things that are universally predicated' (*ta katholou legomena*). If he means, simply, 'universals', then he is evidently saying that no universal is a primary being. So the alternative interpretation is ruled out. But perhaps this phrase serves rather to indicate a certain distinctive type of universals, i.e. those that are universally *predicated*. If so, it is only of these universals that Aristotle denies that they are primary beings. This makes room for the alternative interpretation. So, on the alternative interpretation, the phrase 'the things that are universally predicated' serves to distinguish two types of universals: those that are universally *predicated* and those that are not universally *predicated*. And Aristotle, on this interpretation, argues here (in VII. 13–16) that while the former type of universals cannot be primary beings, the latter type of universals are, precisely, the primary beings.

On this interpretation, Aristotle concludes that primary being with regard to each particular thing is the species to which the thing belongs; and the species is evidently a universal. But he also says that the species is not universally *predicated* of the particulars that belong to it. For example, being human is not universally predicated of Socrates. What does this mean? According to this interpretation, the point of saying that, for example, being human is not universally predicated of Socrates is to draw attention to the fact that the predication relation is a relation between two things – one thing being true of another. But the relation between Socrates and being human is not a relation between two things; for Socrates is a thing at all only in virtue of being human. And this, on the present interpretation, is precisely what Aristotle means when he says that, for example, being human is not universally *predicated* of Socrates. So the alternative interpretation can apparently be reconciled with the text after all.

But let us stand back and consider how the two interpretations in general compare with each other. For the choice between them makes a decisive difference to how we think that Aristotle answers the question, 'What is primary being?' First of all, on our interpretation it emerges that primary being with regard to each particular thing is itself a particular, not a universal. (Or perhaps rather, primary being with regard to each particular thing is primarily a particular and only as a consequence a kind or species, which is a universal. For this point, see §5ix of this chapter.) On the alternative interpretation, by contrast, primary being is, directly, a kind or species, which is a universal. This is a basic disagreement of interpretation about how Aristotle answers the *aporia* that he raised in book III, the book of *aporiai: Are principles one in kind or one in number?* (see the ninth *aporia*, 999^b24–1000^a4). In other words, are there as many principles as there are particular things, so that my principle and yours are different even though we belong to the same kind and species, or are there only as many principles as there are kinds of things, so that my and your principle are the same since we belong to the same kind and species? On our interpretation, there are as many principles as there are particular things (although we will see that these particular principles also generate kinds and species; see §5ix of this chapter). On the alternative interpretation, there are only as many principles as there are kinds of things and in particular species of things.

But there is an even deeper difference between the two interpretations. On our interpretation, a particular, e.g. Socrates, is the very thing it is – it has an essence – simply in virtue of itself, i.e. in virtue of being the particular that it is. In other words, a particular is a determinate and well-defined thing simply in virtue of being the particular that it is. Only as a consequence does the particular also belong to a general kind and to a species. On the alternative interpretation, by contrast, a particular is the very thing it is – it has an essence – only in virtue of its belonging to a general kind and in particular to a species. This is a fundamental difference. It is the difference between thinking (as on the alternative interpretation) that there is a primitive relation between particulars and general kinds, the relation *belonging to*, and thinking (as on our interpretation) that this relation is itself a consequence of a yet more basic relation between a particular and itself.

How is it possible to decide between the two interpretations? There is perhaps no evident way of deciding between them. Perhaps book VII, the core of the *Metaphysics*, is, at the end of the day, open to two fundamentally different interpretations. Still, there are a number of things that appear to us to point against the alternative interpretation.

First, the alternative reading of VII. 13, 1038^b8–12 and VII. 16, 1041^a3–5 (quoted above) may appear forced. Surely it is more natural to take Aristotle's words here as saying what on the face of it they do say, i.e. that no universal is a primary being.

Second, a central thrust in Aristotle's overall argument in book VII is the claim that a particular is the very thing that it is – it has an essence – simply in virtue of itself and not in virtue of its relation to any other thing. But it is natural to understand this as implying that a particular is the very thing that it is not in virtue of its relation to any universal. It is true that the alternative interpretation wants to accommodate this thrust in Aristotle's overall argument. It wants to do so by arguing that the relation between a particular and the species to which it belongs is not a relation between two things; for the particular is a thing only in virtue of this relation. This certainly goes some way towards accommodating the thrust of Aristotle's argument. But does it go far enough? After all, even if the relation between a thing and the species to which it belongs is not a relation between two things, still it is not a relation between a thing and itself. For evidently the particular, e.g. Socrates, is not the same thing as the species to which it belongs. So how can the particular, on this interpretation, be the very thing that it is *simply in virtue of itself*?

Third, we have seen that Aristotle argues that primary being is both the essence and the ultimate subject of predication; and that strictly one and the same thing is both an essence and an ultimate subject of predication. But this directly implies that the essence is not a universal; for evidently the ultimate subject of predication is not a universal. So the essence of a particular thing (e.g. the essence of Socrates, i.e. his being human) is not the general kind, or the species, to which the thing belongs (e.g. being human); for a general kind and a species are universals. Of course, the alternative interpretation will respond that Aristotle does not really think that strictly one and the same thing is both an essence and an ultimate subject of predication. For it will argue that Aristotle, in V. 8, distinguishes between two senses of *ousia* or 'primary being': *ousia* in the sense of 'the ultimate subject of predication'; and *ousia* in the sense of 'essence'. The alternative interpretation will conclude that Aristotle is not really committed to the view that strictly one and the same thing is both an essence and an ultimate subject of predication. This response is very important. For it shows that the alternative interpretation relies on the view that, because Aristotle distinguishes two senses of *ousia*, therefore he does not think that strictly one and the same thing is *ousia* in both these senses. But we have already responded to this line of reasoning. Basically, it is true that Aristotle distinguishes two senses of *ousia*; but it in no way follows that he does not think that strictly one and the same thing can be *ousia* in both these senses (see §5v of this chapter).

Finally, there is a particular and basic problem with the alternative interpretation. It appears that in general Aristotle wants to argue that primary being is likewise the primary object of knowledge. He also argues that the primary object of knowledge is the essence. For all knowledge, and in particular all explanatory knowledge and science, which is knowledge above all, is ultimately derived from knowledge of essence. (See Chapter 2§3.) At the same time, he argues that primary being is the ultimate subject of predication, which is a particular and not a universal. But then, if primary being and the primary object of knowledge are strictly to coincide, the essence, too, must be a particular and not a universal. So the essence cannot be a universal, as it is on the alternative interpretation. (We will return to this point in a moment, in §5x of this chapter.)

ix Is the essence and the form of each particular thing a universal, a particular, or both?

Does Aristotle think that the essence and the form of each particular thing (e.g. Socrates) is a universal, a particular, or both? We recall that, with regard to changing, material things, which are the remit of his consideration here (i.e. in the central books of the *Metaphysics*, books VII–IX), he argues that the essence and the form are one and the same (see §5vii of this chapter). But what is the essence and the form: a universal, a particular, or both? There are really three possibilities, not just two:

(1) the essence and form is a universal only;
(2) the essence and form is a particular only;
(3) the essence and form is both a particular and a universal.

It has emerged that Aristotle thinks that the essence and the form is a particular. For he argues that the essence and the form of a particular changing, material thing (e.g. Socrates) is identical with the ultimate subject of predication with regard to that thing. But the ultimate subject of predication is evidently a particular. The view that the essence and form is identical with the ultimate subject of predication is of absolutely central importance. For it means that the relation between a particular thing (e.g. Socrates), in the sense of an ultimate subject of predication, and its essence and form is the relation between a thing and itself. It is because of the central importance of this view that it is important to recognize that, for Aristotle, the essence and form of a changing, material thing is a particular. It is true, however, that there is a very different interpretation, which argues that, for Aristotle, the essence and form of a changing, material thing is a universal, namely, the species to which the thing belongs. We have set out this alternative interpretation at the end of §5v and especially §5viii of this chapter.

So we may conclude that, for Aristotle, the essence and form of a changing, material thing is a particular. Still, this leaves the question whether the essence and form is only a particular or also a universal. Certainly, the essence and form is *primarily* a particular. For it is identical with the ultimate subject of predication, which is a particular. But perhaps the essence and form is also a universal, *as a consequence of* being a particular. Perhaps this is just what Aristotle thinks.

To decide this question, we need to ask why exactly the essence and the form of a changing, material thing is a particular. The reason why this is so emerges most clearly in the last chapter of book VII, i.e.

VII. 17. There Aristotle argues that the essence and the form of a particular material thing, e.g. Socrates, is the principle that explains why this thing is the particular thing it is, Socrates. It does so by explaining why the matter of this particular material thing, Socrates, constitutes the particular thing that it constitutes, Socrates. So the essence and the form of a particular material thing explains something about a particular material thing, and it does so in so far as this particular material thing is the very particular that it is, e.g. Socrates (as opposed to, for example, Plato). If we add that the relation between a particular material thing and its essence and form is a relation between the particular material thing and itself, then we directly obtain the result that the essence and the form of a particular material thing is itself a particular. In the final analysis, this is why the essence and the form is a particular; i.e. because, first, it is identical with the particular material thing whose essence and form it is, and, second, it explains something about the particular material thing in so far as this particular material thing is the very particular that it is, e.g. Socrates (as opposed to, for example, Plato).

So far, it may appear that the essence and the form is *only* a particular. But really all that has emerged is that the essence and the form is *primarily* a particular. The question remains whether it is also, *as a consequence*, a universal. Consider the way in which Socrates' essence and form explains why Socrates is the particular thing that he is – Socrates. Compare this to the way in which Plato's essence and form explains why Plato is the particular thing that he is – Plato. These forms are two, not one; for they are particulars. Nevertheless, it emerges that the way in which Socrates' essence and form explains why Socrates is the particular thing that he is – Socrates, and the way in which Plato's essence and form explains why Plato is the particular thing that he is – Plato, are really exactly the same way. For the explanation is in both cases the following: the essence and the form of a particular material thing, x, e.g. of Socrates or Plato, explains why this particular material thing, x, is the very particular that it is, e.g. Socrates or Plato, by explaining why this material thing, x, is the determinate and well-defined particular that it is, e.g. a particular human being. The mode of explanation is exactly the same in both cases – the case of Socrates and the case of Plato – because to explain why a particular material thing, e.g. Socrates or Plato, is the very particular that it is is to explain why it is the determinate and well-defined particular that it is, e.g. a particular human being. But evidently Socrates and Plato are both human beings. In general, if something explains why a particular material thing, e.g. Socrates, is the very particular it is by explaining why it is the determinate and well-defined particular that it is, e.g. a particular human being, then apparently this identical mode of explanation is indefinitely repeatable, i.e. it introduces the possibility of indefinitely many particulars that are determinate and well-defined in exactly the same way, e.g. are human beings.

In this sense, the essence and the form of a particular material thing is primarily a particular, but also, as a consequence, a universal. The essence and the form is a universal in the sense that it explains universally, i.e. the mode of explanation provided by the essence and the form is the exact same for any number of particulars. Of course, if we say that the essence and the form of a particular material thing is, in this sense, a universal, i.e. in the sense that it explains universally, then we must take special care not to confuse this with the original sense of 'a universal', i.e. the sense in which a universal is something different from and true of many particulars. For the essence and the form of a particular material thing, although it explains universally, is, precisely, not different from and true of the particular material thing whose essence and form it is.

It is of crucial importance to Aristotle that the essence and the form should explain universally. For the essence and the form are, by their very nature, things that explain – they are principles (*archai*) – indeed they are the basis of all explanation. But, for Aristotle, as also for Plato, it is part of the very nature of an explanation that it should explain universally, i.e. that it should explain any number of things in exactly the same way. (See Chapter 2§3ii.)

So it is not a happy coincidence that the essence and the form explains universally, i.e. that the explanation of why one particular material thing, e.g. Socrates, is the very particular thing that it is – Socrates, should explain this in exactly the same way as the explanation of why another particular material thing, e.g. Plato, is the very particular thing that it is – Plato. Far from being a happy coincidence, this is part of the nature of explanation, and it is part of the nature of essence and form, since essence and form are explanations and the very basis of all explanation. So it is not just a happy coincidence that things, i.e. the changing, material things with which to begin with we are directly familiar from sense perception and experience, are in general intelligible and subject to explanation. Rather, this is part of the essence of things, and hence part of what it is for things to be beings, things that are, in the first place.

It is worth emphasizing that Aristotle's view that

> If something explains why a particular material thing (e.g. Socrates) is the very particular it is by explaining why it is the determinate and

well-defined particular it is (e.g. a human being), then this identical mode of explanation is indefinitely repeatable, i.e. it introduces the possibility of indefinitely many particulars that are determinate and defined in exactly the same way (e.g. are human beings).

This view implies that is impossible to define a single particular without thereby defining a indefinite number of essentially similar particulars – defining a species. In other words, it is impossible that a definition of a particular should be such that it cannot in principle apply to more than one particular. Aristotle sums up this view when he says that 'a definition [*ho horismos*] is of the universal [*tou katholou*] and of the kind [or species, *tou eidous*]' (1036ᵃ28–29). The same point is behind his view that there is no definition of particulars as such and in isolation from species (see e.g. 1036ᵃ5 and 1039ᵇ27–29).

x *Primary being and the primary object of knowledge*

Metaphysics is the search for primary being. But it is also the search for the highest and most explanatory kind of knowledge, indeed for the knowledge that is knowledge most strictly (see Chapter 2§1). So it emerges that primary being is, precisely, the primary object of knowledge. But Aristotle has argued that primary being with regard to each thing is the essence of that thing (see §5iv of this chapter). So the primary object of knowledge is, precisely, the knowledge of the essence of each thing. This is also the conclusion that he states at the opening of book VII, when he says:

> We suppose ourselves to know each thing most strictly [*malista*] when we know *what* this human being is [i.e. its essence] or *what* this fire is [i.e. its essence], rather than when we know its quality or quantity or place.
>
> (VII. 1, 1028ᵃ36–ᵇ1)

But he has also argued that the essence of each thing (e.g. of Socrates) is identical to the ultimate subject of predication and the particular that this thing is (e.g. this particular thing – Socrates). And this means that the essence is itself a particular (see §5v of this chapter). So this – the essence and the particular – is primary being and the primary object of knowledge.

In general, however, Aristotle (just like Plato) argues that it is part of the very nature of an explanation that it should explain universally, i.e. that it should explain any number of things in exactly the same way. (See Chapter 2§3ii.) Here, in book VII, Aristotle appeals to this view especially when he says that explanatory definitions are definitions of the universal (see, for example, VII. 11, 1036ᵃ28–29: 'for a definition [*ho horismos*] is of the universal [*tou katholou*] and of the kind [*tou eidous*]'). The definitions that he has in mind are explanatory in the sense that they provide ultimate explanations. For they are definitions of the essence, and essence is, precisely, what provides ultimate explanations.

But this gives rise to a striking problem. For the following three claims, all of which he commits himself to, seem to be inconsistent with each other:

(1) explanatory knowledge is knowledge of universals;
(2) the most explanatory knowledge, metaphysics, is knowledge of the primary being and the essence of each thing; but
(3) the primary being and the essence of each thing is a particular.

The problem can also be stated as follows. Explanatory knowledge is knowledge of universals; but what primarily and fundamentally exists, i.e. primary being, is particulars. But how can metaphysics, the highest kind of explanatory knoweldge, be of one thing, universals, while primary being is something else, particulars? Surely this is impossible. For metaphysics is just the knowledge of being and especially primary being.

Aristotle states this problem early in the *Metaphysics*, at the end of book III, the book of *aporiai*:

> So we must puzzle over these puzzles about the principles. But also about whether the principles are universal [*katholou*] or of the nature of what we call particulars [*ta kath' hekasta*]. For if, on the one hand, they are universal, they will not be primary beings [*ousiai*, since Aristotle will argue that no universal is primary being]. . . . But if, on the other hand, the principles are not universal but of the nature of particulars, they will not be scientifically knowable [*epistētai*]; for the scientific knowledge [*epistēmē*] of any thing is universal.
>
> (the fifteenth *aporia*, III. 6, 1003ᵃ5–15; see also XIII. 10, 1086ᵇ32–1087ᵃ2)

In book VII Aristotle does not explicitly formulate a solution to this problem. But he provides the materials for a solution, especially when he says that the form of each changing, material thing, which he argues is the essence of that thing, is the same in kind (*homoeidēs*) in different particular material things, e.g. in different particular human beings such as Socrates and Plato. He finds manifest confirmation of this view in the fact that one human being begets another human being, i.e. another particular material thing of the same kind (VII. 7, 1032ª24–25). The kind of solution that he has in mind is clearly stated in book XII:

> It is the particular that is the principle of the particulars; for while *human being* is the principle of *human being* universally, there is no universal *human being*, but Peleus is the principle of Achilles, and your father of you [etc.].
>
> (XII. 5, 1071ª20–22)

But the solution is indicated even more clearly at the end of book XIII – the only passage in the *Metaphysics* in which he appears explicitly to formulate a solution:

> For there can be no demonstration of the fact that this particular triangle is the sum of two right angles, unless [there is thereby demonstration of the fact that] *every* triangle is the sum of two right angles; nor can there be demonstration of the fact that this particular human being is an animal, unless [there is thereby demonstration of the fact that] *every* human being is an animal.
>
> (XIII. 10, 1086ᵇ34–37)

The kind of demonstration that he has in mind here is scientific demonstration – demonstration which is based on definitions of the essence of things.

So what is Aristotle's solution to the problem that, on the one hand, that which primarily and fundamentally exists, i.e. primary being, is particulars, but, on the other hand, explanatory knowledge is knowledge of universals? The solution is to be found in the overall view that emerges from book VII, i.e. the view that the essence and the form of a particular material thing is primarily a particular, but also, as a consequence, a universal (see §5ix of this chapter). The essence and the form is a particular because, first, it is identical with the particular material thing whose essence and form it is; and, second, it explains something about the particular material thing in so far as this particular material thing is the very particular it is, e.g. Socrates (as opposed to, for example, Plato). But, as a consequence, the essence and the form is also a universal in the sense that it explains universally, for the mode of explanation provided by the essence and the form is exactly the same for any number of particulars (see §5ix of this chapter).

So both views can be satisfied at once, i.e. the view which says that what primarily and fundamentally exists, i.e. primary being, is particulars, and the view which says that explanatory knowledge is knowledge of universals. The contradiction between the two views was only apparent.

8

THE ULTIMATE CAUSE
OF CHANGE: GOD

(Book XII)

1 The project of book XII and its place in the *Metaphysics*

Aristotle's overall aim in book XII is to investigate changing things, and nature in general, *as a whole* – to investigate the universe (*to pan*, literally 'the all', i.e. the totality of things) *as a whole* (*hōs holon ti*, XII. 1, 1069ᵃ19). He will undertake this investigation by searching for the principles and explanations of all things, and of the universe and nature as a whole. By nature, *phusis*, he will mean the totality of changing things. But he will argue (in XII. 6–10) for a very distinctive conclusion. For he will argue that the totality of changing things, and nature as a whole, has a single ultimate explanation and cause, which is itself changeless and which is distinct from nature as a whole. What this explanation explains is, in general, why there is such a thing as change in the first place. But in particular it explains why there is such a thing as regular and uniform change, and in general change that is intelligible and subject to explanation – what we may call rational change. He will eventually call this ultimate explanation of rational change: God.

We will consider at length how Aristotle reaches this conclusion, and how he conceives of this ultimate explanation and cause of change: God. But first a word about how (especially in XII. 1) he characterizes this overall project, the project of searching for the ultimate principles and explanations of all things and of the universe as a whole; and how in general this project fits into the project of the *Metaphysics*. This is how he begins:

> [1069ª18–26] The investigation is about primary being [*ousia*]. For we are searching for the principles and the explanations [or 'causes', *ta aitia*] of primary beings. For if the universe is [considered] as a whole, primary being will be its first part; and if [it is considered] as a series of things, in this way too primary being will be first, followed by quality, quantity [etc., i.e. by the non-primary beings]. . . . Further, none of the other things [i.e. the non-primary beings] is separate [*chōriston*].

> [1069ª25–30] Even the ancient thinkers bear witness to this through their deeds. For they were searching for the principles, elements, and explanations of primary being. The present-day thinkers hold that the universals are more properly primary beings. . . . But the past thinkers hold that the particulars are more properly primary beings, such as fire and earth, but not what is common to both, i.e. *body*.

> [1069ª30–33] But there are three [kinds of] of primary beings: one is sense-perceptible – part of it being everlasting, another part being perishable (this latter, i.e. things such as plants and animals, is acknowledged by everyone) – . . .; but another is changeless.

The last lines (1069ª30–33) anticipate what Aristotle will argue later (in XII. 6–10). For the distinction between, on the one hand, sense-perceptible and in general changing things and, on the other hand, changeless things anticipates the distinction between, on the one hand, nature, i.e. the totality of changing things, and, on the other hand, an ultimate explanation of nature as a whole, which will be provided by something that is itself changeless.

Here it is also worth noting straight away that Aristotle also distinguishes the sense-perceptible and changing things themselves into two kinds: those that are everlasting and those that are not everlasting but, on the contrary, perishable. By those changing things that are perishable he has in mind especially things such as plants and animals, and in general the things with which we are directly familiar from sense perception and experience. By those changing things that are everlasting he has in mind, it will emerge, the planets and stars, and in particular the outermost heaven (*ho prōtos ouranos*), which, he will argue, bounds and delimits nature as a whole.

But in general he wants here (in XII. 1) to characterize the overall project in book XII, which is to search for the ultimate explanations of all things, and of nature and the universe as a whole. Aristotle's characterization of this project, we should note, is strikingly similar to, and reminiscent of, the characterization of metaphysics both at the opening of the *Metaphysics* (I. 1–2; see Chapter 2§1) and at the opening of the central books (especially VII. 1–2; see Chapter 7§1). At the opening of the *Metaphysics*, metaphysics was characterized as the search for the ultimate explanations of all things, with the emphasis on *all* things. And early in the central books (in book VII) metaphysics was characterized as the search for primary being (*ousia*). Indeed, in book VII primary being was in general characterized as separate being (*chōriston*) and set against non-primary and non-separate being (see VII. 1, 1028ª33–34; discussed in Chapter 7§4); but this is precisely how primary being is characterized here (XII, 1069ª24, also ª20–21). Furthermore, it is emphasized here (XII. 1, 1069ª25–30) that this search is as old as the trees and is shared by different and various philosophers; but this was likewise emphasized in book VII (see VII. 1, 1028ᵇ2f. and VII. 2).

So the project of book XII is to search for the ultimate explanation of all things, and in particular of nature and the universe as a whole. The aim is eventually (in XII. 6–10) to argue that there is a single explanation of the regular and uniform change that is distinctive of nature as a whole, and that this explanation is provided by something that is itself changeless and distinct from nature as a whole – by God. But apparently this project, as Aristotle characterizes it (especially in XII. 1), is very much part of the project of the *Metaphysics*. It is important to note this, not least because there is, on the other hand, also reason to think that book XII was written as a largely self-contained piece which can, at least to a large extent, stand on its own, and was only later inserted as book XII of the *Metaphysics*.

But there is an important complication. We recall that, earlier in the *Metaphysics*, metaphysics was characterized in three ways:

(1) as the science of all things (I. 1–2);
(2) as the science of being *qua* being (in IV. 1); and
(3) as the science of primary being (in IV. 2 and books VII–IX).

We have seen that two of these three characterizations are also directly present in book XII. 1: the science of all things and indeed of the universe as a whole (see 1069ª19), and the science of primary being (*ousia*, characterized in exactly the same way as in book VII). But the third characterization appears to be conspicuously missing from book XII: the science of being *qua* being, i.e. the search for an answer to the basic question of metaphysics: 'What is being and what is it for something, anything, to be?' So we must ask, is the project in book XII at all intended to contribute to this basic question of metaphysics? There is reason to think that it is. The main reason is that it is hard to understand the question, 'What is primary being?', which (in XII. 1) is part of the characterization of the overall project of book XII, except as a means of addressing the more basic question: 'What is being and what is it for something, anything, to be?' (For this point, see Chapters 4§§1–3 and 7§1.) We will return to this issue later (see §11 in this chapter).

Before we turn to Aristotle's project of arguing for, and his conception of, an ultimate explanation and cause of nature as a whole, a word is appropriate about how in general he undertakes this project in book XII. He begins (from XII. 1, 1069^{b}3 to the end of XII. 5) with an investigation of sense-perceptible and in general changing things, and in particular those changing things that are perishable and not everlasting, i.e. the things with which we are most directly familiar from sense perception and experience – things such as plants and animals. The investigation up to the end of XII. 5 is limited to those things and their fundamental explanations. It does not introduce everlasting things or their explanations, or the question of why we should think that there are everlasting things at all. Neither does it introduce the explanation of nature as a whole, nor the question of why we should think that there is such an explanation at all. Only in XII. 6–10 is this introduced.

We will concentrate on XII. 6–10, i.e. on:

(1) the argument for the existence of a changing thing that is everlasting, and
(2) the argument for the existence of a thing that is changeless, distinct from nature as a whole, and explanatory of nature as a whole.

The first part of book XII (i.e. XII. 2–5) is important, but it does not add anything crucially different from what we already know from the *Metaphysics* (and from the *Physics*). Here is a very brief summary.

XII. 2 considers the nature and principles of change and of changing things especially in so far as they are subject to generation and destruction, i.e. in so far as they are perishable. This is familiar ground, also from the *Physics* (see Chapter 2§4).

XII. 3 considers, in particular, to what extent the main principles of generation and destruction, i.e. form and matter, are themselves subject to change. It also argues that form does not exist distinct from (*para*) the things composed out of form and matter (1070^{a}9–14). But, in anticipation of what is to come later (in XII. 6–10), it is suggested that there may be things that do exist distinct from matter (1070ª14f.).

XII. 4–5 consider whether each changing thing has the same explanation or a different explanation from every other changing thing. The question here is, in particular, whether each particular changing thing (e.g. Socrates) has the same explanation or a different explanation from every other particular changing thing of the same kind (e.g. Plato). This question, it emerges, is closely associated with the question whether forms, i.e. the forms of changing particular things, are particular or universal (see 1071ª19f.; we considered this central question in Chapter 7§5viii–x).

This short summary of XII. 2–5 evidently does not do justice to this first part of book XII. But, setting aside the detailed content of these chapters, the important thing is not to suppose that the first part of book XII (i.e. XII. 2–5) is irrelevant, or even merely secondary, to the further project of the second part (i.e. XII. 6–10). On the contrary, the overall project of book XII is to search for the ultimate explanation of all things, and of nature and the universe as a whole. But evidently nature includes, in the first instance, perishable changing things, and they are the things with which we are most directly familiar from sense perception and experience. So it is natural to start with those things, as Aristotle does in XII. 2–5. Indeed, it is precisely by searching for what ultimately explains these familiar changing things, which are perishable and not everlasting, that Aristotle will argue, first, that there is something changing that is everlasting and not-perishable and, second, that there is something changeless and distinct from nature as a whole. So the overall argument in book XII is that, if we are adequately to explain those changing things with which we are most directly familiar, i.e. perishable changing things (which he considers in XII. 2–5), then it is not sufficient, in our explanations, to appeal only to such things. We will also need (it is argued in XII. 6–10) to appeal to everlasting changing things, such as the planets, stars, and in particular the outermost heaven; and, above all, we will need to appeal to something changeless and distinct from nature as a whole.

Finally, let us straight away draw attention to a question of clarification that is crucial for understanding Aristotle's argument. He will argue that there is a single thing that provides the ultimate explanation of nature as a whole and of all rational change, but this thing, he will argue, is everlasting, changeless and above all *separate* from sense-perceptible and in general changing things, and from nature as a whole (see especially 1073ª3–5; also XII. 10, discussed later in this chapter). But in what sense is this ultimate explanation *separate* from changing things and from nature as a whole? For we need to recall that Aristotle uses the term 'separate' in more than one sense and apparently in three senses: ontological independence; distinctness; and separable existence (see Chapter 7§4, for these three senses).

So, when Aristotle argues that the ultimate explanation of nature as a whole is *separate*, which sense of 'separate' does he have in mind? Evidently, he also has in mind the first sense of separation, i.e. ontological independence. For he argues that every primary being, whether it is primary being with regard to nature as a whole or it is primary being with regard to each particular thing within nature (e.g. with regard to Socrates), is separate in this sense (see XII. 1, 1069ª19–24; also VII. 1, 1028ª33–34). This is because it is part of the very notion of primary being (*prōtē ousia*, often simply *ousia*) that a primary being is a being simply in virtue of itself and not in virtue of its relation to other things. But this cannot be all that he has in mind when he says that the ultimate explanation of nature as a whole is *separate*. For when he uses the term 'separate' of this ultimate explanation and this absolutely primary being, just as when he uses 'changeless' of it, he wants to set this ultimate explanation and this absolutely primary being against any other primary being, i.e. to set it against primary beings with regard to any particular thing within nature (e.g. with regard to Socrates). For he argues, precisely, that primary being with regard to any particular thing within nature (e.g. Socrates or Kallias) is not separate, or distinct (*para*), from the particular thing with regard to which it is primary being (e.g. Socrates or Kallias, see XII. 3, 1070ª13–14). So when he argues that the ultimate explanation of nature as a whole is *separate*, he appears to have in mind also, and especially, the second sense of separation, i.e. distinctness. Perhaps he also has in mind the third sense, i.e. separable existence.

2 Changing, changeless and transcendent things

Like Plato, Aristotle distinguishes two fundamental kinds of things: changing things, which are material, and changeless things, which are not material. Like Plato again, he argues that we are familiar from sense perception and experience with changing things, i.e. they are sense-perceptible things (*aisthēta*), while we grasp changeless things through our intellect and reason, i.e. they are intelligible things (*noēta*, see XII. 1, 1069ª30–34). What we grasp through reason is, above all, that there must be changeless things, if explanation is to be at all possible and if things are to be at all subject to explanation. Further, we can then search for explanations, which are based in changeless things, and this search will involve a combination of, on the one hand, sense perception and experience and, on the other hand, reasoning.

So Aristotle's metaphysics has the following structure:

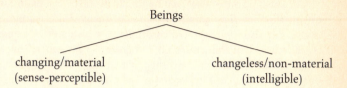

Beings

changing/material (sense-perceptible)

changeless/non-material (intelligible)

Here it is worth recalling that, for Aristotle, matter is part of the explanation of change, so changing things are necessarily material things, and changeless things are necessarily immaterial things. Everyone admits the existence of changing things, since everyone is familiar with the coming into being and passing away of plants and animals (1069^a31–2), but also with the changing seasons and the motion of the planets and the stars – the heavenly bodies (1072^a21–3). But the existence of changeless things is controversial and it is denied by those philosophers who include in their metaphysics only material particulars and their constituents (1069^a28–30); elsewhere he calls them 'the natural philosophers' (*hoi phusiologoi*), and we may think of them as naturalists in general.

But why does Aristotle admit changeless things in his metaphysics? For he is acutely aware of the controversial nature of this commitment. This is perhaps especially clear from the eighth *aporia* in book III, the book of *aporiai*: *Do general kinds [which are changeless things] exist at all, in addition to sense-perceptible things [i.e. the changing things]?* (see 999^a24–$^b24$) The commitment to changeless things is controversial, both because one may argue that explanations must, and perhaps can, be conducted purely in terms of changing, sense-perceptible things, and because one may question the very possibility of explaining anything, i.e. question the view that things are at all subject to explanation. It is perhaps this latter challenge above all that he takes up here, in book XII. (We will return to this point at the end of the chapter.)

His answer in general is indicated at the opening of book XII, when he says: 'The investigation is about primary being [*ousia*]. For we are searching for the principles and the explanations [or 'causes', *ta aitia*] of primary beings' (1069^a18–19). This, as we saw, is also how metaphysics was characterized from the beginning of the *Metaphysics*, namely, as the search for the ultimate principles and explanations of all things (I. 2, especially 982^b7–10). So evidently he thinks that if we include something in our metaphysics and regard it as a primary being, for example sense-perceptible particulars such as plants, animals and the bodies that we see in the sky, then we must likewise include in our metaphysics and regard as a primary being anything that we consider to be its explanation and cause. And he thinks that even the naturalists agree with this, for they admit as beings not only sense-perceptible particulars, but also their material constituents, which are the explanations and causes that the naturalists recognize. So his general line of reasoning against the naturalists is this: you admit of changing things, and you also admit of their explanations and causes, as primary beings; but I will argue that these explanations and causes include changeless beings.

So changeless beings must be admitted in one's metaphysics because they are explanations and causes of changing beings. This line of reasoning is common to Plato and Aristotle. For Plato, too, argued that the changeless forms are explanations of changing things, and this is why they must be admitted as real and primary beings (see Chapter 9§1). So a single project is common to all parties, the non-naturalists, whether Platonists or Aristotelians, and the naturalists alike, namely, how to provide adequate explanations of those things that are recognized by everyone, namely, sense-perceptible, changing, material things. The disagreement concerns whether such explanations can be provided by the changing, material, sense-perceptible things alone, which is the naturalist position, or changeless, non-material, intelligible things are also required, which is the position of Plato and Aristotle.

But once one is committed to changeless, immaterial things, the important question is how they are related to changing, material things. There appears to be just two possibilities: *either* changeless, immaterial things are inseparable from changing, material things, *or* they are, on the contrary, separable and perhaps even distinct, i.e. actually separated, from changing, material things. (We will use the term 'transcendent' for things that are separable and perhaps even distinct, i.e. actually separated, from changing, material things.)

Aristotle's general commitment to inseparable changeless things is familiar, for this is the status that he ascribes to the forms of sense-perceptible particulars (see Chapters 2§4i and 7§5vi–vii). But the reasoning behind this commitment is briefly rehearsed in book XII (chapters 2–5). What is distinctive and new about book XII (although it was anticipated in a promissory way in books VII–IX; see 1028^{b}13–15; 1028^{b}28–31; 1037^{a}10–14; 1041^{a}7–9; and 1050^{b}3–8) is his commitment to changeless things that are transcendent. He calls them 'separate primary being' (*choristē ousia* or *kechōrismenē ousia*, see 1069^{a}34 and especially 1073^{a}3–5; see also XII. 10 in general, discussed below). So the question of book XII (especially chapters 6–10) is whether there really are transcendent changeless beings, and the aim is to establish that there are. For he will argue that there is a single transcendent changeless being which is the ultimate explanation and cause of change, in particular of the motion of the outermost heaven, and which eventually he will call 'God'.

The ultimate cause of change, God, is transcendent not because he is changeless, non-material and intelligible, for that is also true of the forms that are inseparable from changing, material things. He is transcendent because he is separable and perhaps even distinct, i.e. actually separated, from changing, material things and from nature as a whole. The transcendence of the ultimate cause of change is underlined when he summarizes the conclusion of the argument for an ultimate cause of change (at the end of XII. 7): 'thus it is evident from what has been said that there is an *ousia* that is everlasting and changeless *and separate from sense-perceptible things*' (1073^{a}3–5). But it is also indicated when he states that everything else depends on the ultimate cause of change: 'on such a principle depends the heavens and [the whole of] nature', i.e. the entire sense-perceptible and changing world (1072^{b}13–14).

So Aristotle's metaphysics has the following structure:

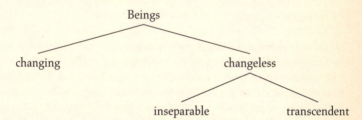

But he wants to distinguish his own commitment to changeless transcendent beings from Plato's. The main difference is that, whereas for Plato all changeless beings are transcendent, for Aristotle some changeless beings are inseparable, namely, the forms of changing, material particulars. But even in Aristotle some changeless beings are transcendent, namely, it emerges, a single thing: the ultimate explanation and cause of change, God. But if we look closer, there is something in Plato which performs much the same function as the ultimate cause of change in Aristotle, namely, the form of the good (*Republic* VI. 506bf.), which is the cause of rational, intelligible order and change in the universe (see also *Timaeus* 29dff.). Moreover, Plato appears to have singled out this form as pre-eminently transcendent when he says that it is even 'beyond real being' (*epekeina tēs ousias*), i.e. beyond the plurality of the other forms (*Republic* 509b). Aristotle recognizes that the form of the good is Plato's rival to his own ultimate cause of change, and he is at pains to point out the difference between the two conceptions of the pre-eminently transcendent being (see especially XII. 6, 1071^{b}16–17). But the similarities are all the more striking. For Aristotle's God, like Plato's form of the good, is ultimately the cause of rational, intelligible order and change in the universe – an order which, for Aristotle, is visibly manifest above all in the orderly, uniform motion of the heavenly bodies.

3 The ultimate cause of change, and the outermost heaven

Aristotle distinguishes between two kinds of changing things: those changing things that come to be and cease to be; and those changing things that are everlasting (see XII. 6, 1071^{b}3–4; also XII. 1, 1069^{a}30–31):

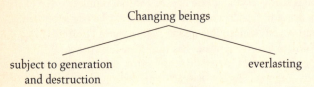

Changing beings

subject to generation   everlasting
and destruction

The former includes the plants and animals around us, which evidently are generated and destroyed in the recurring cycle of their individual lives. It also includes ourselves, or at any rate part of ourselves. For Aristotle argues that a part of ourselves, namely, our intellect, or certainly part of our intellect, is everlasting (see *De Anima* III. 4–5; also *Metaphysics* XII. 3, 1070^{a}24–26). But the latter comprises the planets and stars that we see in the sky, and indeed the whole universe, which he argues are everlasting, i.e. they were never created and will never cease to be. Here it is worth emphasizing his view that the universe is everlasting, i.e. infinite in both directions in time. For it is above all the most comprehensive change of the universe, i.e. the motion of the outermost heaven, that the ultimate cause of change is introduced to explain and cause. This is in itself striking, and it shows that Aristotle's ultimate cause of change is not introduced to create the universe, or to set it in motion. For the universe, he argues, is uncreated and it was always in motion, indeed in the orderly, uniform motion that is manifest to us even now as we observe the heavens. (We will consider his argument later in §4 of this chapter.)

So Aristotle argues that there is a progression or ascent from non-everlasting changing things, which are most subject to change, since they come to be and cease to be; to everlasting changing things, which are less subject to change; to everlasting changeless things, which are not at all subject to change, namely, the ultimate cause of change (see 1071^{b}3f.).

> non-everlasting changing things → everlasting changing things → everlasting changeless things

This progression from more to less change can be understood in an abstract way, as referring to anything that might fit each of the three descriptions. In that case, we should note, the third description would apply not only to the ultimate cause of change, which is transcendent, but also to inseparable forms, which are themselves everlasting and changeless. But there is no doubt that Aristotle rather intends it to be understood in a concrete way, i.e. as referring to certain particulars: plants, animals and humans under the first description; the planets, stars, heavenly spheres and above all the outermost heavenly sphere under the second description; and the ultimate cause of change under the third.

This shows that Aristotle's argument for the ultimate cause of change, although highly abstract, is based on the appeal to concrete particular things with which we are familiar from experience: plants, animals, humans on the one hand, and planets, stars and the heavens on the other. For what the ultimate cause of change is introduced to explain is neither change in general nor a species of change in the abstract, but rather, primarily and directly, the motion of the outermost heaven, and indirectly everything else in the universe that is either carried by or included within the outermost heaven. So his argument is based on the accumulated experience, extending over centuries and millennia, of starlit skies, and on his own scientific interpretation, which involves much abstract argument, of these astronomical data. Two conclusions in the area of astronomy and cosmology are central in his argument for the ultimate cause of change. First, the universe is everlasting, i.e. infinite both backwards and forwards in time (see *On the Heavens*, I. 10–12; see also §4 of this chapter). Second, the universe is finite in space, for it is perfectly spherical and bounded by an outermost sphere which carries the fixed stars and moves in perfectly uniform, circular motion – this is the outermost heaven (see *On the Heavens* I. 5–7).

It may strike us as surprising that Aristotle combines the belief in the temporal infinity of the universe with a belief in its spatial finitude. But here it is crucial to note that, for Aristotle, there is no distinction between the finite universe within space, on the one hand, and space itself, on the other hand. For space, according to Aristotle's conception of space, does not surround the universe, rather it is itself bounded by the universe. Figuratively speaking, if one stood on the outermost heaven and the limit of the universe, one would be standing at the limit of space itself, and there would be no 'outside' into which one could stick one's hand. As Kuhn nicely remarks, in this respect Aristotle's conception of space is closer to Einstein's than to Newton's (see Kuhn 1957: 98–99). For, in Aristotle just as in Einstein, space is not, as it is in Newton, independent of the matter that occupies it; rather space is itself determined by the matter in it. So if the totality of matter is only finitely extended, then space itself will be only finitely extended.

When (at the opening of XII. 6) Aristotle sets out to argue for the existence of a changeless ultimate cause of change, he does so not directly, but rather by first arguing for the existence of everlasting change, in particular everlasting and perfectly uniform circular motion ($1071^{b}3$–11), which he identifies as the motion of the outermost heaven ($1072^{a}23$). This is not the argument for the ultimate cause of change, but it is a crucial step in the argument. For the ultimate cause of change is above all the explanation and cause of the motion of the outermost heaven. And the nature of the ultimate cause of change is rooted in the fact that the change that it causes and explains is everlasting and perfectly uniform.

But there is something puzzling about the fact that Aristotle should offer an argument for the existence of everlasting, perfectly uniform, circular motion. For a little later (at the opening of XII. 7) he says that this motion, which he ascribes to the outermost heaven, 'is evident not only through argument, but in fact' ($1072^{a}21$–23); i.e. it is evident from our sense-experience of the heavens. And in *On the Heavens*, a work dedicated to astronomy and cosmology, he likewise says that 'we ourselves see the heavens revolving in a circle, and by argument too we established that circular motion actually belongs to something' (I. 5, $272^{a}5$–7). But why is an abstract argument needed, if something is already evident from sense-experience? Perhaps because of something that Aristotle appears to overlook, namely, that it is not so evident after all that we directly experience, literally see, that the heavens revolves in a circle. This is rather a hypothesis, even if a very natural one, that we employ to unify the heavenly phenomena that we experience. It is a very natural hypothesis, almost second nature to us, because it appears confirmed continuously and manifestly by our experience of the cyclical, recurring pattern of the seasons, our calendar, and our whole way of measuring time into units that are not only uniform, but cyclically recurring – days, months, years. So habit may render this hypothesis so familiar that we may think that it is evidently exhibited in the phenomena themselves. But it is still a hypothesis rather than a given fact. For the view that the planets and stars revolve in circles with the earth at the centre, the so-called geocentric hypothesis, is after all mistaken and refuted by hard science, we now firmly believe. But just as important, and this is something that Aristotle does not overlook but himself draws attention to, we certainly do not experience, indeed cannot experience, that the motion of the heavens is everlasting. Neither can we experience that this is the motion of a single, outermost heaven that bounds the universe. So an abstract argument is needed for these conclusions.

4 The argument for the everlasting, uniform and circular motion of the outermost heaven

We need to begin by considering Aristotle's argument for the existence of things that change in everlasting, perfectly uniform circular motion – and in particular the outermost heaven. For he begins (at the opening of XII. 6) by indicating that the real aim of this argument is, precisely, to establish the existence of a changeless being, which, it emerges, is the ultimate cause of change:

> Since there were three kinds of *ousiai*, two of them physical and one changeless, regarding the latter we must assert that it is necessary that there should be an everlasting changeless *ousia*.
>
> $(1071^b3–5)$

The things that provide the basis for arguing that there really is an ultimate cause of change are said to be physical, i.e. changing and material; and they are, we saw, divided into two kinds: those that are subject to generation and destruction and those that are everlasting – the former includes plants and animals, the latter the planets, stars, and the universe as a whole. But now he goes on to argue for the existence not of the changeless ultimate cause of change, but of something that changes in everlasting, perfectly uniform circular motion, which, it emerges, is the outermost heaven:

> For *ousiai* are the first of existing things [*ousia* = primary being], and if they are all destructible, all things are destructible. But it is impossible that change should either come into being or cease to be (for it always was); nor can time come into being or cease to be, for there could not be a before and an after if time did not exist.
>
> $(1071^a5–9)$

> Further, change is continuous in the same way as time is continuous; for time is either the same as change or an attribute of change. And no change is continuous except change in place, and indeed only the change in place which is circular is continuous.
>
> (1071^{a}9–11)

Even by Aristotle's standards, this argument is extremely dense. But the reasoning stands out clearly. The subject matter of the argument is changing things, and the introduction of changeless things is for the moment deferred. First he argues that not all changing things are destructible, which means that some changing things are not destructible, but everlasting. For if all changing things were destructible, then time itself would be destructible, which is absurd (1071^{a}5–9). So this establishes that there are changing things that are everlasting. Next he argues that the everlasting changing things change in perfectly uniform ('continuous'), circular motion in space. For time is perfectly uniform, and its uniformity is based on the uniform change of changing things, but the things that change uniformly are things that move in circular motion in space (1071^{a}9–11). So this establishes the overall conclusion that there are things that change in everlasting, perfectly uniform circular motion. At the opening of XII. 7, when this overall conclusion is finally stated, these things are identified as the outermost heaven:

> There is something that always changes in ceaseless change, and this change is circular motion (and this is evident not only through argument, but in fact), so that the first heaven is everlasting.
>
> (1072^{a}21–23)

A number of features are striking about this argument. Especially striking is the prominence in the argument of the appeal to time. Time is conceived as everlasting, indeed it is suggested that to deny this is to be committed to a contradiction: if time were not everlasting, but limited in time, then it would make sense to speak of 'before time began' and 'after time ends'; but evidently such talk is absurd and self-contradictory, since the notions of before and after make sense only within time. Further, time is conceived as dependent on change and changing things, namely, the things whose change provides a uniform measure for time; and in fact we appeal to such things in measuring time, in particular the uniform motions of the planets and stars. So if time is everlasting, and if it depends on the uniform change of changing things, then uniform change must itself be everlasting.

Aristotle appears to conclude that there must be some uniformly changing things that are everlasting, in particular the outermost heaven.

But this may not follow. The everlasting nature of uniform change, even if it implies uniformly changing things, does not require that these things, taken individually, should be everlasting. For presumably a series of things in time, each with a limited life-span, could secure everlasting uniform change, if they forever changed seamlessly into each other.

But Aristotle argues that the uniform change that provides a measure for time must be circular motion; for otherwise it would not be perfectly uniform and could not provide a measure for time. The obvious objection is motion in a straight line, for why should such motion be any less uniform than circular motion? His view that circular rather than rectilinear motion is uniform is based on the view that the universe is spatially finite. For in a spatially finite universe, bodily motion in a straight line in space is limited by the limits of the universe. Hence a body moving in a straight line is evidently not moving in a perfectly uniform way, since it changes direction and hence comes to a momentary halt at the limits of the universe: first one way, then back again, etc. On the other hand, a finite universe allows for uniform motion, if this motion is circular, and if the universe is itself circular, and the circular motion is concentric with it. This again shows how Aristotle's abstract argument relies fundamentally on features of the concrete, actual universe as he conceives it.

Finally, a particular feature of the argument is especially important. From the everlastingness and uniformity of time Aristotle derives not only the everlastingness of the universe, but its everlasting uniformity. This is important, for an everlasting universe may, on the contrary, be such that for its first period (but an infinite period, if the universe is infinite backwards in time) it lacks uniformity and is in a state of chaos, and only at a particular point in time does it acquire uniformity and order. This universe is like Aristotle's in being everlasting, but unlike his in that its uniformity is not everlasting. But he argues not only that the universe is everlasting, but also that the uniform, ordered universe, the cosmos, is everlasting. He drives home this point when he criticizes those thinkers, whether naturalists or those who invoke gods, who claim that order was born out of chaos, a state in which 'all things were thrown together', like day out of night. As he says: 'it is not true that for an infinite time there was chaos and night, rather the same things existed forever, either in circular motion or in some other state' (XII. 6, $1072^{a}7$–9; also $1071^{b}26$–28).

This is the conclusion of a complex argument (XII. 6, $1071^{b}12$f.), which runs along the following lines. Suppose that for its first period the universe lacked uniformity. Then there must be something that explains why, at a particular point in time, the universe changes from a disorderly to an orderly and uniform state. But this explanation and cause must be, by its very nature, active, as opposed to merely having the capacity to act. For if its nature is merely to have the capacity to act, then a similar question can be asked with regard to it: why, at a particular point in time, does it change from a state of not acting to a state of acting (see 1071^{b}17–20). If this cause is, by its very nature, active, then it will always act. But then it will always produce the effect that it produces, i.e. it will always cause order and uniformity in the universe – which means that the universe will always be orderly and uniform. This argument deserves close examination, but we will need to set it aside.

5 The argument for the ultimate cause of change

Let us now turn to the argument (at the opening of XII. 7) for an ultimate cause of change, i.e. for a changeless, everlasting first cause of change, in particular of the everlasting, perfectly uniform circular motion of the outermost heaven. The argument is this: if something changes, then there must be a cause of its changing, but in the case of the change of the outermost heaven, the cause must be changeless.

> There is something that always changes in ceaseless change, and this change is circular motion (and this is evident not only through argument, but in fact), so that the first [i.e. outermost] heaven is everlasting.
>
> (1072^{a}21–23)

> It follows that there is also something that moves it [i.e. something that moves the first heaven, causes it to move].
>
> (1072^{a}23–24)

> But since that which is both itself moving and moves other things [i.e. the outermost heaven] is an intermediary, there must be something that moves it without itself moving [i.e. a changeless ultimate cause of change], and this is everlasting and *ousia* and actuality.
>
> (1072^{a}24–26)

The argument is evidently based on the conclusion, with which it opens (1072^{a}21–23), about the all-encompassing outermost heaven, the limit of nature, and the change distinctive of it. But the reasoning for a changeless ultimate cause of the change that is distinctive of the outermost heaven is conducted in two steps: first Aristotle infers that the changing outermost heaven has a cause – something that causes it to change ([a]23–24), then he concludes that this cause must be changeless ([a]24–26).

Assuming for a moment that the changing outermost heaven has a cause at all, why must this cause be changeless? If the cause were itself changing, then there would be a further cause of it, and so on. Why does Aristotle think that this is a vicious regress? Why is there anything unacceptable about such an infinite series of causes and effects? Aristotle does after all think that the universe is infinite both backwards and forwards in time, and that animals generate offspring in forever recurring cycles. So he argues that there is a series of causes and effects that extends infinitely in time, both backwards and forwards. There is nothing vicious about that. However, there is a difference between time and space, and the argument for an ultimate cause of change is concerned with space in so far as it is concerned with the outermost heaven. For while on his conception the universe is infinite in time, it is finite in space, bounded by the all-encompassing outermost heaven, the limit of nature. So the ultimate cause of change is supposed to cause change in nature as a whole, and nature as a whole is involved in the motion of the outermost heaven. This is indicated when he says that the outermost heaven moves other things and is an intermediary between the changeless ultimate cause of change and the other things (1072^a24). For the first heaven moves in the first instance the fixed stars that it carries, but also everything else within nature. But the same point is underlined when he concludes that 'from such a principle [the ultimate cause of change], therefore, depends the heaven and nature', i.e. nature as a whole (1072^b13–14). But evidently the cause of the change of this heaven must be changeless; if it were itself changing, then it would be a further heaven, so it would not be the cause of the 'first' and 'outermost' heaven. This shows that the spatial finitude of the universe is a crucial premise in Aristotle's argument for the changelessness of the ultimate cause of change – a premise for which he has already argued elsewhere (in *On the Heavens* I. 5–7) and now takes to be established. He draws attention to the spatial finitude of the universe when he calls the heaven whose motion is caused by the ultimate cause of change, 'the first heaven'.

But why does the changing outermost heaven need a cause at all? Aristotle, we should note, sees no problem here and moves directly from 'x changes' to 'something causes x to change' (1072^a23–24). He is clearly working with some version of the principle of sufficient reason, perhaps even the version which states that every event has a cause. To question this principle would really be to abandon Aristotle's overall project, the project of searching for explanations – reasons, causes. Still, we may ask how the principle of sufficient reason applies to the change of the outermost heaven, the limit of nature. Why, we may object, is not change and motion in nature as a whole something basic and primitive which does not require further explanation? The principle that every event has a cause will still apply within nature, but it does not, the objection claims, apply to nature as a whole. But this objection does not really touch Aristotle. For what the ultimate cause of change is supposed to explain is not simply motion and change in general, but a specific change of a particular thing, namely, the perfectly uniform, circular motion of the outermost heaven. And this is evidently one particular event, even if a maximally cosmic one, which contrasts with any other event within nature, such as the growing of the grass in the garden. So the principle of sufficient reason that says that every event has a cause will apply to the motion and the change of the outermost heaven just as much as to any other event within nature.

One may still object that the motion of the outermost heaven does not itself require an explanation, for the simple reason that it is maximally cosmic and coincides with the limits of nature. But Aristotle offers a basic reason for thinking that this particular change, the change of the outermost heaven, does itself require an explanation. The reason is that this change, like any other particular change, is contingent, i.e. it could have been different from what it in fact is:

> If something changes, it could have been different [from what it in fact is]; hence the first motion in space [i.e. the motion of the first heaven], even if it is in a state of actuality [since it always moves in the same way], still, in so far as it changes, to that extent it could have been different [from what it in fact is], i.e. different in respect of place even if not in respect of its existence.
>
> (1072^b4-7)

The point is that the outermost heaven, whether or not we think that it could not have existed, could have moved in a different way from how it actually moves. So we need an explanation of why it moves in the way it does.

Here it emerges quite clearly that Aristotle is working with a very strong version of the principle of sufficient reason: if something could, in a particular respect, have been different from what it in fact is, then an explanation is needed of why it is as it is, and not different, in this respect. That he is working with this principle of sufficient reason is confirmed when he goes on to say that the ultimate cause of change, on the other hand, 'could *not* have been different [from what it in fact is] *in any way'* (1072^b8). So the ultimate cause of change is a necessary being in every respect – an absolutely necessary being. This is why the ultimate cause of change does not in turn require a further explanation, but is indeed 'first' and 'ultimate'. So this is indeed the ultimate cause of change, and in particular of the everlasting, uniform, circular motion of the outermost heaven. If we ask why Aristotle is working with such a strong principle of sufficient reason, the answer is, evidently, because he wants to push the overall project, i.e. the project of searching for explanations – reasons, causes – as far is it will go.

6 The causation distinctive of the ultimate cause of change

But how does the ultimate cause of change cause the outermost heaven to move? There are in fact two questions here. How does the ultimate cause of change cause the outermost heaven to move at all? And how does it cause it to move in the way in which it actually moves, namely, in an everlasting, uniform and circular way? If we are thinking of the first question, it is crucial to recognize that the ultimate cause of change does not set in motion the outermost heaven; for the motion of the heaven is everlasting and it always was in motion. So the function of the ultimate cause of change is not to cause the heaven to change its state – from rest to motion. However, we saw that not only is the motion of the outermost heaven everlasting, but its uniform, circular motion is also everlasting and there never was a time in which it was in a different state of motion than it is now. This shows that the function of the ultimate cause of change is not to cause the heaven to change its state from one kind of motion, disorderly motion, to its present orderly, uniform and circular motion. So the function of the ultimate cause of change is not to cause the outermost heaven to change its state in any way, whether from rest to motion or from one kind of motion to another. For the outermost heaven always was in motion, and in exactly the same motion, namely, uniform, circular motion.

It is crucial to recognize that the function of the ultimate cause of change is not in any way to change the state of motion of the outermost heaven. This shows that the kind of causation distinctive of the ultimate cause of change is very peculiar in a particular respect. For the causation distinctive of the ultimate cause of change does not depend on the cause acting upon the effect or on any interaction between cause and effect. So the ultimate cause of change does not act upon or interact with the outermost heaven. Perhaps this will appear too incredible to us. How, we may ask, can something cause something else to move without acting on it? But if we find this objection compelling, it is perhaps because we suppose that the function of the ultimate cause of change is to change the state of motion of the outermost heaven. For surely it would be right for us to object that something cannot cause something else to change its state of motion, unless it acts on it. But if we bear in mind that the function of the ultimate cause of change is not to change the state of motion of the outermost heaven in any way, since the outermost heaven always was in motion and in the same state of motion, perhaps we will be more ready to envisage that the ultimate cause of change may cause the outermost heaven to move in the way it does, but without acting on or interacting with it. The ultimate cause of change simply does not need to interact with the outermost heaven, for there is no question of its interacting with the heaven and so causing it to change its state of motion.

The reason why the kind of causation distinctive of the ultimate cause of change does not depend on interaction with the outermost heaven is quite simply that the ultimate cause of change is changeless, so it moves other things without itself moving or changing (1072^{a}26–27). For something can interact with something else only if it itself changes or moves; and this is so for the simple reason that interacting is itself a form of changing or moving. So there is, apparently, adequate harmony between cause and effect in Aristotle's conception of the causation between the ultimate cause of change and the outermost heaven. On the one hand, the ultimate cause of change cannot interact with the outermost heaven; for the ultimate cause of change is changeless, and interaction is a kind of motion and change. On the other hand, the outermost heaven does not require interaction from the ultimate cause of change; for the outermost heaven does not change its state of motion, and interaction would only be required if it did change its state of motion. So it appears that Aristotle's account of the causation distinctive of the ultimate cause of change, whether or not it is ultimately convincing, is at least coherent on a central point.

But how can the ultimate cause of change cause the distinctive motion of the outermost heaven without itself moving or changing, and without interacting with the heaven? As an answer to this central question, Aristotle appeals to a familiar context in which the cause of motion and change need not itself move or change, and certainly its causation does not depend on its moving or changing:

> There is something [namely, the ultimate cause of change] which, without [itself] changing, moves [other things]. ... But this is how what is desired [to orekton] and what is thought by the intellect

[*to noēton*] moves [i.e. moves other things], namely, it moves [other things] without [itself] moving.

(XII. 7, 1072ª26–27)

Here we are asked to remind ourselves of how intelligent animals are caused to move and act, in particular animals that are capable of desire (*orexis*, cf. *to orekton*, the object of desire), especially rational desire (*boulēsis*, cf. *boulēton* 1072ª28), and of rational thought (*noēsis*, cf. *to noēton*, the object of rational thought). Such animals, we are asked to recall, are directly moved by their own rational thought and desire, when they deliberate and come to recognize that something is good and worth pursuing. But ultimately what moves them is the object that they recognize is good and worth pursuing (the *orekton/boulēton* and *noēton*). As Aristotle points out here: 'reason [*nous*] is moved by the object that is rationally thought of [*to noēton*]' (1072ª30). But while the thought and desire of an animal changes when the animal moves as a result of its thought and desire, the object of the thought and desire, i.e. what is recognized as good and worth pursuing, need not change, and it does not depend for its causation on its changing. For example, if I reason that a certain kind of exercise is necessary in order to secure health, which I recognize to be a good thing and worth pursuing, then (supposing that I am sufficiently rational) my desires will change and they will cause me to change. But the object that I recognize to be good and worth pursuing, health, does not change, and it does not need to change in order to cause me to pursue it. Aristotle makes the same point more fully elsewhere:

> It is always the object of desire which produces motion, but this is either the good or the apparent good; and not every good but the good that can be achieved by action. . . . That which produces motion is twofold: that which is changeless, and that which produces motion and itself changes. That which is changeless is the good to be achieved by action, and that which produces motion and itself changes is the faculty of desire.
>
> (*De Anima*, 3. 10, 433ª27–ᵇ17)

So it emerges that the ultimate cause of change is supposed to move the outermost heaven by virtue of the fact that the ultimate cause of change is an object of rational thought and desire. This is how the ultimate cause of change can move the outermost heaven without itself changing or moving.

This account of the causation distinctive of the ultimate cause of change is not easy to comprehend, but certainly it serves to dissociate the causation distinctive of the ultimate cause of change from a kind of causation that depends on interaction, and to associate it instead with the way in which an intelligent or rational organism is caused to move when it recognizes that something is good and worth pursuing. So Aristotle conceives of the causal relation between the ultimate cause of change and the outermost heaven in teleological or final terms. For the ultimate cause of change is the good which is the end (*telos*) of the thought and desire of the outermost heaven, and in general of the cosmos that is delimited and unified by this heaven. The ultimate cause of change moves by being an object of thought and desire, not by interaction. We may sum up by saying that the ultimate cause of change is a teleological or final cause, as opposed to an efficient cause that relies on interaction.

But although Aristotle clearly rejects the view that the ultimate cause of change is an efficient cause that relies on interaction, he appears to think that it is an efficient cause in a broader sense. For the ultimate cause of change is not simply the object of thought and desire of the cosmos, it is a supremely real thing and it 'produces' this thought and desire in the cosmos, i.e. it causes the cosmos to have this thought and desire. If the ultimate cause of change had been simply the object of thought and desire of the cosmos, it need not have been different from merely imaginary things; for they can be just as much objects of thought and desire. For example, I may imagine the house that I am planning to build; and this imaginary house, we may say loosely speaking, may cause me to build it. But obviously what causes me to act here is not a real house at all, but my own thoughts and imaginings which represent a house. By contrast, suppose that I am hungry and that I see an apple hanging from a branch; then this apple, the real thing that I recognize, may produce in me the desire for it and the thought of how I may reach it. Aristotle's ultimate cause of change is like the second case, not like the first; and in this sense the ultimate cause of change functions not only as a teleological or final cause, but also as an efficient cause, 'a productive cause' (*poiētikon*), as he calls it. But it is striking that this efficient cause, the ultimate cause of change, does not rely on interaction for its causation.

7 The ultimate cause of change as the object of thought and desire of the cosmos

Aristotle's theory of rational thought, desire and action is an issue in its own right. But what is important for our purpose is that he is ready to use the main elements of this theory in order to clarify the relationship between the cosmos, and in particular the outermost heaven which delimits and unifies it, and the ultimate cause of change, which transcends the cosmos and causes it to move as it does. But, for this analogy to work, the cosmos must somehow be a rational animal, i.e. a rational living organism, and it must somehow be capable of thinking, desiring and acting. Moreover, the ultimate cause of change, which is the ultimate cause of the cosmos, and in particular of the motion of the outermost heaven, must somehow be the good that is thought, desired and pursued by the cosmos. But, naturally enough, it is difficult properly to comprehend this analogy.

There are two questions here. How can the ultimate cause of change be an object of rational thought and desire (a *noēton* and *orekton/ boulēton*)? And how can the cosmos, and in particular the outermost heaven which delimits and unifies it, be a rational living organism that somehow thinks and desires the ultimate cause of change – 'loves' the ultimate cause of change, as he also says (1072^{b}3)?

His answer to the first question appears to be clear enough: the ultimate cause of change is an object of thought and desire because the ultimate cause of change is good, indeed supremely and perfectly good. He emphasizes in a variety of ways that the ultimate cause of change is 'good', 'perfect', 'beautiful', 'loved' (1072^{a}34f.). Of course, this is not moral goodness, but rather the goodness of things in so far as they are rational and intelligible, i.e. in so far as they are subject to explanation. For the ultimate cause of change is the ultimate and most basic explanatory principle, and this is why it is supremely good. The beauty of the ultimate cause of change is also rather abstract and intellectual, although it has a visible counterpart in the beauty of the starry heavens and their rational, orderly, uniform, motion in a circle.

Unfortunately, Aristotle does less to clarify how the cosmos, and in particular the outermost heaven which delimits and unifies it, can be a rational living organism which thinks and desires the ultimate cause of change. It is perhaps less difficult to understand how the cosmos can be a rational living organism. The cosmos is a living organism in the sense that its parts add up to an organic, active whole, such that the activity of the parts contribute to the activity of the whole; and this living, active organism, the cosmos, is rational in the sense that it is, as a whole, intelligible and subject to explanation. What is more difficult to understand is how this rational living organism can think and desire, for it is supposed to think and desire the ultimate cause of change. Clearly its thought and desire does not consist in its speaking to itself or in uttering decisions and choices to itself. So it appears that the rational thought and desire of the cosmos can only consist in its being alive and active in the way in which it is alive and active, a rational way. But here we need to bear in mind a worrying ambiguity in the word 'rational'. It may mean 'intelligible' and 'subject to explanation', i.e. 'an object of rational thought' (noēton), or it may mean 'engaged in the activity that is rational thought' (noēsis). And while it may be clear enough how the cosmos can be rational in the former sense, it is less clear how it can be rational in the latter sense.

Even if we can comprehend how the cosmos can think and desire, we may still ask how it can think and desire the ultimate cause of change in particular. This question is central, for it is because the cosmos, and in particular the outermost heaven which delimits and unifies it, thinks and desires the ultimate cause of change that it moves in the way that it does, namely, in everlasting, uniform, circular motion. In other words, the ultimate cause of change causes the outermost heaven to move in the way that it does in virtue of the fact that the outermost heaven thinks and desires the ultimate cause of change. Now, what the cosmos thinks and desires is the ultimate cause of change, because the ultimate cause of change is the most perfect thing, in the sense of the supremely rational thing and the first principle of explanation; and the cosmos desires to be as like as possible to what is most perfect. But this striving for perfection in nature and the natural cosmos is most perfectly exemplified in the everlasting, uniform, circular motion of the outermost heaven which delimits and unifies the cosmos. This is why the outermost heaven thinks and desires not just any chance thing, but the ultimate cause of change, which is the most perfect thing.

There is, however, an important difference between the perfection of the natural cosmos and the perfection of the ultimate cause of change. For the natural cosmos is a changing, material and contingent thing, whereas the ultimate cause of change is an changeless, immaterial and necessary thing. And this presumably is why, for Aristotle, only the ultimate cause of change is absolutely perfect, whereas the natural cosmos is only as perfect as is possible for a thing of its kind, namely, a changing, material and contingent thing.

At this point we are likely to be struck by the following objection: if the ultimate cause of change, the most perfect being, is changeless, and if the cosmos strives to be as perfect as possible, then why does not the cosmos strive to come to a complete standstill? Why does its perfection consist in perfect motion, i.e. everlasting, uniform, circular motion, and not in a state of rest? This takes us to the heart of Aristotle's conception of the ultimate cause of change. For although the ultimate cause of change is supposed to be changeless, it is also supposed to be engaged in its own internal and most perfect activity, namely, rational thought.

And, as we will see in a moment, the thinking engaged in by the ultimate cause of change is quite unlike the thinking and desire that belongs to the cosmos. For while the cosmos thinks and desires something other than itself, namely, the ultimate cause of change, the ultimate cause of change thinks nothing but itself. Moreover, it is hard to see how God could have any desires at all, since he is absolutely perfect. So what corresponds with the perfect motion of the natural cosmos and the outermost heaven is not the changelessness of the ultimate cause of change, but its activity. This shows that there is after all a proper correspondence and analogy between the most perfect activity of the material cosmos, namely, the everlasting, uniform and circular motion of the outermost heaven, on the one hand, and the most perfect activity of the ultimate cause of change, namely, rational thought, on the other hand. For they are both perfect activities: the one is an activity that is perfect for a thing of its kind, namely, a changing, material and contingent thing; the other is an absolutely perfect activity, the activity that consists in the thinking engaged in by a changeless, immaterial intellect, the intellect that is identical with the ultimate cause of change – God.

8 The activity of the ultimate cause of change: thinking

So far the distinctive characteristics of the ultimate cause of change have included the following: it is the first cause of the motion of the cosmos; it is supremely good; and it is the object of the thought and desire of the cosmos. These characteristics are knit tightly together. For the ultimate cause of change is the first cause of motion in virtue of being something which the cosmos recognizes to be supremely good and which it desires to be like as far as possible. So the cosmos somehow imitates the ultimate cause of change – God, in that God is supremely good and rational and the cosmos is as good and rational as is possible for a thing of its kind.

But we have not yet mentioned what Aristotle undoubtedly considers to be the central characteristic of the ultimate cause of change, namely, activity (*energeia*). It is because the ultimate cause of change is an everlasting, perfect and above all active and living being that Aristotle identifies it with God, since these characteristics, he says, are commonly associated with God:

> For we say that God is an everlasting and perfect living being, so that life and continuous and everlasting duration belong to God; for this *is* God.

> (XII. 7, 1072^{b}28–30)

But the activity of the ultimate cause of change is not just any activity, but the best activity, namely, rational thought (*noēsis*, the activity of *nous*, reason); and this activity is a form of life, indeed the best life (1072^{a}26–28). So the activity of the ultimate cause of change consists of rational thought.

Aristotle goes on (in XII. 9) to argue that what the ultimate cause of change thinks is, precisely, what is best – and this is nothing but itself. So the ultimate cause of change – God, thinks nothing but itself:

> Therefore, it [*nous*, i.e. the rational intellect that is the ultimate cause of change] thinks itself, since it is what is most excellent; and this thinking is the thinking of thinking.
>
> (XII. 9, 1074^{b}33–35; see also XII. 7, 1072^{b}18–20)

So the activity of the ultimate cause of change consists in the rational thought that has as its object nothing but itself – rational thought. It is naturally some task for us to follow Aristotle here.

Let us begin with the view that the ultimate cause of change must be active, setting aside for a moment what the activity is supposed to be. Why must the ultimate cause of change be active? Aristotle emphasizes from the start that the ultimate cause of change must be active; otherwise, he says, it cannot cause and explain the activity and motion of the cosmos:

> But if there is a moving and productive principle [i.e. the ultimate cause of change], but one that is not active, still there will be no motion. . . . Nothing, then, is gained even if we postulate everlasting *ousiai* in the manner of those who believe in the forms [i.e. Plato and the Platonists], unless there is contained in them a principle which can cause change. But even this is not enough, nor postulating some other *ousia* besides the forms [*para ta eidē*]. For if this is not in activity, still there will be no motion.
>
> (XII. 6, 1071^{b}12–17)

We may note that the reference to Plato's view that there is an *ousia* 'besides the forms' (*para ta eidē*) is a reference to Plato's form of the good, which, according to *Republic* 509b, 'transcends' the forms.

So he establishes that the ultimate cause of change must be active by appealing to the basic function of the ultimate cause of change, which is to be the ultimate cause and explanation of activity and motion. But this most basic requirement, he complains, is overlooked by Plato and the Platonists when they postulate the forms, or even something besides the forms, i.e. the form of the good; for Plato's forms, and even the form of the good, do not contain activity, hence they cannot cause or explain activity and motion. Plato, it is true, compares the form of the good to the sun, without whose constant emission of light nothing will move and live (*Republic* 506f.). But Aristotle objects that, unlike the sun, Plato's form of the good, like all his forms, contains no activity, hence it is useless to postulate it as the source of rational, intelligible motion and change in the universe.

But why must the ultimate cause of change be active in order to cause activity and motion in the cosmos? The obvious answer, we may think, is that the ultimate cause of change must be active in order to act on and interact with the cosmos; and without interaction it cannot cause activity or motion in the cosmos. We may also note that the simile of the sun suggests this answer, since the sun appears to interact with the things that it activates and enlivens through the light that it emits. But this is not Aristotle's answer; for we saw that the ultimate cause of change does not in any way act on or interact with the cosmos, rather it is supposed to cause motion by being a final cause and a non-interactive efficient cause. So Aristotle does not think that the activity of the ultimate cause of change consists of interaction with the cosmos, and this makes it all the more striking that he requires that the ultimate cause of change should be active. Evidently, the activity of the ultimate cause of change is not a relational activity, i.e. an activity between it and the cosmos; for then it would be interactive. So the activity of the ultimate cause of change must be, not relational to something else, but wholly internal to it; it is more like the activity of a computer with the screen turned off and less like the activity of the sun.

This is difficult enough to imagine, but it is especially difficult to understand how an activity that is wholly internal to the cause can be necessary for causing motion in the effect. To understand this, we must recall that the ultimate cause of change moves the cosmos in virtue of the cosmos recognizing and desiring the perfection of the ultimate cause of change. But if this perfection did not include perfect activity, then the recognition and desire by the cosmos would not lead it to be active or to move at all, but would, if anything, rather lead it to imitate the ultimate cause of change by standing completely still. What this brings out, once again, is that the cosmos, when it is caused to move by the ultimate cause of change, imitates the ultimate cause of change, i.e. it behaves so as to be like the ultimate cause of change. This is why the ultimate cause of change must be active, i.e. so that the cosmos, in imitating it, can itself be active in the way that is appropriate for a thing of its kind, namely, by moving in an everlasting, uniform and circular motion. This kind of final causation – causation by imitating the cause and behaving so as to be as like as possible to it, shows that Aristotle's conception of the ultimate cause of change, for all its differences, is thoroughly Platonic.

But why does the activity of the ultimate cause of change consist of rational thought (*noēsis*)? It is notable that Aristotle does little to clarify this and seems to assume from the start that rational thought is the distinctive activity of the ultimate cause of change. All he says is that 'reason (*nous*) appears to be the most divine thing that we are familiar with' ($1074^b15–16$), i.e. the most perfect thing. So it is appropriate that the activity of the ultimate cause of change, since it is the activity of the most perfect thing, should consist of the activity of reason, which is rational thought. In fact this goes to the heart of the matter, for the ultimate cause of change is the most perfect thing in that it is the perfect example of something rational – the supreme object of rational thought (the *noēton*). But it appears wholly appropriate that if reason is something active, then its activity should consist of rational thought. This also throws further light on why the ultimate cause of change must be active; this is not just because what it causes in the cosmos is activity and motion, but because what it causes in the cosmos is rational activity and motion, i.e. activity and motion that is subject to explanation. So the activity of the ultimate cause of change cannot after all be distinguished from its rational activity, and this is why this activity is nothing but the activity of reason, namely, rational thought.

But we may also clarify why the activity of the ultimate cause of change is rational thought by pointing out that, for Aristotle, rational thought is the best example of an activity that is immaterial and does not depend on anything material or bodily. This contrasts with obviously material activities, such as the motion in space of material bodies, but also with activities which, although they are mental and belong to the soul, depend on the body, such as sense perception, imagination, and indeed most, if not all, kinds of human thinking. Thus in the *De Anima* (III. 4), when Aristotle considered the human intellect and rational thought, he argued that, unlike sense perception and imagination, which is material, rational thought is immaterial. In particular, he argued that there are two kinds of human rational thought: one kind, although in itself immaterial, depends on something material, since it depends on sensory perception and imagination, but another kind does not even depend on anything material. But God's rational thought is like this latter kind of human rational thought.

However, Aristotle argues that the object of the rational thought of the ultimate cause of change, i.e. what the ultimate cause of change thinks, is nothing but itself. Why does the ultimate cause of change think nothing but itself? The answer that Aristotle gives is clear:

> [If reason, the ultimate cause of change, thought something other than itself, then] it is evident that something other than itself would be more precious than reason, namely, what it rationally thinks [to nooumenon].

$$(1074^b29-30^f)$$

The point is that the object thought by the rational intellect, if it is different from the intellect itself, is more precious than the intellect, in the sense of explanatorily and causally more fundamental. For the object that is thought by the intellect causes the intellect to think and explains why it thinks, and without an object to think, the intellect, although capable of thinking, would never actually think anything and would forever be 'asleep' (1074^b18). To take an example from sense perception rather than thought, one may have the capacity to hear, but unless there are sounds to be heard and unless they affect one's hearing, one will not actually hear anything and one's capacity will lie dormant. So, if the ultimate cause of change thought something other than itself, then this object would be causally and explanatorily more fundamental than the ultimate cause of change. But this is absurd, for the ultimate cause of change is precisely the most fundamental thing, explanatorily and causally. So the object thought by the ultimate cause of change cannot be anything other than the ultimate cause of change itself.

But we should note that when Aristotle argues that the ultimate cause of change thinks nothing but itself, he means that it thinks nothing but the activity that is distinctive of itself, namely, rational thought. In other words, for the ultimate cause of change to think itself is for it to think its own thinking. This is a very interesting move in Aristotle – the move from 'thinking oneself' to 'thinking one's own thinking'. The move goes back to Plato's dialogue the *Charmides*, where Socrates similarly moves directly from 'knowledge of oneself' or 'self-knowledge' – as in the injunction of the Delphic oracle 'Know Thyself' – to 'knowledge of knowledge'. By 'knowledge of knowledge' Socrates means knowing of the things that one knows, that one knows them, and of the things that one does not know, that one does not know them. In general, we should note, this move is far from straightforward, for generally when we speak of self-knowledge or thinking about oneself, we do not mean to confine our reflections to our thinking and knowledge; on the contrary, we may mean to reflect on many other things about ourselves: our emotions, our relationships with others; our identity; our

unconscious desires, etc. On the other hand, since the distinctive characteristic of Aristotle's God is above all rational thought, and since this
accounts for both his perfection and his being the ultimate cause and
explanation of rational activity, it is only natural that God, in thinking
about himself, should be thinking about nothing but his own thinking.

We may say that, for Aristotle, the thought of the ultimate cause of
change, God, is purely reflexive: it is reflexive because it thinks itself,
and it is purely reflexive because it thinks nothing but itself. Aristotle,
helpfully, points out both the similarity and the difference with human
thought and in general the activities of the human soul:

> But it is evident that knowledge and sense perception and judgement
> and thinking have always something other than themselves as their
> object, and themselves only as by-product.
>
> $(1074^b35–36)$

That is to say, the acts and activities of the human soul, such as
perceiving, thinking, judging and knowing, are indeed reflexive, but only
as a by-product; for their main aim is to cognize something other than
themselves. For example, when I hear a bell ringing, I am aware not
only of the bell ringing, but also of myself hearing the bell ringing; so
my hearing is reflexive, i.e. aware of the mental act of hearing. But it
is reflexive only as a consequence of cognizing an object other than the
mental act of cognizing; for evidently I am aware of myself hearing the
bell ringing only as a consequence of my being aware of the bell ringing.

This, Aristotle says, is how things stand with regard to the acts and
activities of the human soul: they are indeed reflexive, but not purely
or primarily reflexive. God's thinking, by contrast, is purely reflexive,
for it cognizes nothing but its own act of cognizing. So God's thought
is the one and only example of a kind of thought that contains no real
distinction between the cognizing subject and the cognized object. As
he says, in the case of the ultimate cause of change, God, 'reason (nous)
and the object of reason (to noēton) are identical' (1072^b21). Or again,
'this rational thought (hē noēsis) is one with what is rationally thought
(to nooumenon)' $(1075^a4–5)$. This extinction, within God's thought, of
the distinction between subject and object, is the ultimate and most
striking consequence of Aristotle's conception of the nature of the
ultimate cause of change – God.

Finally, there is a puzzle about Aristotle's conception of the nature
of the ultimate cause of change, God, which can hardly have failed to
strike us, and whose solution, if there is one, is not straightforward.
How can the ultimate cause of change be both changeless and internally

active? For is not internal activity a kind of change? So there is a threat that Aristotle's conception of the nature of the ultimate cause of change contains a rather striking contradiction: the ultimate cause of change is changeless; the ultimate cause of change is active; but activity is a kind of change. In response to this threat, Aristotle emphasizes that the ultimate cause of change does not change its state or condition in any way; it is always in strictly the same state, and this is why it is completely changeless. It is useful to compare this with the outermost heaven, which changes in so far as it moves, even though its motion is perfectly uniform. The outermost heaven does not change its state of motion, for it is always in the same state of motion, namely, constant circular motion, and its motion is perfectly uniform. But although it does not change its state of motion, it still changes its state or condition, in that it moves. We can see this if we pick out a particular point on the circle that is the outermost heaven and observe that this point will not always be in the same condition. For it will not always be in the same place or position, since it will move in a circle along with the circle on which it is a point. (Think of a speck of dust on a rotating CD or old LP.) Indeed the fixed stars are supposed to move in a circle because they are attached to the outermost heaven which moves in a circle. So, even though the outermost heaven comes very close to being always in the same state, since its shape and motion are perfectly uniform, the fact that it moves spatially implies that it is not completely changeless. The ultimate cause of change, by contrast, is supposed to be completely changeless.

But the puzzle is how the ultimate cause of change can be at once completely changeless and internally active. To try to solve this puzzle, we must concentrate on the kind of activity distinctive of the ultimate cause of change, namely, rational thought. Is not rational thought a kind of change, even if it is wholly immaterial and purely mental change? If it is, then this will establish a contradiction in Aristotle's conception of the ultimate cause of change. Certainly Plato thought that rational thought, or at least human rational thought, is a kind of change, for he argues that if the soul contains reason (*nous*), then it contains change (*kinēsis*, see *Sophist* 249a). It certainly appears natural to think that rational thought is a kind of change, and Aristotle concedes that this is true of human rational thought (1075a5–10). But he argues that God's rational thought is different. It is true, he says, that even human thought can momentarily focus its undivided attention purely on a single and wholly unitary thing without parts; and to that extent even human thought is changeless. But this is only a momentary state, and in general human thought consists in the changing attention of the intellect from one thing, or one part or aspect of a thing, to another. Indeed even when our mental attention comes to a unitary resting point, it does so only as a result of having completed a process of reasoning, i.e. having mentally and through reasoning 'run through' a number of different things. Human thought, we may say, is essentially discursive ('running through'). But Aristotle argues that God's thought is unlike human thought; it is not discursive, in that it is always of one and the same thing, and of something that is perfectly unitary and uniform, namely, God itself:

> For it is evident that it [reason, the ultimate cause of change] thinks the most divine and worthy thing, and it does not alter; for alteration would be for the worse, and that would already be a kind of change.
>
> (1074^b25–27)

He concludes that:

> Just as human reason ... is in this state from time to time ..., so the rational thought that has itself as object [i.e. God's rational thought] is in this state in all eternity.
>
> (1075^a7–10)

This shows, Aristotle thinks, that God's thought is indeed changeless. But we may still be left with the feeling that the puzzle has not gone away. He has perhaps shown that God's thought is completely changeless, since it is always of the same perfectly unitary and uniform object. But then, we may wonder, how can this thought, if it is so utterly changeless, still be a kind of activity? Aristotle may have an answer, but it is not clear what it is.

9 The ultimate cause of change, and the rational order of the cosmos

The ultimate cause of change is in the first instance the cause of the rational motion of the outermost heaven. But Aristotle argues (especially in XII. 10) that the ultimate cause of change is, indirectly and by consequence, also the cause of rational order, in particular rational change, throughout the whole ordered universe, the cosmos:

> But we must also consider in which way the nature of the whole contains the good and the best, whether it contains this as something separated and by itself, or as its order. But perhaps it contains it in both these ways, like an army does; for the goodness of an army

is contained both in its order and in its general. But it is more in the general; for it is not he that is due to the order, rather the order is due to him.

(XII. 10, 1075ᵃ11–15)

He concludes:

The rule of many is not good; let there be one ruler.
(1076ᵃ4; this is a quotation from Homer's *Iliad* II. 204)

So, just as a good general, who is responsible for the goodness of his army, is distinct from his army and by himself, so the ultimate cause of change, who is responsible for the goodness of the universe, is distinct from the universe and by itself: it – or He – is transcendent. But the goodness of the universe, like the goodness of an army, is due also to its immanent order – the arrangement and orderly motion of its various parts. Hence the goodness of the universe, although its cause is ultimately transcendent, also has an immanent cause or explanation, namely, order and orderly motion.

But how can the causation of the ultimate cause of change extend further than its immediate effect, the everlasting, uniform, circular motion of the outermost heaven? And how can the ultimate cause of change also be the cause of the rational order, in particular the orderly motion and change, throughout the universe? The motion of the first heaven is the most perfect example of rational change in nature, but such rational change is present, Aristotle thinks, throughout the universe. But the universe is not only full of motions and changes that are rational, i.e. subject to explanation; it is also full of rational motions and changes that are like the rational change of the outermost heaven in that they are everlasting, uniform and cyclical (even if not circular). For example, the seasons of the year, and the alternations between day and night, repeat themselves in an infinite sequence of uniform cycles, and plants and animals renew themselves and reproduce in an infinite sequence of uniform life-cycles. So, since the ultimate cause of change is the immediate cause of these distinctive features of the motion of the outermost heaven, namely, the everlasting nature, uniformity and circularity or cyclicality of its motion, it will also be the ultimate cause of any genuinely similar features throughout the universe; and Aristotle thinks that the universe is full of such features.

So the universe contains such rational order – rational order that is everlasting, uniform and cyclical, in that it contains things that exhibit these features. Some things exhibit them as individuals, in particular the planets and the stars which are, each of them, everlasting. But other things exhibit them only as a species, in particular animals which, even though the individuals are mortal and finite, as a species renew themselves without end. In this way, rational order is present in the universe, i.e. it is immanent, although its ultimate cause is the transcendent ultimate cause of change. And the ultimate cause of change moves in the first instance the outermost heaven, but through doing so it moves all the other things as well (compare: 'it [the ultimate cause of change] moves the other things *through* a thing moved [i.e. through the outermost heaven]', $1072^{b}4$).

But Aristotle argues not only that many things in the universe exhibit such rational order; he argues that the universe as a whole does so:

> And the order is not such that one thing has no relation to another; rather, they do have a relation [to each other], for all things are jointly ordered in relation to one thing [i.e. to the ultimate cause of change].
> ($1075^{a}17–18$)

So the things that exhibit rational order do so not only each by itself and independently of each other, but all in relation to each other; and in this way the universe as a whole exhibits rational order. But the reason for this, he says, is that all these immanent things, taken jointly and together, stand in relation to and depend on a single transcendent thing – the ultimate cause of change. This view fits perfectly his previous analogy of the army, and he drives home the point by adding the analogy of a well-ordered household, in which every member, from the freemen who rule the household to the most lowly slave and even the household animals, contribute, through their actions and activities, to the common good and activity of the household as a whole ($1075^{b}19–22$).

10 Why transcendence?

Aristotle, it has emerged, thinks of the ultimate cause of change as transcending and lying beyond nature as a whole, i.e. as distinct from the totality of changing, material things. This does not mean that this cause – God – literally occupies a place outside nature. For there is no place, and in general no space, outside nature. But it means that God is not identical with any part of nature, or with the whole of nature. And it means that God is not identical with anything that is inseparable from any part of nature, and likewise not identical with something that is inseparable from the whole of nature. In particular, God is not identical with the form of the outermost heaven, which, like any other form of a changing, material thing, is inseparable from that thing. For the form of the outermost heaven is the form of a single changing, material thing that bounds and delimits the changing, material universe and the totality of changing, material things.

But why in general does Aristotle argue for transcendence? His overall aim in book XII is to search for the ultimate explanation and cause of nature as a whole, and in particular of the kind of change that is distinctive of nature in general, i.e. change that is orderly, uniform and in general subject to explanation – rational change. So his aim is to search for the ultimate explanation and cause of the rationally changing universe and the cosmos. But why does he not think that this aim can be achieved just as well without going beyond or transcending nature? In particular, why does he not think that this aim can be achieved just as well by thinking of the ultimate explanation and cause of rational change as the inseparable form of the outermost heaven? After all, the outermost heaven bounds and delimits nature as a whole.

So why is Aristotle committed to transcendence? One central reason emerges especially in XII. 10, but it is indicated already at the opening of book XII. It is his view that, strictly, there can only be one ultimate cause of rational change in general – only one God. This is because what Aristotle is searching for is the ultimate explanation and cause of rational change in nature *as a whole*. But evidently there can only be one such whole. So there can only be one ultimate explanation and cause of it. It is perhaps above all because there can only be one God that God cannot be identical with the inseparable form of the outermost heaven. It is true that, in virtue of its spatial position, there can only be one outermost heaven. For only one thing can be outermost in space, i.e. can bound and delimit everything that is in space and indeed space itself. But, in virtue of its own nature, the outermost heaven is not essentially singular or unrepeatable. On the contrary, Aristotle even thinks that there are other heavens within nature, each associated with the spatial position and the motion of one or the other of the planets. But these heavens need not differ essentially from the outermost heaven; they need only differ from the outermost heaven in their spatial position. So, if God were simply the inseparable form of the outermost heaven, then there could, apparently, be more than one God. But Aristotle argues that, strictly, there can only be one God, i.e. one ultimate explanation and cause of rational change in nature *as a whole*.

But there may also be another reason why Aristotle is committed to transcendence. For, apparently, his aim in book XII is not only to determine what changing, material things in general must be like in order to be intelligible and subject to explanation. Neither is his aim only to explain why changing, material things in general are intelligible and subject to explanation. His aim includes, crucially, to explain why *there are* changing, material things that are intelligible and subject to explanation. That this is a crucial part of his aim is suggested especially by the fact that he characterizes the ultimate cause of rational change as 'a moving cause' (*kinētikon*) and in particular as 'a producing', 'creating', or 'generating cause' (*poiētikon*). For in general Aristotle conceives of this kind of cause as the cause also of the existence of what it causes. Thus he typically indicates what this kind of cause is like by appealing to the case where one thing causes another by, precisely, 'generating' it; typically he appeals to the example of a father generating his offspring. But, evidently, if one wants to explain why there is a rationally changing universe, it will be natural to think that one must go beyond the rationally changing universe itself – beyond the natural cosmos and nature. For it is natural to think that no part of, or even the whole of the rationally changing universe can explain why there is such a thing at all.

11 Is Aristotle's God relevant to the basic question of metaphysics: 'What is it for something, anything, to be?'?

Is the search for what explains the rational change in nature as a whole, i.e. the project of book XII, part of the search for what it is for something, anything, to be, i.e. part of the basic project of the *Metaphysics*? Earlier in the *Metaphysics* (in VI. 1) Aristotle argued that if there is a divine being, or God, then the science of this being will at once be the science of what it is for something, anything, to be (see Chapter 4§5). So we would expect that when now, in book XII, he argues that there is a divine being, or God, this is directly relevant to the basic question in the *Metaphysics*, 'What is it for something, anything, to be?' But it is striking that nowhere in book XII does Aristotle make explicit what this relevance is. He does not make explicit what the relation is between the question of book XII, 'What explains the rational change in nature as a whole?', and the basic question in the *Metaphysics*. At the same time, there are clear indications in book XII that he thinks that there is a direct relation between the two questions (see §1 of this chapter).

So what is the relation between these two questions, i.e. the question, 'What explains the rational change in nature as a whole?', and the question, 'What is it for something, anything, to be?'? On the one hand, the questions appear too different to be related directly. For we have seen that the former question, i.e. the question in book XII, is associated with the question: 'Why are there changing, material things whose change is rational, i.e. subject to explanation?' This is an example of a question of the type: 'Why are there things that are F?' But the question, 'What is it for something, anything, to be?', is not an example of a question of this type at all. In general, we must not confuse questions of the type, (1) 'Why are there things that are F?', with questions of the type, (2) 'Why are the things that are F F?', i.e. 'What is it for something, anything, to be F?' The basic question in the *Metaphysics*, 'What is it for something, anything, to be?', belongs to type 2, not type 1.

On the other hand, it is striking, and it is surely not a coincidence, that what God fundamentally explains, namely, why changing, material things are intelligible and subject to explanation, is a crucial part of what constitutes what it is for something, anything, to be a being, something that is (see Chapter 7§5 especially ix–x). This shows that there is an obvious relation between the question, 'Why are the changing, material things intelligible and subject to explanation?', and the basic question in the *Metaphysics*, 'What is it for something, anything, to be?' The relation is evidently along the following lines. The answer to the basic question of the *Metaphysics* includes, as a crucial part, the claim that for something, anything, to be a being, something that is, is for it to be intelligible and subject to explanation. Indeed, it includes anything that is in turn required for things to be intelligible and subject to explanation. This answer is about all things, not just changing and material things. But it is also, and in the first instance, about changing and material things – the things with which we are directly familiar from sense perception and experience. And Aristotle thinks that it is especially with regard to such things that it is difficult to establish how they can be intelligible and subject to explanation. So the answer includes in particular anything that is required for changing and material things to be intelligible and subject to explanation. But in book XII Aristotle goes on, naturally enough, to ask, 'Why are the changing, material things intelligible and subject to explanation in the first place?'

Still, if there is really to be a direct relation between the question in book XII and the basic question in the *Metaphysics*, the question in book XII must be understood to mean not only (1), 'Why are there changing, material things whose change is intelligible and subject to explanation?' It must also be understood to mean (2), 'What is it for a changing, material thing to be intelligible and subject to explanation?' For only if the question is understood in this way can the answer to it be at once an answer to the basic question in the *Metaphysics*, 'What is it for something, anything, to be a being, something that is?' So we must ask whether the question in book XII includes not only question 1, but also question 2. There is good reason to think that it does. We saw that the conception of God as a moving and generating cause (*kinētikon, poiētikon*) is associated especially with question 1 (see §10 of this chapter). But we recall that God is a very peculiar moving and generating cause; for it does not move or generate by interacting with what it moves and generates. In particular, God moves and generates the rationally changing universe because the rationally changing universe somehow imitates God – he moves as a paradigm (*paradeigma*). But what the rationally changing universe imitates about God is nothing but what God is – his essence, i.e. reason and rational activity. So God is not only a moving and generating cause; he is also a final and especially a formal cause. For he moves simply in virtue of being the very thing he is, i.e. reason and rational activity (see §§6–8 of this chapter.) But this indicates that what God explains is not only why there are changing, material things whose change is rational (i.e. the answer to question 1); he also explains what it is for changing, material things to be things whose change is rational (i.e. the answer to question 2).

So we may perhaps conclude that the promise made earlier in the *Metaphysics* (VI. 1), namely that theology, i.e. the science of divine being and God, is precisely ontology, i.e. the science of all things and of what it is for something, anything, to be – this promise is kept in book XII.

9

THE CRITICISM
OF PLATO'S THEORY
OF FORMS

1 Plato's and Aristotle's shared project: the theory of essence

Aristotle knows Plato both from his work and from close personal acquaintance. At the same time, it is not always easy to recognize Plato, i.e. Plato as we know him from his dialogues, in the way in which Aristotle represents his views. It is also difficult to decide whether Aristotle represents Plato's views accurately; and whether, when it appears that he does not, this is due to misunderstanding or due to a representation and treatment that is deliberately free. Even if Aristotle accurately understands Plato's views, he may in general want to represent them rather freely. For this may better serve the particular philosophical searches in which he is engaged. We recall that in general Aristotle's aim in engaging with the views of his contemporaries and predecessors is not so much simply to understand these views accurately as it is to make them contribute to the particular searches in which he is engaged (see Chapter 2§4iii and Chapter 3§2). There is, however, also an appearance of deliberate distortion due to polemical purposes. For we sometimes get the impression that Aristotle wants to present a view of Plato's in a poor light for the purpose of disputing it – although perhaps also for the more constructive purpose of challenging Plato and the Platonists, whom he is directly and even personally addressing, to clarify and defend it. We will see that some of his sharpest criticisms against Plato's theory of forms, and perhaps in particular the so-called third man argument, may to a considerable extent need to be understood as deliberately distorting and polemical in purpose.

Should we, therefore, conclude that if our aim is to consider Aristotle's criticism of Plato's theory of forms, then we are really considering the theory of forms only as Aristotle represents it, not Plato's theory; and that, therefore, we must also resist drawing on our acquaintance with Plato's dialogues? That would be unnatural. More natural is to speak of Aristotle's criticisms of Plato's views, not just his criticism of Plato's views as he understands them, and to draw on Plato's dialogues if this appears appropriate, while at the same time bearing in mind the above important complications. Of course, in doing so, we are letting our own understanding of Plato's views enter into our understanding and assessment of Aristotle's criticisms of Plato's views. But this may not be a bad thing, and it is hardly avoidable. We are also supposing that, in spite of the above complications, Aristotle's criticisms of Plato's views can, in one way or another, significantly contribute to our understanding of those views themselves.

The central target of Aristotle's criticism is Plato's theory of essence – the theory of forms. Plato argues that there are essences, i.e. there are things that are what they are, and indeed are beings, simply in virtue of themselves (*auta kath' hauta*) and not in virtue of their relation to other things (*pros ti*). In general, a thing's essence is what the thing is simply in virtue of itself (*kath' hauto* and *auto kath' hauto*); i.e. a thing's essence is what the thing is in virtue of being the very thing that it is. And the essence of a thing is what we know when we know the real definition of the thing, i.e. when we know the answer to the question, 'What is this thing?' and 'What is it to be this very thing?' The originator of this question is Socrates, and especially Socrates as Plato portrays him throughout his dialogues, whose trademark is to ask of things, 'What is it?', i.e. 'What is it to be this very thing?' But Plato also calls the essences, which in general he refers to as the things that are 'themselves in virtue of themselves' (*auta kath' hauta*), 'forms' (*eidē*) and 'ideas' (*ideai*).

Plato's notion, *form* (*eidos*), must not be confused with Aristotle's notion of the form (*eidos, morphē*) of a changing, material thing, i.e. the notion that in Aristotle is correlative to matter. Rather, Plato's notions, *form* (*eidos*) and *idea* (*idea*), may be associated with Aristotle's notion of essence (*to ti estin, to ti ēn einai*). For both Plato and Aristotle are addressing the question of what it is for a thing to have an essence; and they are both addressing the question of what things have an essence. Of course, Plato's notion, *idea* (*idea*), must also not be confused with the modern use of the term 'idea' to mean a mental representation or picture. Plato's ideas are not mental, and they are not representations or pictures. They are, precisely, essences. But the important thing, certainly in Aristotle's criticism of Plato's theory of forms, is that Plato argues that essences are separate and distinct from changing things, i.e. the things with which we are directly familiar from sense perception.

Aristotle, on the other hand, argues that changing things themselves have essences, which are not at all separate or distinct from those things, but are, on the contrary, inseparable from them. Indeed, we saw that he argues that the essence of a changing, material thing is, in a particular sense, identical with that thing; for it is identical with the ultimate subject of predication and the particular that this thing is. For example, Socrates' essence is identical with Socrates in the sense of the ultimate subject of predication and the particular that Socrates is (see Chapter 7§5v). So he rejects Plato's theory of separate and distinct essences – the theory of forms.

We will consider this disagreement in a moment. But first it is important to recognize that this disagreement takes place against the background of a shared notion of essence and in general a shared project. The project is to investigate what it is for a thing to have an essence, i.e. what it is for a thing to be what it is simply in virtue of itself and not in virtue of its relation to other things, and to investigate what things have an essence. In general, Plato and Aristotle share a number of central commitments that in various ways are related to the notion of essence and to the view that there are things that have an essence. The agreement can be summarized as follows. First of all:

Shared, 1. There are things that have an essence (*to ti estin*).

This means that there are things that are what they are simply in virtue of themselves (*auta kath' hauta*) and not in virtue of their relation to other things (*pros ti*). In other words, for a thing, x, to have an essence is for there to be something, E, that x is simply in virtue of itself, i.e. in virtue of its being the very thing that it is. This essence, E, is what we know when we know the real definition of the thing, x, whose essence is E, i.e. when we know the answer to the question, 'What is it for something to be this very thing, x?' Plato and Aristotle agree that there are such things – things that have an essence. So they agree that there are things that have features and determinations simply in virtue of themselves. In other words, there are things that do not depend on other things for their determination. In general, they argue that it is in virtue of having an essence, or depending on things that have an essence, that things are determinate in the first place. They also argue that:

> Shared, 2. We can know the essence of things that have an essence.

So they reject the sceptical view that although things may have an essence, we may not be able to know their essence. On the contrary, they argue that our cognitive capacities, at their best, are adequate for knowing the essence of things. Although the terminology varies, they in general refer to our cognitive capacities, at their best, as our 'intellect' or 'reason' (*nous*). Further, they argue that:

> Shared, 3. Knowledge of the essence of things is knowledge *why* things are as they are, i.e. it is explanatory knowledge.

In general, they refer to explanatory knowledge as *epistēmē*. But they argue that:

> Shared, 4. Explanatory knowledge (*epistēmē*) requires knowing the essence of things.

The view that scientific or explanatory knowledge requires knowledge of the essence of things is particularly important; for it means that it is because things have an essence that they are intelligible and subject to explanation. Further, they argue that:

> Shared, 5. The essence of things is primary being (*ousia*).

This means that not only is it in virtue of having an essence, or depending on things that have an essence, that things are determinate; it is in virtue of having an essence, or depending on things that have an essence, that they are beings, things that are, in the first place.

So it appears that Plato and Aristotle are both addressing the question, 'What is primary being (*ousia*)?', and they both think that primary being is the essence of things. This is certainly how Aristotle understands Plato. In a striking passage, he says:

> But those who say that there are forms [i.e. Plato and the Platonists] in one way speak correctly, i.e. when they conceive of forms as separate – *if indeed* the forms are primary beings [*ousiai*]. But in another

way they do not speak correctly, i.e. when they say that the one over many is the form [i.e. the form as conceived by Plato and Platonists, i.e. as distinct from changing things].

(VII. 16, 1040ᵇ27–30)

This passage is extremely important, because it indicates that Aristotle sees Plato and himself as engaged in a shared project – the project of searching for primary being (*ousia*). And he thinks that there is a shared notion of primary being, which is in general the notion of separate being (see Chapter 7§4). But the passage also introduces an important question of interpretation, namely what Aristotle means by 'separate' (*chōriston*), 'separately' (*chōris*), 'to separate' (*chōrizein*), and 'separation' (*chōrismos*). For when he criticizes Plato and the Platonists for conceiving of forms as separate, i.e. as separate from changing things, he is criticizing the view that essences are distinct from changing things. So he is using the term 'separate from' to mean 'distinct from'. We will see that often he uses the term 'besides' or 'over and above' (*para*) to indicate separation in the sense of distinctness. But here (in the passage just quoted) he is, on the contrary, commending Plato and the Platonists for conceiving of forms as separate. For he says that it is correct to think of forms as separate, *if indeed* (*eiper*) one conceives of them as primary beings (*ousiai*). In other words, he says that if primary being were indeed the forms, which is the view of Plato and the Platonists but not the view of Aristotle, then it would be correct to think of the forms as separate; for it is part of the very notion of primary being that primary being is separate being. So apparently he is using the term 'separate' here not to mean 'distinct', but to mean that primary being (*ousia*), on the shared notion of primary being, is, precisely, separate being. We saw earlier that when Aristotle in general characterizes primary being as separate being, he means that a primary being is a being, something that is, simply in virtue of itself and not in virtue of its relation to other things (see Chapter 7§4). We will return to the issue of separation, and different types of separation, later (see §4 of this chapter).

In a different place in which he is talking about Plato and the Platonists, he says:

The reason why those who say that *ousiai* [primary beings] are universals combined these two views [i.e. the view that *ousiai* are universals and that they are separate] is that they did not make them [the *ousiai*] identical with the sense-perceptible things [*tas autas tois aisthētois*].

(XIII. 9, 1086ᵃ35–37)

This passage again indicates that Aristotle thinks of Plato and the Platonists as addressing, like himself, the question, 'What is primary being (*ousia*)?' But it also indicates a central difference in their answers to this question. For Plato and the Platonists do not, unlike Aristotle, think that the primary beings, i.e. the essences, are identical with the sense-perceptible things and in general the changing things. We saw earlier that Aristotle argues that a changing, material thing is, precisely, identical with its primary being and its essence (see Chapter 7§5v). Plato and the Platonists, on the other hand, argue that the primary beings, i.e. the essences, are universals, and they are not identical with the sense-perceptible and in general the changing things. Indeed, they go a step further and argue that the primary beings and the essences are separate and distinct from changing things.

But Plato and Aristotle also agree that:

> Shared, 6. There are essences that are separate and distinct from changing things.

Plato argues that all essences are separate and distinct from changing things. Aristotle argues, on the other hand, that the essences of changing, material things are inseparable from those things. But he also argues that there is one thing that is separate and distinct from changing things and from nature as a whole. This is the changeless ultimate cause and explanation of rational change and order in nature – God (see Chapter 8, especially §10). But he argues that this ultimate explanation and cause of rational change, God, has an essence and indeed is an essence (we will return to this point at the end of the chapter).

It is against such a shared background that Aristotle criticizes Plato's theory of forms, i.e. the theory which says that there are essences but that they are separate and distinct from changing things. The background is a shared project of considering what it is for a thing to have an essence, what things have essences, and indeed what it is for a thing to be a being, something that is, in the first place. And it is a project of considering how we can know the essence of things, and how this knowledge contributes to our understanding and explanatory knowledge of things.

Recognizing this background of shared commitments is crucial to understanding Aristotle's criticism of Plato's theory of forms. For a central thrust in this criticism is the insistence that his own, i.e. Aristotle's, theory of essence can satisfy the shared commitments and at the same time avoid problems that arise on Plato's theory of essences as separate and distinct forms. In particular, Plato argues that if there were only changing things, then explanatory knowledge (*epistēmē*) would not be possible. For explanatory knowledge is basically knowledge of the essence of things, but changing things do not have an essence. He concludes that explanatory knowledge requires the existence of essences and forms that are separate and distinct from changing things. So he argues that his theory of essences as separate and distinct forms is necessary to ensure the possibility of explanatory knowledge. Aristotle summarizes this Platonic argument in *Metaphysics* III. 4, when he sets out some basic puzzles or *aporiai* that Plato raised. Thus he says, reporting a basic Platonic *aporia*:

> For if there is not something besides [*para*] the particulars [i.e. the changing things], but the particulars are indefinite [*apeira*], how is it possible to attain explanatory knowledge [*epistēmē*] of things that are indefinite? For we know any thing precisely in so far as it is a single thing and the same thing [i.e. in so far as it has an essence or depends on something that has an essence] and in so far as something universal belongs to it.
>
> (999ª26–29)

And again:

> How will there be explanatory knowledge [*epistēmē*], if there is not some one thing over [and above] all the things [i.e. all the changing things]?
>
> (999ᵇ26–27)

The first passage is of particular interest also because it indicates that Aristotle uses the term 'besides' or 'over and above' (*para*) to indicate the distinctness of Plato's forms (see §4 of this chapter). But a particularly clear version of this Platonic argument, as it was understood by Aristotle, for the view that there are separate and distinct essences and forms, is recorded by the later commentator on Aristotle, Alexander of Aphrodisias (second to third century AD):

> Further, the things the sciences are sciences of, these things are. And the sciences are of some other things besides [*para*] the particulars [i.e. the changing things]; for these [the particulars] are indefinite [*apeira*] and indeterminate [*aorista*], whereas the sciences are of determinate things [*hōrismena*, i.e. things that have essences and are essences]. Therefore there are some things besides [*para*] the particulars, and these things are the ideas.
>
> (*Peri Ideōn/On Ideas*, 79. 8–11; trans. G. Fine, but comments added)

This is perhaps Plato's main reason for thinking that there are essences and that essences are separate and distinct from changing things. The reasoning is as follows: explanatory knowledge is basically of the essence of things; but the changing things do not have an essence and there is nothing determinate that they are in virtue of themselves; therefore, essences, which is what explanatory knowledge is basically of, are separate and distinct from changing things. But Aristotle responds that his own theory of essence both satisfies the view that there are essences and that explanatory knowledge is basically of the essence of things (see Chapter 7§5ix), while at the same time it avoids problems that arise from Plato's view that essences are separate and distinct from the changing things.

Finally, when we consider Plato's and Aristotle's shared project of searching for the essence of things, it is natural to ask whether this search is at all conducted along the same lines. We have seen that Aristotle's search for the essence of things begins with changing things as we encounter them through our sense perception and in our experience (see Chapter 2§3i). Is this also where Plato's search for the essence of things begins, i.e. with the changing things with which we are directly familiar? This question is in fact controversial, and it is sometimes thought that when Plato argues for separate essences and forms, his argument entirely bypasses changing, sense-perceptible things. However, there is reason to think that Plato's search for the essence of things likewise begins with changing, sense-perceptible things. This is certainly true in a central argument for the introduction of essences and forms, i.e. the argument at the end of the dialogue *Phaedo* (95e–101c). For there the essences and forms are introduced as the conclusion of an argument that starts with the question, '*Why* (*dia tí*) are things as they are?', i.e. 'What is the explanation and cause (*aitia*) of things being as they are?' But the things of which this question is asked are, at least to begin with, sense-perceptible and in general changing things, e.g. 'why human beings grow' (see 96c7). Indeed, Plato emphasizes here that the question is, at least to begin with, 'Why something is, *and comes to be, and ceases to be*?' (see 96a9–10, 97b5–6, 97c7, 97c8–d1 and 101b9–c7). We may note also that here Plato expressly identifies forms (*eidē* and *ideai*, here generally referred to as the things that are *auta kath' hauta*, 'themselves in virtue of themselves', see 100b) with essences (*ousiai*, see 101c2–4). So it is appropriate to think that although the search for the essence of things reaches very different results in Plato and Aristotle, and although it is in general conducted in different ways, it begins in the same place, i.e. with changing, sense-perceptible things, the things with which we are directly familiar. For the search for the essence of things is, for both Plato and Aristotle, the search for the most explanatory knowledge of things, and in the first instance of those things with which we are directly familiar from sense perception and experience.

2 Central differences between Plato's and Aristotle's theories of essence

We have seen that Plato and Aristotle share the same overall aim, which is to search for the most explanatory knowledge of things, and in the first instance those things with which we are directly familiar from experience. They also share the same general view about how this aim is to be achieved, i.e. by supposing that things have an explanatory essence, and that we can know their essence. The essence of a thing, for both Plato and Aristotle, is what the thing is *simply in virtue of itself* (*kath' hauto* and *auto kath' hauto*); and it is what we know when we know the real definition of the thing, i.e. when we know the answer to the question, 'What is this very thing?' So the essence of a thing is what explains why the thing is the determinate and well-defined thing it is. However, they differ fundamentally over how this essence is to be understood, and they defend very different theories of essence. For Plato, the things with which we are directly familiar from experience, and in general the changing things, do not have an essence; and the things that have an essence, and indeed are essences, are distinct from the changing things. For Aristotle, on the contrary, the changing things themselves have an essence; indeed there is a fundamental sense in which they are identical with their essence. Aristotle's criticism of Plato's theory of forms is a criticism of Plato's distinctive theory of essence. So let us begin with a summary of Plato's theory of essence and especially of those claims in it that Aristotle rejects.

To provide a summary of Plato's theory of essence is not an easy task, for Plato's dialogues are not straightforward or easy to interpret. On the other hand, we may perhaps rely here on Aristotle's representation of Plato; for he provides a precise summary of Plato's theory of essence and especially of those claims in it that he rejects. In that case, however, we run the risk of misrepresenting Plato; for we cannot assume that Aristotle always understood Plato's theory correctly or even that he always chose to present it in the best light – there is an unmistakable element of vigorous polemic in the criticism. But without letting these problems delay us too much, let us set out a number of claims about essence, which we may with some confidence say are characteristic not only of Plato as Aristotle understands him, but of Plato himself.

Plato's theory of essence is above all characterized by a particular view about sense-perceptible and, in general, changing things:

PL1.   Sense-perceptible and, in general, changing things do not have an essence.

This means that:

PL2.   There is nothing that changing things are *in virtue of themselves*.

So it means that:

PL3.   *In virtue of themselves*, changing things are completely indeterminate.

But this negative view about sense-perceptible and, in general, changing things is complemented by a positive view about changeless forms, and about the relation between changing things and changeless forms:

PL4.   To the extent that changing things are determinate, they are determinate not in virtue of themselves, but in virtue of their relation to changeless forms.

Plato calls this relation, i.e. the relation between changing things and changeless forms, 'participation' (*methexis*) and 'communion' (*koinōnia*). He argues that, to the extent that a changing thing has a determinate feature, F, it has this feature, F, in virtue of its participation in or communion with the changeless form, *F*. He also makes this very point by saying that, to the extent that a changing thing is F, the form, *F*, 'is present in' (*paresti, enesti*) the thing. In general, this relation between changing things and changeless forms, i.e. participation, communion, and the converse relation, presence, is part of an account of how some determinate feature, F, can be true of a particular changing thing, x.

So the account of how changing things can have any determinate features, i.e. how they can be determinate things in the first place, is directly associated with the view that:

PL5.   There are changeless forms.

But he also argues that:

> PL6. We can know the changeless forms – not through sense perception, but through reasoning.

Above all, however, Plato argues that changeless essences and forms are separate, i.e. separate in the sense of distinct from changing things:

> PL7. Essences are not identical with, and they are distinct from, changing things.

We will return to this central claim in a moment (see §4 of this chapter). The claim that changeless essences and forms are separate and distinct from changing things is central to Plato's theory of forms, especially as Aristotle understands this theory. For it is this claim that Aristotle especially fastens on in his criticism of Plato's theory of forms.

But although Plato's separation of essences tends to attract most of Aristotle's attention, it is important to recognize that Plato's theory is, exactly, a theory of essence:

> PL8. The changeless forms have an essence. This means that the form F is F *in virtue of itself*, not in virtue of its relation to other things. And the changeless forms are the only things that have an essence.

In general, the changeless forms are what they are in virtue of themselves and not in virtue of their relation to other things. This stands directly opposed to Plato's claim about changing things, which says that changing things are what they are not in virtue of themselves, but in virtue of their relation to changeless forms. But changeless forms do not so much have essences, rather they are essences, i.e. essences conceived as separate and distinct from changing things:

> PL9. A changeless form is identical with its essence – it is an essence.

So the changeless forms are essences, and they are the only essences. It is also worth emphasizing Plato's basic view that:

> PL10. Essences are changeless.

This is a view that he shares with Aristotle. For it is indeed evident that essences are changeless, i.e. this is part of the very notion of essence. In general, the essence of a thing, x, is what we search for when we ask, 'What is this thing, x?', i.e. when we search for the definition of this thing, x. But suppose that x has an essence, i.e. there is something, E, that it is to be this thing, x. Then evidently x will be E for as long as x exists. For example, suppose that the essence of Socrates is being human; then evidently Socrates will be human for as long as he exists. Or suppose that the essence of water is H_2O; then evidently water will be H_2O for as long as it exists. So, in general, if E is the essence of a thing, x, then x will be, without change or variation, E for as long as it exists. It is in just this sense that the essence of a thing is something changeless.

However, the claim that essences are changeless can be understood in two ways. It may be understood to mean that the essence, E, is changeless and everlasting. This will be the natural way to understand it, if one thinks, as does Plato, that the essence is separate and distinct from changing things. On the other hand, it may be understood to mean that the essence, E, is changeless but not everlasting. This will be the natural way to understand it, if one thinks, as does Aristotle, that the essence is inseparable from the changing, material thing whose essence it is. So Plato thinks that essences are changeless, and he thinks that:

PL11. Essences are everlasting.

Finally, Plato thinks that:

PL12. Forms and essences are universals.

Forms are universals at least in the following sense: many different changing things can participate in one and the same form. In other words, one and the same form can be true of many different changing things. So much by way of summary of Plato's theory of forms.

Aristotle rejects Plato's theory of forms. To begin with, he rejects what appears to be the basic motivation behind this theory, i.e. the view that sense-perceptible and in general changing things do not have an essence and do not have any determinate features in virtue of themselves. He argues that changing things, the things that make up what he calls 'nature' (*phusis*), have changeless essences; and they have changeless essences in spite of the fact that they are changing. Indeed, he argues that a particular changing thing (e.g. Socrates), in the sense of the ultimate subject of predication and the particular that this thing is, is identical with its changeless essence (see Chapter 7§§5v and vi).

So he argues that there is no reason to postulate the existence of essences as Plato conceives of them, i.e. as separate and distinct from changing things. He also argues that the essence of a particular changing thing is not a universal; for it is identical with the ultimate subject of predication, which is a particular (see Chapter 7§§5v, viii and ix). Finally, he argues that Plato's theory of essences as separate and distinct forms leads to absurd consequences even on its own merit and independently of his, Aristotle's, alternative theory of essence. But before we look closer at Aristotle's criticism of Plato's theory, let us consider how he understands what appears to be the basic motivation behind this theory, i.e. the view that sense-perceptible and in general changing things do not have an essence and do not have any determinate features in virtue of themselves.

3 Aristotle's diagnosis of the source of Plato's theory of essences as separate forms

In a central and especially interesting passage, in which Aristotle wants first of all to understand why Plato and the Platonists hold the theory of essences as separate forms, he gives the following diagnosis of the source of this theory:

> Those who believe in the forms [*eidē*] came to this belief because they became convinced of the truth of the Heracleitean view that all sense-perceptible things [*ta aisthēta*] are always flowing. So [they concluded] that if there is to be explanatory knowledge [*epistēmē*] and wisdom [*phronēsis*] about anything, there must be certain other natures, besides [*para*] the ones that can be perceived through the senses, which are enduring [i.e. not flowing and changing]. For [they claimed] that there is no explanatory knowledge of flowing things. Now Socrates had been concerned with ethical virtues and had been the first to search for universal definitions about these. . . . But Socrates was justified in searching for what something is [*to ti estin*, the essence]; for he was seeking to reason deductively, and the starting-point [*archē*] of deductive reasoning is the essence [*to ti estin*]. . . . For there are just two things that one might fairly ascribe to Socrates, namely, inductive arguments and giving universal definitions, both of which are concerned with the starting-point [*archē*] of explanatory knowledge. But Socrates did not make universals or definitions separate; the Platonists, on the other hand, did make them separate, and such beings [i.e. separate beings] they called 'ideas' (*ideai*, also *eidē*, 'forms').
>
> (XIII. 4, 1078^{b}12–32; see also XIII. 9, 1086^{a}32–^{b}13 and I. 6, 987^{a}29–^{b}10)

Aristotle goes on to argue against the Platonic view that essences are separate and distinct from (*para*) the sense-perceptible and in general changing things. But for the moment we are concerned not with his criticism, but with his diagnosis of the reasons that led Plato and the Platonists to this view.

The first thing to note about this diagnosis is that Aristotle thinks of Plato's theory of separate and distinct forms as a theory of essence. For he argues that Socrates was among the first to search for the essence of things, or at least of some things: the ethical virtues. He also argues that, unlike Socrates, Plato argued that essences are separate and distinct from sense-perceptible and in general changing things. But Aristotle concludes that it is, exactly, the separate and distinct essences that Plato calls 'ideas' (*ideai*) or 'forms' (*eidē*). It is extremely important that he thinks of Plato's theory of forms as a theory of essence. For this shows that he thinks that he and Plato are engaged in the same overall project, i.e. the project of searching for the essence of things, even if they disagree fundamentally about how this project is to be carried out and what conclusions it will reach.

Aristotle also identifies the motivation behind not only Plato's but also Socrates' search for the essence of things; for he says that this motivation is the search for explanatory knowledge (*epistēmē*) and the view that explanatory knowledge requires knowledge of the essence of things. Here it is particularly important to recognize that Aristotle himself shares this commitment, the commitment to the search for explanatory knowledge, and he shares the view that explanatory knowledge requires knowledge of the essence of things. We know in general that this is his standpoint, but he also indicates here that it is his standpoint. For he ascribes the search for explanatory knowledge, and the view that such knowledge requires knowledge of the essence of things not only to Plato, with whose distinctive view about essences he disagrees, but also to Socrates, who does not, he thinks, hold Plato's distinctive view about essences, i.e. the view that essences are separate and distinct from changing things, and with whom in general he agrees.

If in general we ask why Plato and Aristotle think that explanatory knowledge requires knowing the essence of things, and hence requires supposing that things have an essence in the first place, we may in outline suggest the following answer. Explanatory knowledge (*epistēmē*) is knowledge not only of what things are like, but also *why* things are as they are. But, by reflecting on the very nature of explanation and the requirements for adequate and complete explanations, Plato and Aristotle conclude that in order to explain why a thing is as it is, we need an explanatory account of what the thing is *in virtue of itself*, i.e. an explanatory account of its essence (see Chapter 2§3ii). Such explanatory accounts of the essence of things they call 'definitions' (*horismoi*). Thus it is striking that in our passage he says that explanatory knowledge is based in definitions, i.e. it has definitions as its principle and starting-point (*archē*). It is also striking that he characterizes such definitions as 'universal' (*katholou*); for both Plato and Aristotle think that explanatory knowledge (*epistēmē*) is universal knowledge (see Chapter 2§3ii).

Incidentally, when Aristotle talks about Socrates here, and when he argues that Socrates' view is like Plato's in that they both search for explanatory knowledge and for the essence of things, but also unlike Plato's in that only Plato separated the essences of things, he means the historical Socrates, not Socrates as depicted in Plato's dialogues. However, we may question whether he really succeeds in representing the historical Socrates; we may surmise rather that the way in which he represents Socrates actually fits Plato, or at least part of Plato's work, and that probably Aristotle bases his representation of Socrates primarily on those of Plato's dialogues which we tend to refer to as 'Socratic'. These are dialogues in which Plato depicts Socrates as searching for the essence of an ethical virtue or virtue in general (see, for example, *Euthyphro, Charmides, Laches, Protagoras, Meno*). This confirms that it is Plato himself that is, on the one hand, committed to a general theory of essence – a theory that Aristotle largely accepts – but also, on the other hand, to a more particular theory of essence, which claims that essences are separate and distinct from the changing things, and which Aristotle rejects.

So, according to Aristotle, what is distinctive of Plato's theory of essence, as opposed to what it shares with his own theory, is the view that essences are separate and distinct from sense-perceptible and in general changing things. But in the above passage Aristotle also identifies the reasoning that led Plato and the Platonists to the view that essences are separate. He sets out this reasoning as follows:

P1. Explanatory knowledge is knowledge of something changeless. For it is, ultimately, knowledge of the essence of things; and essences are changeless.

P2. But the things that we perceive through the senses are changing (or even: changing in every way).

Therefore:

C1. Explanatory knowledge is not of the things that we perceive through the senses. But

P3. Explanatory knowledge is possible.

Therefore:

C2. There are changeless things (namely, essences) that are not the things that we perceive through the senses, but are separate from and distinct from these; and these separate and distinct essences, the 'ideas' or 'forms', are the objects of explanatory knowledge.

So this is Plato's argument, as Aristotle sees it, for the claim that essences are separate and distinct from changing things.

One of the most striking features about this argument is that it directly implies the view that:

C3. The things that we perceive through the senses do not have an essence; i.e. there is nothing that such things are *in virtue of themselves*.

This view follows directly from the claims that essences are changeless (which is part of P1) and that sense-perceptible things are changing in every way (i.e. P2). Aristotle appears to be faithful to Plato here. For Plato appears to hold, exactly, that sense-perceptible things do not have an essence, by which he means that sense-perceptible things are inde-terminate in virtue of themselves and depend for their determination on their relation to separate essences – the forms. It is also noteworthy that in a very similar passage in the *Metaphysics* (I. 6, I. 6, 987ª29f.), in which Aristotle likewise sets out a diagnosis of the source of Plato's theory of forms, he concludes as follows:

[Plato claimed that] the sense-perceptible things [*ta aisthēta*] are besides [*para*] these [i.e. they are distinct from the ideas or forms] and that they are all called after these. For [he argued that] the things that are called after the ideas [*ta homōnuma*] *are* [i.e. they are beings, things that are] in virtue of their participation in the ideas.

(987ᵇ8–10)

But does Plato's argument for the separation and distinctness of essences, as Aristotle understands it, succeed? Whether the argument succeeds depends above all on how Plato and the Platonists intend the second premise to be understood. This premise may mean:

> P2–weak. The things that we perceive through the senses are changing in some ways (but they may also be changeless in other ways).

Or it may mean:

> P2–strong.The things that we perceive through the senses are changing in every way (so there is no way in which they are also changeless).

Evidently, for the argument to be valid P2 must be understood as P2–strong, not as P2–weak. Aristotle indicates that this is how P2 is intended by Plato and the Platonists when he says that, according to them, sense-perceptible things (*ta aisthēta*) are 'always' flowing, by which he appears to mean not only that they are changing all the time, but that they are changing in every way.

Suppose that P2 had meant only P2–weak. In that case one may object (against the inference from P1 and P2 to C1) that explanatory knowledge, although it is of changeless things, can still be of the changing things that we perceive through the senses. For if these things are not changing in every way, explanatory knowledge can be of what is changeless about them, in particular their changeless essence. Indeed this appears to be Aristotle's central objection to Plato's argument for the separation and distinctness of essences. For Aristotle argues that P2–strong is false and that only P2–weak is true. This allows him to argue, against Plato, that in spite of the fact that sense-perceptible things are changing and that explanatory knowledge is of changeless essences, explanatory knowledge can be of sense-perceptible and in general of changing things. For there is something changeless even about sense-perceptible and, in general, changing things, and this is their essence (see Chapter 7§5vi).

It may appear to us that Aristotle's response to Plato is eminently reasonable, and that obviously only P2–weak, not P2–strong, is true. But this impression would be precipitate. For we saw (in Chapter 7§5vi) that Aristotle is faced with a particular and pressing *aporia*: how can the essence be changeless, and in particular free from generation and destruction, if it is inseparable from the changing, material thing whose essence it is, and this thing is subject to generation and destruction? It is especially worth noting that this is a problem for Aristotle, who argues that the essence of a changing, material thing is inseparable from that thing. It is not a problem for Plato, who argues that essences and forms are separable and distinct from changing things. Indeed, it appears to be precisely this *aporia* that leads Plato to conclude that essences cannot be inseparable from changing things, but must, on the contrary, be separate and distinct from changing things.

Plato's view that sense-perceptible things are not only changing (so much is obvious), but changing in every way, is perhaps a puzzling view. If sense-perceptible things are changing in every way, does it not follow that they are completely indeterminate? But if sense-perceptible things are completely indeterminate, how can we even perceive them through the senses? For when we perceive something through the senses, we distinguish it from other things that we perceive through the senses; but this surely implies that what we perceive through the senses is determinate to some extent. For example, we may look through our eyes and see a blue expanse extending towards the horizon and blending into the grey above (suppose we are standing by the sea). But although the sea and sky are constantly changing, they are to that extent changeless in this description: the sea is shades of blue, and not, for example, orange; the sky is shades of grey, and not, for example, green; and the grey sky is, in relation to us and our field of vision, above the sea. So there is at least this much constancy and determinacy in what we see here.

So does Plato commit himself to something absurd here, when he commits himself to the view that sense-perceptible things are changing always *and in every way*? Does he commit himself to the view that sense-perceptible things are completely indeterminate? Plato's view may be puzzling, but it need not have this absurd implication. For when he argues that sense-perceptible things are changing in every way, it is arguable that he intends this claim to be about sense-perceptible things only to the extent that we overlook, or set aside, the fact that sense-perceptible things depend for their determination on their relation to changeless forms. For it is arguable that Plato thinks that once we take into account the fact that sense-perceptible things depend for their determination on their relation to the forms, we can admit that they are to some extent determinate. In other words, Plato argues that sense-perceptible and, in general, changing things are determinate not in virtue of themselves, but only in virtue of their relation to the forms. So when Plato claims that sense-perceptible things are changing in every way, this does not imply that they are completely indeterminate; it implies only that they are indeterminate *in virtue of themselves*. For he thinks that sense-perceptible and in general changing things are determinate in virtue of their relation to other things – the changeless forms.

4 The issue of separation, and different types of separation

Aristotle characterizes Plato's essences and forms as things that are separate (*chōrista*). But it is important to recognize that he uses the term 'separate' in more than one way, both in general and in the character-ization of Plato's forms. So more than one characterization is involved. It is also important to recognize that when Aristotle criticizes Plato's view that essences are separate, this decidedly under-characterizes his own positive view of essences. For a number of very different views about essences, and in particular about the relation between a thing and its essence, are compatible with the view that the essence of a thing is not separate from the thing whose essence it is. Let us first consider the different ways and senses in which, according to Aristotle, Plato's essences and forms are separate.

First, Aristotle thinks that Plato considers the essences and forms to be the primary beings (*hai ousiai*). And he thinks that the very notion of primary being, i.e. the notion that he shares with Plato and indeed with other thinkers who raise the basic question, 'What is being?', is precisely the notion of separate being (*chōriston*). Primary being is separate being in the sense that it is a being, something that is, simply in virtue of itself (*auto kath' hauto*) and not in virtue of its relation to other things (see Chapter 7§4). We may also call this type of sepa-ration: 'ontological independence'. It is clear especially from the following passage that Aristotle characterizes Plato's essences and forms as separate beings in this sense, i.e. in the sense in which primary being is, precisely, separate being:

> But those who say that there are forms [i.e. Plato and the Platonists] in one way speak correctly, i.e. when they conceive of forms as sepa-rate – *if indeed* the forms are primary beings [*ousiai*].
>
> (VII. 16, 1040^{b}27–29)

When he characterizes Plato's essences and forms as separate beings, he is not criticizing Plato's view of essence. On the contrary, Aristotle shares the view that the essences are the primary beings and are sepa-rate in the sense of ontologically independent. But he has a different view of what the essences are and in particular how they are related to changing things.

Second, he criticizes Plato for thinking that essences are separate from changing things. Here he is using the term 'separate' to mean 'distinct'. He also commonly uses the term 'besides' (*para*) to indicate the distinctness of Plato's forms – which is the main target of his criticism. So the target of the criticism is the view that changing things and forms are things that are distinct from one another. The notion of two things being distinct from one another is familiar especially when applied to things in space. For such things are evidently distinct from one another if they occupy different and non-overlapping places. But what in general is it for two things to be distinct from one another? This question is pressing; for evidently Plato's forms, if they are in general distinct from changing things, do not as such occupy a place in space. Aristotle does not provide a general account of what it is for two things to be distinct from one another. But he appears to have in mind the following: two things are distinct from one another if, and only if:

(1) they are not identical; and
(2) they are not overlapping, i.e. they do not share any part.

We saw earlier that separation in the sense of ontological independence does not entail separation in the sense of distinctness; and Aristotle does not think that there is such an entailment (see Chapter 7§4). So when he characterizes Plato's essences and forms as separate things in the sense of things that are distinct from changing things, he is not simply drawing a consequence from the characterization of them as separate in the sense of ontologically independent things, i.e. things that are beings simply in virtue of themselves. In particular, the characterization of Plato's essences as ontologically independent beings is simply part of Aristotle's observation that the forms are, in Plato's view, the primary beings (*hai ousiai*). But the view that essences are distinct from changing things, Aristotle thinks, relies rather on a complex argument, which is based on the claim that, while essences are changeless, changing things are changing (see §3 of this chapter).

So Aristotle characterizes Plato's essences and forms as separate in two ways or senses:

(1) they are ontologically independent beings, i.e. they are beings, things that are, simply in virtue of themselves; and
(2) they are distinct from changing things.

Apparently, he also characterizes Plato's essences as separate in a third sense, i.e. as (3) capable of existing even if they are not true of changing things, i.e. even if they are not, as is sometimes said today, 'instantiated in' changing things. In other words, he apparently thinks that a Platonic form, F, can exist even if no changing thing is F. Aristotle is commonly understood in this way, i.e. as characterizing Plato's forms as things, and in particular as universals, that are capable of existing without being true of other things, and, in particular, changing things. For example, the form of justice is a universal, since many things other than this form, and, in particular, many changing things, can be just. But, on Aristotle's characterization of this Platonic form, the form of justice can exist even if no other things, and, in particular, no changing things, are just. It is also sometimes thought that Aristotle's own view is, precisely, that essences are universals, but that they cannot exist if there is not some changing thing of which they are true – they cannot exist without being instantiated in changing things.

Certainly Aristotle thinks that a form, as conceived by Plato, is not a being, something that is, in virtue of being true of an ultimate subject of predication, i.e. in virtue of being true of something other than itself (see, for example, VII. 6, 1031^{b}15–18). This also follows directly from his view that forms, as conceived by Plato, are primary beings, i.e. they are beings, things that are, simply in virtue of themselves and not in virtue of their relation to other things – in particular the relation of being true of other things. Apparently he concludes, directly or indirectly, that a Platonic form can exist even if it is not true of something other than itself. But it is worth emphasizing that this inference ought not to be direct. For it does not directly follow from the claim that a thing, x, is a being simply in virtue of itself and not in virtue of its relation to another thing, y, that x can exist without y existing and existing in relation to x (see Chapter 7§4).

It is another matter whether Aristotle's own view is that essences are universals, but that they cannot exist if they are not true of changing things. For we saw that, on one interpretation (the one that we defended), he does not think that essences are universals at all, and he does not think that the essence of a changing thing is true of the ultimate subject of predication and the particular that this thing is. On the contrary, he thinks that the essence of a changing thing is identical with the ultimate subject of predication and the particular that this thing is (see Chapter 7§5v and viii).

But it is important to recognize that the view that forms are distinct from changing things, which is the main target of Aristotle's criticism of Plato's theory of forms, does not directly entail the view that forms can exist even if they are not true of changing things. In other words, even if Plato's essences and forms are distinct from changing things, it does not follow that they can exist without being true of changing things. That this does not follow can be seen in the following way. The relation of distinctness is necessarily symmetrical. This means that if a thing, x, is distinct from another thing, y, then it follows that y is likewise distinct from x. But certainly it is not true that if a form, F, can exist without there existing a changing thing, x, that is F, then a changing thing, x, that is F can likewise exist without there existing a form, F. On the contrary, even if Plato thinks that a form, F, can exist without there existing a changing thing, x, that is F, he also thinks that a changing thing, x, that is F is F only because there is a form, F, and x is appropriately related to this form – it participates in or communes with this form. So this relation, the relation between changing things and forms, is not necessarily symmetrical, indeed it is necessarily asymmetrical. This shows that we cannot infer from 'Form F is distinct from changing things' that 'Form F can exist without being true of changing things'.

So, if we think that Aristotle characterizes Plato's forms not only as distinct from changing things, which is the central target of his criticism, but also as capable of existing without being true of changing things, we must ask how he moves from the former to the latter characterization. Perhaps he defends this move in the following way: Plato's forms are not only distinct from changing things, they are also, and above all, things that are beings simply in virtue of themselves; but from these two characteristics of the forms, i.e. their being distinct and their being ontologically independent, it follows that they can exist without being true of changing things, and, in general, without changing things existing in relation to them. If this is Aristotle's reasoning, then it may well be cogent. For it is perhaps plausible to think that if a thing, x, is a being simply in virtue of itself and not in virtue of its relation to another thing, y; and if, further, x is distinct from y, then it does indeed follow that x can exist without y existing in relation to x. But it would take us too far to consider this further.

These, then, are three ways in which Aristotle characterizes Plato's essences and forms as separate:

(1) separate in the sense of being ontologically independent beings, i.e. things that are beings simply in virtue of themselves;
(2) separate in the sense of being distinct from changing things; and
(3) separate in the sense of being capable of existing without being true of changing things.

We have also considered how these three types of separation are related to each other.

Aristotle argues against distinctness, and this is the main target of his criticism of Plato's theory of essence – the theory of forms. He concludes that essences are indeed ontologically independent beings, i.e. things that are beings simply in virtue of themselves; but they are not distinct from changing things, and they cannot exist without being true of changing things. But it is important to recognize that this negative conclusion decidedly under-characterizes his own positive view about how essences are related to changing things. For there are very different ways of conceiving of the relation between a changing thing and its essence, even while thinking that a changing thing and its essence are not two things that are distinct from one another. We may distinguish four ways in which, in general, two things that are not distinct from one another may be related to each other. Only the fourth way will fit Aristotle's view about how the essence of a changing thing is related to the thing whose essence it is.

First, evidently two things that are not actually distinct from one another may still be capable of being distinct from one another; i.e. two things may be separable even if they are not actually separated. We may think of the threads in a woven carpet. But clearly this is not Aristotle's view about the relation between a changing, material thing and its essence. On the contrary, he argues that the essence of a changing, material thing is inseparable from that thing.

Second, two things that are not actually distinct from one another may also not be capable of being distinct from one another; they may be inseparable. We may think of a face and its smile. This is closer to Aristotle's view about the relation between a changing, material thing and its essence. But it still under-characterizes his view.

Third, two things that are not distinct and also not separable from one another may still not be identical with one another. Again we may think of a face and its smile. On one interpretation (but not ours), this is just Aristotle's view. For, on one interpretation of Aristotle's view about the relation between a changing, material thing and its essence, the essence of a changing, material thing (e.g. Socrates) is the species to which the thing belongs (e.g. the species, being human). On this interpretation, a changing, material thing is evidently not distinct or separable from its essence and species. For a changing, material thing is a thing in the first place only in virtue of its essence. But evidently a changing, material thing (e.g. Socrates) is not identical with the species to which it belongs (e.g. the species, being human). (See Chapter 7§5viii.)

Fourth, two things that are not distinct and not separable may indeed be identical with one another. On our interpretation, this is precisely Aristotle's view about the relation between a changing, material thing and its essence. For he argues that the essence of a particular changing, material thing is identical with the ultimate subject of predication and the particular that this thing is. (See Chapter 7§5, especially v.)

5 Aristotle's criticism, based on his own theory of essence

Aristotle offers two very different kinds of criticism of Plato's theory of essences as separate and distinct forms. On the one hand, he develops a theory of essence himself, and he argues on the basis of this theory that Plato's theory is mistaken. We may call this the external criticism. On the other hand, he argues that Plato's theory leads to absurd consequences even on its own merit and independently of his, Aristotle's, alternative theory of essence. We may call this the internal criticism. One absurd consequence of Plato's theory of forms, he argues, is that if there is one separate form of, for example, human beings, i.e. separate in the sense of distinct from the changing human beings with which we are familiar from experience, then there are infinitely many separate forms of the human being. This attempt to reduce Plato's theory of forms to absurdity he labels 'the third-man' argument. We will look at this criticism, 'the third-man' argument, in a moment. But first let us consider the external criticism, i.e. the criticism that is based on Aristotle's own theory of essence.

Undoubtedly the third-man argument, and in general Aristotle's attempt to show that Plato's theory of forms leads to absurd consequences (i.e. the internal criticism), is more impressive and memorable than the criticism that is based on his own alternative theory of essence (i.e. the external criticism). But we must not overlook the central fact that Aristotle develops his own theory of essence, and that he uses this as a basis to criticize Plato's theory. If we focus exclusively on the internal criticism, we may gain the impression that Aristotle's criticism of Plato's theory of forms is like that of a sceptic, who has no positive theoretical views of their own. Or we may gain the impression that if Aristotle has positive views about essence, then they arise largely as a natural consequence of his internal criticism of Plato's theory of essence. So we may gain the impression that Aristotle's view, which says that essences are not separate and distinct from changing things, is nothing but a natural consequence, once Plato's theory, which says that essences are separate and distinct from changing things, is shown to have absurd consequences.

But this would be to misunderstand the debate between Plato and Aristotle about essence. For although Aristotle may be right that Plato's theory of essence has problems internal to it, the same may be true of Aristotle's theory of essence; it may have its own internal problems. Indeed, we will see that when he uses his theory of essence to criticize Plato's theory, this also alerts us to problems in his theory. And this is a salutary correction of the impression that his theory of essence is nothing but a natural consequence of his criticism of Plato's theory. So we may rather conclude that the two theories, i.e. Plato's assertion of separation and distinctness and Aristotle's denial of separation and distinctness, are really on the same level. This means that, intuitively and pre-theoretically, there is no more reason to think that essences are not separate and distinct from changing things than there is to think that they are separate and distinct from changing things.

It is also important to recognize, as we saw, that Aristotle's theory of essence is decidedly under-characterized, if we characterize it simply as the view that essences are not separate and distinct from changing things – simply as the view that essences are, as we might say, immanent. For a number of very different views about the relation between a changing thing and its essence are compatible with thinking that changing things have essences and that essences are not separate and distinct from changing things (see §4 of this chapter). Aristotle's distinctive view is that the relation between a changing thing and its essence is a relation between the changing thing and itself; for he argues that a changing thing, in the sense in which a changing thing is a particular and an ultimate subject of predication, is identical with its essence (see Chapter 7§5v). This shows quite clearly that Aristotle's theory of essence is not simply a natural consequence of his rejection of Plato's theory.

Aristotle's external criticism of Plato's theory of essences as separate forms is based on two central Aristotelian claims about essence:

A. Those things that in the strict sense have an essence, i.e. the primary beings, are identical with their essence; and

B. The essence of a thing that in the strict sense has an essence, i.e. of a primary being, is an ultimate subject of predication.

We have considered these claims previously (see Chapter 7§5v). Our aim here is to consider how these claims entail, against Plato, that essences are not separate and distinct from changing things.

Claim A is compatible with Plato's view that essences are separate and distinct from changing things. Indeed, Plato himself appears to hold this claim; for he appears to think, exactly, that separate and distinct forms, which are for him the only things that have an essence, are identical with their essence. Certainly Aristotle thinks that Plato and the Platonists are committed to this claim, A; for he argues that if they do not accept this claim, they immediately commit themselves to an infinite regress:

> For if the good itself [i.e. that which in the strict sense has the essence, *being good*] and what it is to be good [i.e. the essence itself, *being good*] were not identical, and likewise for the animal itself and what it is to be an animal, and being itself and what it is to be [etc.], then there would be other primary beings, or natures, or ideas, besides [*para*] the supposed ones, and *they* would be more primary primary beings [*proterai ousiai*] – if, that is to say, [we suppose that] primary being is the essence.
>
> (VII. 6, 1031^{a}31–^{b}3)

We will look closer at this threat of an immediate infinite regress when we look at the 'third-man argument'. The point to recognize here is that Aristotle is saying that the Platonists themselves, i.e. those who believe that essences and ideas are separate and distinct from changing things, and that it is these separate and distinct essences and ideas that are the primary beings (*ousia*), are committed to the view that (A) those things that in the strict sense have an essence, i.e. the primary beings, are identical with their essence. For example, they are committed to the view that 'the good itself', i.e. that which in the strict sense has the essence *being good*, is identical with this essence, i.e. with 'what it is to be good'. For if those things that in the strict sense have an essence were not identical with their essence (i.e. if claim A were false), then an infinite regress would immediately emerge, such that every time one postulates an essence and claims that this is primary being, a further essence needs to be postulated, which is more primary than the original one – so it is rather *it* that is primary being.

So far, then, Aristotle and Plato agree, i.e. they agree that (A) those things that in the strict sense have an essence, i.e. the primary beings, are identical with their essence. But Aristotle crucially adds that (B) the essence of a thing that in the strict sense has an essence, i.e. of a primary being, is an ultimate subject of predication. So he thinks that we must ensure, in our theory of essence, that the essence and the ultimate subject of predication are not two things, but one and the same thing. But it is, exactly, this requirement that Plato's theory of essences fails to satisfy. For Plato's separate and distinct essences, the 'ideas' or 'forms', are, exactly, not ultimate subjects of predications, since evidently they can be predicated of other things. An ultimate subject of predication, we recall, is something that other things are predicated of, but which is not itself predicated of other things. But Plato's forms are predicated of other things. Or, as Plato would say, other things participate in the forms and depend for their determination, i.e. or having the features they have, on their participation in the forms. So Plato's theory of essences as separate and distinct forms is incompatible with Aristotle's central claim, which says that (B) the essence of a thing that in the strict sense has an essence, i.e. of a primary being, is an ultimate subject of predication.

Aristotle himself points out that if the Platonists think that essences are separate and distinct forms, and that this is what is primary being, then they cannot admit that essence and primary being is an ultimate subject of predication (i.e. they must deny claim B). For he first argues (in 1031^{a}31–^{b}3, i.e. the passage just quoted) that Plato is committed to the view that (A) those things that in the strict sense have essences, i.e. the primary beings, which for Plato are the separate and distinct forms, are identical with their essences. But then he points out that if one thinks that essences are separate forms and that this is primary being, then one cannot admit that (B) essence and primary being is an ultimate subject of predication:

> At the same time it is also evident that if there are ideas such as some people [i.e. Plato and the Platonists] claim that there are, then the ultimate subject of predication [*to hupokeimenon*] will not be primary being. For [the Platonists claim that] these [the ideas] must be primary beings, but not on account of [being predicable of] an ultimate subject of predication; for [if the ideas were primary beings on account of being predicable of an ultimate subject of predication] then they would *be* [i.e. be beings, things that are] only on account of being participated in [so they would not be primary beings after all].
>
> (VII. 6, 1031^{b}15–18)

This in general is Aristotle's external criticism of Plato's theory of essences as separate forms, i.e. the criticism that is based on his own, Aristotle's, theory of essence. The criticism can be summarized as follows. On the one hand, Plato is right to think that primary being is the essence, and that those things that in the strict sense have an essence are identical with their essence. On the other hand, Plato is wrong to think that essences are separate from the changing things; for this view implies that essence and primary being cannot be an ultimate subject of predication. It is easy to see why this criticism is based on Aristotle's own theory of essence. For it is Aristotle, not Plato or the Platonists, that argues that essence and primary being must be an ultimate subject of predication. It is also easy to see (from the passage just quoted) that Aristotle is perfectly aware of this, i.e. of the fact that Plato and the Platonists deny that essence and primary being is an ultimate subject of predication.

To appreciate the force of this criticism we should remember what in general Aristotle is thinking of when he is talking about ultimate subjects of predication; he is thinking of the changing things with which we are directly familiar from sense perception and experience. For he thinks that, at the end of the day, *they* are the things about which we think and speak, i.e. *they* are the things that we signify in predicative thought and speech. Presumably, Plato would agree that our ultimate subjects of predication are the changing things with which we are directly familiar from sense perception and experience. For it appears that Plato and Aristotle are both engaged in the task of explaining how these things – the things with which we are familiar pre-philosophically and from our sense perception and experience, can be something, and something determinate, in the first place. They give very different explanations of these things; for Plato's explanation appeals to separate and distinct essences, whereas Aristotle's explanation appeals to essences that are not separate and distinct, but are, on the contrary, identical with the things with which we are directly familiar. But it is the same things that they are engaged in explaining.

Plato is happy to conclude that the changing things with which we are directly familiar from sense perception and experience do not have an essence, i.e. they are not, in virtue of themselves, something determinate. Rather, he concludes, they depend for their determination on essences that are separate and distinct from them – on the forms. So Plato rejects the view that (B) the essence of a thing that in the strict sense has an essence, i.e. of a primary being, which for Plato is a separate and distinct form, is an ultimate subject of predication. For he argues that the things that have an essence and that are identical with their essence, i.e. the forms, are not ultimate subjects of predications; they are rather separate and distinct from the ultimate subjects of predication and from what we are directly familiar with from sense perception and experience. But Aristotle finds this conclusion unacceptable.

There is a particular benefit in concentrating first on Aristotle's external criticism of Plato's theory of essence, i.e. the criticism that is based on his, Aristotle's, alternative theory. For this brings out that Aristotle's criticism is based on theoretical commitments that may contain their own difficulties. In particular, we saw that it is far from easy to see how Aristotle can satisfy the central requirement that he, but not Plato or the Platonist, sets up; i.e. the requirement that (B) the essence of a thing that in the strict sense has an essence, i.e. of a primary being, is an ultimate subject of predication (see Chapter 7§5v). This is worth emphasizing. For it means that it is not satisfactory to paint the following, simplistic, picture of the debate between Plato and Aristotle about essence: Plato, extravagantly and unnecessarily, made essences separate and distinct from sense-perceptible and, in general, changing things; Aristotle restored essences to where they obviously belong, namely, *in* the sense-perceptible and, in general, the changing things. There is a particular reason why this picture is simplistic. For to say simply that, according to Aristotle, essences are *in* the sense-perceptible things, although it is true as far as it goes, is to overlook that there is a fundamental problem in Aristotle, and one that he himself raises and sets out to answer: how is the essence of a changing thing related to that thing itself and in particular to the ultimate subject of predication? As we saw at length earlier (in Chapter 7, especially §§5v–viii), it is above all this problem that Aristotle raises and sets out to answer in the central books of the *Metaphysics*, and especially book VII.

6 Aristotle's criticism, based on Plato's theory of essence: the third-man argument

But Aristotle also argues that Plato's theory of essences as separate and distinct forms leads to absurd consequences even on its own merit and independently of his, Aristotle's, alternative theory of essence. One absurd consequence, he argues, is that if there is one separate and distinct form of, for example, human beings, i.e. distinct from the changing human beings with which we are directly familiar from sense perception and experience, then there will be infinitely many separate and distinct forms of the human being. He labels this attempt to reduce Plato's theory to absurdity 'the third-man' argument: we start with the human beings with which we are familiar from sense perception and experience (this is the first man); but Platonists postulate a second human being, namely, the separate and distinct form of the human being (this is the second man); but this, Aristotle argues, leads to the absurd consequence that we must postulate a further separate and distinct form of the human being (the third man), and so on without end. The moral that Aristotle wants to draw from this criticism is that we should not postulate a second human being, i.e. a human being that is separate and distinct from changing ones, in the first place.

The polemical intent of Aristotle's criticism is evident already in the label 'the third man'. For to use this label is to portray Plato's form of the human being as simply another human being: a human being which is entirely like those with which we are familiar from sense perception and experience, except that it is changeless and everlasting – as it were in a deep freeze. This is in fact how Aristotle portrays Plato's theory of forms in one of his most polemical moments:

> There are many difficulties [that arise if one thinks that there are separate and distinct forms], but the greatest absurdity is that while they [i.e. the Platonists] claim that there are certain natures besides [*para*] those in the material universe, they at the same time claim that these [i.e. the separate forms] are the same as the sense-perceptible things, except that while the former [i.e. the separate forms] are everlasting, the latter [i.e. the sense-perceptible things] are perishable. For they [the Platonists] claim that there is a human himself [i.e. a separate form of the human being] and a horse itself and health itself, and this is all that they say. But this is to behave very much like those who believe that there are gods, but that gods are like humans. For all they do is postulate everlasting humans, and so too the Platonists make of the forms nothing but everlasting sense-perceptible things.
>
> (III. 2, 997^{b}5–12; see also XIII. 4, 1078^{b}34–36)

So, as Aristotle portrays the Platonists, they think not only that there are essences which are separate and distinct from changing things, namely, the 'ideas' or 'forms', but also that forms are very much like changing things, except that while the changing things are perishable the forms are everlasting. For example, they think that the form of the human being is simply another human being, except that it is not perishable, but everlasting.

Aristotle may certainly be right that if the Platonists think that forms are very much like changing things, then their own reasoning will force them to postulate not only one form in each case, for example, one form of humans, but infinitely many forms. For if the set of human things with which we are familiar from sense perception and experience depends for their being human on there being a form of humans, and if this form is simply another human (except that it is not perishable, but everlasting), then it appears that there will be a new set of humans, the many changing humans plus the one changeless form; and this new set of humans will likewise depend for their being human on there being a second form of humans; and so on without end. We will look closer at this criticism, 'the third-man' argument, in a moment, but first it is worth pointing out that we may doubt whether Aristotle's polemical portrayal of the Platonists is a fair representation. For we must not suppose that Plato thought of the form of humans as simply another human being, or the form of the horse as simply another horse, or the form of health as simply another healthy thing.

But why, let us first ask, is it absurd to suppose that there is not only one form of F, for example, one form of the human being, but infinitely many forms of F? The reason why this is absurd is that a theory of forms is a theory of essence, i.e. a theory of what it is for something to be, precisely, F. But if there are infinitely many essences of human beings, this evidently means that it is impossible to determine what it is for something to be, precisely, a human being. For every time we postulate an essence of human beings to determine what it is for something to be, precisely, a human being, we need to postulate a further essence to determine this, and so on without end. So it is impossible to determine what it is for something to be, precisely, a human being, or any other kind of thing. This is absurd, since the aim was precisely to account for the essence of things.

Aristotle mentions what he calls 'the third-man' argument in a number of places in the *Metaphysics* (990^{b}17, 1039^{a}2, 1059^{b}8, 1079^{a}13; see also *Sophistical Refutations* 178^{b}36–179^{a}10), but he does not spell out what precisely the argument is. Evidently he thinks that this is familiar to his audience, both from his own work and from Plato's. For we will see that it was Plato that originally developed this argument, in the dialogue *Parmenides* (132a–b) – apparently against his own theory of forms. But it is fortunate that a particularly clear version of Aristotle's 'third-man' argument is recorded by the later commentator on Aristotle, Alexander of Aphrodisias (second to third century AD):

If what is predicated truly of some plurality of things is also some other thing besides [*para*] the things of which it is predicated, being separated from them (for this is what those who posit the ideas think they prove; for this is why, according to them, there is such a thing as man-itself [i.e. the idea of man], because the man is predicated truly of the particular men [i.e. the sense-perceptible, changing men], these being a plurality, and it is other than the particular men) – but if this is so, there will be a third man. For if the man being predicated is other than the things of which it is predicated and subsists on its own, and if the man is predicated both of the particulars and of the idea, then there will be a third man besides the particulars and the idea. In the same way, there will also be a fourth man predicated of this [i.e. of the third man], of the idea, and of the particulars, and similarly also a fifth, and so on to infinity.

(*Peri Ideōn/On Ideas*, 84.21–85.3; trans. G. Fine, but comments added)

However, a very similar argument (except that Plato takes *large* whereas Aristotle takes *man* as his example) was originally set out by Plato, in the dialogue *Parmenides*, apparently against his own theory of 'forms' or 'ideas' (see *Parmenides* 132a1–b2). It is remarkable that Plato himself develops this argument, apparently against his own theory of forms. For when he originally puts forward the theory of forms, for example, in the dialogues the *Phaedo* and *Republic*, he emphasizes that there can only be one form in each case, for example, there can only be one form of the many sense-perceptible, changing beds (see *Republic* 596b3–4). So, if he thinks that this argument in the *Parmenides* (let us call it 'the third-large' argument) is successful against his theory of forms, he must think that it reduces this theory to absurdity. For the argument concludes that there is not just one form in each case, for example, just one form of largeness, but infinitely many.

So why did Plato not give up the theory of forms, if he thinks that it leads to absurd consequences? For he seems to have accepted the theory of forms even after he developed the third-large argument against this theory; for example, he accepts the theory of forms in the *Timaeus*, which is probably written after the *Parmenides*. Presumably the answer is that Plato does not think that the third-large argument is successful against his theory of forms, i.e. he thinks that his theory of forms is not really vulnerable to the third-large argument. We will see in a moment why he thinks that his theory of forms is not vulnerable to this argument, and why his theory does not have the absurd consequence that if there is one separate form in each case, then there are infinitely many separate forms in each case.

But let us look closer at how precisely the third-man or third-large argument must work in order to be successful against the theory of forms. It seems that it must rely on three premises:

P1 (the one-over-many assumption, OM):
For any set of things that are F, there is one form *F*, such that each of the members of this set is F in virtue of its relation to the form *F*.

P2 (the self-predication assumption, SP):
A form *F* is itself F.

P3 (the distinctness assumption, DI)

Something that is F cannot be F in virtue of itself; rather it will be F in virtue of something other than and distinct from itself.

In the current literature the distinctness assumption is commonly called the non-identity assumption. But, since distinctness is the target of Aristotle's criticism, it is better to call this the distinctness assumption. If one accepts these assumptions, then one is committed to the view that there is not just one form in each case, for example, just one form of large things or just one form of human things, but infinitely many.

To see why this is so, let us take as our initial set of, for example, human things (or large things), two sense-perceptible, changing things that are human – Smith and Jones. Then (according to the one-over-many assumption, OM), there will be one form, *H*, of things that are human, such that each of the members of this set, Smith and Jones, is human in virtue of its relation to this form, *H*. But (according to the distinctness assumption, DI) this form, *H*, will not be one of the things in the original set of human things: Smith and Jones. So the form *H* will be a third thing, besides and distinct from Smith and Jones. But (according to the self-predication assumption, SP) the form *H* is itself a thing that is human. But now this means that there is a new set of things that are human: Smith, Jones and the form *H*. And (again according to the one-over-many assumption, OM) there will be a form, *H1*, of things that are human, such that each of the members of this set, Smith, Jones and *H*, is human in virtue of its relation to this form, *H1*. And (again according to the distinctness assumption, DI) this form, *H1*, will not be one of the things in the previous set of human things: Smith, Jones and *H*. So the form *H1* will be a fourth thing, besides and distinct from Smith, Jones and *H*. And so on without end. So, on these assumptions, there will be not one form of things that are human (or large, or any other kind), but infinitely many forms. But this is to reduce the theory of forms to absurdity.

This, then, is how the third-man or third-large argument must work in order to be successful against the theory of forms. But is it successful? This evidently depends on whether those who hold the theory of forms, and Plato in particular, accept the above premises or assumptions: the one-over-many assumption (OM); the self-predication assumption (SP); and the distinctness assumption (DI). Plato appears to think that he is not vulnerable to the third-large argument; for he does not give up the theory of forms even after he developed this argument against it. So we may suppose that he rejects one of the assumptions of the argument.

Indeed, it is evident that Plato rejects the distinctness assumption (DI). He accepts this assumption with regard to sense-perceptible, changing things; for he thinks that sense-perceptible, changing things are not determinate (hence are not F, where F is some determination or property) in virtue of themselves, but are determinate in virtue of their relation to something that is separate and distinct from them, i.e. the changeless form F. But he rejects this assumption with regard to changeless forms; for he thinks that a changeless form F is, exactly, F in virtue of itself and not in virtue of its relation to another form. For example, in the dialogue the *Sophist* (255c12–13) he expressly distinguishes between two types of things: the things, which include the forms, that are what they are in virtue of themselves (*auta kath' hauta*); and the things, which include sense-perceptible, changing things, that are what they are in virtue of their relation to other things (*pros alla*).

So Plato accepts the distinctness assumption (DI) with regard to changing things, but he rejects this assumption with regard to separate forms – which are changeless. But then he is not vulnerable to the third-man or third-large argument. In particular, we may argue that although a separate form, F, which is changeless, is required to explain why the changing things that are F are F, no further form is required to explain why this form is F (or why this form, together with the changing things that are F, are F). For, unlike the changing things, the changeless form F is, precisely, F *simply in virtue of itself* (*auto kath' hauto*).

This also shows that when Plato claims that the form F is itself F, for example, when he claims that the form of large things is itself large, he does not mean that the form F is F in the same way as the sense-perceptible, changing things are F. On the contrary, he thinks that the way in which the form F is F is fundamentally different from the way in which the sense-perceptible, changing things are F: the sense-perceptible, changing things are F not in virtue of themselves, but in virtue of their relation to something else, namely, the form F; but the form F is F simply in virtue of itself (*auto kath' hauto*). This also shows that Aristotle misrepresents Plato when he represents him as thinking that separate forms are very much like sense-perceptible, changing things, except that while the sense-perceptible, changing things are perishable, the forms are everlasting. He misrepresents Plato when he represents him as thinking that the form of the human being is simply another human being, except that it is not perishable, but everlasting.

This leaves us with a last question: does Aristotle really think that Plato's theory of forms is vulnerable to the third-man argument? We may think that obviously he does. But this is to overlook the polemical intent behind Aristotle's internal criticism of Plato, i.e. the criticism which says that Plato's theory leads to absurd consequences even on its own merits. It is also to overlook Aristotle's external criticism of Plato's theory of essences as separate forms, i.e. the criticism that is based on his, Aristotle's, alternative theory of essence. For this criticism is much less polemical. Indeed, it is remarkable that in this criticism Aristotle expressly recognizes that Plato and the Platonists reject the distinctness assumption with regard to separate forms. For, as he characterizes Plato and the Platonists, they think that those things that have essences, which, on their view, means the separate forms, are identical with their essence (see VII. 6, 1031^{a}31–^{b}3, quoted in the previous section). So Aristotle does not really think that Plato is vulnerable to the third-man argument. It appears, then, that when Aristotle is in a particularly polemical frame of mind, he represents, or misrepresents, Plato's theory of forms in such a way that it is vulnerable to being reduced to absurdity; but when he is in a more searching and theoretical frame of mind, he recognizes that things are not so simple and that the theory of forms can be presented in a better light.

7 Aristotle's criticism of Plato's separate forms, and his own separate God

So Aristotle rejects Plato's view that essences are separate and distinct from the changing things, the things with which we are directly familiar from experience and which Aristotle calls 'nature' (*phusis*). At the same time, however, he himself argues that there is something that is separate and distinct from nature as a whole, namely, the changeless God – which is the ultimate cause and explanation of rational change and order in nature (see Chapter 8). Furthermore, he argues that God is nothing but its essence.

This suggests that Aristotle's theory of essence is not so completely different from Plato's after all. Plato argues that all essences are separate and distinct from changing things. Aristotle argues that all essences are, on the contrary, inseparable from changing things. But he makes room for a single exception, God, who is separate and distinct from nature as a whole. Furthermore, there are striking similarities between Aristotle's God and Plato's form of the good. For both are separate and distinct from nature as a whole; and both provide the ultimate explanation of why things in nature are rational and intelligible. In fact, Aristotle is at pains to distinguish his conception of God from Plato's conception of the form of the good. He makes a point of emphasizing that while his God is wholly and perfectly active (*energōn*), indeed active in the way in which reason, and rational thought, is active, and so can cause and explain rational change in nature, Plato's form of the good is wholly inactive, and so cannot cause or explain this (see XII. 6, 1071^b12f; and XII. 7, 1072^b26f.).

This shows that when Aristotle criticizes Plato's view that all essences are separate and distinct from changing things, his objection is not directed against the very possibility of there being things that are separate and distinct from changing, material things. So his criticism is not at all like the criticism of certain modern naturalists, who object precisely to the possibility of there being things that are separate and distinct from nature and in general from changing, material things. Rather, his objection is directed against the view that *all* essences are separate and distinct from changing, material things. In particular, he argues that the essences of changing things need not be thought of as separate from those things (which is how Plato thinks of them), but may be thought of as inseparable from, and indeed as identical with, those things. He also argues that if (as Plato does) one thinks that the essences of changing things are separate from those things, this leads to difficulties; and that his own view avoids such difficulties and is in general better off.

But we may wonder why Aristotle is confident that his own commitment to a single transcendent being – God, is not subject to similar difficulties. In particular, why is he confident that his own commitment to a single transcendent thing – God, is not vulnerable to the third-man argument, which he employs unsparingly against Plato and the Platonists? Formally, the answer is evident: while God explains rational change, and while God is rational activity, this activity does not consist in rational change – indeed, God is completely changeless (see Chapter 8§8). Formally, this may succeed in deflecting the third-man argument. For to direct this argument against Aristotle's God would be to argue that because God is subject to the same rational change as the change that he explains in the universe, therefore, a further God is needed to explain the rational change that is common to the first God and the universe, and so on without end. Aristotle's response appears to be, precisely, that God is not subject to the same kind of rational change as the universe. Indeed, God is changeless. But although this response is formally successful, it highlights our original puzzle: how can God be active yet changeless? (see Chapter 8§8).

CONCLUSION

What would we have to do in order to look for an overall assessment of Aristotle's *Metaphysics*?

First, we would have to assess the basic question of metaphysics as Aristotle conceives it: the question, 'What is being?', i.e. 'What is it for something, anything, to be a being?' We recall that he thinks that when we raise this question, we raise it of beings with which we are already directly familiar, pre-philosophically and from our ordinary experience. For beings are directly apparent to us and present to us, they are all around us and make up the world which we inhabit. So we would have to ask whether Aristotle does enough to motivate this basic question of metaphysics.

Second, we would have to assess Aristotle's method of searching in metaphysics, the method that is based in puzzlement and particular puzzles – *aporia* and *aporiai* – prompted by our thinking about being in general.

Third, we would have to assess Aristotle's central claim that we can address the question, 'What is being?', only by addressing the question, 'What is primary being?' (*prōtē ousia*, often simply *ousia*). We recall that a primary being is something that is a being simply in virtue of itself and not in virtue of its relation to other things; and it is what explains what it is for anything to be a being. So we would have to ask whether, if we want to search for what being is, we must do so by searching for a privileged kind of being that explains what it is for anything to be a being.

Fourth, we would have to assess the parameters within which Aristotle searches for an answer to the question: 'What is primary being?', i.e. the parameters set by what he considers to be the main candidates for primary being. These candidates were: the particular; the universal; and the essence (see VII. 3, 1028^{b}33–36, discussed in Chapters 1§4 and 7§3). So we would have to ask whether these are indeed the natural parameters.

What if we follow Aristotle this far? Should we also follow him in answering the question, 'What is primary being?', in the way in which he answers it? His answer was that primary being with regard to each thing, i.e. with regard to the things with which we are already directly familiar, is the essence of that thing. It is the essence in the sense that it is what each thing is in virtue of itself and in virtue of its being the very thing it is. But the essence of each thing, Aristotle argued emphatically, is not something different from and true of that thing and of things like it – so it is not simply a universal. For suppose that the essence of each thing, i.e. of the things with which we are already directly familiar, were simply a universal. This would mean that the things with which we are already directly familiar, the so-called particulars, would be indeterminate in virtue of themselves and would depend on certain other things, the universals, for their determination. This is Plato's view – but Aristotle wants to avoid it. For Aristotle wants to ensure that the things with which we are already directly familiar, the so-called particulars, are primary beings, i.e. they are beings in virtue of themselves and not in virtue of their relation to other things.

However, if we work within the parameters of Aristotle's main candidates for primary being – the particular, the universal, and the essence – Plato's view is not easily avoided. This view says that the things with which we are already directly familiar, pre-philosophically and from our ordinary experience, are indeterminate in virtue of themselves and depend on the universals for their determination. Of course, if we find Plato's view attractive, still it does not immediately follow that we must conceive of universals as Plato does, i.e. as distinct from changing particular things and as capable of existing even if not true of any changing particular things. Whether we must take these further steps is a further question.

So the choice among Aristotle's main candidates for primary being, and especially between the essence and the particular on the one hand (which is Aristotle's choice), and the universals on the other hand (which is Plato's choice), is a particularly difficult one. Perhaps this is just what Aristotle indicates when he says that the question, 'What is primary being?' – like the basic question, 'What is being?' – 'is always a source of puzzlement' (VII. 1, 1028^{b}2–4).

FURTHER READING

On Chapter 1

For general introductions to metaphysics in a broadly Aristotelian spirit, see Loux (1998) and Lowe (1998). For general books on the *Metaphysics*, see Owens (1951), Loux (1991) and Reeve (2000). For some general papers on the *Metaphysics*, see Cresswell (1971, 1975). For Aristotle's essentialism, see Cohen (1977/1978). For recent works in metaphysics in a broadly Aristotelian spirit, see Kripke (1972), Armstrong (1978, 1997), and Fine (1994, 1995).

On Chapter 2

For Aristotle's distinction between experience and explanatory knowledge, see Frede (1996). For a different interpretation of this distinction, see Bolton (1991). For Aristotle's general conception of science, see Ruben (1990, chapters 2–3), Moravcsik (1991) and Hankinson (1995). For the relation of metaphysics to the other sciences, see Wieland (1975) and, for a very different interpretation, see Bolton (1994, 1996). For the theory of the four causes, see Bostock (1982). For Aristotle's conception of matter, see Cohen (1984) and Fine (1992).

On Chapter 3

See translation and commentary by Madigan (1999). See Code (1980), Nussbaum (1982), Owen (1986), Halper (1988), Wians (1992), Cooper (1999) and Pritzl (1999).

On Chapter 4

See translation and commentary by Kirwan (1993). For Aristotle's general conception of metaphysics, see Irwin (1977/1978), Frede (1987) and Barnes (1995). For the problem of conceiving of being as a whole, see Loux (1973). For the focal theory of being and the notion of primary being, see Hamlyn 1977/1978), Ferejohn (1980), Irwin (1981), Owen (1986b), Morrison (1987) and Kung (1999). For the *Categories*, see Frede (1981, 1987b). For the relation of the *Metaphysics* to the *Categories*, see Lewis (1995, sections I–II) and Wedin (2000). For the relation between ontology and theology, see Patzig (1979) and Frede (1987).

On Chapters 5 and 6

See Noonan (1977), Lukasiewicz (1979), Code (1986, 1999), Halper (1984), Cohen (1986) and Wedin (2000b). For recent criticism of the principle of non-contradiction, see Priest (1998, 2000).

On Chapter 7

For an excellent, but difficult, commentary on *Metaphysics* VII, see Frede and Patzig (1988). For general books on *Metaphysics*, books VII–IX, see Gill (1989), Witt (1989), Loux (1991), Scaltsas (1994) and Wedin (2000). For the notion of primary being (substance), see Frede (1987c). For Aristotle on predication, see Moravcsik (1967), Owen (1978/1979), Weidemann (1980) and Code (1981). For ontological independence and dependence, see Fine (1995). For the claim that primary being is not simply the ultimate subject of predication, see Schofield (1972). For the claim that primary being is essence, and on how the essence is related to the ultimate subject of predication, see Woods (1974/75), Hartman (1976) and Code (1986b). On the relation between form and matter, see Sokolowski (1970), Loux (1979), Mansion (1979), Modrak (1981), Charles (1994) and Scaltsas (1994b). On whether the primary being of each thing (and its essence, and its form) is a universal, see Sellars (1957), Woods (1967, 1991), Sykes (1975), Code (1978, 1980) and Loux (1979). On book IX, see Frede (1994) and Witt (1994).

On Chapter 8

See Kahn (1985), Ackrill (1991), Judson (1994) and Kosman (1994). See also the collection of scholarly articles in Frede and Charles (2000).

On Chapter 9

See Fine (1984, 1985, 1993: chapters 4–5 and 7–8), Fine (1985), Morrison (1985) and Spellman (1995).

BIBLIOGRAPHY

Translations of the *Metaphysics*

1. Translation of the *Metaphysics* by W.D. Ross (Oxford: Oxford University Press, 1923). Also in J. Barnes (ed.), *The Complete Works of Aristotle*, vol. 2 (Princeton, NJ: Princeton University Press, 1984).
2. Translation of the *Metaphysics* by H.G. Apostle (Bloomington, IN: Indiana University Press, 1966).
3. Translation and commentary of *Metaphysics*, books III and XI, 1–2, by A. Madigan (Oxford: Clarendon Press, 1999).
4. Translation and commentary of *Metaphysics*, books IV, V, and VI, by C. Kirwan (Oxford: Clarendon Press, 2nd edn, 1993).
5. Translation and commentary of *Metaphysics*, books Z and H, by D. Bostock (Oxford: Clarendon Press, 1994).
6. Translation and commentary of *Metaphysics*, books Zeta, Eta, Theta, Iota, by M. Furth (Indianapolis, IN: Hackett, 1986).
7. Translation and commentary of *Metaphysics*, books XIII–XIV, by J. Annas (Oxford: Clarendon Press, 1976).

Other

Ackrill, J.L. 1991. 'Change and Aristotle's theological argument'. *Oxford Studies in Ancient Philosophy*, suppl. vol. I, 57–66.

Armstrong, D.M. 1978. *Nominalism and Realism* (Cambridge: Cambridge University Press).

Armstrong, D.M. 1997. *A World of States of Affairs* (Cambridge: Cambridge University Press).

Barnes, J. 1995. 'Metaphysics'. In J. Barnes (ed.), *The Cambridge Companion to Aristotle* (Cambridge: Cambridge University Press), 66–108.

Bolton, R. 1991. 'Aristotle's method in natural science: *Physics* I'. In L. Judson (ed.), *Aristotle's* Physics: *a Collection of Essays* (Oxford: Clarendon Press), 1–29.

Bolton, R. 1994. 'Aristotle's conception of metaphysics as a science'. In T. Scaltsas, D. Charles and M.L. Gill (eds), *Unity, Identity and Explanation in Aristotle's Metaphysics* (Oxford: Oxford University Press), 321–54

Bolton, R. 1996. 'Science and the science of substance in Aristotle's *Metaphysics* Z'. In F.A. Lewis and R. Bolton (eds), *Form, Matter, and Mixture in Aristotle* (Oxford: Blackwell), 231–80.

Bostock, D. 1982. 'Aristotle on the principles of change in *Physics* I'. In M. Schofield and M.C. Nussbaum, *Language and Logos* (Cambridge: Cambridge University Press), 179–96.

Charles, D. 1994. 'Matter and form: unity, persistence, and identity'. In T. Scaltsas, D. Charles, and M.L. Gill (eds), *Unity, Identity and Explanation in Aristotle's Metaphysics* (Oxford: Oxford University Press), 75–105.

Code, A. 1978. 'No universal is a substance'. *Paideia*, 65–76.

Code, A. 1980. 'The aporematic approach to primary being in *Metaphysics* Z'. *Canadian Journal of Philosophy*, 10, suppl. vol., 1–20.

Code, A. 1981. 'On the origins of some aristotelian theses about predication'. In J. Bogen and J.E. McGuire (eds), *How Things Are* (Dordrecht: Reidel), 101–31.

Code, A. 1986a. 'Aristotle's investigation of a basic logical principle: which Science investigates the principle of non-contradiction?'. *Canadian Journal of Philosophy*, 16, 341–56.

Code, A. 1986b. 'Aristotle: essence and accident'. In R.E. Grandy and R. Warner (eds), *Philosophical Grounds of Rationality* (Oxford: Oxford University Press), 411–39.

Code, A. 1999. 'Metaphysics and logic'. In L.P. Gerson (ed.), *Aristotle: Critical Assessments* (London: Routledge), 167–85.

Cohen, S.M. 1977/78. 'Essentialism in Aristotle'. *Review of Metaphysics*, 31, 387–405.

Cohen, S.M. 1984. 'Aristotle's doctrine of the material substrate'. *Philosophical Review*, 93, 171–94.

Cohen, S.M. 1986. 'Aristotle on the principle of non-contradiction'. *Canadian Journal of Philosophy*, 16, 359–70.

Cooper, J.M. 1999. 'Aristotle on the authority of appearances'. In J.M. Cooper, *Reason and Emotion* (Princeton, NJ: Princeton University Press), 281–91.

Cresswell, M.J. 1971. 'Essence and existence in Plato and Aristotle'. *Theoria*, 37, 91–113.

Cresswell, M.J. 1975. 'What is Aristotle's theory of universals?'. *Australian Journal of Philosophy*, 53, 238–47.

Ferejohn, M.T. 1980. 'Aristotle on focal meaning and the unity of science'. *Phronesis*, 25, 117–28.

Fine, G. 1984. 'Separation'. *Oxford Studies in Ancient Philosophy*, 2, 31–87.

Fine, G. 1985. 'Separation: a reply to Morrison'. *Oxford Studies in Ancient Philosophy*, 3, 159–65.

Fine, G. 1993. *On Ideas* (Oxford: Clarendon Press).

Fine, G. 1993. *On Ideas* (Oxford: Clarendon Press).

Fine, K. 1992. 'Aristotle on matter'. *Mind*, 101, 35–57.

Fine, K. 1994. 'Essence and modality'. *Philosophical Perspectives*, 8, 1–16.

Fine, K. 1995. 'Ontological dependence'. *Proceedings of the Aristotelian Society*, suppl. vol., 269–90

Frede, M. 1981. 'Categories in Aristotle'. In D. O'Meara (ed.), *Studies in Aristotle* (Washington, DC: Catholic University of America Press), 1–24.

Frede, M. 1987a. 'The unity of general and special metaphysics: Aristotle's conception of metaphysics'. In M. Frede, *Essays in Ancient Philosophy* (Oxford: Clarendon Press), 81–95.

Frede, M. 1987b. 'Individuals in Aristotle'. In M. Frede, *Essays in Ancient Philosophy* (Oxford: Clarendon Press), 49–71.

Frede, M. 1987c. 'Substance in Aristotle's *Metaphysics*'. In M. Frede, *Essays in Ancient Philosophy* (Oxford: Clarendon Press), 72–80.

Frede, M. 1994. 'Aristotle's notion of potentiality in *Metaphysics* θ'. In T. Scaltsas, D. Charles and M.L. Gill (eds), *Unity, Identity and Explanation in Aristotle's Metaphysics* (Oxford: Oxford University Press), 173–93.

Frede, M. 1996. 'Aristotle's Rationalism'. In M. Frede and G. Striker (eds), *Rationality in Greek Thought* (Oxford: Oxford University Press), 157–73.

Frede, M. and Charles, D. 2000. *Aristotle's Metaphysics Lambda* (Oxford: Oxford University Press).

Frede, M. and Patzig, G. 1988. *Aristoteles. 'Metaphysik Z'* (Munich: Beck).

Gill, M.L. 1989. *Aristotle on Substance* (Princeton, NJ: Princeton University Press).

Halper, E. 1984. 'Aristotle on the extension of non-contradiction'. *History of Philosophy Quarterly*, 1, 369–80.

Halper, E. 1988. 'The origin of Aristotle's metaphysical *aporiai*'. *Apeiron*, 21, 1–27.

Hamlyn, D.W. 1977/78. 'Focal meaning'. *Proceedings of the Aristotelian Society*, 98, 1–18.

Hankinson, R.J. 1995. 'Philosophy of science'. In J. Barnes (ed.), *The Cambridge Companion to Aristotle* (Cambridge: Cambridge University Press), 109–39.

Hartman, E. 1976. 'Aristotle on the identity of substance and essence'. *Philosophical Review* 85, 545–61.

Irwin, T.H. 1977/78. 'Aristotle's discovery of metaphysics'. *Review of Metaphysics*, 31, 210–29.

Irwin, T.H. 1981. 'Homonymy in Aristotle'. *Review of Metaphysics*, 34, 523–44.

Judson, L. 1994. 'Heavenly motion and the unmoved mover'. In M.L. Gill and J.G. Lennox (eds), *Self-Motion* (Princeton, NJ: Princeton University Press), 155–71.

Kahn, C.H. 1985. 'The place of the prime mover in Aristotle's teleology'. In A. Gotthelf (ed.), *Aristotle on Nature and Living Things* (Pittsburgh, PA: Mathesis publications and Bristol: Bristol Classical Press), 183–205.

Kosman, A. 1994. 'Aristotle's Prime Mover'. In M.L. Gill and J.G. Lennox (eds), *Self-Motion* (Princeton, NJ: Princeton University Press), 133–54.

Kripke, S. 1972. *Naming and Necessity* (Cambridge, MA: Harvard University Press).

Kuhn, T.S. 1957. *The Copernican Revolution* (Cambridge, MA: Harvard University Press).

Kung, J. 1999. 'Aristotle on "Being is said in many ways"'. In Lloyd P. Gerson (ed.), *Aristotle: Critical Assessments* (London: Routledge), 186–202.

Lewis, F.A. 1995. 'Substance, predication, and unity in Aristotle'. *Ancient Philosophy*, 15, 521–49.

Loux, M.J. 1973. 'Aristotle on the transcendentals'. *Phronesis*, 18, 225–39.

Loux, M.J. 1979. 'Form, species and predication in *Metaphysics* Z, H, and θ'. *Mind*, 88, 1–23.

Loux, M.J. 1991. *Primary OUSIA* (Ithaca, NY: Cornell University Press).

Loux, M.J. 1998. *Metaphysics. A Contemporary Introduction* (London: Routledge).

Lowe, E.J. 1998. *The Possibility of Metaphysics* (Oxford: Oxford University Press).

Lukasiewicz, J. 1979. 'Aristotle on the law of contradiction'. In J. Barnes, M. Schofield and R. Sorabji (eds), *Articles on Aristotle*, vol. 3 (London: Duckworth), 50–62.

Mansion, S. 1979. 'The ontological composition of sensible substances in Aristotle'. In J. Barnes, M. Schofield and R. Sorabji (eds), *Articles on Aristotle*, vol. 3 (London: Duckworth), 80–7.

Modrak, D.K. 1981. 'Forms and compounds'. In J. Bogen and J.E. McGuire (eds), *How Things Are* (Dordrecht: Reidel), 85–100.

Moravcsik, J.M.E. 1967. 'Aristotle on predication', *Philosophical Review*, 76, 80–97.

Moravcsik, J.M.E. 1991. 'What makes reality intelligible? Reflections on Aristotle's Theory of *Aitia*'. In L. Judson (ed.), *Aristotle's Physics: a Collection of Essays* (Oxford: Clarendon Press), 31–47.

Morrison, D. 1985. 'Separation in Aristotle's metaphysics'. *Oxford Studies in Ancient Philosophy*, 3, 125–57.

Morrison, D. 1987. 'The evidence for degrees of being in Aristotle'. *Classical Quarterly*, 37, 382–401.

Noonan, H.W. 1977. 'An argument of Aristotle on non-contradiction'. *Analysis*, 37, 163–69.

Nussbaum, M.C. 1982. 'Saving Aristotle's appearances'. In M. Schofield and M.C. Nussbaum (eds), *Language and Logos* (Cambridge: Cambridge University Press), 267–94.

Owen, G.E.L. 1978/79. 'Particular and general'. *Proceedings of the Aristotelian Society*, 99, 1–21.

Owen, G.E.L. 1986a. 'Tithenai ta phainomena'. In M.C. Nussbaum (ed.), *Logic, Science and Dialectic* (London: Duckworth), 239–51.

Owen, G.E.L. 1986b. 'Logic and metaphysics in some earlier works of Aristotle'. In M.C. Nussbaum (ed.), *Logic, Science and Dialectic* (London: Duckworth), 180–99.

Owens, J. 1951. *The Doctrine of Being in the Aristotelian Metaphysics* (Toronto: Pontifical Institute of Mediaeval Studies).

Patzig, G. 1979. 'Theology and ontology in Aristotle's *Metaphysics*'. In J. Barnes, M. Schofield and R. Sorabji (eds), *Articles on Aristotle*, vol. 3 (London: Duckworth), 33–49.

Priest, G. 1998. 'What is so bad about contradictions?'. *Journal of Philosophy*, 98, 410–26.

Priest, G. 2000. 'Truth and contradiction'. *Philosophical Quarterly*, 50, 305–18.

Pritzl, K. 1999. 'Opinions as appearances: Endoxa in Aristotle'. In L. P. Gerson (ed.), *Aristotle: Critical Assessments* (London: Routledge), 73–83.

Putnam, H. 1983. 'There is at least one a priori truth'. In H. Putnam, *Realism and Reason* (Cambridge: Cambridge University Press), 98–114.

Quine, W.V.O. 1953. 'Reference and modality'. In W.V. O. Quine, *From a logical Point of View* (Cambridge, MA: Harvard University Press).

Reeve, C.D.C. 2000. *Substantial Knowledge. Aristotle's Metaphysics* (Indianapolis, IN: Hackett).

Ruben, D.-H. 1990. *Explaining Explanation* (London: Routledge).

Russell, B. 1973. *Essays in Analysis*. Edited by D. Lackey (New York: George Braziller).

Scaltsas, T. 1994a. *Substances and Universals in Aristotle's Metaphysics* (Ithaca, NY: Cornell University Press).

Scaltsas, T. 1994b. 'Substantial holism'. In T. Scaltsas, D. Charles and M.L. Gill (eds), *Unity, Identity and Explanation in Aristotle's Metaphysics* (Oxford: Oxford University Press), 107–28.

Schofield, M. 1972. '*Metaphysics* Z3: some suggestions'. *Phronesis*, 17, 97–101.

Sellars, W. 1957. 'Substance and form in Aristotle'. *Journal of Philosophy*, 54. 688–99.

Sokolowski, R. 1970. 'Matter, elements and substance in Aristotle'. *Journal of the History of Philosophy*, 8, 263–88.

Spellman, L. 1995. *Substance and Separation in Aristotle* (Cambridge: Cambridge University Press).

Sykes, R.D. 1975. 'Form in Aristotle: universal or particular?'. *Philosophy*, 50, 311–30.

Wedin, M.V. 2000a. *Aristotle's Theory of Substance* (Oxford: Oxford University Press).

Wedin, M.V. 2000b. 'Some logical problems in *Metaphysics* gamma'. *Oxford Studies in Ancient Philosophy*, 19, 113–62.

Weidemann, H. 1980. 'In defence of Aristotle's theory of predication'. *Phronesis*, 25, 76–87.

Wians, W. 1992. 'Saving Aristotle from Nussbaum's Phainomena'. In A. Preuss and J.P. Anton (eds), *Essays in Greek Philosophy V. Aristotle's Ontology* (Albany: SUNY), 133–49.

Wieland, W. 1975. 'Aristotle's *Physics* and the problem of inquiry into principles'. In J. Barnes, M. Schofield and R. Sorabji (eds), *Articles on Aristotle*, vol. 1 (London: Duckworth), 127–40.

Witt, C. 1989. *Substance and Essence in Aristotle* (Ithaca, NY: Cornell University Press).

Witt, C. 1994. 'The Priority of actuality in Aristotle'. In T. Scaltsas, D. Charles and M.L. Gill (eds), *Unity, Identity and Explanation in Aristotle's Metaphysics* (Oxford: Oxford University Press), 215–28.

Woods, M. 1967. 'Problems in *Metaphysics* Z, Chapter 13'. In J.M.E. Moravcsik (ed.), *Aristotle. A Collection of Critical Essays* (New York: Anchor Books), 215–38.

Woods, M. 1974/75. 'Substance and essence in Aristotle'. *Proceedings of the Aristotelian Society*, 75, 167–80.

Woods, M. 1991. 'Particular forms revisited'. *Phronesis*, 36, 75–87.

INDEX

Greek terms (and titles of works) in italics